GOD'S DOMINION

GOD'S DOMINION

A Sceptic's Quest

Ron Graham

An Adrienne Clarkson Book

M&S

Canadian Cataloguing in Publication Data

Graham, Ron, 1948–
God's dominion

Includes bibliographical references.

ISBN   0-7710-3522-5

1. Canada – Religion.   I. Title.

BL2530.C3G73   1990   200'.971   C90-094671-7

p.60 Excerpt from *Beautiful Losers* by Leonard Cohen. Used by permission of *The Canadian Publishers*, McClelland and Stewart, Toronto.
p. 83 Quotation by Northrop Frye from "History and the New Age" by David Cayley, broadcast by "Ideas," CBC Radio. Used by permission of CBC Radio.
p. 165 Excerpt from *Belonging* by Lucinda Vardey, © 1988. Reprinted by permission of Lester & Orpen Dennys Publishers Ltd., Canada.
p. 375 Lines from "Time Corrected" translated by F.R. Scott. From *The Collected Poems of F.R. Scott* by F.R. Scott. Used by permission of *The Canadian Publishers*, McClelland and Stewart, Toronto.

An Adrienne Clarkson Book

McClelland & Stewart Inc.
The Canadian Publishers
481 University Avenue
Toronto, Ontario
M5G 2E9

Printed and bound in Canada by
T.H. Best Printing Company Limited

CONTENTS

My thanks to the Canada Council for its good graces, and my gratitude to the three Graces for their good counsel: Adrienne Clarkson, Mary Adachi, and my darling Gillian.

To S.N.G.
– with metta –
and to the memory of
Father Sean O'Sullivan
(1952–1989)

Everything begins in mysticism and ends in politics.

Charles Péguy

One may conquer millions in battle, but he who conquers himself, only one, is the greatest of conquerors.

Gautama the Buddha

The Great Perhaps

"Truly, to come here, much strength and patience are needed," wrote Jean de Brébeuf from Huronia in 1635, "and he who thinks of coming here for any other than God, will have made a sad mistake."

No student of Canadian politics and history can ignore the extraordinary impact God has had on those who have come here. Spirituality governed the aboriginal tribes of America before the Europeans. Bishops dominated French Canada from Laval to Léger. Religion ruled the issues and parties of English Canada from the Quebec Act through the hanging of Louis Riel to the programmes of "Bible Bill" Aberhart and the Reverend Tommy Douglas. Denominations shaped our education system, our social services, many of our laws, even the ethics of our business élites. An obsession with sacred themes has characterized our culture from the wood carvings of New France to Jean-Paul Lemieux and William Kurelek, from Sinclair Ross to Margaret Laurence and Denys Arcand, from St-Denys Garneau to E. J. Pratt and A. M. Klein, from Goldwin Smith to Marshall McLuhan and Northrop Frye. No less an authority than the Bible gave Canada its designation and motto, from the seventy-second psalm: that God "shall have dominion also from sea to sea, and from the river unto the ends of the earth."

Much has changed in the second half of the twentieth century, of course. Where once everything in French and English Canada seemed about religion, now little of importance does. While almost 90 per cent of the population declared themselves Christian in the 1981 census – 47 per cent Roman Catholic, 16 per cent United Church, 10 per cent Anglican, 3 per cent each for the Baptists and Lutherans and Presbyterians, 1.5 per cent Pentecostal, 1 per cent Eastern Orthodox, plus a variety of smaller denominations – sociologist Reginald Bibby's 1985 survey showed only 60 per cent affirming all the Christian fundamentals of God, the divinity of Christ, and life after death, and only 40 per cent judging themselves "committed" followers. Before 1950 approximately two-thirds of adult Canadians were said to attend a church or synagogue regularly; after 1980 the estimate went down to one-third. And while almost 90 per cent professed some faith in a Supreme Being, more than 40 per cent did not think there is an answer to the meaning of life.

Behind the murk of such statistics there exists indubitable evidence of the secularization of Canada by industrialization, urbanization, science and technology, mass communication, and pluralism. Prayers are under siege in our schools, courts, and public ceremonies; giving thanks for our food has gone the way of antimacassars; universities tend to lump religious studies in with sociology, anthropology, or philosophy; and even many committed believers do not care a hoot what the Pope thinks about condoms or what the pastor preaches about South Africa. If there are exceptions to such a generalization, in parts of Atlantic Canada or Quebec, in pockets of Ontario or the West or the North, amid the non-Christian religions imported by immigrants or cultists, they are seldom to be found in my experience among the élites, and that is a significant change from the days when our politicians, tycoons, educators, artists, and generals jostled to be seen at the side of God.

When I considered exploring the state of religion and spirituality in Canada today, many of the businessmen and political movers I had encountered as a journalist were blunt in suggesting that I was abandoning the field of money and power for a hinterland as remote and irrelevant as Huronia itself. Though they still summon archbishops to perform at their weddings, funerals, and state dinners, and still bestow on religious institutions heaps of cash (often accompanied by the perpetual gift of their own names), they usually regard religion as little more than a business or lobby group. They envy the churches' ability to sell nothing for something (and, miracle of miracles, pay no taxes on it); they appreciate the prelates' authority to mobilize masses of votes (and take pressure off the system with promises of better days in the world to come); and they are nonplussed to find the same fellows who are always putting the touch on them for fat donations now storming into corporate annual meetings or leading demonstrations on Parliament Hill for one "communist" case or another. Like all mere mortals they might wonder about the universe one night at the cottage after the sixth martini. Certainly no set has more desire for membership in the exclusive and everlasting country club that is Heaven, and Rosedale Catholics may flock to Toronto's Our Lady of Perpetual Help because they *know* how hard it is to get even temporary help these days. But generally the modern élites distrust anything that cannot be bought, put on a balance sheet, or sacrificed to political expediency. "I'd like to have faith, and certainly I'd be a happier man with it," a retired senator told me recently, "but I just never could get the swing of it."

That is understandable: most of the powerful obtained their wealth and position by clever manipulation and shrewd knowledge of this material realm, not by clinging to medieval notions of predestination, conscience, and self-restraint. So when some presumptuous bishop suggests they have won the world but lost their soul, when he advises them to share their gains with the needy and temper their greed with wisdom, when he smugly implies that their mastery of profit and power means little because they must die, their instinct is to screech with Henry II, "Who will free me from this turbulent priest?"

And yet – and yet – success often teaches its own emptiness. When we can still dream of money and fame, we have less need to pursue a more ethereal consolation from our miseries. To experience the poverty of money and fame can be as upsetting as to know that they are beyond our grasp. Both push us toward drastic help. But while the poor usually have to make do with prayers and candles, the rich have the time and means to hunt out swamis in India, sorcerers in Peru, gestalt therapists in California, yogis in the Bahamas, psychics in London, and whirling dervishes in Istanbul to supplement the regular comforts found in the psychiatrist's study, the gin bottle, and the Valium capsule.

What is true for well-to-do individuals is true for well-to-do societies. For all the talk of Canada as a secular and materialist country there seems to be more and more attention to spiritual issues. Hardly a day passes without a front-page headline directly or indirectly about religion: the Supreme Court decisions on abortion, the Ontario government's decision to extend public funding of Catholic schools, sex scandals in Newfoundland and Quebec involving priests and preachers, Jewish lobbies protesting Ottawa's policies toward the Middle East, Sikhs standing trial in British Columbia, Christian racists in Alberta and New Brunswick, provincial debates on Sunday closings and religious instruction in the schools, church groups opposing free trade and nuclear weapons, the ordination of gays in the United Church, and cult activity from Halifax to Vancouver. Some of this comes from the world at large, whether the morals and politics of televangelism, the role of religion in India and Ireland and South Africa, the impact of the Pope in Eastern Europe and Latin America, or the rise of New Age spiritualism through the books of Marilyn Ferguson and Shirley MacLaine. Some of it is a leftover from ideas and battles of the past, when behaviour codes were inherited from Victorian times and constitutional laws were designed for denominations. And some of it exists because the great questions of being, meaning, behaving, and dying can never go away.

14

"You've put yourself in a very dangerous position," a Hutterite preacher once warned me, "to be a writer going around asking about Truth and knowledge. What happens if you find them? You'd stop being a writer going around. As John the Baptist said, what good are pretty leaves on a tree if you don't put down strong roots?"

I had many occasions to remember his warning as I went around, for more than two years, from prophet to guru and primate to priest. One night, for example, on a visit to Newfoundland, I attended a performance of Benjamin Britten's *Noye's Fludde* in the cathedral and city named after that same saint who had cried in the wilderness and prepared the way of the Lord. A cool and impenetrable fog engulfed the gothic Anglican church set on the hillside overlooking St John's and the harbour. Inside, as if huddling from the terrors of the dark within the high and massive walls, a packed crowd sat listening to the music and choirs, both rapt and enwrapped with the sacred atmosphere and spiritual tradition. When the flood came, rocking Noah's boat and intimidating its creatures with thunder and lightning, the entire audience rose to sing "Eternal Father, Strong To Save."

> *O sacred Spirit, who didst brood*
> *Upon the chaos dark and rude,*
> *Who bad'st its angry tumult cease,*
> *And gavest light, and life, and peace;*
> *O hear us when we cry to thee*
> *For those in peril on the sea.*

The night, the fog, the smell of the sea, the voices of the Newfoundlanders, the children at the altar in animal costumes, the huge and eerie stone building, the thought of the sailors and fishermen and rig-workers out on the waves – perhaps a little fatigue, a little loneliness, a little cosmic sorrow – quite overwhelmed me. It was not just an aesthetic feeling based on the old hymn. It was a religious empathy. I was touched by the dignity of human beings calling out to their unknown Creator to pray for the well-being of others who were suffering. I was jealous of their faith. It seemed to be their ark, a small dory of wisdom and compassion amid storm and fog and night. It seemed to come from no reason, like God's message to Noah that he should gather together his family and the living creatures before the world was destroyed for its sinfulness. It seemed to go toward hope, which was the dove and the olive branch and the rainbow. It may only have been an illusion, like this amateur production's sets and effects, but for a minute it reduced me to tears.

What these people had faith in, why they had faith in it, how they expressed their faith, even the effect of it, all were marvellous, but much more marvellous to me was the mere fact of faith. The philosophers say that everything is an act of faith – that the airplane will lift on take-off, that the light will come on with the switch, that the sun will rise at tomorrow's dawn. They are probably right, but my attraction was to these beliefs that were beyond empirical evidence or scientific measurement.

I had held them myself once, when I used to sing this very hymn at school. Indeed, part of the emotion I felt came from a nostalgia for childhood, for innocence, for the desire to be taken up into a father's arms again for comfort and protection. Why not put down strong roots again? Why not let go of pride and doubt to pass the burden of knowledge back to God and the work of salvation back to the Saviour? I was too ignorant, I was too tired, and this was the time of day when, in William Faulkner's words, "man approaches nearest of all to God" and there is "something of that peace which is the promise and the end of the Church." I would feel it often in my travels at this hour: when the monks in Saskatchewan and the Hutterites in Manitoba sang at the end of their labours, when the Dene danced around a fire under the stars and Jews gathered in a Montreal synagogue to remember Kristallnacht, when a Sikh priest chanted from the Guru Granth Sahib at the temple in Vancouver and Buddhists meditated in a Cape Breton monastery during a howling rainstorm, when my friends died and my son was born.

It is not as if my faith had ever been founded on intellect. I had been enlisted in the Roman Catholic Church as an infant, after all, and though I had been taught the catechism, I picked up the stories and the picture cards more than the business about transubstantiation and purgatory. When my grandmother asked me what I would like as a gift for my First Communion, I replied, "A gun." Shortly afterwards, I was sent to an Anglican school, so I was spared both the best and the worst of Roman Catholicism. I developed a preference for English carols over Gregorian chants, I became more familiar with the *Book of Common Prayer* and the King James Bible than with the Rosary and papal infallibility, and Sunday Mass did little for my mind because the service was in Latin and the sermons were in French. By my second year in university humanist reason – abetted by some powerful urges to sin – led me to conclude that there is no God, and I directed what was left of my Christian ethics into radical politics and the remainder of my spiritual fervour into literature, art, and opera.

Newton, Marx, Freud, and their boys have made exotic and eccentric what once was commonplace and crucial. In this I remain their product. I do not dance for the Great Spirit, I do not worship the God of the Jews, I have not accepted Christ as my personal saviour, I give no credence to the Heaven and Hell of the Muslims, I reject the eternal soul of the Hindus, I do not wear the five attributes of a baptized Sikh, I have not done the mantras and prostrations of Tibetan Buddhism, and I maintain a basic scepticism about New Age spiritualism. On the other hand, I have been practising a philosophy and a technique – about which more in due course – for over fifteen years. Though they have spiritual dimensions, they do not add up to a religious faith. They do not bring me the solace of a supreme and benevolent Other; they do not pardon me through prayer or ritual from the consequences of my actions or the responsibility for my salvation. But neither do they preclude religious faith. I now *know* that our existence is infinitely more mysterious, more miraculous, and more complex than the average atheist and agnostic would suppose.

Even rational science says that the hands before us, the pages we behold, and the chairs in which we sit are nothing but masses of tiny particles! If we truly understood that, we would not be so complacent about this mundane experience.

To put it another way, I came to look at faith with an attachment to reason and plenty of reasons to doubt – as all seekers should – but I brought too a keenness to learn, a willingness to be startled, and an awesome respect for everyone whose soul panteth after the Truth as the hart panteth after the water brooks. Though usually I could not leap the chasm that separates believers from doubters, in fact I think that the first duty and great purpose of our lives is to find the Truth.

If I say Truth instead of God, Christ, Allah, Brahman, Buddha, or the Great Spirit, it is in order to include all the names of the ultimate reality without exalting any one tradition in particular. Even in Christianity alone, God conjures up so many descriptions, from an old man who lives in the sky to the blind force of life, from Nature to George Burns, that the name has become practically useless in religious dialogue. All believers can agree that Truth describes their deity, and doubters may rest assured that it does not prohibit the possibility that creation is a cosmic freak conceived by accident and existing without meaning.

If it is such a freak, however, history indicates that many human beings would consider that insufficient even if true. "So long as man remains free," Dostoevsky wrote, "he strives for nothing so incessantly and so painfully as to find someone to worship." For where is the succour in the midst of an accident, where is the alleviation of suffering in the swirl of random meaninglessness? Those who dismiss religion as the opium of the people just do not know the sense of pleasure and purity that opium can create amid filth, toil, despair, and perpetual disappointment. An unproductive fantasy, perhaps, but is it more unproductive than the dictatorship of the proletariat or more fantastic than the pursuit of happiness? I confess to times when, sitting at the feet of gurus and preachers while they prattle utter nonsense about the divinity of Haile Selassie or the wisdom of Joseph Smith, I have been carried off by the very beauty of the human imagination, by the poignant pathos behind the need to transcend reason and fact, by the sheer power of rhetoric and vision and hope. I became a primitive again, hunched near the warmth and light of the fire, hypnotized by the voice telling of how we came to be and revealing the stories written in stars on the night heaven and teaching the way back to perfect oneness.

Some of this was the potency of the narrative myth, the epic poem, the symphonic chorus. Intellectual belief was not required for me to be stirred by a Baptist sermon, an evensong hymn, a Requiem prayer, an Ojibwa legend, the lament of a cantor, the cry of the muezzin. But another part was the hope that Truth may be attainable. Reports of a path to knowing and peace, rumours of people who have travelled that way, these make us patient with the most preposterous prophets. We will climb mountains, take bread from our children to give to thieves, sleep in hair shirts or on nails, and spend the brief miracle of life alone in silence for just a glimmer of God and a moment of tranquillity.

Canada is not so far in time from the religious influences of its beginnings that it has lost completely all spiritual values and concerns. They are echoed in our character as a polite and tolerant people. They are in our politics as a liberal and compassionate culture. They are in our arts as a formidable and silent landscape. They are in our environmental movements, our debates over abortion, even our anti-smoking rules. They are in the fundamental differences between Canadians and Americans, based on the fact that, unlike the United States, Canada got French Catholics rather than English Puritans in the seventeenth century, missed the formative influence of the Age of Reason that permeated the American Constitution in the eighteenth century, and congealed as a political and social entity under the religious revivals of the nineteenth century. (In affiliation alone the contrast is remarkable: in 1984 only 28 per cent of Americans were Roman Catholic, the largest Protestant denomination was the Baptist at 20 per cent, and the Episcopalians accounted for a mere 3 per cent.) As the liberating individuality of secularism increasingly reveals its dark side – alienation from nature and community, sterile love, moral anarchy, neurotic vanity, the limits of reason and science, corruption in business and self-service in politics, the paralysing purposelessness – Canadians seem to be calling back those old values and concerns to their assistance.

"I see Canada as a country torn between a very northern, rather extraordinary, mystical spirit which it fears," the novelist Robertson Davies once remarked, "and its desire to present itself to the world as a Scotch banker."

I knew the faces of those who sit on Bay Street and in Parliament. But their mystical spirit was a puzzle to me, only hinted at by the Timothy Eaton Memorial Church, the ruins at Mackenzie King's estate, or the orthodoxy of the Reichmanns. So I resolved to set out across Canada to seek what Rabelais called the "Great Perhaps" and explore the relationships between religion and politics, the tensions between religion and culture, the differences between religion and spirituality, the debates between divine authority and personal conscience, the conflicts between mainline churches and minority beliefs, and the huge question of Truth. I went to all the regions and a representative number of faiths, from episcopal palaces to sacred tents, through church organizations and the temples of immigrants, into Bible colleges and spiritual communes, up mountains and down dirt roads, to discover the soul of God's Dominion.

"Who knows," said my good friend Farley Mowat, "if you discover that, maybe you'll discover a reason for Canada to exist."

ONE

And the Bow Shall Be
in the Cloud

"Yes, we'll gather at the river, the beautiful, beautiful river – "
I found myself singing that wet and chilly dawn. It is not my
habit to sing in the early morning, particularly on mornings as
dark and miserable as this one. But my spirit had been aroused
by the palpable excitement of the hundreds of men, women,
and children who were walking down the long and muddy
main street of Fort Simpson in the Northwest Territories.
" – Gather with the saints at the river – " As for the subconscious choice of song, it was obvious: we were heading for a
stretch of low flatland just south of town on the western bank
of the Mackenzie River (Deh Cho) to await the arrival of Pope
John Paul II. " – that flows by the throne of God!" Or its local
equivalent: a papal chair made from moose antlers, moose
hide, and a beaver pelt sitting within an enormous white
teepee that was actually a theatrical set, with a raised stage, an
open proscenium, and klieg lights in the apex.

From time to time life tosses up such peculiar circumstances that we are lifted momentarily beyond the mundane,
like rounding the aisle of a supermarket and running cart to
cart into the Queen of England. This was shaping up to be one
of those occasions. Popes, after all, were supposed to hang out
in the Vatican. That was where, as a boy, I had seen John XXIII;

21

that was where, in the fall of 1982, I had last laid eyes on John Paul II. "*Veni, sponsa Christi*," the Sistine choir had sung as he proceeded up the length of St Peter's amid a crescendo of applause and the flash of hundreds of cameras, wound with his majestic concelebrants round Bernini's magnificent baldachino, and arose out of the incense on the high altar above the tomb of St Peter himself. It was mystical, magical, almost hallucinatory, but not improbable given the context. Despite all the images of this pontiff hobnobbing with half-naked tribesmen in Papua New Guinea or only slightly better dressed actresses in Los Angeles, a papal mass in a gigantic teepee in a mud field outside of a town of fewer than 1,000 people on the Canadian frontier, with drums and native chants and Indians in parkas, seemed something else.

I was also experiencing the eeriness of a prolonged *déjà vu*. This was perhaps because I *had* in fact been here before, also to see the Pope, also in September, also at dawn, also in fog and drizzle on this long and muddy road with most of these same excited people. At that time, in 1984, the Pope was scheduled to make a three-hour visit to Fort Simpson during his twelve-day journey across Canada, en route from Edmonton to Vancouver. The teepee had been finished at the last moment, some 4,000 Indians had travelled vast distances at great expense and effort, three days of Masses and drum dances and enforced sobriety had been concluded as spiritual preparation, and by daybreak everyone was shivering under blankets, strips of plastic, and garbage bags waiting for the Pope to come. But he didn't. His aircraft could not land because of the thick fog.

The Indians of the North are used to sitting out bad weather, and time is not a priority for them. If conditions did not allow the Pope to arrive that day, he could come the next morning on his way to Ottawa, or the morning after that before returning to Rome, or whenever the fog lifted. Most would wait, because their promise to meet him at his request seemed as inviolable as his promise to meet them. Things did not look as simple among the papal entourage, however. Though the Pope was reported to have said that he wanted to drop into Fort Simpson even if it meant getting up at three o'clock the next day, the

Vatican officials were reluctant to set the precedent of changing his programme, the Canadian officials were frightened by forecasts of more poor weather, and no one wanted to jeopardize the Ottawa events.

"I guess the Pope wanted to ride a boat down the Rideau Canal and be with all those politicians and diplomats rather than be with us," one man fumed.

Others did not blame John Paul II at all: they blamed themselves. Someone must have thrown garbage in the sacred fire burning beside the concrete monument that had been built to commemorate the historic encounter. Or wicked men, such as gamblers and bootleggers, must have turned away the Holy Father. Or a bad prophet must have brought the fog to prevent the Pope from delivering Christ's message. Or perhaps the cancellation was a sign of divine retribution because the Indians are unworthy, as they had been taught for so long.

"Maybe the Pope was scared of Indians," Stanley Isaiah joked. A former river pilot who lived in the old people's home beside the Mackenzie, Stanley was respected as a very spiritual elder. Oddly enough he bore a startling resemblance to the Pope, though older, more wizened, and wearing a cloth cap rather than a mitre. "They picked the wrong time of year. There's often fog in the mornings at this time of year. Or it would have been better to wait until the afternoon, when the earth warms. But they were in a rush. They should have waited and heeded the law of nature, but they only heeded man-made time."

If the Roman Catholic Church deliberately had set out to twist the minds and hearts of a gentle, trusting flock, it could not have devised a crueller method. So many hopes had been raised, none had been realized. Many of the young priests were ashamed of their church that day ("The Church is finished in the North," one lamented); its native stalwarts, especially the elderly who did not expect such an opportunity again, felt wounded and betrayed; and what was the promise of Heaven if that of a rendezvous on earth could no longer be believed?

"It's a sad occasion, it's emotional," Jim Antoine, the young and handsome chief of the Fort Simpson band, had said to the crowd. "But we have come together and we can still make this into something for ourselves. We've always had ourselves and we always will have ourselves."

Later Antoine became part of a delegation that went to Rome three times to remind the Pope and Vatican officials of the papal commitment to visit Fort Simpson someday. At last, in June 1987, a five-hour stopover was arranged for Sunday, September 20, at the end of the Pope's tour through the United States. The native co-ordinators had only three months to organize the programme, the logistics, the financing, the security, the accommodation, the media, and all the other details of a half-million-dollar "world event," but they benefited from the 1984 run-through – as well as from $40,000 the town had received as its share of the insurance payment made after the Pope's cancellation under the "no-show" clause of a performer's contract, similar to one used by the Rolling Stones.

The determination of the young native leaders such as Jim Antoine and Stephen Kakfwi to get John Paul II to the Canadian North had more to do with their politics than with their piety. In 1969 the five tribes of the Mackenzie Valley – Hare, Chipewyan, Dogrib, Slavey, and Loucheux – had formed the Indian Brotherhood of the Northwest Territories, which in 1978 changed its name to the Dene Nation and opened its membership to all status and non-status Indians and Métis of Dene ancestry. Dene, which means "the people," refers to those who live within the western part of the Territories known as Denendeh, "the land of the people." The primary objectives of the alliance had been recognition of the Dene as a nation within Canada, of their aboriginal rights to the land, and of their right to determine the development of the land and the future of their people. Clearly the very appearance of the Pope in Denendeh would be a boost for those objectives. For once, after years of receiving the images and messages of the world via satellite, the Dene would be sending out an image and message of their own. The world would see the Indians in their homeland, would see the wide and graceful Mackenzie, would see the poplars and birches as yellow as butter in the autumn sunshine, and would realize at last that a people had been here for more than 10,000 years and still loved their land.

"For the first time since the coming of the Europeans," said Stephen Kakfwi, a former president of the Dene Nation, "a very special recognition is being given to our people by such a powerful leader. In a way we're being blessed again as we were at creation, as having a special place in the world community. We want to imprint a picture in everyone's mind that we are real, so that every time someone talks of putting in a pipeline or stopping the harvesting of furs, people will remember we're here."

As someone who had grown up in Quebec during the 1950s, I was hardly naive about the political utility of religion; nor was I unaware of the intimate connection between native spirituality and the land upon which native politics and economics are centred. There seemed more than the usual opportunism in these manipulations, however. When I asked Jim Antoine about his faith in Jesus Christ, for example, he simply replied, "Oh, I'm not into that kind of stuff." Kakfwi often cited foreign religions along with foreign governments and corporations as the historic cause of Dene oppression. "We didn't ask to be saved," he told me with an edge, recalling how the Christian churches had undermined native culture by forbidding Sun Dances and potlatches, wrenched native children from their families and traditions by placing them in residential schools and beating them for speaking their own languages, and often worked in conjunction with the government agencies to strip the Indians of land and power in order (as Bishop Joseph-Octave Plessis put it in 1818) "to draw from barbarism and the disorders that follow it the savage nations scattered in this vast country."

There was an irony in this. Many of the important young leaders in Denendeh had been singled out at an early age by the Church as the best and brightest of their villages. By giving them an intensive education under close scrutiny, the Church hoped they would complete high school and perhaps go on to university, so that at least some of them could become priests. Instead, most of them emerged as intelligent, articulate, and vociferous critics of the Church's record.

As every Canadian schoolchild is taught, it was the fate of the native peoples that their discovery by the Europeans in the early sixteenth century should have occurred when, in the words of E. J. Pratt, "The winds of God were blowing over France." In the wake of the Protestant Reformation, though not entirely because of it, there had arisen within the Catholic states of Europe a spiritual energy that became known as the Counter-Reformation. If it shared with the Protestants a desire to cleanse the Church of corruption and error, it chose to do so not by schism and conflict but by a return to faith, piety, obedience, mystical experience, and good works. While the Reformation turned against pope, priests, and pomp, the Counter-Reformation reacted with ultramontanism, holy vows, and a rage for traditional saintliness which produced several enthusiasms of extraordinary consequence for the unsuspecting tribes of the Americas: a thirst for evangelization, a romance about self-abnegation to the point of martyrdom, an emphasis on moral discipline, and a dedication to the founding or revitalizing of religious orders. Nothing could have been more illustrative of these enthusiasms – or more consequential to Canadian Indians – than the formation in 1534 of the Society of Jesus (the Jesuits) and in 1535 of the Company of St Ursula (the Ursulines). Those were the years of Jacques Cartier's first two voyages to the place he named Canada; that was the context within which he planted a cross at Gaspé to claim the land for his King and God – to the bewilderment and consternation of the Iroquois who had stumbled upon him during a seal hunt.

Though furs and fish accounted for most of the interest, the harvesting of heathen souls was not a negligible concern. The King made that a condition for the fur monopoly; and Samuel de Champlain made it his business to bring those "living without God and without religion like brute beasts" to a knowledge of Christ. Like Champlain the missionaries did not credit as true religion the beliefs and rituals they found among the Indians. The native cosmology was "fable," the native holy men were "sorcerers," and the native ceremonies were "superstitions." Nor did the missionaries appreciate why their own cosmology, holy men, and ceremonies might have struck many shamans as nonsense at best and bad medicine at worst. Certainly if strange diseases broke out in my town after every visit by foreign cultists all dressed in black, if the sick and elderly in my family were almost sure to die whenever such cultists administered spells as esoteric as the last rites, then I might have reasonable cause to wonder what in God's name was happening.

In some ways the surprising outcome was not that Father Brébeuf was tortured and burned but that the Jesuits made any inroads at all. Even in Europe it was an age when burning heretics was more popular than putting up with kooky religious ideas. An opening skirmish in France's Wars of Religion had occurred just weeks after Cartier's return from his first trip, when Francis I was goaded by Protestant propaganda into burning thirty-five Huguenots. As F. R. Scott asked in his ironic little poem about the Canadian Martyrs, given the similarities between what the Hurons did to the Jesuits and what the Jesuits were doing under the Inquisition, "is priest savage, or Red Indian priest?" Nor could I ignore the spiritual masochism that attracted many of the missionaries to Canada, to imitate Jesus Christ by seeking suffering and death.

"We shall die, we shall be captured, burned, butchered; be it so," wrote Father Charles Lalemant. "Those who die in their beds do not always die the best death. I see none of our company cast down. On the contrary they ask leave to go to the Hurons, and some of them protest that the fires of the Iroquois are one of their motives for the journey."

The Hurons were not unaware of the role they had been given in this macabre Passion play. They "baptized" Brébeuf with boiling water to speed him on to Paradise. Torturing him with red-hot hatchets and belts of fire, they said, "Thou seest plainly that we treat thee as a friend, since we shall be the cause of thy Eternal happiness. Thank us, then, for these good offices which we render thee – for, the more thou shalt suffer, the more will thy God reward thee."

If conversions were possible at all, the reason may have had less to do with Christianity's filling a void than with the fact that the Indians already had a genuine spirituality. Brébeuf himself noted the "great love and union" they revealed among themselves, their remarkable hospitality to strangers, and their constant equanimity in the face of sickness, famine, and death. Though they had difficulty with the concept of Hell and could not accept why Catholicism had to be the only truth, their own faith prepared them to understand God, Saviour, Heaven, immortal souls, visions, prayers, priests, and all the most colourful and complicated rituals. And though they sensed that the Black Robes undervalued the world of nature for the world beyond – most evident in the white man's klutziness as hunter and explorer – they were impressed by the magic of clocks and writing, by the wisdom in the simple pedagogical techniques the missionaries invented, and by the courage and tenacity that came with the Christian faith.

Too, as with all conversions, there were personal, social, and economic factors that had little to do with theology: old people seeking knowledge or comfort, young people rejecting the norm for the exotic and difficult, ambitious people worming their way to the power and money, families being dragged in by a fervent parent, tribes facing change and crisis. Sometimes baptism came for a few trinkets; sometimes it came from a transcendental illumination; and sometimes it came because Brébeuf had predicted an eclipse.

In the long run the most effective agents were the education of native children and the gathering of nomadic bands into segregated settlements. Both permitted a more total, intense, and constant indoctrination, producing mystical flagellants such as Kateri Tekakwitha and native evangelists such as Joseph Chihwatenha. As early as 1636 the Jesuits sought to secure the hearts and minds of select Indian boys by removing them from their pagan homes to a seminary at Quebec, and a year later they established a controlled settlement at Sillery to promote faith and farming. In 1639 the Ursulines under Marie de l'Incarnation took in native girls. The desire, she admitted, may have been "to make the little savages French or civilized" as well as Christian, though after three decades of effort she rued that they still preferred to run in the woods than live in comfortable French houses. From the first days of New France there had been a strong, often dominant view that to make the Indians good Christians meant to make them good Frenchmen. The further they were taken from their traditional ways – whether beliefs, occupations, languages, or family life – the closer they would get to Jesus Christ.

"In leaving our houses these children have nothing more of the savages than their blood; they have even forgotten their maternal language so well that savage life is no longer possible for them," Bishop Vital-Justin Grandin wrote proudly in 1876. "We will instill in them a pronounced distaste for that kind of life, so that they will be humiliated when reminded of their origin."

Not all missionaries shared this view, especially those who underwent enormous personal hardship to live among the tribes, learn their languages, and develop techniques for teaching the Gospel in harmony with native customs. Many Jesuits, in particular, saw the segregated communities as *protection* from exploitation and assimilation by traders who were no better Christians for being French, and Bishop François de Laval waged an aggressive campaign against those colonists who encouraged the ruin of Indians by the selling of alcohol. Long after the Conquest, in the West and the North, not a few priests and nuns maintained that concern. Themselves a minority as francophones and Catholics, engaged intimately in the lives and sufferings of native families, they had little reason to identify with the English Protestants who were moving into Indian land as farmers, miners, and government agents. In fact, many Catholic missionaries expressed sincere sympathy for the causes of the Métis uprisings and for Louis Riel, himself a former seminarian who came to believe his people had a divine mission to establish a Christian kingdom under a pope of the New World. Ultimately, however, even the best intentions only paved the road to Hell. From that regard the missionaries were less the bearers of salvation than the shock troops of oppression.

The Roman Catholic Church was not the only guilty party. If the founding of French Canada coincided with the Counter-Reformation in France, the settling of English Canada occurred during an era of Protestant evangelism in England. Driven by spiritual conviction, moral crusade, and imperial confidence, the Anglicans and Methodists in particular fanned out among the tribes of British North America to save native souls from the damnation of heathenism and popery alike, just as the Pentecostals, the Seventh-Day Adventists, and the Jehovah's Witnesses still do. By 1900 almost three-quarters of the Indian population were estimated to belong to a church; and in 1981, among the 413,375 the census counted as native peoples, there were 219,130 Roman Catholics, 83,840 Anglicans, 35,615 United Church, 13,890 Pentecostals, 5,360 Baptists, 4,690 Presbyterians, as well as a smattering of Lutherans, Mennonites, Mormons, Salvation Army, Jehovah's Witnesses, and so on. (More mysteriously, perhaps, there were also 2,075 Hindus, 1,755 Muslims, 1,120 Sikhs, 185 Jews, and 75 Buddhists!)

"To an extent that is seldom recognized," observed the historian John Webster Grant in his excellent book on missionary activity in Canada, "the assault on Indian culture bemoaned by social activists today was led by social activists of an earlier era." For the Protestant do-gooders agreed with their Catholic rivals that the eradication of squalor, disease, immorality, and ignorance required the native people to become European as well as Christian. They launched the same attack on traditional beliefs and customs; they too gathered bands into settlements and on to reservations, including William Duncan's controversial community of Metlakatla in British Columbia; and they too subverted families, language, and the passing down of skills by exiling the children to residential schools. In fact, unlike the Catholics, they had the full force of government, trading companies, and English numbers to assist them.

"The wild boys persist in beating the drum," whined the Reverend William Spendlove, the Anglican missionary at Fort Simpson in 1884, taking a break from ranting against the

Romish darkness, "but I hope the time is not far distant when this relic of heathenism shall be a thing and practice of the past, when they shall give the horrible Drum a passage on the current of this beautiful river and never make any more of them."

I found something of that attitude still alive in Fort Simpson in 1984 when talking with Bishop Paul Piché, at the time seventy-five years old, fifty years a priest, and soon to retire after more than twenty-five years as Bishop of the Mackenzie. "At first we admired the few priests who were working closely with the Indians, but soon they had all the other fathers against them," he said. "They thought the old Indian religion was as worthy as the Christian religion, so the missionary feels, 'Why am I coming here and disturbing them?' But we were *sent* by Christ. If we admit that the Indians' religion is enough, that they don't need us to bring Christ because they have the Big Spirit, well, that's *ignorance*."

His frown creased his round bald head, then his laugh shook the glasses on his nose and the cross hanging upon his chest. "They say we oppressed the Indians, we killed them, we destroyed their culture. But the Church *saved* the Indians. In 1902 when the first bishop came, there were only 5,000 in all the Northwest Territories, and they were all dying of T.B. We opened the hospitals and the residential schools and we started to rebuild their health. We suffer what they say rather than insult them or give them an inferiority complex, but we know what we have done and what they were. We're encouraged by the progress they're making. We rejoice in their awakening and the personality coming out. But we have to be very careful. It's like parents with their children: they seek what is best for them."

Since 1962, however, when the Second Vatican Council initiated a radical modernization of Roman Catholicism, Piché's paternalism has become increasingly outmoded. Though the bishops reaffirmed that the Church had been "divinely sent" to bring all nations to Christ as the "unique way to salvation," their decrees had the general effect (if not the exact intention) of breaking down the exclusive, defensive, and reactionary mentality of the Counter-Reformation and nineteenth-century Roman triumphalism. Power and responsibility were to be shared with the people of each diocese; language, symbols, and ceremonies were to be adapted to the various cultures; pluralism within the Church and tolerance toward other faiths were to be encouraged; and individual dignity and community creativity were to be esteemed.

Moreover, as the Church moved closer to the lives of its parishioners (now more numerous in Asia, Africa, and Latin America than in Europe and North America), as it grew alienated from power and prestige in the materialistic and militaristic societies of both communism and capitalism, as it opened itself to modern economics and sociology and the experiences of other churches, the Roman Catholic hierarchy shifted from a vehement political conservatism to something resembling social democracy. Though John Paul II and his most influential advisers are considered reactionaries on social and theological issues, they remain radical in their criticism of unbridled individualism and bottom-line myopia; and the strongest pressure on them from priests and theologians, especially in the Third World, is to embrace the Marxian analyses contained in the prevalent thought known as "liberation theology."

Liberation theology first developed in Latin America, primarily during the 1970s, to link Christ and the Gospels to specific situations of military dictatorship, class struggle, multinational exploitation, extreme poverty, and human suffering. It sought to apply Christian ideals of freedom and justice to political action, economic reorganization, and social transformation, and it did not rule out revolutionary means if necessary. Its "preferential option for the poor" and its "base communities" soon gained popularity around the world, even in rich industrialized democracies which they hardly suited, and it was not long before many Canadian Catholics brought them to the problems of the poor, the unemployed, the working class, and especially the native peoples such as the Dene.

"The Dene want to decolonize themselves, their government system, and their economy. They also have their plans to decolonize their church," wrote René Fumoleau, a priest who went to the North from France in 1953. "The missionaries must forget their own liturgical concerns, their own administrative worries, the fear that their religious system may not survive, and their hope of perpetuating the only type of church they know. All these are secondary details when compared to the survival of the Dene Nation, the struggle of the Dene for self-determination, and their hopes and anxieties."

Even the bishops took up the cry in the face of oil exploration and other economic and cultural crises. In 1975, for example, the Canadian Conference of Catholic Bishops issued a statement asking, "Northern development – at what cost?" It demanded a just land settlement with the native peoples, effective consultation with them on development, and aboriginal control over their future economic destiny. "In the final analysis what is required is nothing less than fundamental social change," it said. "Until we as a society begin to change our lifestyles based on wealth and comfort, until we begin to change the profit-oriented priorities of our industrial system, we will continue placing exorbitant demands on the limited supplies of energy in the North and end up exploiting the people of the North in order to get those resources."

By that time most Christian churches had undergone "a conversion experience" regarding their role in the sorry condition of Canada's native cultures. Also in 1975 an alliance of Roman Catholics, Anglicans, Presbyterians, Lutherans, Mennonites, Quakers, and the United Church formed Project North to combat the threat of northern development; and in 1987 the leaders of those churches in Canada issued a strong plea for "a New Covenant" that would give constitutional recognition and protection to aboriginal self-government.

Probably the most abject apology was given by the United Church, the heirs of the Methodist preachers, at its General Council meeting in Sudbury in 1986. Amid drums and chants and a dance around the fire, the Right Reverend Robert Smith as Moderator declared, "Long before my people journeyed to this land your people were here, and you received from your elders an understanding of creation, and of the Mystery that

33

surrounds us all that was deep, and rich, and to be treasured. We did not hear you when you shared your vision. In our zeal to tell you of the good news of Jesus Christ we were closed to the value of your spirituality. We confused Western ways and culture with the depth and breadth and length and height of the gospel of Christ. We imposed our civilization as a condition of accepting the Gospel. We tried to make you be like us and in so doing we helped to destroy the vision that made you what you were. As a result you, and we, are poorer and the image of the Creator in us is twisted, blurred, and we are not what we are meant by God to be. We ask you to forgive us and to walk together with us in the spirit of Christ so that our peoples may be blessed and God's creation healed."

The day before the Pope's arrival, I wandered without much aim around the village and the camp sites. The sky was blue, the sun was warm, the mood was festive, and the bell summoning the faithful to eleven-o'clock Mass at the Sacred Heart increased my feeling that God was in His Heaven and all was right with the world. The small church was filled to overflowing, mostly with elderly Indians casually dressed, their weather-beaten faces solemn with piety, and I was touched to hear them singing the hymns so fervently in their own language.

On the southern edge of town, among the birches and spruce, camps had been set up by those from afar. In tents and vans, around fires and picnic tables, families were enjoying the life they love to live when they leave the settlements for the bush. Old friends lingered together, women sliced raw caribou and slabs of fish into chunks and hung them to be smoked over the fire, husbands played checkers or gambled at cards, sons found excuses to roar around in the pick-up trucks, daughters teased the barking dogs, small children kicked up dust playing ball or tag, and there were few wails from the babies. The impression that beautiful Saturday morning was of grace, good humour, and peace.

In this scene, shortly before noon, I came upon eight priests (including a bishop) celebrating an outdoor Mass with a hundred or so Indians. The altar was a picnic table, the pews were logs and plastic folding chairs, and most of the priests wore sunglasses and jeans. Prayers in Cree were followed by "Ave Maria" and "Alleluia," a native medicine bundle of sweet grass, tobacco, and sacred whatnot was placed beside a cross, and the Communion wine was poured from a maraschino-cherry jar. Watching the enthusiasm and devotion with which the young unshaven priests were singing the Cree hymns, I understood how the opening to native forms of worship had deepened their own faith. Seeing the Eucharist prepared on a picnic table, I realized why the symbol of cannibal sacrifice had reached the so-called pagans. In fact, because of the pri-meval setting with the autumn foliage and camp smoke and barking dogs, I felt I had been transported back to the essential sources of the Christian religion, to its own pagan and super-stitious origins and to its first appearance amid the forests of Huronia.

Whereas three years before, Bishop Paul Piché of the Mack-enzie had lorded his way through the Dogrib camp like some-thing from another planet surrounded by a phalanx of priests in white and himself aglitter with golden vestments, mitre, and crosier, now Archbishop Peter Sutton of Keewatin-Le Pas and his holy band of ragamuffins were comfortable sharing hamburgers on the "altar" once the Mass was over. When the service ended, one of the priests picked up the embroidered medicine bag, and scores of Indians lined up in front of him for blessings and cures.

"That's Father John Hascall," a bystander explained. "He's recognized as a powerful medicine man."

"Actually I call myself a *medicine priest*, no hyphen," said Father Hascall when I tracked him down later in the day. "I think I'm the only one there is, and it's kind of lonely."

In fact, he did look kind of lonely. Even during the Mass I had noticed him because he was taller, darker, and bulkier than the other priests – and a great deal more woebegone. He moved as if weighed down by his past, his work, and his spiritual striving, as well as by his large and unhealthy body, and neither his pallor nor his voice was made less mournful by his chain-smoking. We sat on a log, which may have accounted for some of the pain in his expression.

Hascall is an Ojibwa who grew up on a reserve on the Ontario-Michigan border. His clan is the White Crane, the bearer of physical and spiritual healing. Though he can remember elders teaching by parable about nature and the medicine way, he was raised a Catholic and at fourteen entered a seminary to become eventually a Capuchin friar. It was a hard path, characterized by obedience and silence, and it almost pushed him to suicide. Torn between two cultures, two paths, he found some relief in the late 1960s when he was allowed to develop his native self by praying in the Indian way and training as a medicine man, while still working as a parish priest in Michigan. He flirted with the radical politics of the American Indian Movement, he wrestled with alcoholism and depression, and he battled the bishops who were afraid of the changes he was promoting. By 1978, on the verge of leaving the Church, he had a heart attack.

"I just couldn't go on, and I got mad," he said. "Three times I asked Christ to tell me who he is, and then the answer came: 'I AM.' He took me through the Scriptures, he took me among the Israelites and the Africans, he took me into the lodge of my own people, and he was there. He is at the centre of everything. There is no separation between whites and natives, between the medicine and the sacraments. Jesus gave us the pipe and the White Buffalo Woman just as he gave us the Eucharist and the Lord's Prayer. For Jesus is God and has all the names of God."

From this vision a sort of peace and understanding settled over the troubled soul of John Hascall, and he picked up the burden of integrating the two ways. "There was a medicine man who had a dream. In it there was a young lady, blind from birth, who wanted to see again. All the medicine people were called to her. When I touched her, she got sight. Then the scene switched: there was a long line of native people and I was leading it. When I heard of this dream, I prayed, and I knew that the lady is the Church, to whom I have been called to heal her blindness."

In 1986 he left his parish (he cried telling me of the farewell powwow) to work with the Tekawitha Conference, a Montana-based institution dedicated to the development of aboriginal Catholicism throughout the Americas, though in practice he spends most of the year bringing his experience to native communities. "The first step is to get my people to love themselves again – love is the strongest medicine – by whatever works, whether the sweat lodge or a charismatic meeting, whether through the healing of a Sun Dance or the Mass. I put drums and naming ceremonies into the Mass, and I give confession and absolution in the sweat lodge. When young people ask me the way to Christ, I send them on a native vision quest to learn who they are. Only after that do I instruct them about Jesus. They can't skip; they have to see the fullness of both Christianity and the Indian way. But my single purpose is to draw out the Christ who's already there."

Father Hascall is just part of a broad effort to create a genuine native Church, genuinely Catholic and genuinely indigenous, an effort propelled by the dying off of the white missionaries. Its symbols, ceremonies, and special rules would come up from the people and their traditions, so that the fundamental message could penetrate deeply and directly into the culture. With this approach the world-renewing purpose of the Sun Dance is exactly the same as the regenerative meaning of Holy Week. The tree at the centre of one circle is the cross at the centre of the other. The fast of the vision quest is the lenten period in the wilderness. The pipe is the tabernacle, its smoke the body and blood of the Great Spirit, its passing the Communion, its turning the prayer of incense. The twelve posts of the teepee are the twelve apostles, the spirit helpers are the angels and our hopes, the bad medicines are the devils and our neuroses, the dreams and prophecies are the inspirations of the Pentecost, the land is the Bible, and the sweat lodge is the confessional. The priest is the medicine man, the pope is the shaman, Jesus is the perfect healer, and God is the Creator.

In the past twenty years all the major denominations have designed educational programmes, national and local councils, and administrative structures to give power and expression to native members. The Roman Catholics have set up the

Kisemanito Centre in Northern Alberta and allowed married deacons in Northern Ontario; the Anglicans have a theological school at Pangnirtung, the Council for Native Ministries, and a native bishop in Saskatchewan; and the United Church established the All Native Circle Conference and the Jessie Saulteaux Centre under native control, for example. Generally, however, the results have been disappointing, for various reasons. There are barely a handful of native priests among the Catholics, because of a cultural aversion to celibacy; natives still feel marginalized in the Anglican Church, despite their large numbers; and the natives of the United Church have yet to accept the Sudbury apology, until its words are proven by actions. "If it's structured, it's not Dene," I was told by way of explaining the clash between cultures.

At the heart of the tensions is the cold reality that the whites have the final authority. However tolerant they may have become, they still have their "God-given" responsibility to promote and protect their own viewpoints. If Rome surrenders control to a native Church, for instance, it risks losing the authority to dictate morality, ward off false gods, and save souls, and however sympathetic the Pope may be to affirming aboriginal culture for the sake of justice and development, Christianity believes it can never accept any culture completely. Since cultures are temporal and made by humans, they must be purified by the Truth that is eternal and divine. While bishops and theologians are willing to put up with measured doses of sweet grass and drums, therefore, they are not beyond snide comments about how unhealthy Father Hascall seems for a medicine man. And while native Christians are willing to behave like good parishioners, many of them may actually be holding two distinct and conflicting theologies simultaneously.

"It's claimed that Catholicism completely replaced the native traditions for a couple of generations, but perhaps the priests and anthropologists were only told there was nothing left," said Jean-Guy Goulet, a former Roman Catholic missionary, now a professor of anthropology at Calgary. "In Meander River I knew a missionary, fluent in the native language, who was sure there was nothing left – his church was full and all that – but at night I used to go to the homes of medicine men for ceremonies! And in Assomption I know elders who are equally comfortable in church and at a Prophet Dance."

In a paper for the *Canadian Journal of Anthropology* Goulet described one of his own vivid encounters with what is termed "religious dualism." One day he was invited to join a young Dene and his mother at the grave of a brother who had been killed at the age of twenty-two in an industrial accident. "In the cemetery Andrew, his mother, and I knelt by David's tomb. We took out our rosaries and prayed a full rosary in English. We concluded with a sign of the Cross, and we rose to our feet. We had accomplished a typical Catholic act of devotion for the deceased, and we prepared to return quietly to our homes. But the unexpected occurred.

"As we neared the gate of the cemetery a deer appeared at the edge of the wood. It bounded towards us. It neither ran away nor appeared frightened. It headed towards us and stopped fifty feet away. At the sight of the deer Andrew's mother threw herself down and pounded the earth with clenched fists. She cried loudly, pulling the grass out of the ground with rage and tears. Andrew addressed the deer in Dene. The deer stood there, moving only his ears, as if trying to find the best position to pick up what Andrew was saying. Andrew twice turned to me saying, 'It's our brother's power, he knows we are here, he sends it to us.'"

Andrew talked to the deer for a few minutes, until it gently walked away, and then he told his mother to stop crying "lest she bring death upon another member of the family." Afterwards no one wanted to speak about what had happened, and it took Goulet almost a year to penetrate the mystery. "What Andrew's family knew was that since early in his childhood David had had a deer as an animal guardian. When David was twenty-two the deer had appeared to him in the bush and said, 'I have come to say farewell, for this is the last time I will see you in this world, you are almost dead.' David reported this vision and message to his family. Two days later he died in an accident on an oil rig. Ten years later David's animal guardian was at David's grave to remind us of their continuing relationship."

But how can a person believe in two opposing systems at the same time, in reincarnation and eternal afterlife? There may be Christians, of course, who go to church on Sunday, consult their horoscope on Monday, attend their yoga class on Tuesday, see their psychiatrist on Wednesday, practise Transcendental Meditation on Thursday, affirm reincarnation on Friday, and break most of the Ten Commandments on Saturday, but I have always assumed that is possible because they do not really believe or understand anything. Among the native peoples, however, especially among the elders, there often seems to be a depth of faith and knowledge that precludes such an explanation.

"They seem to have made Christianity part of a larger whole that we are unaware of," Goulet suggested to me. "In that sense they've already begun what the missionaries and theologians are only talking about doing. So far the Roman Catholic Church isn't free enough to allow for the variety of faith's manifestations, because of the burdens and mistakes of her past. She can't even accept the Anglicans and Eastern Orthodox yet. And because she still dismisses those who may be shacked up or using contraceptives, they speak their truth somewhere else, where our priests never hear it."

Nevertheless, the Pope did want to signal a dramatic change of heart with his appearance in Fort Simpson. "In keeping with the teaching of the Second Vatican Council," he said of the missionaries in 1984, "they have striven with greater awareness to show you, as the Church earnestly desires, even greater respect for your patrimony, your language, and your customs." Indeed, he said, "Christ himself has become Indian and Inuit in you, his members."

This was the spirit that brought him back in 1987. While John Paul II's authority comes from his position as God's chosen successor to St Peter himself, his charisma comes from his personality. With his combination of intelligence and devotion, with his handsome looks and kind manner, with the energetic grace and articulate voice that suggest the actor he once was, his Masses make all other Masses seem like provincial road shows. When he bows to kiss the altar or swings the censer or raises the chalice, there is a dramatic beauty to stir the soul of an agnostic. When he intones, *"Mysterium fidei,"* the mystery of faith is indeed proclaimed. And all his travels have lent him the aura of a TV celebrity, which may be a greater attraction in these times than any spiritual blessing. For John Paul II is the first satellite pope. His genius is to understand that he can go to the remotest corners of Christendom and still speak live to the entire world. In fact, the more exotic the locale, the more likely is his message to reach TV screens in Kansas City, Seville, and Colombo. Even a pope with wanderlust would have had trouble justifying the time and money absorbed in addressing a few thousand people in the wilds of Canada if they had not been the live audience for a production not unlike a Home Box Office special.

So, despite the betrayal of 1984, back came the pick-up trucks and school buses full of native Catholics from Fort Providence and Snowdrift. Back came the charter flights from Watson Lake and Fort Smith, and back came the river boats from Norman Wells and Fort Good Hope. Back came the long-gone children from Edmonton 1,400 kilometres to the south, and back came the seldom-seen friends from as far away as Ontario. Back came the elderly whose way was paid by more raffles and bingo, and back came the hunters on their way to the bush. Back came the native camps, the press tent, and the CBC (bitching this time in army tents, not luxuriating in Atco trailers, because of government restraint). Back came the four Lebanese from Calgary to sell Elvis tapestries, Confederate flags, costume jewellery, and hashish pipes beside their van on the main street, and back came those men who thought the presence of Dogrib women held out hope for a good weekend. Back came many of the undelivered gifts: the moccasins from Hay River and Canoe Narrows, the soapstone carving from Coppermine, the paintings, the moose-hide jacket, and the ten-dollar offering "to help us from alcohol."

Stanley Isaiah did not make it back, however. He had picked up what he teasingly referred to as "the Pope's cold" when waiting that September morning three years before, and a month afterwards he was dead.

But I came back, and back came the bad luck. As in 1984, the days leading up to the momentous arrival had been clear and crisp, with sun on the yellow leaves at noon and frost on the ground at night. Even science put the odds of rain on Sunday, September 20, at 20 per cent. Someone must have put garbage in the sacred fire again. Down came the rain at dawn, in dribbles and in buckets, and in rolled the fog. Though we knew there was special radar at the airport now, reducing the chances of another papal fly-past, our spirit could not help but be dampened. Even when the loudspeakers informed us that the Pope's plane had indeed landed, our cheers were rather sodden and the droplets coursing down our cheeks were not all tears of joy.

Then something astonishing happened. Shortly before eleven o'clock, as the Pope's cavalcade drove up to the monument by the edge of the river, the rain stopped, the sky began to clear, and a huge and radiant rainbow appeared overhead. "I do set my bow in the cloud," God had said to Noah after the Flood, "and it shall be for a token of a covenant between me and the earth." Neither the priests nor the elders missed the symbolism. And so this miraculous coincidence was taken for a token of the New Covenant between God and the aboriginal peoples, between the churches and the faithful, between mankind and the land. Under this transcendental arch even the cursed rain became the sign of purification, baptism, and fresh beginnings, reinforced by the fact that the Dene call the rains of this season when the moose mate and are hunted, "the rain that washes away the blood."

"It's better not to hurry," I remembered Stanley Isaiah saying. "It's better to listen and to learn, to learn from nature. Look at the power of nature. Such a mere thing as a little fog stopped such a mighty man. If he had moved slower, he might have learned something. The fog would have lifted, and he would have seen something beautiful."

TWO

_____

Not Only Looking
But Seeing

"What did that rainbow mean?" I asked the elderly Cree prophet, Albert Lightning.

"It meant good weather," he grumped. Then he laughed at his own *bon mot*, which I would hear him repeating around town for the rest of the day. He knew I was expecting a more cosmic answer, especially since there was a bold rainbow painted above the entrance to his ceremonial teepee, but Albert liked to be opaque and he was not about to concede to the Pope any supernatural power to summon heavenly signs. I had been curious about him for a couple of days. He was obviously ancient. (Once he told me he had been born in 1898, but when I tried to confirm that later, he dismissed the question as of utterly no importance, as if I should not waste our time on temporal details.) But he had a strength, an energy, and a brightness that contradicted his years. For hours upon hours I watched him instructing his helpers on how to erect his sacred tent in the field near the Pope's stylized one, his back straight, his eyes missing no intricate peg or tiny error, his voice stern and certain. Despite his glasses and hearing-aid, he had the puckish face of Lord Beaverbrook under a red peak cap; and despite his taciturn nature and other-worldly vagueness, he had the portentous eloquence of Churchill doing an imitation of Grey Owl.

It took me several tries to get him to speak. He usually had some chore to perform, some preparation to arrange, till I sensed he did not care for my reporter's approach. Perhaps I should have brought him some tobacco, the traditional gift when answers are sought from an elder; perhaps he was too deaf, rather shy, and somewhat confused; perhaps he was just plain rude, which sometimes looked to be the case; perhaps it had to do with the style of native teaching. The truly wise seldom announce themselves as such. They are modest and reticent about what they know. Their knowledge rarely comes quickly or directly or without much prodding. A supplicant, therefore, must demonstrate eagerness and persistence while being coy and patient. I learned this by accident early one afternoon when I happened upon Albert sitting on a log in the sun by himself. Since I had given up trying to get a useful quote from him, I simply sat silently at his side. Then he spoke.

"The Spirit speaks to me. I can summon it so that a whole group will hear it. It doesn't always come. It won't come if someone has been drinking alcohol or something like that. It speaks through a round stone. Its voice comes out of that and carries everywhere. The Spirit tells me things of the past and the future. I have seen everything. I can see without turning my head.

"I always travel with the Lady Spirit. In the circle of people at the beginning of time, a woman walked away. She was put somewhere by spirits, where she could see everything and know everything. She had five daughters – I know them all – and one comes to travel with me.

"The Spirit first came to me when I was two years old. Then it came back when I was thirty-six. I was out threshing in a field and I lay down for a rest. Then I was taken *upstairs* for seven and a half hours. I saw Christ with his outstretched hands and I was taught many things. I couldn't move the whole time. When I was brought back, I was placed very gently on the grass, 200 yards from where my jacket still was. A dog came over and licked my face and hands, and I started walking.

"Many people don't know: when the Spirit appeared to the people in Europe, he appeared here too, north of Vancouver. He lived among our people and taught us many things and told us what to do. When he was killed, he chose to leave us too. We begged him to stay, but he said he had taught us what to do, and he left for the East. (I have seen where he stopped. He slid down a hill and left the mark of his body.) He told us that he would come again. I know the time, I have seen the place. It's soon, it's near.

"The Spirit tells me how to heal too. Once a girl died. I tried something. I went out and collected some grass and other things. I told the girl's mother, who was weeping, to mix these things into a liquid and give it to her daughter. That was hard to do, she had to pry open the jaws. Then the girl's eyes opened. That girl was only told about this a few years ago. She's still alive."

I did not blink. It was too soon in my wanderings for me to presume to tell wisdom from lunacy. I was, after all, moving into the realm of faith, where water is turned into wine, Ignatius Loyola sees the mysteries of Heaven while sitting in a cave at Manresa, and Pat Boone is considered a holy man. Nor can anyone reach forty years of age without becoming more or less inured to the unbelievable things people will believe – that Brian Mulroney is a good prime minister, that baseball is an interesting pastime, that money can buy happiness, that Bob Hope is funny, and so on. In fact, from certain angles and in certain moods, a flight with the Lady Spirit strikes me as considerably more plausible than half the items on the nightly news.

Albert had met his fair share of scepticism, of course, especially from Roman Catholic priests and his sister who had been a nun. About a year after our encounter on the log in Fort Simpson, I met him again at his home on the reserve in Hobbema, Alberta, and after the same initial reluctance he continued his story.

"The priests saw us as savages, pagans, heathens, idol worshippers. They said to me, 'We are priests, you are an Indian, so listen to us: you have to stop what you're doing, there's nothing in whatever you're doing.' They did not know our way of religion. Our worship is better than theirs, because theirs was made in a book while ours was given by the voice of the Spirit. That nobody knows. But I was up there for seven and a half hours, I've got the pictures to show the people that what I'm talking about is the truth.

"There was a time when I met with different priests. One said to me, 'You say there are people who are given to know something by certain spiritual information, but I don't believe it because the Bible says the opposite.' He got me boiled up. So I said, 'In ten minutes that door over there will open. A man will come in, stop, look around, and ask who's the boss here. Someone will point to the one who's running this meeting. The man will go up and pull out a long envelope. It will contain a cheque for $15,000 for our meeting. If that doesn't happen in that time, you can call me a damned liar.' Ten minutes later the door opened, a man came in, he asked for the boss, he went up and pulled out a long envelope, and it contained a cheque for $15,000. So the priest got up and said he owed me an apology. I said, 'Don't tell it to me, tell it to our Creator.' People clapped. That showed I was telling the truth."

So that explained Albert's hostility toward the Pope's rainbow: a clash of visions, professional competition, and not a little jealousy. Not for Albert or the voice from the round stone had thousands of Indians journeyed for days over tortuous roads and chilly waters; nor did the rainbow and the vivid buffaloes that the Lady Spirit had commanded him to paint on his teepee during one of his 827 "flights" offer the power and magic of that covenantal revelation in the sky. Moreover, Albert had the defensive vehemence of an apostate, for he had been raised a Roman Catholic before the Spirit took him up, caused him to return to the native religion, and inspired him to change his name from Leclair to Lightning.

"What does the Pope's visit mean to you?" I once asked him.

46

"Nothing! He has his traditions, we have ours."

Many elders are not wild about blending their spirituality with Christianity, even if they know that all religions are one Truth. For they believe the Creator gave the aboriginal peoples certain gifts and a special mission to sustain mankind's relationship with nature. If they compromise those gifts, if they forget their main mission, they fear they will forfeit their power, their identity, and their place near God. When the white man came, he made off with everything except their religion, because he saw no value in it. It remains as their one distinction, the springboard for their political and social renewal. Now it seems as if the Christians are turning up to look over the elders' house, extract the better pieces to help build their own church, and in the process destroy the integrity of what exists. If the priests regard the pipe as merely an exciting new toy, for example, if they do not handle it properly or respect its power, the elders believe that death itself will result. These things are not metaphors, they are potent realities.

"It's impossible!" one Canadian archbishop thundered when pressured to enter into an inter-faith exchange with native elders. "They're Christians!"

But Christians in their own way. "Our people had knowledge of Christ long before the coming of the white man," a Cree told me. "We had ceremonies and traditions that re-enacted Christ's story. Now the churches are willing to accept that we had some knowledge of God, in an Old Testament way, but they won't accept that our teachings had Christ too. But that's why the Indian people welcomed the missionaries, because the message and story were so close to what we already had. We don't disagree on the reality of Christ's life, but on the idea that we needed someone to come to bring that to us. In fact, Jesus may have come especially to save the whites because they had lost God's way."

That was why Albert Lightning was in Fort Simpson, showing the young people precisely how to erect the teepee poles and leading the Dene elders in the lighting of the sacred fire beside the monument by the river. Boughs were placed round the circle of stones; no cameras or menstruating women were allowed nearby; drummers chanted (*and* crossed themselves afterwards); a pipe, an eagle feather, sweet grass, and other auspicious objects were produced from a medicine bag in the form of a black briefcase; and the fire was lit.

"All different tribes were given their ways of worship," Albert told the small gathering, recovering from his fit of pique that the wood and the axe had not been exactly where they were meant to be. "At the beginning of time when the first people were created on Mother Earth, certain spirits were given to them to explain how to conduct their ceremonies. Everything that was created was created to speak. Many people don't know that. The rock speaks. It was given the power to understand people, to know what they think about, to interpret our desires into the presence of our Creator. The fire speaks. The water speaks. So it is important to respect everything that was created and given to the first people for survival." Then, after filling, lighting, turning, and passing the pipe, he shouted, "Some departed souls have appeared, *now!*"

The fact that these departed souls were neither seen nor heard by anyone else, Albert grumbled to me later, was no doubt due to the sloppiness and inexperience of the participants. Someone had snuck a photograph, another had been suspected of drinking, and the tardy arrival of the wood and axe was all the excuse any soul needed to get out of a manifestation. Native rites, I was to appreciate, had a duration, etiquette, and meticulousness to make the Roman Catholic Mass seem like a high-speed impromptu.

"I'm beginning to suspect Kwanza," said Herb Denton, who was reporting the Pope's visit for the *Washington Post*.

Kwanza?

"Kwanza." And he explained. In the 1960s, in the throes of the black-consciousness movement, there arose in some quarters an aversion to Christmas as a "honky" holiday. Happily someone in California discovered an African feast that the enslaved would have celebrated, Kwanza, which also occurred toward the end of the year and involved the exchange of gifts.

48

So a fashion sprung up among black activists to replace Christmas with Kwanza, and no doubt it included Kwanza presents, Kwanza cards, and Kwanza carols. About a decade later, of course, it was admitted to be a complete fabrication, but apparently that did not bother the pockets of revellers who continue to wish each other a very merry Kwanza.

When Herb suspected Kwanza in the Indian ceremonies, he was reacting to the evidence that so few seemed to have a clue about what was meant to happen, more media were usually in attendance than native elders, and most of the chants in Slavey and Cree contained clear appeals to "Jesus, Mary, and Joseph." In fact, he had stumbled upon the greatest controversy in native religion (apart from the general one about the improbability of the whole business): how much knowledge had been lost through the systematic persecution of the aboriginal beliefs and rituals by the missions and laws, and how much had been saved underground?

Just as there is tremendous variety within what is generally termed native religion, with different tribes and regions having radically different legends and customs, there is no one answer to that question. Some groups proved more open than others to the Christian message and its European forms; some suffered under a longer and more intensive inculcation; some had leaders who converted the rest by threat or example; and some harboured individuals who never abandoned the sacred mysteries of their ancestors. Broadly speaking, more was preserved in the West than in the East because the missionaries had less time to do their damage, and more was preserved in the United States than in Canada because the native populations were more numerous, more isolated, and less evangelized. But everywhere much was in peril.

"The missionaries were good in some ways and I don't blame them," Stanley Isaiah had said to me in 1984, as he sat at the Arborite table in the kitchenette of his spare, bright room in the old people's home beside the Mackenzie River. "They taught a lot that the natives already knew, just a little bit different but it meant the same thing."

Are there still natives who know a lot of things?

"There are prophets. There used to be good prophets, who could tell what was ahead, and bad prophets, who didn't tell the truth. Now there are very few, maybe one or two. They didn't keep the law, I guess."

What law?

"The Ten Commandments. The Ten Commandments were written in the wilderness, not in the big cities where there are a lot of government people. They are the same as the laws of the bush. We used to live with nature and know about it. We were happy people then."

What happened?

"Too many things got in the way. Too many temptations. Man created temptations, so it's hard to live with the Ten Commandments. Now there is nothing but man-made law, and man-made law carries nothing but trouble. Now there is too much wickedness. Nations are rising against nations. Things are getting out of control like a forest fire. People are going out of their minds, and they can't blame others or liquor or anything but themselves. The earth is really a terrible place to live now."

His low and shaky voice fell silent for another while. "The Indians used to keep the earth clean. Now the earth and the air and the water are getting dirty from the cities. But the earth is a living thing. If you put pipelines on it, you will choke it just like Judas choked himself by hanging because he hadn't done the right thing."

Is it too late?

"Maybe we'll have to wait until the Creator comes back to clean everything that man has made a mess of. But Adam and Eve were only two, so maybe two or three people can begin to turn things back. Maybe the Pope's visit is our last chance to change. They say he's a holy man, but I'm not sure why he's coming to Fort Simpson. There's nothing here but a few drunks. Maybe he's heard about us and pities us."

As Stanley revealed, spiritual despair can be both the cause and effect of political and economic despair. Certainly there is despair among the native communities, arising out of poverty, unemployment, alcoholism and drug abuse, suicides, migration to the cities, cultural assimilation, crime and prison, racism, paternalism, and the profound loss of self-respect. In the 1960s, however, a new phenomenon emerged from those depths: the revival of native religion. With desperation as its parent, it was nurtured by a host of influences, including the civil-rights and Black Power agitations in the United States, the global rebellions against colonialism, the growth of ecological consciousness, the new wave of radical sociologists and anthropologists, and the romantic exaltation of tribal ways in the hippie cults. While some of these inspired political action such as the formation of the American Indian Movement (AIM), others inspired spiritual quest based on a back-to-the-land, vision-oriented metaphysic. And while white kids were turned on by the books of Carlos Casteneda to stalk Indian sorcerers for peyote enlightenment, young native leaders began to seek their traditional elders for political as well as personal reasons.

In Canada at that time the best-known native activist was a young Alberta Cree named Harold Cardinal. Born in 1945 on the Sucker Creek reserve near High Prairie to devout Catholic parents, he went through the residential-school system, attended a priest-run college in Ottawa, and at twenty-three was elected president of the Indian Association of Alberta, a post he held until 1977. Though he had become an Indian "nationalist" in college, affected by the ideas of the times and his own studies of his people, he was only exposed to native spirituality after his election in 1968. Before that, he admitted when I visited his home on the reserve, he had accepted the Church's view of it as pagan superstition. In Northern Alberta many of the teachings and ceremonies had been lost in 1918 when so many elders died from an influenza epidemic; many of the remaining practices had been outlawed; and the missions and schools had made almost everyone strong Christians.

"But soon after I became president," he said, "elders from various tribes in the province sent their helpers with the message that they wanted to make me aware of the things that were important to them. I responded to that, and the initial experience of sitting down with these elders convinced me that our people should go back to them to learn. Until then, politically at least, they had lost their position of respect."

Significantly, because he had been raised a Catholic and because his office gave him a responsibility for all Alberta Indians, Cardinal approached native religion with an intertribal eclecticism. As a politician he brought together elders whose tribes had had serious historical differences, and as a seeker he picked up knowledge from Iroquois, Sioux, Dene, Ojibwa, whomever, but especially in Wyoming from an Arapaho elder named Raymond Harris.

His own people gossiped that Harold had become a devil-worshipper. His own parents, as strong Catholics, were upset. One weekend, as he was in his sweat lodge, praying with tobacco, and preparing for a pipe ceremony, Father Roger Vandersteene came by. He was one of the rare Oblate missionaries who spoke impeccable Cree, enjoyed living in Cree style, and demonstrated early interest in Indian spirituality. He was also Harold's "brother," having been adopted by the Cardinals in the native way. When Harold shocked his mother by inviting the priest to share the sweat and a pipe, Vandersteene surprised him by agreeing at once.

"I have my own pipe," he added as another surprise. "An old man gave it to me. He came to me with the pipe in two pieces. A priest had broken it. I fixed it and gave it back, and the old man continued to pray with it. When he was near death, he passed it to me along with his songs and ceremonies."

When Harold's mother mentioned all the talk on the reserve, Vandersteene asked, "Which of us can claim to have seen God?"

"No one," she answered.

"True. So white men paint a picture with fair hair, blue eyes, and a white complexion. Your people create and use a different image. Why should our image of God be more valid than yours? When we think of angels as fair and blond, is that truer than the elders who use an eagle or a raven as an angel? And why is our way of praying more valid than the way your people have learned?"

"So Mum had no more qualms," Harold told me. "And when Father Vandersteene died, he passed his pipe and ceremonies to me."

How much was lost?

"That's a difficult question," he said. "Some elders went underground, and it wasn't until the 1960s that they were convinced to come out again. They're still very cautious. So, while some rituals certainly have gone, many spiritual practices are returning. At the individual level, people are taking from different traditions or specializations and putting them together in new ways. But one of the functions of the elders is to make sure that what we do is done the way it should be done by our own tribes. So, at the collective level, the central ceremonies are kept very traditional, with few innovations."

Throughout the Americas, on reserves and skid rows, in schools and prisons, this regeneration is taking place. Though the numbers may still be small, their impact is not. Just before I visited Albert Lightning in Hobbema, he had been guiding some young Cree through a four-day Sun Dance in the bush nearby; and I was to meet Indians who had been influenced by him from Halifax, Nova Scotia, to Alkali Lake, British Columbia. In Morley, Alberta, I saw elders gathering by the hundreds to share their knowledge, as they had been doing each summer since 1970; in Saskatoon I met a storyteller who now feels it is safe to reveal the "songs of power" his family had preserved for generations; and in Toronto one weekend I found a native conference with crowded workshops on the drum, the Medicine Wheel, and "How To Approach an Elder."

"It was as if we had been tied to a tree and forced to watch our house burn down, with all our valuables in it," said Art Solomon, an Ojibwa from Northern Ontario. "Now we have been released, and we are looking for bits among the ruins in order to start again. When I started thirty years ago, there were no teachers around, so my university was creation. I learned how not to live mindlessly, and the spirits came in different manifestations. Now we're in a whole new time. The spirits are giving visions like never before. People are not only listening but hearing. People are not only looking but seeing."

As he described it, the goal is to regain "the sacred way to walk upon the earth." That way is the one in harmony with the Creator, alias the Great Spirit, alias the Supreme Being, which seems better defined as the natural life force than as a bearded old man in the sky. While the creation myths vary tremendously, all are to be found in nature, all take place in a circle, and all give mankind an intimate relationship to animals and spirits. And while there are myriad techniques for regaining the sacred way, all involve rituals of purification, all demand practices to expand knowledge, and all produce powers to transcend the separateness of ordinary existence.

Among the rituals there are sweet grass, fasts, taboos, silence, and the sweat lodge (which is rather like attending a chapel service totally naked in a primitive sauna). Among the practices there are praying, chanting, storytelling, drumming, dreaming, seeking visions in the wilderness, apprenticing under an elder, passing the pipe, naming, orating, and dancing (especially the cosmic dances such as the Sun Dance, the Ghost Dance, the Medicine Dance, or the Prophet Dance). Among the powers there are prophecy, healing, astral travel, reincarnation, medicine bundles, spirit helpers, hunting success, hexing, and total unity with the entire universe.

In general, native spirituality has an Old Testament flavour, evoking the history of nomadic tribes struggling for survival in a harsh but beloved landscape. Beyond everything there is the omnipotent Creator, who established with a special people a covenant in which land and wisdom were exchanged for obedience and devotion. History, politics, genealogy, poetry, music, and geography are not distinct from "religion," for which I was told there is no specific word in most Indian languages. The laws and rites are set out with intricate precision, and the penalties for offending them can be severe. There are prophets (named Isaiah!) and priestly sages (named Solomon!) to guide the people and the ceremonies, and there is a messianic conviction that the Creator gave his chosen ones the duty to keep and proclaim the truth for the sake of all humanity. Small wonder so many explorers thought they had found in the aboriginal nations of North America the ten lost tribes of Israel.

"The land is our Bible," Stanley Isaiah told me. "What's in the Bible was already on the land. There are legends in the rivers and the mountains, and there's a meaning to them that has to be read. That's why you have to live with it. Like the Bible, if you don't go to school, you won't know how to read it. Reading the land is like reading signs, so you won't get lost."

Though more and more books are being written about it, though there are college texts and shaman memoirs and instruction manuals, the teaching is still an oral tradition, primarily passed down by the elders to their helpers. Most of it is given very gradually, often after an initial reluctance and long silences and an initiation ordeal, and most of it comes in the context of practical experience in the bush. Practice is always more important than theory, experience is always more important than belief, and the bush is always more important than any church or classroom. As a result there are debates about how effective the traditional ways can be for Indians in modern times or in the cities and how much non-natives can – or should – be taught. And since there are no theological degrees or ordination certificates in native spirituality, beyond the demonstration of certain powers gifted from the Spirit and an instinctive recognition of wise persons "who know a lot of things," there is a range of responses. Some elders insist on taking their apprentices back to the wilderness; others are adapting their rituals for use in prisons and community halls. I heard of one man who conducted sweetgrass ceremonies in front of the oil furnace in the basement of his Edmonton apartment building.

"All people who walk on the earth have equal access to the sun, and all spiritual paths are valid for every individual who decides to walk better," Art Solomon said. "The spirit people know all about us, where we've been and where we're going. They won't give us a gift if we're not ready for it or if it will harm us. And if we're getting ourselves together just for ourselves, selfish motives won't work. We have to get ourselves together for all in creation."

The native way is characterized by openness, an acceptance of the natural rightness of things as they are, and a reluctance to assume the spirits' role of judging "good medicine" from "bad." It even embraced Christianity, which may be characterized as dogmatic, averse to nature as the sinful precondition to one or another eternal abode, and eager to denounce all other paths as inadequate at best and demonic at worst. In fact, many elders shy away from labelling anything "bad medicine" precisely because that was the notion by which the missionaries condemned all native practices. However, Indians do acknowledge that spiritual powers can be and have been abused for wicked reasons. The very tolerance within the native way, therefore, makes its travellers especially vulnerable to physical danger, psychic harm, and the more outrageous forms of Kwanza.

In November 1988, for example, I came across an item in the Toronto *Globe and Mail* about a secret native rite, "spirit-dancing," that had just recorded its seventh victim since its revival in the 1970s. A thirty-five-year-old alcoholic died on the Cowichan reserve north of Victoria, B.C., at the end of a four-day ceremony involving fasting, strenuous exercise, solitary confinement, and beatings by "friends and relatives" with heavy rattlers made out of deer hooves. Death came from bruising and dehydration.

But it would be European arrogance to use such tales – of charlatanism, of diabolic possession, of spells and ineptitude and sexual assault in the sweat lodge – to single out native religion as unworthy of wisdom. *All* religion may be nothing but Kwanza, a series of beliefs and practices invented by human beings for political or social purposes. Even if some of it is divinely ordained or mystically revealing, *every* religion has elements of Kwanza. Certainly the Roman Catholic Church has had saints who would have been delighted to be whipped to death by deer-hoof rattlers if such an opportunity had presented itself. Certainly the United Church has lost, discarded, and adapted to modern culture more sacred ceremonies than the Indians ever have. And certainly some Pentecostals could give the elders lessons in spiritual chicanery, mental manipulation, and emotional hocus-pocus.

The reality is that native religion can work as a healer and a power. How it works, whether as a real medicine or a type of placebo, will always remain a mystery deep in the heart of Truth and psychology; but the evidence of its effect is clear. Since its revival whole communities of alcoholics have sobered up after submitting to the purification rites, native convicts and drug-users have been reformed by the sweet grass and the chant, and a resurgence of dignity and pride has followed the pipe and the dance. The tradition has brought back an absent meaning, and the meaning has brought back a forgotten purpose, and the purpose has brought back discipline and confidence and pride. To clean the mind, to give thanks for creation, to respect nature, to pay attention to dreams, to seek contact with the spirits that empower and the demons that torment, to make sacred the mundane and make complete the individual, that is the healing of the native – and every other – way.

"Their ceremonies are to experience that we humans are very small, that great things are happening around us, that *we are not the masters,*" said Jean-Guy Goulet. "When they learn that at all levels, then they have learned everything."

After being ordained in 1978 at the age of thirty-two, Goulet studied anthropology at Yale, then lived almost a year in a totally isolated aboriginal village in South America. Back in Canada he divided his time equally between teaching at St Paul's University in Ottawa and living among the Dene in Northwestern Alberta as a priest and researcher, until he left the priesthood in 1985 to marry. His work on native spirituality, therefore, has been academically rigorous and remarkably intimate. By learning their language, entering into their ceremonies, and approaching their elders with humility and curiosity, he came to experience with the Dene what he called "ways of knowing with the mind," such as dreams and visions. That personal experience let him conclude that the powers claimed by the elders were in fact real.

Among his accounts of life-like visions of the dead, prophetic dreams that came true, and ceremonial teachings given by mental projections instead of by words or example, he told of the strange events that took place over a two-week period in Ottawa in July 1982. "Every time I entered my bedroom I sensed immediately that two Dene elders were somehow present. This thought would automatically come to mind, no matter what I had been thinking just before stepping into the room. Each time I would stop in my tracks and look around uneasily. I could not dispel the conviction that I was sensing something unusual. I reported this experience to an elder who was attending a conference in Ottawa. This elder knew one of the two elders I thought were present in my home. He confirmed that the elder he knew had the power to travel, and encouraged me to acknowledge their presence without fearing them."

Six months later, back among the Dene, Goulet met one of the elders he had sensed in Ottawa. Immediately the elder said, "You know, I went to see you in your house this summer." Later he described Goulet's house correctly as a large one with a hedge all around it. "I had never travelled that far and was afraid," he said. "My helpers then told me, 'Do not be afraid. You are going to Jean-Guy's house.' So I kept going and finally saw you in your house." Though sceptical, Goulet could not think of any picture or conversation that might have given the elder that description.

Despite more than three centuries of persecution and brainwashing, this private spirituality has survived, and now it is spreading out among all peoples in response to the world's ecological crisis and spiritual hunger. For, above all else, native religion teaches harmony with nature by means of real experience and actual healing. That is why the elders began to open up once more in the 1960s. That is why there were many ready to hear them, to fast and sweat and seek visions. Ultimately the greatest sign of the Truth in native religion may be less its supernatural phenomena than its persistent vitality.

I had felt that vitality myself in 1984 in the aftermath of the Pope's cancellation. As the media packed their equipment and scrambled for the fastest flights out, as the attention of the TV audiences shifted from scenes of tearful natives in a cold and shrouded hinterland to happier events in Vancouver and Ottawa, the Indians danced round their fire in the temporary arena of wood and cloth that had been erected near the teepee by the river, a circle open to the black night brilliant with stars and northern lights but enclosed by a narrow ring of protected bleachers now packed with spectators. Around and around the bonfire, hour after hour for most of the night, a throng wheeled to the fierce pounding of half a dozen drums and the hypnotic cries of the singers. Ancient women in blue parkas and magenta kerchiefs, hunters just in from the bush, show-off adolescents wearing Black Sabbath jackets, girls chewing gum, cousins come home from the cities, everyone hopped from foot to foot, clockwise, independently, backs generally straight, heads generally high, faces generally impassive, soles patting the earth with steps like soft kisses. Behind and beside each other, free to express their individuality but united by the beat and tightly moving together for community and warmth, they revolved like the stars and planets above their heads, flowed like the river that ran near them, passed like the parade of humanity around its own hot light in the cold, empty darkness.

Song followed song, set followed set, with barely a rest: such was the love of a drum dance. It was more than a Bunny Hop, just as the drums – round as tambourines, made of caribou hide stretched on a wooden hoop, held where two gut-strings cross at the back, and beaten with a wooden stick – are more than musical instruments. Made from plants and animals, they are considered sacred instruments of prayer, able to set free the song of the spirit inside. Dancing to them need not be a devout occasion, almost any social excuse will do, but a drum dance can produce some of the harmonizing, healing effects usually ascribed to holy rites. And seldom have those effects been felt more powerfully than during the night of the Pope's broken promise. Even the spectators experienced the comfort and solidarity of the dance, the subtle alleviation of the sorrow by the rhythmic trance and pressed bodies, the taking of power from the earth and giving it back to the earth. Soon the tribes would disperse, soon the rest of the world would forget them once again, soon winter would settle in, but for the moment they were dancing together in a circle and nothing else mattered.

At the beginning of time, the teaching says, the Creator came to consciousness in the darkness of endless space. So it created a place to receive its thoughts, by building a fire and drawing around that light a huge circle, the universe, which the Great Spirit then set in ever-changing motion. And it created people, pure and gifted and with the means to develop their gifts, making them of four colours, placing them in the four directions, and giving them four ways to the Truth. The White Man, whose gifts are movement and doing, moved out the fastest, loudly and linearly, into creation; while the Red Man, whose gifts are vision and respect, did not want to leave the Creator's side because creation is kind and loving and in perfect balance. So the Red Man moved out slowly, spoke slowly and softly, thought things through before moving or speaking, danced around the fire and kept the perspective of the circle, and as a result has not lost his way to the Creator. That is the way the elders are being asked to share with those who have lost theirs.

Thus the day has come when Roman Catholic bishops sniff sweet grass during Mass, Anglican priests parade around in Nishga blankets, and United Church members pass the pipe at sunrise ceremonies. And it was a Jew from Montreal, Leonard Cohen, who wrote in his novel about Kateri Tekakwitha, "God is alive. Magic is afoot. God is alive. Magic is afoot. God is afoot. Magic is alive. Alive is afoot. Magic never died. God never sickened. Many poor men lied. Many sick men lied. Magic never weakened. Magic never hid. Magic always ruled. God is afoot. God never died."

The Pope was afoot anyway, out from his limousine, on to the muddy field at Fort Simpson. As the drums drummed the Dene welcome song, he walked to the concrete monument, a low structure climbed by stairs on its four sides which were the four directions of creation, surmounted by a dome to represent the beaver lodge and the sweat lodge and the igloo which were themselves symbolic of the universe. Standing at it, John Paul II did something so rare and subtle that its wonder was lost amid the handshakes, political gestures, and Catholic extravaganzas to follow. In the rain that washes away the blood, under the rainbow that is the sign of holy blessing, he paid homage to the native way by performing an Indian ceremony, written by a local elder and containing no reference to Jesus Christ or the Gospel or the Cross.

Facing east to the Mackenzie River, he gave thanks for water. "As the waters cleanse and heal and strengthen the air and the land," he prayed to the Creator, "so too let your flowing love cleanse and heal us, bring us together as one people, and strengthen us."

Then he turned north toward the sacred fire burning nearby and said, "We give thanks to you, gentle lover, for this fire, for all home fires where offerings of love and kindness, understanding and caring are made. Let this fire burn all impurities from this land and from our minds and hearts and spirits, and send a pure prayer of love from this land and from each of us to you."

Then he turned to the west and thanked the Great Spirit of life for the air. "As the winds awaken and caress the land in spring and summer, as they prepare the land for rest and sleep in fall and winter, so too let the winds of your spirit awaken our lives so that we may always be as the seasons of your love, constant as the land in our expressions of your great creative power."

Then he turned south toward the magnificent fork, the shape of a divining rod, created by the Liard flowing into the Mackenzie. "We give thanks to you, Creator of all, for this land and all she produces, for the animals of the land and water and sky, for the plants which help us to live healthy lives, for the lives we live in caring for this beautiful land you have given to our care."

Albert Lightning could not have said it better.

THREE

Prophets
in the Wilderness

If I understood the poster properly, the Virgin Mary was going to be speaking in the Mississauga Ballroom of the Toronto Airport Hilton that Sunday afternoon one April ($12.50 for the session, $75 for the three-day seminar, special prices for students and senior citizens). Not exactly in person, I was disappointed to discover, but through the person of Elizabeth Clare Prophet, Guru Ma of the Church Universal and Triumphant, Messenger for the Ascended Masters, and self-proclaimed reincarnation of the Martha who got Jesus Christ to resurrect her brother Lazarus.

According to the blurb I received at the door (along with a FREE 44-page booklet and 92-minute cassette of prayers and chants dictated to Mr and Mrs Prophet by Jesus himself for world peace), the Virgin Mary is an Ascended (Lady) Master – along with Confucius, Moses, the Buddha, Jesus, Mohammed, and lesser known beings such as Kuan Yin, St Germain, and El Morya, "to name but a few" – who mastered "outer conditions and earned the right to ascend into the very Presence of God." Collectively called the Great White Brotherhood – "white" referring to the light around the soul, not the colour of the body, and "brotherhood" including the sisterhood of spiritual lightbearers – these "immortal, God-free beings living in the joy of the Eternal Now" are in charge of guiding "this system of worlds" and its "billions of souls yet abiding in the veils of time and space" on "the path to soul freedom," often by means of teaching through embodied messengers or prophets. And that is basically what the Virgin Mary and Mrs Prophet were up to at the Airport Hilton.

Apparently they go back a long way, maybe to Atlantis and the court of King David, certainly to conversations in Bethany at the time of Christ and in Boston in the early 1960s (when the Mother of God gave Elizabeth Wulf, a pretty, political-science major from Red Bank, New Jersey, a rosary to help raise her spinal energy). It was in Boston too, in 1961, that Elizabeth met Mark Prophet, then a forty-two-year-old medium for the Archangel Michael. After a mystical experience one night, they joined psychic forces to receive and transmit the eternal truths of the Ascended Masters, particularly St Germain (an eighteenth-century French alchemist, Knight Commander of the Keepers of the Flame Fraternity, and reputedly the seventh angel prophesied in Revelation 10:7 as well as incarnation of the prophet Samuel, patron of the United States of America, and hierarch of the Age of Aquarius) and El Morya (Chief of the Darjeeling Council of the Great White Brotherhood, Lord of the First Ray, and Master of the Lodges of Perfection).

According to a letter dictated by St Germain, El Morya and the Darjeeling Council wished the Prophets to form the Keepers of the Flame Fraternity. It was to gather together men and women who would teach, serve, and "reconsecrate their lives to the rekindling of the flame of Life and the sacred fires of freedom in the souls of God's people," just as these same people had done long ago when they had been with Sanat Kumara ("one of the Seven Holy Kumaras") at Shamballa, his island retreat in the Gobi Sea (now the Gobi Desert). The Father-Mother God had placed in each heart this flame – a divine spark, one-sixteenth of an inch high, seat of cosmic consciousness, link to Reality and Being, composed of the blue Father-Power and the yellow Son-Wisdom and the pink Spirit-Love – so that all people might remember their source and realize their divinity. Since 1973, when "the soul of Mark Prophet made the transition from the planes of time and space and ascended into the sphere of the I AM Presence" under the name Lanello, Mrs Prophet has carried on as Mother of the Flame, with some 10,000 followers in dozens of centres around the world.

The first step for a disciple ("chela") is to apply for a seven-month probationary membership (which requires pledges to both the Knight Commander and the Mother of the Flame, $33 for monthly dues and a card, and a colour passport photograph of one's lesser self), which brings the first seven Keepers of the Flame lessons about karma, reincarnation, and transmutation through invocation of the violet flame, access to certain meetings and functions and practical instructions, and a FREE 500-page book on alchemy by St Germain. If the student wishes to continue after this "experiment with the Teachings in the laboratory of his own soul," he may apply for ongoing membership (which requires a handwritten letter to St Germain c/o the Mother of the Flame, another $33 plus $5 a month, and an annual "love offering" of $40 plus postage for weekly letters known as Pearls of Wisdom), which brings more lessons, access to more conferences and seminars and prayer vigils and changing sessions, the chance to attend the twelve-week programme at Summit University on the Church's 33,000-acre ranch in Montana (with courses by Jesus, the Buddha, El Morya, and others using Mrs Prophet's voice), and out-of-body trips to the "etheric retreats of the Brotherhood." Serious students can apply later for admission into the Church.

The Toronto seminar was part of this methodical training. By the time I entered the Mississauga Ballroom, about 400 people were chanting ("decreeing") along to a loud tape. "Light, set me free! Light, set me free! Light, set me free! Light command, Light command, Light command, command, command! Light demand, Light demand, Light demand, demand, demand! Light expand, Light expand, Light expand, expand, expand!" The voice on the tape was like a high-pitched computer with a bad cold, and its pace accelerated like "Bolero" on fast-forward into a hypnotic and blurry fever.

"Light I AM, Light I AM, Light I AM, I AM, I AM, I AM a being of Violet Fire, I AM the Purity God desires!"

At the height of the cool frenzy Mrs Prophet glided to the podium, set amid portraits of Jesus and St Germain (also blond, blue-eyed, and bearded, but with a dapper haircut), crystals, flowers, American and Canadian flags, and figures of Mary and Kuan Yin and the Statue of Liberty. Slender and elegant in a white robe and blue chasuble, perfectly coiffed and comfortably poised, with two fistfuls of sparkling rings and a nasally enunciation capable of cutting glass, she resembled a severe Mary Tyler Moore now out promoting some rejuvenating carrot-juice formula across Middle America. Her presentation was impressively professional, her smile was disarmingly warm, and her manner was intimidatingly Junoesque, but the content let me down. It seemed less a revelation from the Mother of God than a well-researched lecture on the feminine force throughout religious history delivered by a glamorous high priestess of the New Age, the loose and controversial term broadly used to describe a loose and controversial mishmash of unusual cosmologies, spiritual practices, and health-food recipes.

"The term New Age springs from the astrological knowledge that the vernal point will enter the sidereal constellation of Aquarius in approximately 2375 AD," wrote Alexander Blair-Ewart, publisher of *Dimensions*, a New Age monthly in Toronto. It therefore anticipates the end of the 2,000-year Age of Pisces, which "is characterized by religious faith in and scientific explanations of the forces of nature and life" and by the control of those forces and mankind by technology. "What we now call the New Age is in fact not the New Age. What we now call the New Age is the gathering and distilling of the highest and best from the age of religions and ideologies. We are gathering and distilling the raw stuff out of which the seed of the real New Age will form and germinate."

In the 1960s the concept of the New Age was advanced by the hippie movement, a Broadway song, and the press as the dawning of the Age of Aquarius, a planetary shift in cosmic consciousness that would usher in spiritual wisdom in place of religious cant, love not war, individual freedom in harmony with community feeling, organic health, respect for nature, magical powers, and plenty of guilt-free sex. It certainly seemed as if something massive was shifting in an irrational way, as a generation of pampered and educated kids chose LSD over IBM, peace demonstrations over military enlistment, communes over suburbs, and gurus over professors. For many, anxious to escape the banality of corporate materialism or eager to stay on the mystery tour of chemical enlightenment, familiarity with the words, symbols, and forms of mainstream religion bred ennui (contempt requiring at least a modicum of interest and energy). Some took the route toward the lively and fascinating traditions of lamas and yogis, shamans and roshis – which makes Eastern religion and native spirituality one aspect of the New Age – while others rejected all established traditions to explore unknown or poorly charted paths.

All paths have to come from somewhere, of course, and a few of these paths seem to have come from everywhere. Partly as a conscious reaction against the narrowness and arrogance of most religions, partly as a subconscious revolt against the discipline and integrity of most traditions, the fashion was to try a bit of this, add a bit of that, toss in a bit of something else, and come up with a personal metaphysics and a made-to-order regimen. Some of these were packaged then for others, including the Unification Church of Rev. Sun Myung Moon, the Church of Scientology of L. Ron Hubbard, the gestalt Hinduism of Bhagwan Shree Rajneesh, the *est* seminars of Werner Erhard, and the Church Universal and Triumphant of Elizabeth Clare Prophet.

In the case of Prophet, for example, the syncretism ranges from the obvious borrowings from Christianity, Buddhism, Hinduism, and ancient Egypt to the more esoteric pilferings from Nicholas Roerich on El Morya, Guy and Edna Ballard on St Germain, Madame Blavatsky and the Theosophical Society on the Ascended Masters, and ancient Gnosticism. Her teachings cover astrology, macrobiotic diets, alchemy, healing by touch or crystals or herbs, sun worship, Hindu mantras for chakra meditation ("Om Aim Hrim Srim Klim Sou Hu Om"),

Buddhist visualizations, reflexology, a waltz for St Germain, matchmaking, Christian prayers (a version of "Hail Mary" within a chant of "Aum Buddha, Aum Ma-Ray"), Jesus' seventeen lost years studying Buddhism in the East, communal living, and virulent right-wing politics based on the belief that the United States of America is a reincarnated civilization reassembled by St Germain to rebuild the golden age of freedom-loving Lightbearers who had existed "more than 50,000 years ago in a fertile land where the Sahara desert now is."

(This last aspect explains why St Germain is given to quoting American presidents and why the Statue of Liberty is used as a modern symbol for the Keepers of the Flame. In my favourite mantra of the Ascended Masters, "Hail, Freedom Flame," chants to St Germain and Sanat Kumara are woven into snatches of "Home on the Range," "Keep the Home Fires Burning," "Yellow Rose of Texas," "Swing Low, Sweet Chariot," "Oh, Susanna," "Michael, Row Your Boat Ashore," "Yankee Doodle Dandy," "You Are My Sunshine," "I Wish I Was in Dixie," "Anchors Aweigh," "Star-Spangled Banner," and "California, Here I Come." Less amusingly, there is lots of prophecy about an imminent nuclear attack by the Soviet Union, as a result of which the Church is building huge fall-out shelters at the ranch, and Mrs Prophet's fourth husband was found guilty in December 1989 of conspiring to buy fifteen paramilitary weapons illegally "for use in self-defense in the event of a war on American soil.")

Whether as Eastern and native religions, as cult and sect packages, or as revived and invented occultisms, during the past twenty-five years the New Age has been crawling from the flower-power edges toward the centre of North American and European culture. Americans barely blinked when they learned that some of Ronald Reagan's decisions had been influenced by Mrs Reagan's astrologer – probably because so many in the population themselves consult horoscopes and believe in psychic predictions. About a quarter-century after wondering if God is dead, *Time* announced the birth of the New Age on its cover, citing the eight million books Shirley MacLaine

67

has sold about her spiritual adventures, and the widespread fuss made around a dubious thesis that August 1987 marked a Harmonic Convergence in which a 5,000-year cycle of history ended in a twenty-five-year prelude to 2012, when "a galactic synchronization phase" would usher in the New Age of peace and wisdom. It became relatively normal for the middle class to do yoga and Transcendental Meditation, to sing the virtues of organic food and herbal medicines, to hunt out fortune-tellers and channellers, and to hop from UFOs to self-help manuals to pyramid energy.

"A Vancouver numerologist says he has been offered a $1,500 contract from Premier Bill Vander Zalm's office to predict B.C.'s economic fate," *The Province* reported in July 1988, and though the Premier is a devout Roman Catholic, the newspaper claimed he admitted consulting the "Kabalarian philosopher" before the 1986 Social Credit leadership convention. Meanwhile, in Ontario, an arbitration board ruled that Charles Arnold, a clerical worker at Humber College of Applied Arts and Technology, a second-degree high priest of witchcraft, and Elder of Spendweik Coven, was entitled to paid leave for Wicca's two major holidays, November 1 (Samhain) and May 1 (Belthane). "Everyone has the right to be weird," he was quoted as saying, overjoyed at the quasi-official recognition of his faith as a religion after centuries of Christian persecution and misrepresentation. He is one of some 5,000 witches in Canada, belonging to different sects performing different rituals – from dancing around a maypole to entering trances during nude ceremonies – mostly in Southern Ontario and British Columbia. (If B.C. seems to have more than its fair share of New Age activity, that is probably because it has a higher proportion of atheists and agnostics than any other Canadian province. As well, I was told, people often migrate there to escape their traditional past, and witches have a particular fondness for water.)

According to a survey conducted by Reginald Bibby, 35 per cent of Canadians believe in astrology, 63 per cent believe in psychic prophecy, and 58 per cent claim to have experienced premonition. There are New Age bookshops (Banyen in

Vancouver, Self-Connection in Calgary, 100th Monkey in Toronto, for example), New Age magazines (including *Dimensions* in Toronto, *Le Guide Ressources* in Montreal, *Intervox* in Halifax, *Networker* in Calgary, *Common Ground* in Vancouver, and *Interior Source* in Kelowna), New Age music racks, New Age natural-food and holistic health centres in almost every medium-size town, and New Age entrepreneurs pushing crystals, dream interpretation, acupressure therapy, iridology, rebirthing, past-life memories, totem poles, dolphin sounds, green politics, and chicken-bone readings at mystic fairs and ESP expos, which have become both common and popular in cities across the country.

The three-day event I attended in Toronto one Sunday needed a vast convention hall near the airport to accommodate the display booths and the thick crowds. The scene reminded me more of a carnival midway than a spiritual assembly, except that the line-ups were for tarot-card readings instead of games of skill and chance. I wondered how many of these excited families, giggling youths, and romantic couples had been near a church that morning. There was a High Priestess Ainajugoh, "Africa's foremost psychic," hereditary healer and occultist of the Yomba religion, as well as a "royal aristocrat from Sierra Leone who is a trance-medium in two worlds – this one and the one beyond." There was Rovena, a Seneca Indian seer, born on Halloween and trained by "traditional masters" of native spirituality and "the great masters" of India. There were twelve people sitting around a woman in white for a free, ten-minute lesson in raja yoga meditation; there were three men lying on massage tables being pressed by three Oriental women in a free demonstration of shiatsu, "acupuncture without needles"; there were lectures on karmic patterns, biofeedback, and hypnosis; there were entrepreneurs selling incense, rocks, relaxation music, cosmic art, talismans, and herb sachets (one for prosperity, one for fertility, one for "all-purpose love attraction," and one for wishes, which required you to hold the sachet in both hands, press it to your nose, close your eyes, wish for three minutes, then put the sachet under your pillow and sleep on it).

That was not all. There were aura readings by the "internationally acclaimed Artist and media personality," Alex Samchuk, and by Pamela Kristen, clairvoyant to many "inventors, entertainment personalities, doctors, lawyers, government leaders, entrepreneurs and corporate heads," who also does "parties, weddings, bar-mitzvahs, country clubs." ALaun, a "daughter of Demeter" from Hamilton, was offering Chinese divination; Ginger, the "well-known psychic in North York and Scarborough," was ready to gaze into the future with her crystal ball; Soundara, "Panacea for Problems of Life and Love," was willing to apply her mastery of Hindu Horary Astrology to answer all your questions and advise you on sex, money, marriage, health, travel, and lucky numbers.

Yogi Narayana, born Alfred Schmielewski in Berlin, now the "Super Psychic" of Mississauga, was taking appointments (fees from $150 for ordinary folks to $3000 for corporations), using his press clippings as bait: "Mulroney as PM," he told the *Calgary Herald* in 1982, but he also predicted that Brezhnev would be followed by hardliners who would plunge the world into global warfare, that Prime Minister Trudeau would be the target of an assassination attempt, and that Margaret Trudeau would become a born-again TV evangelist ("what else is left but God after Pierre Elliott Trudeau and the Rolling Stones?"). "I've pulled a number of boo-boos in my time," he confessed, though he claimed an accuracy rate near 85 per cent. He also claimed that the cosmos blooped when he was made: where other men are glued with Krazy Glue to the time continuum, he is connected with a very stretchable rubber band. "ESP has provided me with a gentleman's income for life," he once said. "Without ESP, I'd be pushing cat food cans onto shelves at Mac's Milk."

Some, like David John, are born to psychic greatness. His mother read tea cups, he learned to read palms when he was seven, and at sixteen he warned of his father's death the very day his father sternly told him not to say such things, and drowned. Some, like Keith ("not known for his tact"), achieve psychic greatness, in his case through the removal of "blocks" and a swift blow to the "third eye" (pineal gland). Some, like

Claude Vorilhon, now Raël, have psychic greatness thrust upon them. "On December 13, 1973, in a volcanic crater located in the centre of France," he reported, "I met with a spacecraft from which emerged a small human-like being." This being, who spoke perfect French, announced that Claude "had been chosen to spread the greatest message ever revealed to humanity": we were created in scientific labs millennia ago by an advanced civilization from another planet, the Elohim, which Genesis misinterprets as God the Creator when it in fact means "Those who came from the sky." Over time the Elohim sent us Moses, the Buddha, Jesus, Mohammed, Joseph Smith, et cetera, to prepare humanity for the Age of Apocalypse, which began on August 6, 1945, with the Bomb. Now they have commissioned Claude to build an embassy where they can "meet with our political leaders to give us their wisdom as well as their technology," to help us flee our solar system shortly and attain eternal life. I resisted spending $11 for Raël's *Space Aliens Took Me To Their Planet*, but it was damn tempting.

Meanwhile, over at the ISKCON (Hare Krishna) booth, I came upon a rather unpleasant argument between a passing sceptic and an acolyte with shaved head and white robes about the touchy matter of brainwashing. This was no place for a serious sceptic, I thought, and why pick out this bunch? Star Enterprises, for example, was presenting messages from entities called the Transcendors (not to be confused with another group of entities called the Transeekers); the Concept-Therapy Institute was promising HEALTH, HAPPINESS, SUCCESS, and PEACE (Absolute Money-back Guarantee); Potentials Unlimited, Inc., was selling over 160 kinds of Subliminal Persuasion Self-Hypnosis tapes to fight weight, improve memory, earn money, and so on; the Namaste Institute was using its unique Mind Mirror EEG to give you a brainwave profile and help you conquer stress; Neuro Linguistic Programming was going to work on your communication skills; AVATAR (est. 1987) was offering a programme to change your life in thirty hours for the better (except you'll be out $2500); the Order of the Blue Star was promoting Light and Sound healing using pyramid energy and tuning forks; the Oraeon Society was tutoring in applied dowsing, body decoration, and contemporary paganism; and the Aetherius Society was touting two items – a book on spiritual healing and a beechwood Radionic Pendulum – by its founder-president, His Eminence Sir George King, who is also, it seems, a count, an archbishop, a yogi, a doctor, and an expert in Shape Power.

If I had been a judge at the fair, I would have awarded the blue ribbon to Shawnäh Johnson, a certified accountant from Vancouver. According to her book, *Entity from Another World*, she used to be a woman named Yvette; but in 1982, while visiting a friend near Montreal, Yvette fell down a stairwell and broke her neck – whereupon her body was entered by Shawney, a male non-manifested being originally from the village of the Usha clan near Tryne City on the planet Utrey in galaxy Tryut, though more recently a student in the holy city of An-rah on the planet Uticah in the galaxy Kana. Shawney had "graduated" into the physical dimension on Earth, and though he had some initial difficulty with being a woman and with Yvette's taste in clothes, once he feminized his name and went shopping he settled in quite nicely. There he was, as fresh as new wine in an old bottle, whipping off aura paintings ($25) and offering "discerning investors" an opportunity to help build a City of Light ("a place where dreams and reality meet") in the Okanagan Valley.

Just before leaving, I did succumb to a SHOW SPECIAL (all THREE for $7) to have a computer read my future, my love and sex life, and my personality, based on my birthday and the number of letters in my name. Much of its report was the usual generalities, too imprecise to be accurate or foolish: "You are not usually lost for words," "You experience your emotions deeply," "This is a good year for consolidating your energies." Some of it was in the category of a safe guess: "You will own real estate," "You may have to change your wardrobe a little in order to spark up your romantic life," "You may be taking a trip towards a tropical location." But some of it was uncanny: "There may be secretive activity around your love and sex life," "There may be an end to an era in your life," "You

72

may have met the one of your dreams – there could even be a wedding, scary, isn't it?" I snickered, I smirked. True, I had just become involved in a clandestine affair, but marriage seemed a long way off. That was in October. By Christmas I was engaged. Scary, isn't it?

There is nothing new about all this, of course; it is very, very old. It goes far back into the primal ooze of the primitive mind, when visions and chants directed the hunt and assuaged the demons, when magic was the power of good and evil. Despite the great efforts of religion and science and civilization to eradicate – or, more accurately, to usurp – this power, it survived, in native spirituality, in occult practices and beliefs, in mystical traditions, in folklore, in the imagination of every child. It was banned, it was burned at the stake, it was rationalized, it was ridiculed, but it was never extinguished, because it represented unleashed desire and raw terror, it spoke to everything that is unknown and unknowable, and it stayed alive in the soul and experience of everyone.

Thus, in Canada, it remained among the native peoples; it was in the miracles and hallucinations of the Jesuits and Ursulines of New France; it was present at the ouija-board seances Susanna Moodie attended in the bush of nineteenth-century Upper Canada; it was part of the "cosmic consciousness" (in his famous phrase) that Dr Richard Bucke, the Ontario psychologist who died in 1902, encountered as "one momentary lightning-flash of the Brahmic Splendor" in his brain and "one drop of Brahmic Bliss" upon his heart; it was in the influence of Nicholas Roerich's mystical landscapes on the spiritual art of Lawren Harris; it was with William Lyon Mackenzie King when he consulted his dead mother on state policy through mediums and crystal balls; it propelled the "magic sandals" with which the wife of another Canadian prime minister ran around Morocco in the 1960s; and it inspired a sister of the current prime minister to live in an ashram in India in the 1980s.

Much of the current passion for magic and mysticism has to do with the decline of the mainstream churches in a secular age. The less a society shows respect for all religion, the more

73

it grants space for any religion; and as the old faiths falter and fade, new ones grow faster and brighter. Moreover, these opportune conditions have coincided with shifting needs, provoked by dramatic social change, the fall of empires, technological and economic revolutions, moral and sexual uncertainty, ecological crises, pessimism, and even the approach of the end of this millennium. Some trace a connection to the rise of superstition in all dark epochs, or to the tom-tom effects of too much rock and roll, or to a mass mid-life crisis among the baby-boomers; others postulate that urbanization has undermined the agrarian roots of the priestly religions, by turning modern man into a nomad again, with more need for shamans and sorcery than for seasonal ceremonies. For whatever reason, having walked out of their old rituals and beliefs toward individual freedom and modern thought, many people found the initial euphoria dissolving into loneliness, fright, confusion, stress, vacuity, and a cosmic lack of meaning to their pain and joy. Some ran back to the old reliables with relief and remorse, but some found they could not go home again. They tried alcohol, drugs, and money; they tried psychiatry, tennis, and daytime television; and when those divinities failed, they tried creative visualization, homeopathic medicine, and the art of motorcycle maintenance.

Running like common themes throughout the panoply of ideas and techniques are the mighty incentives for power and health. Insecure, alienated, victimized by the colossal forces of governments and corporations and media, more and more individuals are seeking ways to *empower* themselves, to find the knowledge and balance with which to cope and thrive; and faced with illness, death, and the limits of medical science, more and more individuals are seeking to *heal* themselves (or at least find hope in reincarnation). The ways may be myriad, but in essence all of them share a remarkable number of philosophical assumptions. God is the energy of the natural universe. This cosmic energy is a unity, so that everything is a manifestation of it. Everything is therefore a deceptive illusion, behind which swirls this changing energy. To get behind the illusion of things is to grasp the full force of the energy and be able to direct it anywhere. In that sense, though our tiny selves are illusions, we are the energy, we are nature, we are expressions of God. That gives us the potential to create our own reality, escape our own death, and pick up all sorts of tricks on the way.

The wish for mental and physical healing is understandable. When shrinks and surgeons hold out no further hope, when the neuroses and pains are no longer bearable, people will do almost anything. They will go to Fatima, send money to Oral Roberts, listen to the songs of humpback whales for ten hours, have needles put in their ears, hang a two-pound quartz around their necks, and drink potions prepared by Haitian sorcerers. Indeed, even the threat of neurosis and pain is enough to send many to self-help programmes, flower-essence boutiques, native elders, and ayurveda consultants. While many of these alternatives never work or work only as placebos, some do succeed. The effects of stress and bad diet are alleviated regularly by yoga and nutrition, for example; doctors are learning the force of mind over matter; and recently a friend of mine amazed her doctors by reversing the damage done by bone cancer through a combination of conventional medicine and herbs, macrobiotic foods, bioelectric healing, salt-water flushes, meditation, yoga, positive attitude, and love. "I got in touch with the powerful healer within myself," she said.

Empowerment is not so straightforward a desire, though it may be as attainable as health. Without totally dismissing as fraud or delusion the experiences Jean-Guy Goulet documented involving the Dene elders, for example, one would have to admit, with William James, "the presence, in the midst of all the humbug, of really supernatural knowledge." Reason did not allow the feudal mind to believe that men could fly to the moon, after all, and no doubt there are more things in Heaven and earth, Horatio, than are dreamt of in your philosophy.

Take as another example the popular technique known as channelling, in which voices from ethereal times and places give spiritual discourses and advice through a tranced medium. Some say it is an unexplained mental state similar to multiple-personality disorders; some say it is a real communication from disembodied beings in other dimensions; but no objective witness of a genuine channelling can say it is an elaborate ruse. I myself have seen relatively inarticulate and uneducated people speak flawlessly for an hour, with insight and nuance, about material that would challenge a doctoral candidate in religious philosophy. Within New Age circles, however, legitimacy is not the debate. The serious issue is whether trances, prophecy, and other psychic hocus-pocus are useful in attaining the Truth, except as introductory enticements to miracle and wonder. Supernatural powers do not necessarily indicate wisdom, especially if the magician is not conscious when they are operating, and those who set out for powers may become possessed by their demonic aspects.

"I'm not into self-improvement, I'm into self-realization," said Alexander Blair-Ewart, a bright-eyed and highly educated spiritualist who is no fan of trance mediumship. "Unconsciousness and blind following are incompatible with the New Age, which is about getting people to *think* about what they're doing. Every individual has to learn to separate the true from the false, to nourish his critical faculty in new territory. In this transition period of some 300 years I use the term 'negative psychism' to describe all the opiates that threaten to put people back to sleep. We're still in the early stages, like Christianity in the first century, moving toward a new world covenant between God and a more conscious humanity. There will be a weeding process before that happens, but the seeds are emerging now."

His own thinking about the Truth began early, when he was a child in Scotland. One afternoon in 1954, aged seven, he had a transcendental experience that marked him for life. "I was standing in a field," he recalled, still with a Scottish accent, his face as pale and intriguing as Brando's in *Apocalypse Now*, his manner part greying altar boy and part cunning Rasputin. "It was a beautiful day in May, and I was thinking that all of it

– including me – is God. At the same time I said, 'I,' to myself, with full consciousness, and that's when I *awoke*."

Though he cannot remember a moment of scepticism about God's existence, he fell into a darkness at the age of thirteen, now in London, torn between his disenchantment with the fear and nastiness of Roman Catholicism and the soul-destroying alternatives of Darwinism and Marxism. "If they were true, I was better off dead, and I remember sitting in a park in North London, staring into a duck pond, wondering how to kill myself, when a man walked directly toward me and said, 'There is an answer to your question.' I never knew his name or where he lived, but he became my spiritual teacher. He directed me to books and lectures for two years, and then he disappeared."

Eventually, through an eclectic study of comparative religions and meditation and "a remarkable chain of events," Blair-Ewart became a disciple of Theosophy, especially Madame Blavatsky's *Secret Doctrine*, and a master of esoteric astrology. He taught about both after his arrival in Canada in 1972. "Then, in 1973, I had what I can only call an initiation experience, an experience of dying and coming back to life," he said, puffing on a cigarette. "It shattered the membrane between the spiritual and physical worlds and gave me a direct awareness of my existence in other parts of time, such as ancient Egypt. It was a fork in the road: I could withdraw to become a full-time holy person or I could go back into the blood and guts of the world. It took me years to reassemble myself."

In the secular world, the New Age is a fool's paradise operated by elixir salesmen and religious quacks. While it certainly contains its fair share of con artists and lunatics, it is probably no more corrupt than any business or most politics – and a great deal less harmful. A lot less money has been thrown away on idiotic predictions from psychics and useless chants from yogis than on cocaine, prostitutes, and science-fiction movies, I would guess, and a lot more good has been achieved by Transcendental Meditation and Pagans for Peace than by football and Stephen King novels. If sceptics can point to the case of John Tiernan, the British Columbia resident who cut off the head of his former Hare Krishna guru in order to rid the world of the Antichrist, believers can point to the case of Réal Simard, the cold-blooded killer in the Montreal Mafia who became a police informer after reading Shirley MacLaine. "The book made me realize I had a soul," Simard was quoted as saying.

In the religious world, however, the New Age causes deeper concerns. It does not just threaten to steal a few bucks or waste a few years; it threatens the soul for eternity. Far from dabbling in utter nonsense, it is seen as playing with real fire without the safety of tradition, lineage, and proper authority. Ancient sources get misinterpreted and adapted; self-anointed prophets mix authentic methods into worthless or lethal compounds; yuppies rush from one disappointing quick fix to another marginal fantasy; and the emphasis on power and health degenerates into narcissism, political apathy, spiritual consumerism, and self-absorbed salvation. Though I have heard such criticisms by Roman Catholic bishops, United Church ministers, Jewish rabbis, and Anglican theologians, the most concerted and passionate attacks have come from Christian conservatives, who condemn the New Age for setting up man and beast as God, rejecting the unique divinity of Jesus Christ, and reducing sin to moral relativism. They even have a Canadian organization, the Christian Research Institute, headquartered in Calgary since 1985, dedicated to taking on the "cultists and occultists now opposing the church."

There is an irony in this, because some sociologists see Christian fundamentalism itself as another aspect of the New Age. Though it goes back to the Bible and Christ rather than out to yoga and El Morya, it surges from the same historical and social turmoil and expresses itself in similar ways. Like many of the New Age movements, it lets go of reason and science, emphasizes experience and emotion, promises empowerment and healing, pushes individual salvation and community feeling, downgrades political action and material ambition, dotes on legendary prophets with peculiar names and charismatic preachers with fancy watches, promotes devotion and communication with the spirit, and warns of the coming apocalypse. (People forget that Jonestown was a Christian sect.) In this light, Christians may be railing so aggressively against the New Age movement not because it is a diabolic instrument, but because it is an effective competitor.

"But the fundamentalists should be happy if the New Age becomes pervasive," Blair-Ewart argued. "Unlike unmitigated technological statism, we're creating a climate for them to live in freedom. In fact, it's a shame that Christendom is in such a mess now. This could be a period of tremendous revitalization for Christianity if its votaries weren't so vulnerable to satanic energies such as fear and guilt and blame. That's not Christ. We can't talk about Christ in this culture because of the damage done by Protestant fundamentalism."

However preposterous Sanat Kumara and the Radionic Pendulum may appear on the surface, deep in the heart of faith they are no more so than Ezekiel and the Communion wafer. Familiarity with Obadiah, Habakkuk, and Zephaniah may make them more credible than Seth, Ramtha, and the Great White Brotherhood; the Garden of Eden, the parting of the Red Sea, and the Resurrection of the Lord may be no more literal (or no less mythic) than Shamballa, all-purpose love attraction herbs, and the entering of Yvette's body by the Entity From Another World; but once you have slipped the surly bonds of logic and accepted one absurdity, why not go on to accept the most absurd?

Within the mainstream churches, therefore, there are those who want to absorb the New Age rather than resist it. It is an old device: Judaism borrowed from pagan rites, Christianity borrowed from Jewish prophecies, Catholicism borrowed from Pentecostal enthusiasms, the United Church borrowed from Fabian tracts, the Anglicans borrowed from native rituals. Now all of them are borrowing from the New Age. The Roman Catholics have Father Matthew Fox, for instance, teaching African dance, massage, and aikido in California. He often lectures in Toronto under the auspices of the Applewood Centre for Spiritual Studies, co-founded by an Anglican priest and offering seminars in Myers-Briggs personality analysis,

Jungian dream interpretation, and the art of movement. Fox has also led a workshop at the Naramata Centre for Continuing Education, near Penticton, B.C., where the United Church sponsors courses on personal empowerment, t'ai chi, and breath and sound exercises. "There Is An Exotic Culture Out There That Embraces Meditation, Pursues Mysticism, Talks Of Inner Light And Has A Diet All Its Own," the newspaper advertisement trumpeted on behalf of the Institute for Jewish Learning, and Rabbi Zelman Schacter of Philadelphia has Canadian followers of his special blend of Judaism and the New Age. And, while a Benedictine priory in Montreal practises forms of Hindu meditation, I met a Cree medicine man doing the Progoff Intensive Journal therapy in Alberta.

Personal and sociological reasons aside, much of the energy comes from the neat fit between the New Age and the secular age. At the obvious level it uses images and techniques with which secularism is comfortable: psychological games, aerobics, cybernetic metaphors, diets, commercial pizzazz, power. At the obscure level it touches upon secularism's worst fears about science, nature, and the Day of Judgement. In that sense, New Age spirituality is the religious side of secular materialism. "The New Age deals with issues of planetarization and the emergence of an awareness that we are all one people living on one world that shares a common destiny," wrote David Spangler, formerly a co-director of the Findhorn community in Scotland. "The New Age represents social, political, economic, psychological, and spiritual efforts to recognize and include all that our modern society has tended to exclude: the poor, the dispossessed, the feminine, the ecological, and inwardly, all the painful, repressed, and unintegrated material that Carl Jung called the Shadow."

Thus, while the New Age seems to be turning its back on science and reason, science and reason are not quite what they used to be. If once they stood strong on empiricism and rationalism in defiance of religious beliefs and pagan superstitions, now they have had the ground cut from under their feet by the results of their own explorations. Things no longer are what they seem, as science has demonstrated, and what they are no longer makes sense. As Fritjof Capra wrote in his famous book, *The Tao of Physics*, "Two separate developments – that of relativity theory and of atomic physics – shattered all the principal concepts of the Newtonian world view: the notion of absolute space and time, the elementary solid particles, the strictly causal nature of physical phenomena, and the ideal of an objective description of nature."

In other words, science itself – the god that challenged God, with its own high priests and esoteric tomes and fancy temples – has been coming to some rather mystical conclusions: space and time are relative, nothing is solid and eternal, natural *laws* may be only natural *tendencies*, and the underlying unity of all creation in which every particle influences every other particle belies the apparent separation of objects. Just as the transcendent God of eternal verities and absolute laws is being challenged by those who see Truth as immanent and contextual and relative, so the mechanical god of measurable constancy and fixed pattern is being challenged by those who find evidence of chance and change and contradiction. While the first challenge often leads into worldliness and culture and politics, however, the second often leads into mystery and awe and holiness.

In fact, it leads directly into the cosmology shared by Eastern religions, native spirituality, and the New Age movements. "Everyone who is seriously involved in the pursuit of science becomes convinced that a spirit is manifest in the Laws of the Universe," Albert Einstein said, "a spirit vastly superior to that of man." And because it was Einstein, using mathematics and experiments, the message seeped into the civilization that worshipped the wizards who had given it the automobiles and airplanes and television. If these guys say that things look pretty miraculous and sacred out there in the universe, well, maybe things are worth another look.

Not a moment too soon, either, because these same guys are saying that things look pretty disastrous and desperate down here on the planet. Nature is taking a terrible beating at the hands of science and industry, with the Bomb and acid rain and holes in the ozone layer, and mankind is in danger of destroying itself as well as its precious galactic carrier. So, with the fading of the stern Law-giver and all separate matter, there has sprung up in their place a new cult of Gaia, the Greek goddess of the earth, the personification of the planet, Mother Nature herself, loving rather than legalistic, changing rather than eternal, intuitive rather than rational, our other and long-suppressed self.

It is as if we have been out of harmony for too long with God the Father and the laws of the high priests of science, as a result of which we are paying the price in garbage and pollution and alienation. It is as if the male Yang is completing its vast cycle of ascent and descent – hundreds of years in the rising, hundreds of years in the falling – and the female Yin is beginning to restore the cosmic balance. Whatever is happening, the lady is everywhere. She is sighted as the Virgin Mary in Yugoslavia, she is in the feminist theology of the United Church, she is popping out of Jewish mythology, she is with Elizabeth Clare Prophet in Montana and ALaun the "daughter of Demeter" in Hamilton, she is Kali and Kuan Yin and the Divine Light, she is prominent in native spirituality and Wicca and save-the-whales, she is behind quantum physics and the peace movement and organic lettuce.

Some groups talk directly about the Goddess, under different names; and with the need people have to worship some specific image, it is likely that there will be more and more devotees of Her in the decades or centuries to come. But many others speak of Her unconsciously, when they speak about ecological systems, biological evolution, neo-Darwinism, the Big Bang theory, creation spirituality, or process theology. Even the most hardened atheists can see the effect of secular materialism on the earth, their bodies, and their minds and feel the need for values, ethics, and meaning that science cannot provide. While once they used to laugh at those historical Christians who worked themselves into a panic from the belief that the world would end in AD 1000, now they are working themselves into the same panic on the eve of AD 2000. This is not a religious madness, they argue, it is common sense based on nuclear weapons, overpopulation, and industrial pollution. Yet those convincing rationalizations may be the same psychological forces as existed a thousand years ago, wrapped in the language and faith of today. More importantly, the solutions usually involve more than reason and technology: they involve respect for creation, the unity of nature, sharing, moderation, compassion, holiness. No less a figure than Mikhail Gorbachev has called recently for "a spiritual regeneration" to solve the problems of the world.

"I believe that the New Age is God's doing," said Alexander Blair-Ewart. "What else could have produced this phenomenon in an intellectual climate that totally opposes it? We need a new social and political paradigm that will replace power with participatory harmony. The state won't do it, Christendom can't do it, so I think it will come out of the New Age as serious people start to create new institutions."

Whether because of divine intervention or social utilitarianism, the result is evident in the shift of global consciousness toward sacredness, however wacky or marginal it may seem at times. "I think that man is a concerned animal, and he has certain primary concerns which are extremely simple," Northrop Frye once remarked on CBC-Radio. "Life is better than death, and happiness is better than misery, and freedom is better than slavery. He also has secondary concerns which are ideological and have to do with the ascendency of classes or nations, priesthoods or bureaucracies, or what have you. And consequently, all through history, the secondary concerns have had an edge over the primary ones, because although we prefer to live, we still go to war. And I think that the twentieth century, what with the atom bomb and a pollution that threatens to cut off the air we breathe, is the first period in history which confronts man with the conclusion that primary concerns must become primary, or else."

FOUR

The Lord Is My Light

I had not heard of Peter Castonguay for about a decade. We had
been in high school together, and though we had not been
close friends, I had always liked him. I could not say that Peter
stood near the top of our class, nor was he a football star or
hockey hero; but he had a coltish humour and attractive
charm that many brains and jocks might have envied. Once
we graduated, our paths separated completely until rumours
began to reach me in the mid-1970s: Peter was on the West
Coast, he had married and then suddenly abandoned his wife,
he had fallen into the clutches of a strange cult run by a British
lord, he was living on a commune in the interior of British
Columbia, and his parents were in despair.

I was less shocked than curious. By that time I knew a fair
number of people whose parents were in despair – Moonies,
Marxists, Krishna devotees, organic farmers, Rajneesh group-
ies, transcendental poets – and Peter's fate seemed much more
interesting than the usual descent into law school, station
wagons, and alcoholism. Still, when I happened to encounter
Peter's mother at a cocktail party in Ottawa around 1980, I
prepared my longest face for her tale of disappointment and
woe. I knew her to be a proud woman, of proper elegance and
distinguished poise, and I suspected that her least ambition

for her eldest son was that he follow in the footsteps of his father and grandfather as Canada's Chief Electoral Officer. So, upon broaching the subject of Peter with the utmost delicacy, I was startled to see her face light up with enthusiasm and joy. Peter had married the British lord's daughter – which, she told me, meant access to one of the grandest homes of England, a private jet, and the bluest of blood for her grandchildren!

She and Peter's father had even gone out to 100 Mile House, British Columbia, for the wedding. "It's a lovely place, with lovely people. Not what I had imagined at all," she said. "At the dinner I sat next to Lord Martin and I said to him, 'I'm so relieved. I was worried this was going to be another Jonestown.'"

And that is how I came, after another eight years and after a long drive from visiting Albert Lightning and Harold Cardinal in Northern Alberta, to be unpacking my bag at the Red Coach Inn in 100 Mile House. I had written to Peter and received a warm invitation to visit. "I'm sending you a couple of publications of ours," his reply stated, "but if you really want to discover what we are actually doing, it's better to come with fewer preconceived conceptual frameworks. Nobody can actually discover anything that is new and heretofore unknown if they seek to understand it by translating the new item through the old consciousness." (Oh-oh, I thought ominously at the time, it sure sounds intense, whatever *it* is; and though every reporter is taught to leave his preconceived conceptual frameworks at the door of every story, I felt a certain nervousness just before meeting Peter. People had warned me that the group was everything from a science-fiction cult to a CIA front. If science had come up with a pill against malarkey as it has against malaria, I would have popped a couple in that hotel room.)

The publications proved more helpful in preparing me with facts than with frameworks. One was a question-and-answer booklet, *What Happens at 100 Mile Lodge*. The other was a glossy yearbook full of group photographs, individuals at work and play, activity reports, and little essays about community life. I learned, as a start, that Peter belongs to the Emissaries of

Divine Light; that the British lord was Martin Cecil, 7th Marquess of Exeter, Hereditary Grand Almoner, and Lord Paramount of the Soke of Peterborough; and that Lord Exeter had died in January 1988, at the age of seventy-eight, and been succeeded as marquess and chief Emissary by his son, Michael Burghley.

I had known of the great name of Cecil, of course, since studying British history at school with Peter. William Cecil, the 1st Lord Burghley, was Elizabeth I's famous statesman, and from him two branches ascended to the rank of marquess – Exeter and Salisbury – because of their public service. The Exeter branch still retains Burghley House, the sixteenth-century glory of Elizabethan architecture, built by William Cecil and boasting some 240 rooms, superb Italian art, and a park designed by Capability Brown. Here Lord Martin Cecil was born in 1909, the second son of the 5th Marquess. As such, he expected the title, house, and properties to go to his older brother (who made his own reputation as a track star by winning an Olympic gold medal in 1928); so Martin joined the navy and then got the bug at the age of twenty-one to manage the cattle ranch his father had bought in 1912 in the Cariboo country of British Columbia.

"His move was partially prompted by the lure of the unknown, but also because deep inside himself he did not feel at home in the aristocratic 'establishment.' He wanted to discover who he was as a person in his own right," I read in the yearbook. "During these early days the Bridge Creek Ranch comprised the original stopping house built in 1863, a general store with a post office, a log-building carpentry shop, and a barn built around 1915. The population was about twelve. For his first two years Martin lived in a tiny room in the roadhouse. He had a cot and a small cook stove for heating – a far cry from the luxuries of stately Burghley House."

The far cry physically was followed by an even farther cry spiritually. Out of a personal yearning for the Truth, out of the hardships of the Depression, perhaps out of exile and isolation and the unique alienation of being a reserved aristocrat among rowdy cowboys, Martin began exploring the mysteries of life, character, and faith beyond the formal structures of the Church of England. By 1940 his desultory search led him to Lloyd Meeker, a warm and magnetic American who had experienced a mystical illumination in 1932 that inspired him to preach widely and organize kindred spirits into the Emissaries of Divine Light. As it was explained to me in the simplest terms, Meeker's three-day epiphany involved witnessing the energy of life (alias the Holy Spirit, alias God) as light, seeing himself and everyone as expressions of that light, and realizing that human forms can unleash their full potential by aligning their hearts and minds to the natural flow of that light. Apparently this made more immediate sense to Lord Martin Cecil than it did to me, and even though he was not known to have had such a dramatic enlightenment, he recognized at once the wisdom of Meeker's vision.

Even today Emissaries are not defined by those who have seen the light or undergone instruction. "The name Emissary of Divine Light applies to anyone who brings a stable, true, and loving spirit into his or her life," I continued to read. "An Emissary has acknowledged that there is a great deal more potential to human beings than is usually actualized. Our approach is to take full responsibility for ourselves as individuals, to face and let go of attitudes that limit the release of our own potential."

Martin was already this kind of "natural" Emissary, it seems, concerned with developing in himself such qualities as integrity, honesty, compassion, discipline, and nobility in tough conditions. "Stay steady," he used to say, "and do well what is immediately at hand to do." He formed a strong bond with Meeker as soon as they met in Vancouver in 1940. Others too were being attracted to this effusive, bearded, yet very practical prophet, whom they now called Uranda, and in 1945 some began to gather around him in a spiritual community called Sunrise Ranch at Loveland, Colorado. As well as being an administrative centre for the movement, Sunrise was to serve as a proving ground for the message of inner alignment and responsible living. For years it was poor, rugged, and makeshift, but it grew under the compelling laugh, oratorical inspiration, dynamic personality, and competent command of its "bishop," Uranda. In 1948 Lord Martin invited a handful of Emissaries to duplicate the experiment on his ranch, thus joining the august ranks of British aristocrats such as Lords Baltimore and Selkirk who have attempted to establish utopian religious communities in the wilds of Canada.

By that time the ranch included an adequate house for Martin and the log inn he had built to replace the old stopping house for travellers on the gravel road to Prince George. There were also the beginnings of a town on land leased from the ranch near the inn: a few cabins, a couple of businesses, a garage, and about two dozen people. As the lumber industry developed in the area after the war, 100 Mile House continued to grow under Martin's paternal supervision and the management of his right-hand man, Ross Marks, who had gone as a teenager with his parents to Sunrise in 1946 and then moved from Toronto to the Cariboo in 1948. When the town was incorporated in 1965 and its residents were able to buy their land from the Bridge Creek estate, Marks was elected mayor, a position he held for twenty-one years – though the booklet Peter sent me took great pains to show how the Emissaries neither control, exploit, or have advantage over the townspeople.

In 1954 a couple of tragedies had major consequences. Martin's wife (and the mother of Michael, who was born in 1935) died after a long illness. Then Uranda and his wife were killed in a plane crash. Martin became leader of the Emissaries; he married Lillian Johnson, a young woman from Milwaukee who had grown up at Sunrise; and he and Lillian took responsibility for Uranda's three children, Nancy, Lloyd, and Helen. In 1956 they had their own child, Marina, who eventually married Peter; and in 1967, as if to complete the circle, Michael Cecil married Nancy Meeker.

Meanwhile, Emissaries had begun to crowd Martin's inn, the Lodge. "Every Christmas there were seven more for dinner," I was to be told, and more stayed than left. By 1957 there were more than thirty people living together. By 1965 the Red Coach Inn was built for the public, and the Lodge became the centre of a complex of houses and communal buildings set on ten acres carved out of the ranch's 12,000 acres. It grew organically, as people came and room was made and viable employment was found, all under the quiet authority and pragmatic attention to detail of Lord Martin Cecil.

It was my impression that, during these early years, the spiritual content was evolving as organically as the physical arrangements. The cosmology was based on flux, after all, and the practice was to adapt to natural change. As the son of a fire-and-brimstone Seventh-Day-Adventist preacher, as someone who sought instruction and inspiration from the Bible, Meeker seemed to cloak the spirit in the style and rhetoric of Christian evangelicalism, though he was more interested in living the way of Jesus than in creating another religious structure. He added an unusual dimension, however, after he made contact in the 1940s with – truth being stranger than fiction – a number of Canadian avant-garde chiropractors.

Chiropractic is a method of natural healing based on manual adjustment of the spinal column, and within it there developed a kind of spiritual movement that saw it as God's gift, a way to connect mankind to the source of life, a power given some people who must use it without fee or ambition to serve the suffering. Under the influence of an American named George Shears, who invented the GPC (God/Patient/Chiropractor) philosophy, came three Canadians: John Oshanek in Winnipeg and Albert Ackerley and Lorne French in Toronto. Each came to experience that healing could take place with little or even no touch, just by moving their hands over the patient's body; each came to hear of Uranda's message of alignment to the life force; and, on a mattress in the Marks' living-room in Toronto, experience and message came together when Uranda underwent an "attunement" at the hands of Ackerley and French. After that, attunements became part of the Emissaries' practice at Sunrise and 100 Mile House.

"Uranda may have been doing something like attunement even before Sunrise, when people came to him for physical healing," said Lorne French, when I met him much later in

Victoria, "but we were the ones who gave expression to it in our daily living. Some people are born with this talent, but many of them sludge it up with a big show and religious mumbo-jumbo till you want to throw up. We just provide a means by which the life force comes into focus. We can feel it."

French did admit that Uranda himself used a certain amount of religious connotation. "In those days people were being attracted out of orthodox religious fields, so you needed to use religious forms – on an undistorted basis – to enter their consciousness. In my case I had grown up in the United Church, I had seen the suffering and destruction of the war, I was looking for the meaning of life, and I felt the answer wasn't in religion and faith. I guess I looked through about fifteen 'isms' and 'ologies' before Uranda's material just turned me on fire. It made sense. With him, for instance, the Bible came to life in a simple way, without a lot of theological complexity. He pointed to the keys of Truth amid all its filler."

There was an inherent contradiction, an unresolved confusion, that the first group had to work out in the Lodge in the 1950s and 1960s. Almost all, including Martin, had come out of traditional Christianity (Protestantism mostly) because of a feeling that the form had smothered the essential spirit. Yet, crammed together in pioneer conditions, trying to define the elusive nature of their beliefs, trying to live it and earn a living, they risked creating another empty structure of organization, dogma, and rite. They even had "services" in a "chapel" (once an engine-repair shed) under the direction of their "bishop," Martin Cecil. Their very earnestness produced a noticeable gap between the tight control they practised and the relaxed approach they preached. Many of their young people detected hypocrisy and left.

But, by the end of the 1960s, other young people began to arrive. They too had given up on traditional religious forms and Christian hypocrisy; and though most of them had gone through the fires of rebellion and drugs rather than of depression and war, they too were searching for meaning and transcendental experience. It was the Age of Aquarius, of communes in the country, of tuning in and dropping out, so inevitably some would hear of this far-out spiritual community in the back and beyond of B.C. with this phantasmagoric name, the Emissaries of Divine Light.

This was when Peter came in, and I left it to him to recount the story. We met in the lobby of the Red Coach Inn, and he was easy to recognize despite the twenty-five years. The moustache was new, the face a little fuller, but he had the same darkly handsome looks, the same lanky frame, and the same frolicsome energy and laugh. He still downplayed his own intellect, he still could cut by a brutal frankness or insensitive jest, but he had gained a confident authority over ideas and a managerial competence over people or things that I did not remember. The most obvious difference was that he had metamorphosed from a privileged schoolboy into a working cowboy, driving around in a pick-up with a dog in the back, talking about roping calves and riding the range, and sporting a fancy buckle on the front of his jeans. As he drove me across the beautiful landscape of rolling hills and grazing pastures and wild forests to check salt licks for the cattle and shoot gophers, he hardly needed a question to fuel his monologue.

In 1967 he had gone to Simon Fraser University, "a totally programmed kid, with no self-awareness, ready to follow the scenario provided every upper-middle-class WASP." In his first year he concentrated on beer-drinking and girl-chasing. In his second year he "minored in political radicalism and majored in psychedelics and spiritual understanding." Then he got married, a short-lived folly that managed to upset his parents, his hippie friends, his wife, and himself. In his third year, with most of his classes cancelled by strikes and demonstrations, he read Baba Ram Dass, Zen, Jonathan Livingstone Seagull, and one day he drifted into a lecture on "Oneness, the Way of Life" because it had an "Alan Wattsian ring." It was put on by something called Ontology, and it was given by a straight-looking young man named Michael Cecil.

"He may not have fitted the counter-culture's image," Peter remembered, "but he had an attractive presence and philosophically he was right on the money. Halfway through he said, 'All this is fine, but do any of you experience this in your daily living?' Lights went on in me. After a couple of years of asking myself who I was, what was I doing, what wasn't me, I knew too much and had burned too many bridges to go back and become a doctor or lawyer. A glow like a homing device at my core compelled me to keep moving toward a greater understanding of the Truth. That core had had ten pounds of granite around it, of programming and conditioning, but psychedelics and all my reading had blown them up. I now knew my identity centred on nothing. I had discovered the illusion and the problem. I still needed the answer, but I didn't know where to go for it. Baba Ram Dass had said: if you want to be a motorcycle freak, hang around motorcycle freaks; if you want to be an intellectual, hang around intellectuals; if you want to be a divine being, hang around divine beings. But where were the divine beings who were exemplifying the answer, not just talking about it? After the lecture I went up and asked Michael about the community. If your car is full, I asked him, is there any room in the trunk?"

About three weeks later Peter went to 100 Mile House. He lived and worked in town for a winter, then in the spring of 1970 moved into a cabin on the ranch. He traded his car for a horse, passed a happy "Walden Pond" summer, and turned himself into a cowboy. "I was like a kid at the circus," he said. "I was smiling all the time, my eyes were wide open, it felt like being reincarnated." The next winter he was back in Vancouver and soon back into his old ways, but he pulled himself away from both, entered a series of Emissary courses, and within a year had returned to the community for good.

"Meeting Martin, looking into his eyes, I saw a *real* person. He was a strong being, with a clarity and depth that was almost scary. Talking to him about substance was like being stoned. His attitude to me (or anyone) was totally welcoming, whatever my idiosyncrasies. They weren't relevant. In fact, the circumstances of my past had been the very ticket I needed to wake up to reality. Drugs had been my history, my opportunity, the door I was able to walk through. Now I had to go through the fact that there were no hippies here. There were

92

people reading *Reader's Digest* and doing other things I found bizarre. I had to relinquish my own identity as a hippie and pay attention to substance, not form. I found here people I could trust. I sensed that a certain percentage of them had come to experience in their living what they were talking about."

Perhaps, but a certain percentage of them had trouble with the arrival of Peter and other hippies who landed in their bliss. "There was some individual concern and dismay, because of the difference in lifestyle," Ross Marks told me. "Lots of our long-haired, freedom-loving friends came and went, and it caused some head-scratching. Obviously people couldn't just come and camp, there were practical matters as to how many we could accommodate, but the process proved almost self-regulating. Some just seemed to fit, some moved on. Martin had a big influence, naturally, but we tried to develop an internal discipline, largely free of rules and regulations."

In many ways the hippies were the perfect test of how much the older group had absorbed of their philosophy, of how much hypocrisy remained to be expunged. It was one thing to feel the light, to get beyond form and suspend judgement and flow with the life force, while living in a small, precious, and isolated environment of similar types with similar ideas. It was another thing to be invaded by dirty, promiscuous, bug-eyed anarchists who wanted to move in. On the whole, the Emissaries seemed to have passed the test, and by passing it they seemed to have gone through a door into greater vitality, greater numbers, greater prosperity, and greater spiritual confidence.

When I visited, more than a third of the 120 Emissaries at 100 Mile House fell into the general category of hippie veteran, now entering middle age, clean-cut, hard-working, and parentally responsible. Often bright and well-educated, generally energetic and enthusiastic, they account for much of the expansion that has taken place in the community and the movement since 1970. Behind the Lodge there sprung up a communal dining-hall and kitchen, a new meeting hall beside the small log chapel, a "sanctuary" for attunements, a few unobtrusive apartment residences, and a variety of cabins, cottages, and bungalows surrounded by gardens of flowers and vegetables. To support these facilities there arose several businesses, such as the Red Coach Inn (co-owned with the Cecil family's private company, Bridge Creek Estate), Tip Top Radio & TV, the *Free Press*, and Cariboo Carpet ("The Wug Washer").

These community businesses are separate from the Cecils' personal holdings in land or investments and from the non-profit society known as the EDL. The salaries earned by Emissaries working in them are pooled to pay for the capital and operating expenses of the group, commonly referred to as the Lodge, the unit, the Lodge unit, or sometimes the Lodge family. Significantly, inheritances and other forms of outside income are not pooled, as in the case of Lord Martin's heirs, whose company is worth millions. This is not an egalitarian world, therefore, though everyone lives very comfortably on the Lodge compound or in town. (Nor is it all work. The yearbook was full of ski marathons, art classes, dance performances, choir and music concerts, book projects, children's programmes, community socials, as well as all the outdoor activities the ranch offers.)

As the Sunrise and Lodge units grew to optimum size, new units sprouted: King View near Toronto in 1972, Edenvale near Vancouver in 1973, one each in England and France and Australia and South Africa, and several more across the United States. By 1990 there were twelve altogether, plus a network of centres and individuals in a score of countries around the world. As I had learned, the Emissaries do not describe themselves by their community living (as monks or Hutterites do) or even by their mailing list (estimated at 3,000 names). In *form*, however, to use their lingo, the EDL society organizes a series of courses on the Art of Living, Spiritual Expression, Leadership, Assembly, and World Service – designed (according to one Emissary) "to reinforce the innate reality that's been hidden by fear and shame" – and the more serious participants are encouraged to spend some time in a unit to mature their ideas in a focused setting. If once the Emissaries had believed that everyone would have to end up in a commune somehow, they came to consider those who could not or would not. Now many drop into the units for short periods and return to a multitude of ordinary situations.

"We aren't selling community as such," Peter told me. "If people belong here, they're here. If they don't, they aren't. We just come to an agreement in spirit that this is where we should be, and we become an active part of it. No one has to tell us to stay or leave."

The hippies and those who followed them to the units and the courses did more than change the physical operation. They affected the spiritual direction too, by bringing to it a new generation, a new metaphysics, a new vocabulary, a new style, a new ethics, and new views on leadership and society. It had already been shifting under Martin's influence. One student who had studied the teachings of Uranda, Martin, and Michael went so far as to conclude that Uranda was a Christian fundamentalist, Martin was a Hegelian, and Michael is a Buddhist. ("Who's Hegel?" Martin had asked when told of this insight.)

Whatever the subtleties, all agree that the unit became more relaxed and joyful, less pressed by survival and urgency, more outgoing to the rest of the world, and less overtly religious. Christ and the Bible moved from the front and centre; and terms such as bishop, chapel, ontology, even Divine Light began to be downplayed to avoid the false trappings of a religion or cult. I met Emissaries who did not know that Christ was mentioned in their charter; there are townspeople who believe that the Lodge is the Antichrist, full of voodoo and free love; and Lord Martin's own family back in Burghley House was suspicious of his preachings.

"Because the Cecils had been central to the foundation of the Church of England," Michael Exeter said when I met him in his ranch-style house just off the Lodge compound, "they see themselves as stalwarts of the Church. And here Martin was, doing something entirely outside that, saying essentially that the basic precepts of Christianity ring true, but who's living them? They didn't like that very much."

It might not have mattered much, except that in 1981 his older brother died without male heirs and Martin inherited the title (thereby, according to custom, becoming Martin Exeter, while Michael Cecil became Michael Burghley until his father's death made him Michael Exeter. The phone book lists him as "Exeter Lord" between Exeter Forest and Marine Sales and Exeter Parts and Supplies.) There were fears that Burghley House would fall into the clutches of the Emissaries, but Martin was not interested in returning and a trust was established by the 6th Marquess to manage its 27,000 acres for the benefit of maintaining the estate itself. Still, the great line of Exeter and Burghley did move to the Cariboo, though both Michael and his son Anthony (once Cecil, now Burghley, someday Exeter) were educated at Eton.

While Michael admitted there had been an evolution in format and terminology, he insisted that the underlying message had been consistent. "What connected with people in Uranda's day had a different style than required to meet the thinking of the flower-power era. At first everyone connects to us by evoking the belief system he or she comes from, despite our warning that it isn't necessary. Also, in the early days, there were few people, so there was a sense of *preciousness*, of needing to contain things, of creating a greenhouse in which to find the point of equilibrium. That point was found, so it was increasingly possible to relax, not to carry expectations and judgements as to what people should be doing or where they should be. Our whole thrust is to encourage people to find the still inner place which is beyond structures of organization and belief systems, to be set free by what's fresh and alive and not bound in the moment. When the spirit comes upon you, when you experience being in the flow, you know it. If you stop and act the observer, there is a separation, and you know that too, because things become more difficult."

I was not being deliberately stubborn, but I could not help noting that the Emissaries still had both an organization and a belief system. Both were centred in practice around Michael and Nancy Exeter, and though I was told time and again that their authority had evolved naturally from their spiritual qualities and personal dedication, I could not ignore who their fathers had been. Indeed, the Cecils and the Meekers seemed to dominate the community psychologically, so that they did not have to dominate it more blatantly. Though both the Lodge and the EDL have a variety of councils and committees to share responsibility, I sensed that the buck stopped with the Exeters, not least because they had the lineage, the style, and the ranch.

"In principle," Michael said, "there is a right way and a wrong way of doing anything, and we'll come to the right way if we're open to it. But we have learned that trying to work things out strictly by consensus is an awful pain. There needs to be someone, a chairman, who will help draw everything to a point, who will remind everyone of where we're going. It's like flying a small aircraft: there are hundreds of factors affecting it, we have to make constant adjustments, but we still have a general direction."

Ross Marks called that general direction the tone or standard set by the community. "Some of the hippies felt we didn't need anyone in charge – do your own thing – but we would fall apart without some connection," he said. "There have been some conflicts on an individual level, some hard nuts to crack or some head-banging, but we tried to deal with them in a way that permitted the individuals to come clear of whatever the hang-ups, on a basis of love."

As an example of this flexibility, there was a shift in the standard about pre-marital sex. As long as it does not upset the harmony of the group – as happened when two couples swapped spouses and fled in the night – it is usually deemed appropriate. "There are no hard and fast lines," Marks said. "But there is a significant control pattern present. Usually people don't have to be taken aside. They come to talk often. They realize they have a responsibility to the whole, and they're *keen* to do the right thing. The key is the common spiritual base that allows space and time for things to emerge." When I asked him, to clarify this, if homosexual relations would be appropriate, he replied, "It's never been an issue here, but I think the group could probably encompass them. People are just people, after all, and if they have an aberration, then healing is possible. Look at the hippies and drugs. Some people were bothered by them, but in the end it all worked out."

The Emissaries offer a range of healing, from chanting to attunements, from long-distance running to talking things through, whatever works best for the individual. (Peter recalled having a knot in his chest one night after his two children had been thrown from a horse. His therapy was to get up, turn on David Letterman, and have a double scotch. Neither smoking nor drinking are forbidden, by the way, though moderation is encouraged in all things.) A major focus is on the four weekly services (or meetings, as the less religious prefer to call them), which take place on Wednesday and Saturday evenings and on Sunday mornings and evenings in the modern theatre known as the meeting hall. They bring everyone together in a more formal way as if to remind the group of why it is together, through personal testimonials, inspirational talks, guest lectures, singing and music, and creative presentations. The service at eleven o'clock Sunday morning tends to be more reverential than the others, with everyone showered and dressed up, with flowers and candles and hymns (such as "The Tide of Life," the Emissary anthem by Uranda), and normally with a low-key sermon by Michael Exeter, who has a low-key voice and low-key pace to match his low-key niceness. His sermons are often picked up by other units by videotape or telephone, just as Martin's were collected into books (available in the lobby of the Red Coach Inn) such as *Being Where You Are*, *On Eagle's Wings*, and *Beyond Belief*.

Whether directly by the services and courses or indirectly by the continual reaffirmation of the cosmology and its buzz words in everyday life, the Emissaries' spiritual practice seemed centred in trying to maintain the vision by constant mental adjustments. It was not like praying or meditating or whirling in the manner of dervishes. It was developing a different way of viewing life, the world, and oneself. But, when we were driving around in his truck, Peter objected to the notion that the process was a mind game.

"If you focus your identity on the mind, that's static, because everyone has judgements and opinions about what's true," he said. "But if you focus your identity into life's energy, you see that Truth isn't an object to be sought: it's a dynamic process which you can access when you tune into the moment by listening to what life has to say. That isn't intellectual, it's *vibrational*. When you know how to flow with life, everything is perfect. You understand what's going on, and it all makes total sense."

In the microcosm of the unit it certainly makes sense, because the rest of the world looks like madness. Whether Truth or lunacy, the Emissary vision has constructed a few happy, peaceful, and prosperous corners of the globe, helped by the strong character and sizeable fortune of both Lord Exeters, by the goodwill and spiritual determination of the pioneers, and by the education and pep of the bourgeois kids who followed. It functions as smoothly as a Club Med through efficient organization and collective effort, without much dark theology or heavy authority. The Lodge rules are pragmatic and malleable. Members work in town, their children go to local schools, business travel and annual vacations are customary, families and individuals are allowed the space to be themselves, and the lifestyle is as urban and yuppie as possible in a small, hinterland town. There are, of course, the natural tensions of people living in close and constant proximity: a loss of privacy, petty feuds and shifting factions, sexual undercurrents, a pressure toward homogeneity, and from time to time an overwhelming claustrophobic urge to get on the next bus and escape these all-too-familiar people who know you all too well.

"We're not some weird cult," Peter said, "though we're totally weird in terms of what other people are doing. Some people look at us and see they would have to give up all sorts of things they want, but we don't see those things as worth wanting, so there's no real giving up. They say we don't live in the real world, and we say we tried life out there – in the unreal world – and we decided to reorient."

Good for them, the chorus of conscience sang louder and louder, but what of those they left behind? It was the same terrible question that no doubt tormented Noah and his family as they watched the drowning of the cities from the ark; no doubt it obsesses the old age of the Holocaust survivors; no doubt it will give anguish to the few who will witness the destruction of the world from behind the barred doors of their fall-out shelters. The Emissaries live in an environment where Indians dwell in squalor nearby, where poverty and militarism are bred by government and business policies, and where there are no natives or refugee families or mental patients in their midst. But, as they see it, their important work is to tackle the spiritual decay at the root of political and social problems rather than make token gestures, offer Band-aid solutions, or add fuel to the fire.

"There are too many Boy Scouts helping old ladies who don't want to cross the road," Michael Exeter said. "We go through the doors that open to us. Whenever we can contribute something – to bring attunements to the Indians of Alkali Lake, to transcend the separation of blacks and whites in South Africa, to be a serene presence amid the tense negotiations between East and West – we'll do that. But all these problems are only a reflection of what is going on inside people, and that's what has to change. You can go around rubbing the image off the mirror, but it won't make any difference until the image changes."

"It is the sense of separation, of elemental loneliness, that stimulates within people this frantic endeavour to fill up: fill up the world with people, fill up their bodies with more food, fill up their experience with more things," he wrote in a booklet called *My World, My Responsibility*. "It all has to do with the gnawing sense of spiritual emptiness. So, thank God for hunger. Thank God for the crisis in population, for starvation, for disease, for the shadow of Armageddon that haunts everyone these days. Bring on the pressure! This sounds cold and inhumane, but pressure can be of great value. It prevents us from lying back with our hands folded and our eyes shut, assuming that all is as it should be. We are forced to face the fact of our own personal misalignment."

Yet it seems, in Zen-like contradiction, that the way out of personal misalignment is to assume that all is as it should be.

In other words, as I read it, we somehow have to turn on and tune in, but not drop out of problems altogether. "It is not that they don't need to be dealt with," he continued, "but the crux of the matter always is: WHO is dealing with them? What is the calibre of the person? How able are we to see what is really going on and to take appropriate measures relative to the things that are seen?"

I had learned long ago – at least since the days when the Anglican chaplain at school was revealed as a sadistic paedophile – to check what preachers say against what they do. History is full of saints (and revolutionaries) who loved the hungry and the homeless with such perfect purity that they had no love left for their own children, no time left for their neighbour in need, and no penny left for the beggar on the corner. Alternatively, others have insisted that charity begins at home, and interpreted it to mean feeding oneself with money from the poor box, taking care of the family and the business, and damning the rest of humanity to oblivion.

In the case of Michael Exeter and the Emissaries, as evidenced by what I saw, the practice is to begin with what they have – themselves, the Lodge family, the ranch, the town, the other units, the kindred spirits – and cleanse them with as much honesty and selflessness as possible. That does not mean giving up all worldly possessions, sex, meat, or gopher-killing, apparently, but neither does it mean getting rich, laid, chemically beefy, or trigger-happy about communists after the fashion of TV evangelists. Then, from that moderate decency, they reach out to touch whatever hands are reaching out to them.

If the Emissaries are unlikely to arm guerrillas in South Africa or demonstrate against pulp mills, neither have they fallen into a lotus-eating passivity. Their major activity is the dissemination of ideas. "Our service isn't to proselytize or convert," Michael said, "but we are seeing increasing numbers who have come naturally to our kind of thinking and we encourage them to carry on. We confirm that their thoughts aren't crazy. We've been beating this drum for years, and the sound is being heard out there."

The drum includes the lectures, the courses, the books and pamphlets, the information centres, and the word of mouth. Recently other instruments have been introduced. There have been conferences on earth stewardship, health, and peace. There is Educo, a wilderness summer school "with specific adventure/challenge activities" to lead youth "from the known into the unknown." There is the Association for Responsible Communication to help make the media, the arts, and communication technology "a responsible and unifying force in the world." There are the Whole Health Institute (to transcend "the basic mechanics of health care"), the Renaissance Educational Associates (for "honesty" in the classrooms), the Renaissance Business Associates ("to extend the influence of integrity into the business arena"), all with their own lectures and conferences and newsletters. There is "Integrity International," a journal of "practical spirituality" put together in 100 Mile House and concerned with bringing out "the qualities of integrity and nobility in people" for "positive, creative change in our world."

In it I caught a headline – "Life Purpose Party" – and I feared for an instant that the Emissaries were going into mainstream politics. But it was not that: it was a real party, in Boston one February, an evening of "entertainment, conversation, dancing, and an opportunity to discover new personal and professional associations that will enhance your life work," amid complimentary hors d'oeuvres and sparkling wines. Apparently more than 115 assorted strangers showed up for "some fun ice-breaker activities" and a chance to share their life purposes more deeply than "a straight card-swapping session." They were also introduced to the "official, but low-profile, sponsor of the event," the Emissary Foundation International, which later collated their names, addresses, and life work into its networking files. "Magic and music were in the air," the report stated, "and it did seem that we were sharing in social renaissance."

It may not have been social work as defined by the liberation theologists or even the Salvation Army, but it was a door to pass through, a focus to point at, a form to use. It was part of the gathering together of the family and the animals, two by two. "People come in through the door and allow the ark to be built, second and third stories, because there are those who are drawn," Martin, the 7th Marquess of Exeter, once wrote, "not because someone is out there with a whip saying, 'You get in here now,' but because a window is opened above. There is something pouring out of heaven into the earth and there is that in people which will respond. If the response is enough, a person will begin to gravitate into the space where this ark is to appear. This is not to say that floods of people are liable to put in an appearance; it certainly hasn't happened so far. But this is the way it works, this is the truth."

FIVE

The Very Rich Hours

I am sitting in Notre-Dame Basilica in Montreal. It is one of the most sumptuous rooms in North America and among the most beautiful churches in the world: a dark and rich extravaganza of magnificent woodwork and polychrome decoration, elegant columns and gilded arches, superb carvings and fine paintings, stained-glass windows and a mighty organ, all spanned by a ceiling of stars glittering in a blue-green sky. Unashamedly theatrical, with two tiers of galleries on three sides and a slight incline of the nave for better viewing, it forces attention toward the sanctuary, where a soaring Neo-Gothic reredos of ornate spires and wooden statues glows like a celestial city above the altar against the illuminated dazzle of a heavenly blue radiance. And though I realize the seduction of my senses – by the splendour and the darkness, the lingering incense and the votive candles, the lovely objects and the mystical silence – I succumb willingly for a while to its pleasures.

As a soul seeking a few minutes' refuge from the stress and squalor of the city outside, I differ little from the few devotees nearby on this ordinary Monday morning, though they are on their knees murmuring prayers or fingering rosaries. I sink into the warm voluptuousness of the place without worrying whether its costs should not have gone into helping the peasants of nineteenth-century Quebec or whether its sacred purpose is not a vain folly constructed to glorify a folk tale. (In fact, at the point where religion meets aesthetics, both churches and theology can seem even more wondrous if they serve as pure art, without pragmatic end or selfish function.)

It is not possible to speak of religion in Canada, its history and politics and thought, without speaking of Catholicism in Quebec. Nor is it possible to speak of Catholicism in Quebec, I would argue, without coming to this city and this church, which has seen the great funerals of George-Etienne Cartier and Pierre Laporte and heard the great speeches of Henri Bourassa and Archbishop Charbonneau. While the population and wealth of Montreal gave clout and prestige throughout the province to its clergy and theologians, the origin and majesty of Notre-Dame made it known as "the parish church of French Canada" or simply "The Parish."

To my right there is a stained-glass window that depicts a ceremony held in the Church of Notre-Dame in Paris in 1641. Two men, Jérôme Le Royer de La Dauversière and Abbé Jean-Jacques Olier, are seen dedicating the new settlement about to be established on the island of Montreal in New France to the honour and protection of Christ, St Joseph, and especially the Virgin Mary. They named it Ville-Marie, no less – a name preserved by the central office complex, Place Ville-Marie, which is shaped as a cross! – and its *raison d'être* was neither fish nor fur nor military strategy but the salvation of heathen souls. It was intended to be a sacred place: the founders sought Heaven rather than profits, their associates were actually forbidden to engage in the fur trade, and the site was deliberately selected deep in the region of hostile Indians in order to bring them the Gospel. Angels were to tread where even fools feared to rush in.

There cannot be many major cities that were ordered into existence, without any commercial or imperial benefit, by the direct command of God. Both Dauversière and Olier were ardent offspring of the French Counter-Reformation. The former had been taught by the Jesuits, knew many of the missionaries who would become famous in Canadian history (as well as René Descartes, a classmate), and balanced his life as a provincial tax official and pious father of six with spiritual devotions involving whips made of small chains and a belt sporting over 1,200 sharp points. His zeal was rewarded by a voice requiring him to found first an order of nuns and then a hospital, on an island in the wilds of Canada, where they would work. A humble man of modest means, he was not sure how he could accomplish either, especially in a place where there was not yet a colony, but he set off to Paris to do God's work and was reassured by an ecstatic vision that the Holy Family was behind him all the way.

Shortly afterwards, Providence threw him into the arms of Olier, a young priest with a similar taste for self-mortification and a similar experience with a voice. God's talk for him was to found a society of priests and send them off to proselytize – also on an island in the wilds of Canada! Though the two men were complete strangers, history records that at their accidental meeting they ran across the room to embrace like long-lost brothers. From this encounter would arise the organization and finances from which sprang, in 1642, the settling of Ville-Marie by the small band of devout men and women under Paul de Chomedey de Maisonneuve with hymns of praise and an immediate Mass. There is a stained-glass window in Notre-Dame showing that Mass, and another showing Maisonneuve carrying a heavy cross up to the top of Mount Royal in 1643 as he had vowed to do if God spared the tiny colony from a flood that had threatened it several months before. The huge, electric cross that dominates Montreal today is a reminder of that magic.

"What shall we say of these adventurers of Montreal," asked Francis Parkman, the nineteenth-century historian, "of these who bestowed their wealth, and, far more, of these who sacrificed their peace and risked their lives, on an enterprise at once so romantic and so devout? Surrounded as they were with illusions, false lights, and false shadows; breathing an atmosphere of miracle; compassed about with angels and devils; urged with stimulants most powerful, though unreal;

their minds drugged, as it were, to preternatural excitement," they could only be compared in his judgement to the saintly soldiers and ideal damsels of the first Crusades.

Certainly the epic accounts of how the colonists slew the Iroquois in the name of Christ evoke the legends of the knights battling the infidels for the Holy Land; and certainly the beatific portraits of such women as Jeanne Mance, Marguerite Bourgeoys, and Madame de La Peltrie – or Marie de l'Incarnation and Marie de Saint-Joseph at Quebec – suggest virtues and superstitions looking back toward the Middle Ages rather than ahead to the Enlightenment. Not only did Jeanne Mance by chance meet Dauversière for the first time with the same charge of recognition that Olier had experienced – thereby convincing Dauversière that she was the person destined to run his hospital at Montreal, appropriately to be named the Hôtel-Dieu – but years later she apparently regained the use of her crippled arm by touching the relic in which Father Olier's heart had been stored upon his death.

My favourite story involves Marie-Madeleine de Chauvigny de La Peltrie, a young widow whose piety never dampened her energy, determination, and somewhat manic behaviour. Once a Jesuit report about New France put the bee in her bonnet, nothing could prevent her from giving her life and her fortune to the cause of converting the Indians. She faked a marriage to "a man pure as an angel" in order to escape her father; she battled her family in court to prove she was not insane to spend her money on good works; and she chartered her own boat to transport herself and all her baggage to Quebec in 1639. All this was because of a vow she had made to St Joseph when, ill to the edge of death, she promised to serve in Canada if she recovered. When the doctor who had given her up for dead found her cured, he exclaimed (not knowing of her vow but using a contemporary expression for a sudden disappearance), "Your fever must have gone to Canada!"

"Yes, Monsieur," she is said to have replied with a little smile, "it has gone to Canada."

And then there was Marie de l'Incarnation, the foundress of the Ursuline order in New France, another young widow imbued with the mysticism of the period and the spirituality of the Jesuit *Relations*. Jesus used to appear in her dreams when she was a child; as a girl she used to converse at length with God; and when an adult she was whacked by the Holy Spirit one day on the street and found herself up to her neck in the blood of Christ. As a result she developed an ardour for hair shirts and nettle whips, and though she was eager to kiss the infected foot of a servant, she would not allow herself to kiss her little son. When she was led finally by a series of visions and voices into entering an Ursuline convent, the boy stood beneath her window and shouted, "Give me back my mother, give me back my mother!" But his mother only heard that pitiful cry as a temptation of the Devil.

In 1633 she had a dream in which she and a female companion were walking in a dangerous land when they met a man who showed them a spacious place as white as alabaster and wonderfully silent. They saw there a small house on whose roof sat the Blessed Virgin and the Infant Jesus, who turned from looking out upon the afflicted landscape to shower Marie with smiles and kisses. The place was Canada, of course; the man was St Joseph; and when Marie met Madame de La Peltrie in 1639 on the eve of their voyage to Quebec, she knew her at once as the companion on the walk.

"It is true that there are ice-floes, brambles, and thorns there," Marie wrote to her new patroness (in a series of letters brilliantly translated and introduced by Joyce Marshall), "but the Holy Spirit has a sovereign power to consume all these – and even to split rocks. It is this divine fire that inspires and strengthens holy souls, makes them pass through the greatest travails, makes them despise themselves and give unsparingly of their wealth and their lives for the conquest of souls redeemed by the blood of Jesus Christ."

At first, because Canada offered so few material comforts, Marie saw "a sort of necessity to become holy; one must either give one's assent to this or die." But as the colony grew in population and prosperity, with traders and soldiers and settlers arriving for reasons unconnected to any divine vision, her letters made clear that holiness had eluded many of the inhabitants. In 1661, for example, a sorcerer showed up in the guise of a miller. He plagued a girl who had spurned him with demons, goblins, and phantoms; he caused invisible drums to pound in her ears and stones to fly past her head; and he was held responsible for the sickness then devastating the colony. (And these were the folks who were accusing the natives of being superstitious, terrified by shamans and bad medicine, and obsessed by dreams and visions!)

By the time the great earthquake hit in 1663 like the eve of Judgement, Marie was prepared to accept it as God's wish "to punish the country for the sins committed here, especially the contempt for the ordinances of the Church." She meant, in particular, the liquor trade with the Indians. Since the arrival of François de Laval in 1659, and especially after his appointment to the Sovereign Council in 1663 as the second most powerful man in New France after the governor, this issue pitted the spiritual values of the Church against the political aims of the state and the commercial interests of the traders. Bishop Laval took this crusade as far as the court of Louis XIV, the theologians of the Sorbonne, and the excommunication of anyone giving intoxicants to the native people; and he too noted with gratitude God's help in scaring the daylights out of the traders in 1663.

"One would have said," wrote Marie de l'Incarnation, "that, even while God shook the mountains and marble rocks of these regions, he took pleasure in shaking consciences. The days of carnival were changed into days of penitence and sadness; public prayers, processions, and pilgrimages were continual, fasts on bread and water very frequent, and general confessions more sincere than they would have been in the extremity of sickness."

As usual, however, it did not take long for the general piety to pass with the memory of the calamity. Bishop Laval's biography is a lengthy record of battles waged against the governors and the intendants, among the Sulpicians and the Jesuits and the Récollets, in Paris and Rome, involving ridiculous questions of protocol and sublime matters of faith. At heart was a power struggle between religious and secular authority, for if

God ruled over the French king himself in New France, would pope or bishop or priest rule over the king's agents there? No less a person than Louis XIV declared that the state must prevail over the clergy, lest they "establish their authority too firmly through the fear of excommunication and through an excessively severe way of life that they wish to maintain."

New France cannot be considered a theocracy, therefore, however powerful or prominent the Church was in the affairs of state and the lives of the settlers. While a fair share of religion can be highly useful to the state, in terms of moral behaviour or social cohesion or the rewards to come in the next world, few politicians in history have felt comfortable with too much religion – and not just for selfish reasons. It is always surprising, given the spiritual push toward universal love and compassion, how quickly and brutally theocracies routinely degenerate into intolerance, oppression, and corruption. Those who have their heads in the clouds seldom have their feet on the ground; the pursuit and exercise of secular power usually are enough to twist even the souls of saints; and the legislation of holiness when all else fails is just too easy.

Though Bishop Laval and his successors won many of their battles, and though the parish priests assumed an early and firm leadership of the agrarian society, it is worth noting that French Canada has never been a monolithic community of the righteous. Rowdy *coureurs de bois* were going native, and few *habitants* had the fervour of the priests and nuns who had sacrificed their lives to religion. Even today, while most Quebeckers would agree that their province was "priest-ridden" before the Quiet Revolution of the 1960s, they caution English Canadians against dismissing them as dull and timid sheep. Quebec never elected as premier a religious fanatic like William Aberhart in Alberta, they hasten to suggest, and even in the grimmest days of Catholic Jansenism, Montreal was never as uptight and puritanical as Toronto the Good.

In fact, they make a good argument that Quebec's priest-ridden condition was inflicted upon them by the British Conquest in 1763. With the defeat of the civil authorities and the most important merchants, the British had only the Roman

Catholic hierarchy as a possible ally in the maintenance of peace and control. They moved fast to secure such a *roi nègre*. First, the new English governor helped arrange a replacement for the Quebec bishop who had died in 1760 (apparently of a broken heart due to the fall of Quebec), even though Roman Catholicism was still not tolerated in England and no Anglican bishop had yet been appointed anywhere in North America. Then, by the Quebec Act of 1774, the Church was allowed to maintain its essential rights and privileges in French Canada. That pragmatic concession had extraordinary consequences: logically it opened the way for Roman Catholics to hold public office in British North America decades before they were permitted to do so at Westminster, and politically it was to bind religion and the state in Canada by a diversity of quasi-established churches. In the immediate term, it caused Bishop Briand and his priests to rally French Canadians around the British flag during the American Revolution.

Bishop Plessis performed the same service during the War of 1812. Indeed, viewing what had happened to the Church and the King in France during its revolution, he lauded Great Britain as the best protector of French Canada's faith. "Almost the whole of Europe has been given over to carnage and destruction, the holiest cloisters have been violated, virgins dishonoured, mothers and children slaughtered in several places," he had said in a famous sermon delivered in 1799 to celebrate Nelson's victory over Napoleon at Aboukir. "Is it not evident, and can it not be said, that at the height of this war you enjoy all the advantages of peace? To whom, my brothers, aside from God, do you owe these favours, if not to the paternal vigilance of an Empire which, in peace as in war, I dare to say, has your interests closer to its heart than its own?"

Though Plessis had some sympathy for the nationalist causes of the early French-Canadian radicals in the Assembly, by the time of the rebellions the Church hierarchy turned against Papineau and the *patriotes* as tainted with liberalism, republicanism, anticlericalism, and plain insubordination. If the Church had to share its authority to speak on behalf of

French Canadians, it preferred to do so with devout conservatives. Backed by the orthodoxy of the nineteenth-century popes, allied to the political machinery, influential in education and culture and parish life, it supported Confederation and settled down to more than a century of power in Quebec.

Not unchallenged power, of course: modern ideas kept creeping into the system through ideas and industry, and the Church had to wage a ceaseless campaign to contain them. Though many moderate Catholics and a few liberal bishops sought an accommodation with what they sensed was inevitable, if not precisely desirable, the prevailing mood well into the twentieth century was belligerent. Its fiercest champion was Ignace Bourget, the Bishop of Montreal from 1840 to 1876. Reacting to the waves of freedom that swept Europe and splashed French Canada in the first third of the century, spurred on by Pope Gregory XVI's savage attack on liberal ideas in 1832 and Pope Pius IX's comprehensive denunciation of everything from progress to modern civilization in the *Syllabus of Errors* in 1864, enthusiastic about the declaration of papal infallibility by the First Vatican Council in 1870, Bishop Bourget never hesitated to use his position and authority for political ends.

"Be faithful to God and respect all legitimately constituted authorities. Such is the will of the Lord," he told his people in 1849. "Do not listen to those who address seditious remarks to you, for they cannot be your true friends. Do not read those books and papers that breathe the spirit of revolt, for they are the vehicles of pestilential doctrines which, like an ulcer, have corroded and ruined the most successful and flourishing states."

When the people did not heed his advice – by electing to the Assembly in 1854 eleven members of the Institut Canadien, a liberal club with a library full of pestilential books – Bourget went to war against the *rouges*, with tirades against ideas such as the separation of church and state and the secularization of education. Every Quebec Catholic, therefore, was instructed to repeat Bourget's neat formula: "I listen to my curé, my curé listens to the bishop, the bishop listens to the pope, the pope listens to our Lord Jesus Christ, who aids with the Holy Spirit to render them infallible on the teaching and government of his Church." On one front, he moved against the members of the Institut Canadien directly as Catholics; on another front, he inspired some lay followers to issue the *Programme catholique* in 1871. In practice that meant voting for the Conservative Party, except when another local candidate was even more sympathetic toward the programme.

By the time Wilfrid Laurier became leader of the Liberal Party in 1887, the situation had changed fundamentally, mostly because of the Conservatives' role in the hanging of Louis Riel two years before despite the protests of Quebec Catholics. The Conservative Party no longer seemed their natural home, and it became even less comfortable once it gave in to Protestant bigotry by failing to protect the Catholic schools of Manitoba in 1890. The presence of a Quebec Catholic at the head of a party dedicated to such protection in the 1896 election took the punch out of any more sermons to the effect that Heaven is *bleu* like the Tories and Hell is *rouge* like the Grits.

Intrinsic to Quebec's support for Laurier was a mounting concern for the survival of French Canada in the wake of Confederation, industrialization, and modern thought. The *Programme catholique* had summed up itself as "Religion and Fatherland," and many Catholic thinkers were concluding that the best safeguard for their faith (and for their power, no doubt) was a Quebec-centred, Church-controlled, agrarian nationalism. In Europe Rome had tended to combat nineteenth-century nationalism as another aspect of liberalism, but in French Canada the Church picked up the failed nationalism of the middle-class and peasant rebellions and turned it toward its own conservative designs. As postulated by the popular histories of Abbé Faillon and Abbé Ferland (and later Abbé Groulx, the most popular of all), and articulated in the sermons of Bishop Laflèche of Trois-Rivières and the renowned theologian L.-A. Pâquet, the spiritual and mystical circumstances surrounding the origins of French Canada proved that God intended French Canadians to persist as a nation in their own homeland for a divine purpose.

"I cannot doubt that this religious and civilizing mission is the true vocation and the special vocation of the French race in America," Pâquet agreed in 1902. But he made a significant addition. "French Canada will accomplish God's purposes and respond to its sublime calling only to the extent that it maintains its own way of life, its individual character, and its truly national traditions." In reality this meant the preservation of the French language, the exaltation of spirituality above materialism, and "a complete submission" to the authority of the Church leaders. "Let us not step down from the pedestal, where God has placed us, to walk commonly among those generations who thirst for gold and pleasure," he said. "We must leave to other nations, less inspired with the ideal, the kind of feverish materialism and vulgar bestiality that rivets them to material things. Our own ambition must aim higher; our thoughts and aspirations must be loftier."

In this vision agriculture was closer to God than industry, the colonization of desolate corners of Quebec was more His will than migration to Montreal or the United States, and Roman Catholicism was to protect the French language because French isolated the faithful from the evils of Anglo-Saxon Protestantism. These themes found power as early as 1886, when Honoré Mercier's Parti National formed a nationalist, Catholic government in Quebec as a reaction to Riel's hanging. Not only did he put a priest in charge of the colonization department and ask the Pope himself to hand out provincial funds to settle a dispute among competing religious orders, he pressed the idea of Quebec as the homeland of the French-Canadian nation that remains on the agenda today.

Later, when industrialization and urbanization proved invincible forces, the Church attempted to influence what it could not actually control. Catholic trade unions were promoted to steer workers away from multinational, socialist movements; parish priests helped organize local cooperative societies and credit unions as alternatives to the corporations and banks; youth groups for students and farmers and workers, lay associations, and corporatist ideas were mobilized in the battle against modern statism; newspapers, publishing houses, and radio programmes broadcast ecclesiastical propaganda; and, above all, there was religion's grip on the education system. "If there is a ruling class here," said Henri Bourassa, with strong appreciation, in 1902, "it is certainly the clergy."

About fifty years later another Catholic polemicist, Pierre Elliott Trudeau, concurred – but with rather less appreciation. "In this way," he wrote in 1956, "the social doctrine of the Church – which, in other countries, had openly welcomed popular democracy, the emancipation of workers, and social progress – in French Canada was called upon to support authoritarianism and xenophobia. And, worse still, our 'doctrine' helped make it impossible for us to solve our problems. For, on the negative side, it rejected all solutions that could be successful against our 'enemies': the English, the Protestants, the materialists, etc. And, on the positive side, it remained content with elaborating theoretical systems, devoid of any objective link with reality and often totally inapplicable in practice."

If that was the economic result, the social and cultural result was expressed in the famous *cri de coeur*, *Refus global*, issued in 1948 by Paul-Emile Borduas and other artists. "We are a small people sheltering under the wing of the clergy – the only remaining repository of faith, knowledge, truth, and national wealth; isolated from the universal progress of thought with all its pitfalls and perils; and raised (since complete ignorance was impossible) on well-meaning but grossly distorted accounts of the great historical facts. We are a small people, the product of a Jansenist colony, isolated, defeated, left a powerless prey to all those invading congregations from France and Navarre that were eager to perpetuate in this holy realm of fear (fear-is-the-mother-of-wisdom!) the blessings and prestige of a Catholic religion that was being scorned in Europe. Heirs of papal authority, mechanical, brooking no opposition, past masters of obscurantist methods, our educational institutions had, from that time on, absolute control over a world of warped memories, stagnant minds, and crooked intentions."

No revolution, even a quiet one, blooms without seeds and a period of underground maturation. The Roman Catholic Church and French Canada had both. In the Church there survived a somewhat liberal opposition that felt the Inquisition had been an inadequate reply to the questions of the Protestant Reformation and the First Vatican Council had been a vain defence against the pressures behind Europe's political turmoil. At some point, these priests and theologians maintained, the Church would have to deal more realistically and more rationally with the issues of modern economics, scientific discovery, individual liberty, national freedom, and papal authority. These subversive ideas entered Quebec through Church circles, whether through the "social Catholicism" of Pius XI, through the influential philosophies of Jacques Maritain and Emmanuel Mounier, through the Faculty of Social Sciences set up at Laval in 1938 by the Dominican priest, Georges-Henri Lévesque, or through student activists and lay or clerical liberals; and there they met individuals and movements keeping alive the flame of reform passed along by the French and American Revolutions, the Papineau rebellions, the moderate French-Canadian *rouges*, and Wilfrid Laurier. This small minority, mostly intellectuals, existed in an atmosphere where Italian and Spanish fascism were lauded as the defence of Catholic values against godless socialism, where the highest-ranking bishops forbade their flocks from joining the CCF Party in the 1930s, and where much of the Church hierarchy preferred the corrupt stability of Maurice Duplessis's regime to the uncertainties of true democracy.

By 1950, however, serious cracks had appeared in the conservative fortress. Until Rome forced his retirement (not least because of lobbying by Duplessis and right-wing Catholics), Archbishop Joseph Charbonneau of Montreal was a prominent advocate of social and ecclesiastical reform, most spectacularly when he and several other bishops supported the Asbestos strike of 1949 in the face of government bullying.

"The working class is the victim of a conspiracy that wishes to crush it," he said in a sermon at Notre-Dame, "and when there is conspiracy to crush the working class, it is the duty of the Church to intervene." And in the unions, in the press, in the universities, in the arts, in Church circles too, voices arose to confront Duplessis and his clerical allies on behalf of democracy, civil liberties, and the separation of church and state as Quebec met the modern world through business, the media, the unions, and theory. "MAKE WAY FOR MAGIC! MAKE WAY FOR OBJECTIVE MYSTERY!" shouted the *Refus global*. "MAKE WAY FOR LOVE! MAKE WAY FOR WHAT IS NEEDED!"

The traditional structure did not exactly *make* way: it *gave* way under the weight of its own inflexibility, obsolescence, and corruption. The victory of the provincial Liberal Party occurred on the eve of both the Second Vatican Council and the social, political, and cultural wildness of the 1960s, and these three forces coincided to make the Roman Catholic Church in French Canada virtually unrecognizable by the end of the decade. While the world Church popularized the Mass and many of the antiquated rules, pulled away from triumphal domination toward pluralism, and sought to replace fearful submission with joyful belief, the Quebec Church encountered an activist provincial state determined to secularize the school system, the hospitals, and the welfare agencies, as well as intervene in the economy and propel Quebec into the industrial age. The secularization that had taken place in Europe over a hundred years happened in Quebec in about five years, and ordinary parishioners were left exposed to a world in which television shook up the old values, political and sexual freedom was the fashion, and all those Fridays of abstaining from meat turned out to be an unnecessary effort.

It is impossible to untangle these intricate causes, but their combined effect is evident. In 1965 an estimated 88 per cent of Quebec Catholics attended Mass at least twice a month. By 1975 the figure was 46 per cent, and by 1985 it was 38 per cent – more than 10 per cent lower than attendance by Canadian Catholics outside Quebec. During this twenty-year period hundreds of priests and nuns quit and new vocations fell by some 75 per cent. Quebec now has one of the lowest birth rates in the Western world, which suggests that even practising Catholics are ignoring the Church's teachings on artificial contraception and abortion, and surveys have shown Quebec Catholics to be often the most tolerant religious group in the country regarding moral issues such as adultery, divorce, homosexuality, and premarital sex.

In the face of this extraordinary mutation the Church hierarchy abandoned its power over education and social services, lost most of its political and union influence, and even forfeited much of its authority over its own clergy and laity – all symbolized by Cardinal Léger's resigning in 1967 from the perks and powers of being Archbishop of Montreal in order to go off to work among the lepers of West Africa. In fact, the Quebec Church today has been described as an anarchy. Some priests give Holy Communion to the divorced and baptize the children of unwed parents, despite Rome's regulations; some theologians teach all sorts of Protestant heresies in the seminaries, despite the bishops' instructions; and groups of women, Marxists, charismatics, and old-fashioned traditionalists continually challenge the status quo. Even a bunch of bishops crowded around the altar at René Lévesque's funeral, though he had been divorced and remarried.

Some argue that the hierarchy surrendered too quickly and gently to the secular, materialist ideology of the Quiet Revolution. By not resisting more vehemently the loss of its influence over the society, they contend, it gave the field to public opinion and social pressure and thereby lost the battle for the minds and souls of the people. Sometimes accusing Léger of abandoning his post in a funk after his failure to contain the revolt against all authority, they draw a parallel to Eastern Europe: while the Church may have suffered defeat and persecution there in its opposition to communism, it has remained a fighting force that cannot be ignored in the way that the Quebec Church is ignored.

"The Church gladly renounced the authority and power that had placed it under the tutelage of people like Duplessis, who used it in a ruthless and ultimately counterproductive way," a senior Canadian bishop once confided to me. "But it suffered from a sense of alienation and a fear of falling into the trap of connecting religious authority with social authority. So it lapsed into silence often, and therefore fell into the opposite extreme of not taking religious and moral leadership. They still are cowards, afraid of their own shadows."

But this is North America, goes the response, and the graceful concession of power for the sake of democracy and freedom may have been Roman Catholicism's finest hour in Quebec. The writing was on the wall; a vigorous last stand may simply have made the Quiet Revolution considerably less quiet in terms of social peace and Church prosperity; and, more important, the spiritual essence was relieved at last from the burden and decadence of worldly preoccupations. "The Quebec Church behaved magnificently," Gregory Baum, the McGill theologian, told me. "The tendency in Europe had been to react by a hardening of positions. In Quebec, largely because of Vatican II, there was an opening toward change. What conservatives describe as anarchy may just be the Spirit moving in different directions 'to let a thousand flowers grow.'"

What happened in Quebec demonstrates the danger to a religion when its institutions are mistaken for its faith. The *public* religion of Christendom, propped up for social, political, or economic reasons, is not the same as the *true* religion of Christianity. How else can anyone explain the pace and conviction with which so many Quebeckers walked away from their churches, in spite of extraordinary indoctrination? They must have sat as "baptized pagans" through the sermons, attended the schools, memorized the catechisms, obeyed the priests, and taken Communion as social norms, without intelligent understanding or deep belief. The moment the norms shifted, these people fled the pews for politics, sex, money, cults, or the lazy cosmology of "bad Catholics" who tell pollsters they believe in God and Christ but never pray or go to confession.

Catholic atheists are not the same as Protestant, Jewish, or Sikh atheists, however, and those who go to church out of blind faith are different from those who do not go to church at all. Their religions mark them with indelible attitudes – about the relationship of the individual to society, whether the universe is benign or malevolent, how confidence is balanced with guilt, or what is important in life, for example – which then are applied to new pursuits. The medieval Catholicism that shaped French Canada was characterized by a strong and centralized authority preaching obedience above conscience, order above freedom, the collective above the individual, ideals above realities, future rewards above present gratifications, and tradition above innovation. With the overthrow of God the Father (and His earthly agent, the Church), sovereignty passed immediately to His natural children, "the people," along with most of the old traits. The state replaced the hierarchy, language replaced faith, and nationalism replaced religion. Thus, having created the abstract context and the rhetoric of ethnic survival, the Roman Catholic Church left as a legacy the Quebec independence movement.

Whether from the right or the left, positively or negatively, Quebec nationalists owe more to the Church than they usually admit. Where else did their notions of community and idealism come from? What else conditioned their ideas of authority and tradition? Who else preserved the dreams and memories of French Canada for two hundred years and provided so many of the images and obsessions of French-Canadian culture? Even though the Quebec bishops supported Confederation in 1867 and tried to remain neutral during the referendum in 1980, many of their priests and theologians stoked the nationalist flames during this whole period. Certainly the number of ex-priests in the Parti Québécois, within the media, among the intellectuals, suggests the metamorphosis of one faith into another, as does the change of St Jean Baptiste Day to the *fête nationale*, and even yuppie businessmen have become nationalistic. It has always been my theory that the October Crisis of 1970 was so cathartic because, as a kind of elaborate Passion play, it touched the religious soul of Quebec. The kidnapped diplomat was named Cross; the murdered cabinet minister was named Laporte ("I am the door," Jesus said); two of the abductors were named Rose (the symbol of Resurrection and Redemption); and the sadistic horror of Laporte's murder, among the bloody leaves of autumn, conjured up the Jesuit martyrs whose tortures are so ingrained in every French-Canadian child.

"Every revolutionary action has a spiritual dimension," Pierre Vallières said in 1989, accounting for his own passage from seminarian to FLQ theorist to radical Christian. "It goes back to the essence of Christianity as a movement that was on the side of the excluded, of the slaves, and which called for liberation."

Even Quebec liberalism, when not absorbed in fact by nationalism, owes as much to Catholic personalism as to any English or American philosophy. By seeking to avoid the worst aspects of self-centredness and alienation, it permitted more authority and collective will than generally conceded by classic liberalism. Far from being an intellectual gymnastic of no real consequence, this difference transfused the thinking of Pierre Trudeau, Marc Lalonde, Jean Marchand, Gérard Pelletier, Jeanne Sauvé, and many others who governed Canada in the heyday of "French Power." Trudeau's imposition of the War Measures Act, his obsession with the constitution, and his application of the National Energy Program would have been less puzzling in Toronto or Calgary if more English Canadians had understood they were dealing with a Catholic intellectual who had grown up, along with many of his closest advisers, amid Catholic colleges and youth associations, with Catholic unionists and journalists, under Catholic values and ideas. Interestingly, despite the anticlerical vitriol with which they fought the power of the Church in the 1950s, few of them gave up their deep faith.

The same cannot be said for those who substituted religion for revolution, on the one hand, or those who quit the worship of Truth for the pursuit of Lifestyle, on the other. Neither the utopian nationalists nor the pragmatic materialists have much time, energy, or heart left for God, though they are more likely to be agnostics than atheists. On Place d'Armes outside Notre-Dame, dwarfing the church's two beautiful towers

121

("Perseverance" and "Temperance"), soars black and bold and blank the Banque Nationale like a dark symbol of Quebec's new creed; and around the statue of Maisonneuve, holding high the flag of faith in the centre of the square, secretaries and accountants sit in the sun speaking of their mortgages, vacations, and horoscopes. Except on special occasions such as Christmas Eve, Easter Sunday, weddings, funerals, and concerts, most of those who enter the magic of Notre-Dame these days are tourists.

In 1987 a report to the Quebec bishops on the state of their Church described each parish as three circles: a central nucleus of 250 convinced and active Catholics, an intermediate "clientele" of 1,500 regular but quite passive "consumers," and an outer group of perhaps 4,000 who demand occasional services. "The central nucleus has dwindled to such an extent that parishes can no longer count on anything but a reduced number of active members to assume pastoral responsibilities which are becoming more and more onerous. Can we estimate the number of these active Christians? Perhaps only 1 per cent of the total number of the baptized? The intermediate circle, where in the past the largest number of baptized persons used to be found (about 80 per cent), has itself been reduced to a minority of between 10 to 20 per cent of those baptized. The outer circle has in turn become just as inflated."

As the politics of the nationalist state failed to produce either salvation or satisfaction, as individual conscience and personal freedom challenged even God's authority, the ideals of soul, community, service, and sharing – MAGIC! OBJECTIVE MYSTERY! LOVE! – got trampled in the stampede toward consumer goods, self-advancement, hedonism, and profit. When the Church fell, the moral teachings fell, and all the exhortations toward caring and sharing were dismissed as the repressive devices of the clergy to keep people from enjoying the fruits of North American capitalism: money and sex, only tempered by cultural nationalism. This was not exactly what the liberals of the 1950s and the radicals of the 1960s had in mind when they began their revolutions, of course, and it is odd to find many of them now making cause with the bishops and priests who are among the most progressive voices in the society.

This society has been portrayed vividly in *The Decline of the American Empire* and *Jesus of Montreal*, two films by Denys Arcand. In the first, a group of intellectual men and women grope for meaning and happiness in an age of collective decay. Politics contains no inspiration or hope; the beads and trinkets of yuppie pleasure prove a poor exchange for the land of the spirit; the illusion of freedom has captured their lives in pathos and silliness; and all that is left is sex, love, or talking about them. Amyl nitrate just before orgasm is as close as they can get to the ecstasies of St John of the Cross; the torture of Christ inspires only sadomasochism; the legacy of faith has been reduced to pain and guilt in relationships, ennui and discontent amid earthly beauty and comfort, and emptiness and lies in words. "In our personal lives," a character concludes, "unless one's a mystic or saint, there are no models to live by." In fact, in the second film, to be a mystic or saint in modern Quebec seems merely a model to die by. Surrounded by the triumph of stupidity and cupidity, by corrupt bishops and cynical priests as well as trendy intellectuals and entrepreneurial fools, the Christ figure must be crucified once more.

Yet three centuries of mysticism do not evaporate in three decades of materialism. Though Arcand offers little hope, his films touch upon the limits of selfishness and consumerism. The Gospel message is whispered again in secret cells. The Passion story has again the power to excite and move. Even the theatrical rites of the institution are given credit for alleviating misery as effectively (and more cheaply) than psychiatry and drugs. In the same way, hundreds of thousands of pilgrims still trek to St Joseph's Oratory, Ste Anne de Beaupré, or Cap de la Madeleine (where a plaster statue of the Virgin Mary was reported to have rolled its eyes about a hundred years ago) for cures and blessings – but please, a booklet begged those crawling up the steps of the Oratory to get spiritual favours from the heart of Brother André, "refrain from the superstitious practice of throwing coins in the fountain." In 1984 tens of thousands jammed the Olympic Stadium to cheer Pope John Paul II – but one priest dismissed that as a "tribal festival" more than a religious reawakening. In 1988 charismatic Catholics filled the Montreal Forum twice in one day to speak in tongues and witness the miraculous healings by the popular lay televangelist, Pierre Lacroix – not long before he was convicted of gross indecency with a male minor. Cells of Catholic traditionalists popped up around the province as followers of the ultra-conservative European bishop, Marcel Lefebvre – despite his excommunication by the Vatican for provoking a schism.

On the whole, many of the Quebec bishops are heirs of the tolerant spirit of Vatican II; many of them are sympathetic to the political and theological developments of the Third World and feminism; many of them understand the social passage necessary as French Canadians learn to handle freedom, wealth, and external influences after centuries of rigidity and isolation; almost all of them know that a heavy hand or conservative tilt would only push more away from the Church.

"Often the bishops have been ahead of the people," said Julien Harvey, the well-known Jesuit activist. "When something is new and decent, not against the poor or the Gospel, they react by saying nothing, as they did in the 1960s. That is typical of Quebec. Now, when the head office in Rome is moving to the right, they oppose it with the same silence. It's a humane and polite church. Sometimes people get scolded, but heads don't fall here. The bishops are more concerned with building a local network of influence through their episcopal organization than thinking about what the Vatican is saying. That comes out of the past, when the Quebec Church felt responsible for the whole life of the people at the civic level."

Though there are small signals of a hardening of attitude in accordance with the Vatican's recent shift toward authority, the Quebec bishops seem to be waiting for the tide of history to turn inevitably. The Roman Catholic Church is accustomed to moving in great oscillations across history, of course. It has been up and down, persecuted and potent, political and holy, papal and episcopal and clerical and laical. Yet, if it should ever experience a major revival in Quebec, both optimists and pessimists agree that it would be a very different beast. The critical disappearance of priests – with their average age now above sixty and their replacements not in sight – is already seeing to that. It is forcing the parishes, the seminaries, and the bureaucracy to open up to the laity, especially to women, who in turn are putting new pressures on the hierarchy and the doctrine. The revolt of Catholic women in Quebec against a patriarchal structure, against Rome's stand on divorce and birth control and female ordination, has been instrumental in making their bishops among the most sympathetic in the world, for example, and lay Catholics have been effective in pressing liberation theology through their youth groups, workers' movements, social-justice centres, and international-aid agencies. The present fashion is toward small "base" communities for prayer, Bible study, and social action, in which faith and fellowship supersede imposed rules and private salvation, and if the bishops still lust for influence, they seem prepared to accept it at the local level of family and workplace than among the bourgeois élites.

"The Church in Quebec today is extremely lively, very tolerant, very ecumenical," said Benoît Lacroix, a Dominican teacher. "It's going back to the source, the Word of God more than the word of the Pope, and slowly it's restructuring at the base, with lay involvement and new ways of worship and more personal conscience. This will take time, there will be risks, and the Church will *never* be the majority again, but experimentation is better than more discipline and experience is better than more rules. Now Quebec Catholics have to make a series of personal moral decisions for themselves. The law can come later."

More important than the internal situation is the external one. The state, the business sector, the education system, and other religions are no longer weak in relation to the Church's authority. Quebeckers have a very tempting offer to worship Mammon instead of God, and even those who prefer God have plenty of opportunity to worship Him in the Anglican Church (where their contraceptives and divorces do not matter), with the Pentecostals (who bring many of the advantages of tradition along with a personal fire, jazzy singing, and few grim priests), or among an estimated 600 sects and cults active in the province. Moreover, even those who choose to remain nominal Roman Catholics may decide that their beliefs do not require them to attend Mass, obey the Pope, or contribute to the parish. As much by choice as by circumstance, even a strong Church would be simply one more player struggling for power and influence in a pluralist, secular culture.

"Pluralism seems to be making us more Protestant," Julien Harvey observed, "and it's a question how we can build a strong Church with the sheer multiplicity of ideas and attitudes. The youth movements aren't strong, liberation theology is still a small and middle-class affair here, the charismatics are no longer growing, the priests have no authority in the cities, the immigrants are multiplying the 'solitudes' all the time. But the ancient tradition of community is still alive, in hope and charity. People who never go near church still want the last rites, and whenever you touch something that concerns the whole group, people get out of their lethargy. We'll have to await the new forms, which will be influenced by Latin America and Eastern Europe and the return of political involvement by the Church here, not as a powerful lobby but as a humble witness to peace and justice."

The story of the Roman Catholic Church in Quebec is, in many ways, the story of all religions. As Max Weber outlined, they usually begin with the experience and authority of one person, whose mysterious charisma attracts others and makes them obedient. They create a small community, a movement grows, institutions arise, the original fire is transformed into rituals and teachings, laws replace personal will, tradition interprets the laws, and the faith is usurped by politics and culture. Either there are outbursts of the founding vision and spirit to keep the faith true and alive, or the faith dies for lack of spiritual power. The people no longer want it, the state no longer needs it, the priests and magicians disappear, the treasures get spent, the wisdom is lost, and a palpable energy disperses.

I have walked among the temples of Zeus, seen children sport in Jupiter's sanctum, looked on the deserted city of Nalanda where tens of thousands of Buddhist monks once meditated. The world is littered with dead gods. And though Notre-Dame still has awe, silence, mystery, beauty, peace, and old Cardinal Léger praying most of the day next door, I could not help thinking what H.G. Wells once said of New York, "What a lovely ruin it will make."

SIX

Come Hell or High Water

"Everyone kept asking me about my health," Emmett Cardinal Carter chortled to a friend soon after a meeting of all the priests in the Archdiocese of Toronto a couple of years ago. The Archbishop's eyes twinkled with mischief and he grinned the charming grin of a sly old leprechaun, for he knew at whose expense he had made his subtle little joke: Aloysius Ambrozic, already named by the Vatican to become Carter's successor and already nicknamed by his colleagues "Big Al" for his black-bear appearance and "The Ayatollah" for his dogmatic faith.

Cardinal Carter is too astute and well informed not to know of his failure to have won the hearts of most of the men under his command. His first bold move after coming to office in Toronto in 1978 had been a major diocesan rehaul that struck many veterans as a bloodbath; and though he had arrived from London, Ontario, with his reputation as a liberal son of the Second Vatican Council, he soon alienated the younger and more progressive clergy with a series of actions, attitudes, and symbolic gestures they felt were conservative and undemocratic. Reassuming a bishop's right to chair certain meetings may not have been the real matter, however. To those who yearned for a fatherly mentor, a spiritual inspiration, or a paragon of faith His Eminence often appeared as an aloof administrator, a political gamesman, and a very worldly socialite.

"Pius XII used to say there are two hierarchies in the Church: the hierarchy of ordination and the hierarchy of sanctity," said Gregory Baum, who had left the priesthood to become a radical critic of the institution. "The bureaucrats tend to focus on the logic of *maintenance*, which is necessary for the institution to survive. But we also need the élite who teach and inspire, which is the logic of *mission*. Cardinal Carter would not be among those."

For those who do not know him well – and few are allowed to get close – Carter seems a stiff old school principal. At Mass, set apart and somewhat fantastic with his dazzling robes, jewelled cross, golden crozier, and tall mitre, he has a manner that once caused a trembling boy to address him as "Your Majesty." His face is a stern mug, his voice an authoritative baritone, and even the paralysis of his left arm and leg emphasizes a formidable determination more than any obvious vulnerability. At the office and in meetings around town, though less intimidating in a black suit only distinguished by the heavy gold chain and cross around his neck and the enormous gold ring on his right hand, he ruled over Canada's largest, wealthiest, and most influential English-speaking diocese (in the words of one priest) "like a benevolent monarch" until his retirement in March 1990. (As cardinal, an honorific title bestowed on some bishops, giving them the special power to help select the pope, he is in fact a "prince" of the Church as well as a "successor to the apostles" for life.)

"People always know where I am on issues, what I'm thinking," he told me. "There's no doubt about the leadership I've tried to give."

A critic put it differently. "Emmett Carter is seldom right, but he's never uncertain."

There is a thin line between certainty and arrogance. Carter once described himself as "a self-propelled, take-control guy," and he had a tendency to be gruff in his decision-making, immovable in his convictions, and even argumentative for the sake of a good brawl. He has a sharp mind, and as a child in a working-class Irish family in Montreal, he honed his tooth-and-nail debating techniques around the dinner table on Sunday nights during "discussions" so loud and vituperative that visitors fled in terror. It is apparent why many mistake the sport he finds in intellectual and personal competition for animosity, ambition, and rudeness.

He tends to reserve his better side for the comfort of home, the company of friends (who often call him "Min"), and the ear of God. Though he never seems to relax totally, he has a vivid sense of humour and a warm laugh, a loyalty and kindness that make him loved by those who know him best, a keen intelligence that can range over philosophical wisdom and Vatican intrigue, and an inspiring patience and courage in the face of his infirmity. Easily fatigued, often frustrated, to a degree humiliated by his lame arm and awkward shuffle, he betrays his fragile humanity most clearly when he tries to hide it behind his fierce stamina and shy silences.

"His health is bad, he had a difficult job, he's terribly misunderstood, and he's very lonely," said one intimate. "Yes, he was an executive and a politician. Yes, he can be cold and impenetrable. But he's a man of faith who deeply loves the Church. It's as if he's uncertain what to do with his feelings. He shows his heart in small, thoughtful acts, but he shows his affection only to his dog."

His infirmity, the result of a stroke he suffered while at work in 1981, produced what is probably the only true insight the priests of Toronto ever have obtained into the soul of Emmett Carter. A workaholic, an avid tennis player, with a proud and self-reliant nature, suddenly he had to learn again how to walk and dress. Afterwards, in a letter to the clergy, he admitted how painful it was for a person with his need to dominate to be led like a little child. "Don't lose sight of your spirituality," he warned them. "Believe me, my friends, it is all you have. All your strength, all your brains, all your achievements, your honours, your parish – nothing really matters. You have the Lord and you don't have anything else."

It was not an easy letter to write, for Carter is a private person who comes from the Irish tradition in which one's faith is a private matter, but it touched and impressed a lot of Catholics who had been craving just such a simple affirmation of spirituality. Probably no one was more touched than Carter's older brother, Alexander, a merry and much-loved liberal who had been Bishop of Sault Ste Marie for more than twenty-five years. He and Emmett went through school together, sometimes jockeying for first place in the same class; both went through the Second Vatican Council as bishops, sometimes startling their peers with intellectual disputes that usually degenerated into the yelling matches they had practised as kids; and though their intense sibling rivalry caused some to speculate that Emmett purposefully had climbed over Alexander to become Archbishop of Toronto or that Alexander spitefully had boycotted Emmett's installation as cardinal, their love and friendship remain deep.

"I used to pray for him," Alexander told me about a year after the Cardinal's stroke. "Positions of honour and eminence are spiritually dangerous, and it takes a lot of grace to be elevated to the rank of cardinal with the adoration of lots of poor, simple people and not get arrogant or proud or self-centred. I think he has received a tremendous grace with his stroke. He has more depth in his spiritual perception, and he's more tolerant of disagreement and of people who are annoyingly stupid or awkward. He has become a much more humble man. It's as if he had a meeting with our Lord, a great *healing* experience, a new injection of the profound values."

The Cardinal explained the healing experience in another way. Passing through an ordeal so long and painful that he came to understand suicide for the first time, he saw the wonderful, mysterious plan of a loving God. "If you accept the belief that Christ had to die in order to save the world, then we have to die ourselves in various ways. Startling ways – in a case like this – or other ways that come with the ordinary things with which we get frustrated. We get beaten up as we go along the road, but we can turn it to positive value, just as Christ did.

But that will not explain the mystery of faith, and I don't pretend to have the answer."

If any of his flock thought the revelation would transform Cardinal Carter into Francis of Assisi, provoking him to abandon his rich lifestyle and political manoeuvres in order to preach to the birds about the mystical beauty of God's creation, they had another think coming. It did not take long for His Eminence to get back into the episcopal rat race with a vengeance, as if to make up for lost time or beat the clock that suddenly was ticking very loudly. (In this respect he was not unlike his old friend, John Paul II, since the assassination attempt.) Not only did overwork seem to be an occupational hazard, but Carter personally enjoyed doing fifteen things at once for all his complaints about the load. *Laborare est orare*, to work is to pray, seemed to be his motto. He even had the disconcerting habit of glancing through his notes during the prayers that preceded a speech or meeting.

"It's what the French call *'les qualités de ses défauts,'*" he once admitted to me. "I was always so damned busy, and that was probably a mistake. I probably would have been a deeper person if I hadn't been so busy."

Certainly, for every religious leader, the world of power and money contains dangers more subtle than the great doubt about whether the whole rigmarole is nonsense. The superficialities overrun the fundamentals, and the wear and tear of executive management can strangle "the open lines to God," which is Carter's definition of prayer. Even in Montreal in the 1950s he had been known for his ambition and as a "consoler of the rich," to borrow the term applied to Clement of Alexandria in the third century. Some of the Cardinal's closest friends had felt that his spiritual side was "undernourished," and Carter himself one day shouted, half angry, half pleading, upon seeing his agenda, "Enough! I've got to have some time to myself. I've got to save my own soul too, you know."

Yet, far from craving the simple parish duties to which his predecessor returned upon retirement, Carter gave his staff the dreadful impression that he wanted to die trying to clear the hurdle of paper on his desk; nor could anyone imagine him following Cardinal Léger's dramatic path to a leper colony in Cameroon. "I'm too busy running this incredible outfit to make plans for my retirement," he told me well after celebrating his seventy-fifth birthday, the official age at which he could have laid down his weary head with pride at having gone the distance and delight in having retained the Rosedale mansion for his own use for the rest of his days.

What his friends saw as selfless service and heroic effort, his enemies saw as an unseemly clinging to the power, the glory, and the goodies of the office. No event illustrated the mixed feelings about him more clearly than the dinner held in May 1987 to mark his seventy-fifth birthday, his fiftieth year as a priest, and his twenty-fifth year as a bishop. Three thousand people paid $200 each to join him for lobster bisque and beef Wellington; there were 120 dignitaries at the head table, including four cardinals, four dozen or so bishops, a couple of lieutenant governors, a gaggle of mayors, and a herd of tycoons; and His Eminence was toasted by the Governor General, Prime Minister Brian Mulroney, Pierre Trudeau, and the Premier of Ontario.

To his admirers this was the apogee of Carter's success, an awesome testimonial not only to his own social achievements and political clout but also to those of all Roman Catholics in Toronto, Ontario, and Canada. The archbishop of Quebec may remain the senior bishop in Canada, because his see was the first one, but the archbishop of Toronto has become the more significant. To Carter's detractors, such as the members of the Catholic Worker movement who protested the conspicuous consumption of the evening at the door, it was the nadir of his failure, a spectacular display not only of his own "preferential option for the rich" but also of those of the Roman Catholic hierarchy in Rome, North America, and the Third World. They did not miss the fact that, in his speech, the Cardinal quoted William Shakespeare twice, George Burns once, and Jesus Christ not at all.

"My mother taught me how to pray and my father taught me how to argue," Carter admitted to that audience. "And of the two, I'm afraid my father was the more successful."

There is, as people used to say of a distinguished nineteenth-century prelate, "a lobster-salad side to the Cardinal." There were times in our conversations when Carter referred to Newman and I was not sure whether he meant the famous English cardinal or the author of *The Canadian Establishment*. His priests claimed that he gave only seven minutes for pastoral interviews, yet they saw him regularly in the newspapers, gracing the tables of the politicians and financiers. In one story that made the rounds, Carter was holidaying with Conrad Black in Palm Beach and was reported to have exclaimed at the sight of all the white mansions and flowering gardens, "This is just what I've always imagined Heaven to be like!" (I myself suspect that the Cardinal has too lively a mind and spirit to view Palm Beach as anything better than purgatory, in which the living dead who have spent their existence rolling in greed and self-gratification are given a final chance to escape eternal damnation by spending the remainder of their days and fortunes planning, attending, and recovering from charity balls.)

There is another telling tale, which Black himself told me, about his recent conversion to Roman Catholicism.

"It took place in Emmett's study," he declared proudly. "I told him I was ready to join, and he said that I would be welcome."

"Ah," Black had replied, "but would I be invited?"

"All right," the Cardinal responded. "I invite you."

But Black had some problems with the Creed: he thought parts of it purely allegorical. So the two men entered into a kind of negotiation about the Truth, and eventually they struck a deal. "Then Emmett called for champagne, to celebrate," Black concluded. *"So I didn't exactly go to them on my knees."* Though I was curious about what parts of the Creed the Cardinal had conceded as allegorical, I was astounded that he had neglected to instruct such a clever convert that the essential point of faith is to go down on your knees.

While some of this hobnobbing was the very human pleasure any typesetter's son would find in being wined and dined by the Eatons, the Westons, and the Bassetts, much of it came with the job. In a town like Toronto the élites cultivate their friendship with an archbishop for understandable reasons. The politicians seek votes, moral messages, and the social integration of immigrants and the dispossessed. The businessmen seek contracts, an assurance that camels can pass through the eye of a needle, and the social prestige of having a leader of the Church bless their babies and lamb chops. ("I hope he comes in his red outfit," the hostesses always said of Carter, "and not that depressing old black suit." And, in his case, they always looked forward to the cunning, informed, and amusing individual whom John Turner once described as "a fun guy.") In return, the archbishop gets an incredible amount of information, the company of people with whom he can spar on an equal footing, the rewards of quiet diplomacy, vast sums for his operations and charities, and the personal satisfaction of wielding power.

"We're not angels," said Bishop Leonard Wall, the Archdiocese's chief administrative officer (probably the only executive of a multimillion-dollar corporation whose previous experience was teaching theology and philosophy). "Our people need churches, schools, and seminaries, and those things aren't provided by miracles. They're provided by hard work and the application of God-given talents. I can fight with architects, lawyers, developers, or contractors – 'You're one tough baby,' they say – because I'm working for those who know God and who love Him. They're counting on somebody who won't be taken for a pious fool."

The archbishop is legally entrusted with final authority over the assets, liabilities, personnel, and work of a civil entity known as the Roman Catholic Episcopal Corporation (for the Diocese of Toronto in Canada). It has a board that meets weekly, an elected senate of priests, and 210 parishes serving more than a million people. In 1988 its revenues – mostly from parish collections and diocesan investments – exceeded $62 million. Its bank loans were almost $24 million, its properties totalled nearly $150 million, and its investment portfolio was worth over $8 million. These figures do not include the affiliated schools, hospitals, social agencies, religious orders, or provincial and national associations.

"We're like a head office with 210 branches," Bishop Wall explained. All the parish revenues, after expenses, go into the head-office kitty, which is used to build new parishes or lend money at low rates to the struggling ones.

Cardinal Carter, who drew no salary *per se*, responded with typical bluntness to the cynics who emphasize the contrast between the poverty of Jesus Christ and the wealth of the Mother Church. "They want us to go around with our backsides out of our pants. And then they'd have no use for us anyway. Generally they are not very holy people themselves."

Indeed, when I asked him what he considered his greatest achievements in Toronto, he thought they had been organizational. "To have kept the organization together through a decade of hectic activity is a *tour de force*. When I arrived, the see had become too big, the bishop was absent from too much, and the mechanisms were floating and disunited. So I restructured the archdiocese, set up the episcopal board that meets every Tuesday morning, and put the whole thing on a firm financial footing."

To most Toronto Catholics, however, such mechanics are as remote and opaque as the Archdiocese's modern, two-storey headquarters in the dingy downtown across from the Donut Castle on Church Street. ("Like the doors of Heaven" the receptionist once said of the intimidating entrance to the building. "Getting heavier each day.") If people had any assessment of Carter other than as the magisterial old guy hobbling around St Michael's Cathedral at Christmas and Easter, it would have been as a superb political operator. History, I would guess, will judge as his major triumph the decision taken in 1984 by his good friend Premier William Davis to extend public funding to all levels of Ontario's Roman Catholic school system. Not only did it represent the vindication of the Cardinal's person-to-person, behind-the-scenes strategy, it heralded how far Roman Catholics had come as a social and political force in the city and province under Carter's leadership.

Traditionally Toronto, like Ontario in general, had been a Protestant stronghold, with Anglicans ruling the social and political establishments, Methodists pervading the business and education élites, and Roman Catholics relegated to a second-class status. According to historian William Kilbourn, almost all of the city's mayors between 1845 and 1972 were members of the anti-papist Orange Order; Toronto had a Jewish mayor more than twenty-five years before it elected its first Catholic one; and it was not until 1988 that a St Patrick's Day parade was allowed to compete with the historic Glorious Twelfth procession held each July to celebrate the victory of the Protestant King William over his Roman Catholic enemies at the Battle of the Boyne in 1690. In the 1930s anti-Catholics placed a burning cross on the lawn of my grandparents' house in Toronto.

In the early 1950s Mayor Leslie Saunders, a former Salvation Army bandmaster who was later to be world head of the Orange Order, warned Torontonians of a conspiracy to open immigration to those from Catholic nations and flood the place with papists. Whether a conspiracy or not, that was exactly what happened as families rushed in from Italy, Eastern Europe, the Philippines, and Latin America, pushing Roman Catholics to the edge of becoming the majority in both the city and the country. Surely not even in his wildest nightmares could Mayor Saunders have imagined a pope riding triumphantly down Yonge Street to the cheers of the multitudes. As Cardinal Carter once put it, "I'm told Timothy Eaton wouldn't hire Catholics in his store. Now some of my best friends are Eatons, and some of his own descendants are Catholics."

As a consequence Carter's term coincided with the ascendancy of his Church in English Canada's most powerful city. While religions throughout North America were selling some of their buildings to developers and discotheques because of the decline in attendance, the Archdiocese of Toronto was constructing seven or eight churches a year to accommodate the doubling of the Catholic population in two decades, much of it still sincerely committed to the faith. It was not long before municipal, provincial, and federal politicians saw the votes in those numbers. Thus, when the Queen visited Toronto in 1984, Cardinal Carter was placed with her at the head table at Premier Davis's banquet, pushing to the side poor Lewis Garnsworthy, then the Anglican Archbishop, who was reported to have sputtered, "But don't they realize that *I'm* her archbishop?"

That and other humiliations – including an intentionally extravagant meal Carter once threw as a kind of potlatch for Garnsworthy, with the words "Let's show him whose town this is" – may have accounted for the rather hysterical attack the Anglican made against Davis soon afterwards, comparing the process by which the Premier decided to fund fully the Catholic schools to the methods of Adolf Hitler. "That came from his sense of pique that no longer are the Anglicans calling the shots here," the Cardinal suggested to me. "He was obviously obsessed by the idea that they hadn't been consulted."

On the other hand, His Eminence was quick to rebuff the common opinion that the Catholics are calling the shots now. "We don't have any real political clout. Politicians are aware that we have votes, so they're careful and conscious of us, but we haven't attempted to organize any real movement. We have intervened in the abortion issue, we put pressure on the school question, we did a little bit to oppose Sunday shopping, but we try to stay clear of politics."

As for the school-funding decision, Carter said, "I never made a deal with Davis. But he and I were good friends, and I did say, 'Bill, you're going to get into a fight if you don't do something before your next election. My neck is on the line, and I hope you'll help us.' I never threatened to line up all the troops and attack him from every pulpit."

The illusion of power is often the essence of power, however, and both Carter and his Church benefited from the old prejudice many non-Catholics hold that Catholics are cowering children completely in the thrall of their pope, their bishops, and their priests. The myth that one decree from Carter could have mobilized all Toronto Catholics behind one party or issue was no doubt more effective than any such decree would have been.

Carter had many critics, on the left and on the right, who argued that he should have used his political potential and his love of politics more aggressively. In most ecclesiastical or state matters he prided himself as a man of the centre. "As old Pope John XXIII used to say, '*Un demi-tour à gauche, un demi-tour à droit.*' The Barque of St Peter is not a steamboat, it's a sailing ship. If the wind is blowing one way, you lean against it. If it's going the other way, you lean against that. That's my philosophy in life, particularly as a bishop. People ask me if I'm a liberal or a conservative, and I say, 'What's the issue and where are we at this point?' In the Second Vatican Council I was counted among the liberals because I felt we needed liberal reforms. But now I see what people are doing to the Council that might destroy the Church, and I go the other way. I think social activism is carrying us into Marxism, so I go against it. But if another group arises to say that we shouldn't give to the poor, then I'll go against that. I'll go wherever I have to go."

So some days he lectured businessmen that "Capitalism unrestrained and unregenerate has obviously not taken into consideration the proper distribution of the goods of this earth," and other days he lambasted fellow bishops for presuming to preach specific remedies to economic problems. If his flexibility confused the ideologues to fury, it was not always much clearer to him. "We should get involved in moral issues like abortion or general principles like social justice. On the application of general principles, I don't pretend to know any more than anyone else. But it's very frustrating. Where does the principle stop and the application apply? I don't see priests on the barricades. I think we have to awaken consciences and let the people decide. But if you say, 'That's a nice statement, what are you going to do about it?' – I don't know, and that bugs me a lot."

To the left in particular, influenced by liberation theology to translate Christ's love for the poor into their Church's battle on behalf of the hungry and oppressed, such vacillation from such a potent and decisive figure was nothing less than proof of his surrender to the élites of the status quo. Carter's efforts to feed the street kids or provide low-rental housing to the poor remained for them simply reactionary gestures when not accompanied by a radical Christian critique of post-industrial society; and Carter's reluctance to take on the Vatican's conservatives (including the Pope) on issues such as the marriage of priests or the ordination of women confirmed for them the doubts about his liberal conscience, his personal charm, and even his spiritual faith. By the time his reign drew to a close, it was hard to find many who would follow him to any place more transcendental than a first-class restaurant in Rome.

But then, in May 1986, Aloysius Ambrozic was appointed by the Vatican as Coadjutor Archbishop of Toronto, the heir to the see once Carter retired. That was when everyone began to express inordinate interest in the Cardinal's health.

Though Ambrozic is only the second Torontonian in history to become archbishop of the city (having settled there with his family from Yugoslavia as a teenager in 1948 and having been an auxiliary bishop there since 1976), he is not very well known. What is known strikes terror in the souls of liberal clergy and laity. For his reputation is as an unapologetic conservative in doctrine and tradition, an unabashed authoritarian regarding the teachings of the Pope and the Church, and an uncompromising opponent of all that smacks of Marxism. His appointment to such a key diocese was seen as part of a worldwide push by Rome to empower right-wing loyalists to combat institutional dissent, liberal heresy, and political radicalism. In this light, whatever quarrels they had had with Emmett Carter, whatever concerns they had had about how much he *cared*, many Catholic liberals came to prefer the devil they knew to the one they did not.

As evidence of the shape of things to come, they usually point to a report Ambrozic wrote in 1985 after visiting Catholic high schools in the archdiocese. While he had kind comments for most of the principals, religious teachers, and students (whom he described as "Sloppy Catholics well disposed towards the Church"), he detected some who seemed "infected" by the "disease" he called "liberal orthodoxy" – what Bishop Bourget had compared in 1875 to "a serpent that glides through the terrestrial paradise to entice and destroy the human race" with "a liberty and knowledge that leads to death."

"This orthodoxy," Ambrozic wrote, "is characterized by an insufficient attention to God's absoluteness and that of His revelation, and to the authority of the Church in doctrinal and moral matters. It contains the tendency to turn doctrine into poetry and to downplay specifically Catholic doctrines; it tends to be individualistic (for all its emphasis on community) and voluntarist. Its language is an amalgam of history-of-religions, existentialist, sociological, psychological, and, in some cases, Marxist jargons."

These are fighting words for those who claim to carry the spirit of the Second Vatican Council. For them Vatican II brought the oldest institution in the world kicking and screaming into the modern age, all the way from feudalism to the Protestant Reformation, the French Revolution, industrialism, Marx, Darwin, Einstein, Freud, two world wars, multinational capitalism, the atom bomb, television, black holes, and the technology to go from human cells to Mars. This process, which the liberals would call progress, was biased toward individual conscience rather than hierarchical obedience, political liberation rather than personal salvation, social action rather than private prayer, scientific reason rather than mystical experience, religious unity rather than sectarian dogma, situational morality rather than universal codes, and a relative Truth rather than an absolute God. If all this whittles triumphant medieval Catholicism down to the size of contemporary Protestantism or even modern agnosticism, as many critics charge, many other theologians and lay people would assert that is so much the better.

Because Vatican II unleashed several centuries of pent-up liberalism, and because its direction meshed with the secular values dominating much of the educated world, no aspect of the Church's thought and structure was left unshaken by change or controversy. The language of the Mass was translated from Latin to the vernacular; radical bishops joined grape boycotts, advocated armed revolution, and denounced the power of the pope and his bureaucracy known as the curia; priests demanded the right to marry, women demanded the right to be priests, and both demanded the right to elect their bishops. Since everything had been taught with the same voice of authority, the repeal of some laws put the validity of the others into question. If the concept of limbo was now in limbo, was the birth-control pill about to be permitted and is God really Three Persons in One?

The immediate upshot was a dramatic drop in church attendance, in obedience to the hierarchy, and in uncritical faith. Though the intent of Vatican II had been to make the Church more attuned to modern, democratic Catholics, both priests and laity responded by quitting in droves. The traditionalists argued that the Council had encouraged the very scepticism, radicalism, and materialism it wanted to curb by reform. To them Catholic self-confidence and belief suffered irredeemably as the rites and dogmas by which Catholics had identified themselves were transformed into "Coke and cookie" Masses, confused catechism, and divisive languages. The progressives argued, on the other hand, that the situation would have been much worse without the Council. Authority was challenged in every institution in the 1960s, the sexual revolution confronted every moral restriction, and the political and spiritual idealism of the period attacked all established religions. Furthermore, the greatest desertion among North American Catholics took place in the wake of *Humanae vitae*, Pope Paul VI's 1968 encyclical dashing all hopes for a liberalized attitude toward artificial contraception.

Such was the energy, euphoria, and intellectual momentum of the Council that Aloysius Ambrozic himself was infected with enthusiasm for its liberal rhetoric. Born in 1930 on a small farm in Slovenia (part of the Hapsburg empire until it joined Yugoslavia in 1918), he described the religion of his region and youth as typical Austrian Catholicism: firmly shaped by the devotions and dogmas of the Council of Trent during the Counter-Reformation, Baroque in style, Jansenist in morals, at one time intolerant toward heretics but not as inhumane as the Spanish Inquisition, somewhat modified during the eighteenth century by the rationalism of the Enlightenment but consistently strong on authority and sentiment. The priests were involved in everything from co-operatives to schools, the laity were active and knowledgeable, and the deep devotion to Mary as a loving mother was expressed by the singing of emotional hymns.

There was a political side too. Largely as a result of Pope Leo XIII's 1891 encyclical, *Rerum novarum*, which advocated a kind of social Catholicism to promote the interests of workers without the evils of liberalism or socialism, Christian democratic parties arose throughout Europe. In Slovenia one such populist party began in opposition to high interest rates and other capitalist inequities, and Ambrozic's father was an organizer for it. Because of its rural base, the party neglected the union movement in the industrial towns, so labour fell under the influence of the socialists and communists; and when Yugoslavia was occupied during the Second World War, first by the Italians and then by the Germans, it was the communists who were able to draw the Catholic, liberal, and cultural patriots into a united liberation front. Ambrozic's father had been against the communists from the start, however, and he suspected that they were less interested in patriotism than in their own revolution.

One day in 1942, with the Italians in Slovenia and patriot guerrillas in the hills, some communists coerced Ambrozic's father into hiding propaganda for them, then reported him to the police as an agent of the partisans. He was jailed for four months and would have been shot except for an Italian colonel who took compassion at the sight of the farmer's seven children, of whom Aloysius was the eldest boy.

"So from the age of eleven I couldn't help but be interested in politics," Ambrozic said. (On recent holidays he has even taken a radio in order to keep abreast of developments in Eastern Europe and the Soviet Union.) "I was awake to real dangers and I had to get used to continual fear. I remember asking myself then if I would ever feel safe again, and I answered no, that's impossible, that world is gone forever."

In 1945, as the communists prepared to take over the country, his father prepared to leave it. The family got a horse, loaded what they could onto a wagon, and walked into Austria. For three years they lived there in a series of displaced-persons' camps, usually in crowded misery and unalleviated hunger. Aloysius discovered the indignity of begging for food, attended a makeshift school without books or pencils, and developed a passion for hiking in the mountains. In time the dream of going home faded, and the hope of joining an uncle in Wisconsin collapsed because of the American quota. But that uncle, a priest, had Church contacts in Canada, including an auxiliary bishop in Toronto, and so the family was sponsored by some local Carmelite nuns as refugees in 1948.

"The whole experience marked me for the rest of my life," Ambrozic said. "At one point we missed being handed back to the commies by the British in Austria by one day. They sent more than 10,000 Slovenes back, including many people we knew from home, and everyone over eighteen was killed. For a long time I shared with some Irish and French Canadians a pleasure every time Britain got a kick in the shins. And for five years after I came to Canada, the fear of being sent back kept returning in my nightmares. There was a sense of being abandoned, of total helplessness, and I knew what was happening to those left behind, all the kicking around and indoctrination and nonsense with which communism sought to transform the world in its first enthusiasm."

Among the first things he noticed in Canada, along with the bright lights and abundant food, was a certain political naiveté. "Security has its own advantages," he told me one day over a long Italian lunch at his house. "People are more trusting, they're likely to see the good side of things, and generally that's positive. But I grew up knowing the importance of ideology, aware of perpetual ideological struggles."

Perhaps the only mystery as mysterious as Truth and faith is religious vocation, why some people not only seek and believe Truth but dedicate their whole lives to serving it. Ambrozic's vocation grew slowly and quietly before he came to Canada, and it blossomed the moment he caught himself thinking he did not want to be a priest. "Why not?" he immediately asked, and he could not find a good reason, especially since the Church had been the one institution that had not let him down during the war. His first ambition was to join the Jesuits, because of their reputation for scholarship, but he went to study for the priesthood at St Augustine's seminary, mostly to avoid offending the Toronto bishop who had helped his family. By the fourth year of the seven-year programme much of his doubt and ambition had dissolved.

"The war had thrown up many questions," he said. "Why was I not a communist like one of my uncles? Why was I not a non-believer like another of my uncles? Is there a God? Why do I believe so? At first I expected philosophy to give me more of a defence of belief than it could. Some of my questions didn't have purely rational answers, for the act of faith is an act of will as well as of mind. Can I prove that God is my Father? I think I can make some fairly decent arguments for God's existence, but I can only believe that He is my Father. Jesus said so, and I say yes, but I could also say no."

Some of his questions disappeared because the culture was not conducive to them. "Many of my classmates didn't have them, because their faith was more unquestioned. They weren't pushed up against it. There was a cohesiveness to the Catholic Church in Canada that had disintegrated in Yugoslavia where many Catholics found other ideologies, other faiths, such as communism and secularism. Someone once accused Jackie Gleason, the comedian, of being an apostate. 'I'm not an apostate,' he said. 'I'm a sinner.' Here there were sinners, those who don't keep to what they believe is true. In Yugoslavia there were apostates, those who deny what they once believed to be true."

Ambrozic was an exception to most of the norms at seminary. Though he spoke Slovene and could manage Italian and German, he knew very little English; and while few of the other young men shared his passion for philosophy, he did not share theirs for sports. He found their sense of humour different; he thought their complaints about the food incomprehensible; he resented the strictness with which the seminary treated the students as kids rather than as gentlemen. Endowed with a powerful intellect and a Central European delight in ideas and literature, he took his refuge in books and got his revenge by topping the class regularly. He still gives the impression of many hurts, many humiliations, covered over by a thick hide of moral strength, personal conviction, and intellectual confidence that edges on pride. Often he behaves as if he is smarter than anyone else in the room, that he has read more in more languages, and that he is likely to win any argument with the same ease he showed when he used to read *War and Peace* instead of studying for his exams. And though such presumptions are often well founded, the fact that he displays them suggests an insecurity in his character, a need to prop up a defence against a world that knocked him about, alienated and underestimated him as an immigrant, and continues to marginalize him as a right-wing outsider.

He is, by nature, an intellectual. His earliest fantasy as a priest was to teach at the university level, and most of his career between his ordination in 1955 and his appointment as auxiliary bishop in 1976 was as a teacher at St Augustine's or a graduate student in Rome and Germany. His talk is laced with quotations from William Faulkner or Heinrich Böll; his thought is shaped by monumental tomes in German about celibacy or some Bosnian novel he read about Moslems; his mind is serious, scholarly, abstract, and deeply theological. While Cardinal Carter likes to portray himself as an egghead *manqué* – having written a couple of books, having taught catechetics for twenty-five years, having been known as "Mr English Catholic Education" in Quebec in the 1950s – he comes across like a well-read lawyer or street-smart politician when compared to Ambrozic. (The presence in the diocesan boardroom of two men who both considered themselves the smartest person at the table may explain many of the rude put-downs delivered by the Cardinal to the Archbishop, according to witnesses; or perhaps they were simply a matter of no man accustomed to power enjoying the all-too-visible reminder, in the form of a dark and heavy heir, that his time was nearly up.) In January 1990, for example, he read *Menschen werden Christen: Das Drama der Bekehrung in den ersten Jahrhunderten* by Gustave Bardy, *Maya: The Riddle and Rediscovery of a Lost Civilization* by Charles Gallenkamp, *Priesthood: A History of the Ordained Ministry in the Roman Catholic Church* by Kenan Osborne, *Les Prêtres* by Mgr. E. Marcus, *Eglise et ministères* by Pierre Grelot, *Das Christentum als absolute Religion* by Ulrich Mann, *The Liberal Catholic Movement in England: The "Rambler" and its Contributors 1848–1864* by Josef Altholz, *Heimatmuseum* (a novel) by Siegfried Lenz, *Rainbow's End* (a mystery) by Ellis Peters, *Pefau: Spomini* (memoirs) by Milos Vauhnik, and *Faith* by Keith Clements.

In fact, Aloysius Ambrozic needs books a lot more than he needs people. His Heaven is to be alone in the study of his comfortable home with a glass of rye and a metaphysical treatise. His Hell is to be stuck making awkward talk at tedious functions with school kids or Knights of Columbus, however pious. Shy more than arrogant, solitary more than disdainful, he admits to having only a narrow circle of people with whom he feels comfortable. Sometimes he watches TV with them, sometimes he hikes with them in Europe or holidays with them in Prince Edward Island or shares with them his excursions to Mayan ruins, but generally he seems (like many priests) a loner. If there can be great peace in serving God, there can be great sadness too, for the Truth seldom embraces as tightly as a spouse or delights as directly as a child or speaks as warmly as a buddy.

While Ambrozic claims not to have had the intense periods of doubt that afflict most priests during their lives (though he must still grapple with sexual desire and rekindle his faith from time to time), there is a hint of haplessness in the burdened way he moves his large frame, in the vulnerable eyes behind his black-rimmed glasses, in the resolve of his high forehead and stern expressions, in the depth of his very deep voice. Unlike his big appetite and big laugh and big ideas, his big heart and big hurts are rarely seen, except by family, the few companions, and those fortunate enough to experience the care and feeling he reveals as a private spiritual adviser.

In his own judgement the most important and wonderful part of his life was passed between 1967 and 1970 as a doctoral student in Würzburg, Germany. Instead of being dragged down in the daily crises of the post-Council Church in Toronto, he devoted his days to an intense study of Mark's Gospel, to rigorous debates at the university and in the beer halls, and to a profound examination of the ideological foundation of his beliefs.

"It was an unexpected blessing," he told me, "for it gave me time to think. I knew what was happening back home, where so many friends were leaving the priesthood, and I knew I was becoming disenchanted with some of the ideas and expectations I had had in connection with the Council. It may have had something to do with my approaching forty, and it certainly had something to do with the Soviet invasion of Czechoslovakia in 1968. 'I've just lost my goddess of reason,' I said then, because I had always believed that enlightened humanity would triumph – and it didn't.

"Also around that time there was an auxiliary bishop in Minneapolis who delivered a long attack on *Humanae vitae*. Three weeks later he quit the Church to get married! 'That's the last damn liberal I'm going to defend automatically,' I thought. I began being disgusted by all the highfalutin criticisms from people who weren't going to stick with their calling or faith. So I asked myself what I was *for*. I knew what I was against, I could bitch for the rest of my life, but there must have been something good about the Church. What could I do to uphold that?"

When Ambrozic got back to Toronto in 1970, a colleague said to him, "Most of our guys go to Germany to become liberal. You went to become a conservative."

"It was awful," Ambrozic recalled. Instead of the warm welcome he had received when he returned from Rome ten years earlier, he met discouragement and distrust. Nobody invited him to anything, some of his classmates were quitting, and he felt scarred and betrayed. A friend asked, "Are we the last of the Mohicans? Are we priests condemned to die as a body?" All Ambrozic could do was take his increasingly conservative message to the seminary and to the priests' retreats. Then, after becoming an auxiliary bishop in 1976, he took it to his work with the immigrant communities and the education system.

"Even when I was going with the liberal stream in the 1960s, even in the most heated arguments, I depended on our having something in common. If I shot off my mouth against Roman centralism, it didn't mean I was questioning papal infallibility. But some were, so I had to say I couldn't go with them. Things I had taken for granted were being questioned, so I had to defend them. Without rejecting ecumenism or a scientific approach to the Bible, when people play around with the Scriptures or the prayers to the point of denying what the words say, then I'll risk the price of looking or being conservative."

Taking on the liberals in the Church is only a part of his determination to take on secularism throughout the society. "When I visited our high schools, I used to ask what they were doing to prepare the kids to challenge, or withstand the challenge of, the intellectual onslaught against their faith at the secular universities. Most didn't understand my *question*, and that bothered me. Moral training isn't enough. The intellectual side of the discourse is immensely important. The University of Toronto is a greater threat to Christianity than Bay Street, because Bay Street has sinners while the University of Toronto tends to produce agnostics. British pragmatism can be very realistic, but it doesn't give enough attention to ideas. I think that ideas matter."

Suddenly, in 1986, without warning or expectation, Aloysius Ambrozic was given a mighty platform for his ideas. For reasons known only in the Vatican – though the rumour mills spewed forth speculations that archconservative allies and Yugoslav connections in Rome had overpowered the liberal opposition in Canada – he was designated to become Archbishop of Toronto, and thus a player of provincial and national significance.

"When I asked myself if I could do it, I answered, 'Yeah, but in my own way,'" he said. "I can't keep measuring against Cardinal Carter, because we have different gifts. For one thing, I'll have to get to know the financial oligarchy far better than I do, and though I'm insecure about that, I'll just have to do it as I've done other things that scared me. Also I don't know much about finances, but there will be enough people in the diocese to look after that. And then there's the public-relations side, which already has hit me much more than I ever expected."

In September 1987, for instance, *Toronto Life* magazine described "a lack of enthusiasm for Ambrozic" and "the utmost apprehension" about his appointment among Toronto Catholics; and in July 1989, a profile in *The Toronto Star* went further by declaring that the "rigid, authoritarian, provocative hardliner" was meeting "fear and loathing" behind the closed doors of the Archdiocese. "Where's your sense of fair play in condemning a man before he really gets into the game?" Cardinal Carter replied in a public letter to the newspaper in defence of his coadjutor. "Character assassination is never attractive, but in advance?" (Actually, while some of this assassination was the obvious work of the secular press and the unhappy progressives, some of it could be traced to the Carter men, those priests and politicians and financiers whose self-interest is threatened by Carter's loss of power to the unknown guy with the "weird" name. A few insiders have even suggested that, consciously or not, the Cardinal himself had been less than helpful in arranging a smooth passage for his heir into the duties, hearts, and salons that were Carter's personal territory.)

At last, in the spring of 1990, Aloysius Ambrozic got into the game. The Vatican, which had been sitting on Carter's automatic resignation at the age of seventy-five, finally retired His Eminence to suit its own agenda more than his, and Ambrozic's frustrating wait was over. (The three-year delay had been the cause of much rumour, from Rome's desire to milk the Cardinal's big-money buddies for as long as possible to a strategical ploy to let the heat on Ambrozic cool down. Almost every month there had been fresh gossip that the Vatican, realizing it had made a mistake, was about to ship Ambrozic to Rome instead. "Wishful thinking," the Archbishop used to say.) But the new archbishop was not ready to move quickly or dramatically. He still had the important files to master, he still had to connect with the "fat cats" and politicians, he still had to redecorate his office to something less modern and bland.

Perhaps that was a metaphor for what he intended to do with his position as well. "But I'm not prepared to make Ambrozic a horror story," said Mary Jo Leddy, a well-known Toronto nun and theologian. "He's not just an administrator, he's not in the pocket of Bay Street, he's honest, and he has a spiritual side. His style is out of the typical Eastern European academic mode, where he says something and expects you to say the opposite and you both go from there, so it's important that he doesn't surround himself with people who always agree. Pastorally speaking, the main problem is that, as a European, he despises this culture. That's dangerous for a public figure, and he's going to have to be careful."

"As much as the next person I like to be popular and have the crowd on my side," Ambrozic said, "but if I'm convinced I have to proclaim something that has to be proclaimed, then I'll do it, come Hell or high water. I'll try to do it in a way that is as attractive as possible, but I know that some people will be alienated for all sorts of reasons, sincere, insincere, and half-sincere. I hope I won't be too harsh on them – no doubt they have to follow their own conscience, such as it is – but I have to say that their conscience is *wrong*."

Against the problems, Ambrozic thought, there are the possibilities. He consoled himself by remembering the end of Robert Graves's novel, *I, Claudius*, when Claudius is dragged away to be emperor. He is resisting, but then he thinks, "So, I'm Emperor, am I? What nonsense! But at least I'll be able to make people read my books now."

SEVEN

Between the Devil and the Deep Blue Sea

The penis is the Achilles heel of the Roman Catholic Church.

The faithful will put up with an awful lot from Rome about the Immaculate Conception or social justice, but each time the Church's teachings touch their private parts, all hell breaks loose. Thus, while a small number of traditionalists leaves for the sake of the Latin Mass, vast numbers leave for the sake of sex – which includes, in its broadest definition, premarital affairs, birth control, homosexuality, abortion, divorce, the celibacy of priests, and the ordination of women.

At the heart of this exodus is the question of authority. By what authority does the Roman Catholic Church rule on right and wrong? Does that authority demand of the flock ovine obedience, or is there room for personal decision? And if there is room for individual conscience, how much deviation is compatible with remaining in the Church? As abstract as the concepts seem, they hold a tremendous weight to those who believe in God, Christ, Heaven, and Hell. The Protestant Reformation, the Catholic Inquisition, and the two Vatican councils were provoked by them, and their fierce power is felt whenever a young woman has to choose between an unwanted child and the possibility of eternal damnation.

Matters of authority are not confined to the Roman Catholics, of course. Every organization, sacred and secular, must face them to some degree. Nor are they confined within the Church to issues of sexuality. But there is no clearer way to explore the conflict between religious authority and individual conscience than through the struggle between Rome's magisterium and contemporary Western attitudes toward sex. On the one hand, there is the unambiguous vigour with which the Pope opposes abortion, artificial birth control, married clergy, and women priests. On the other hand, there is the social obsession with sexual expression, brought on by the cultural revolution of the 1960s, women's liberation, gay liberation, the Pill, and the advertising techniques of the mass media. Caught between the Devil and the deep blue sea is the ordinary believer.

To get the theoretical background, I went to have lunch with Archbishop Ambrozic at his home in an affluent, leafy neighbourhood just north of downtown Toronto. It is a substantial, old-fashioned house, provided by the Church as appropriate to his status, with dark and heavy pieces in the living-room, a study and chapel upstairs, and prints of Rome in the elegant dining-room. Rome was also brought to mind by the meal, course upon course of pasta and veal and salad and wine, served by another new perk of office, the Sicilian cook. Better than all the creature comforts, Ambrozic implied, was the privacy. At last he could read and think without the purgatory that is other people.

"The ultimate authority is God revealing Himself," he said. "Christ speaks with a divine authority, and his fundamental command to every disciple is 'Follow me.' The Church is the body of the disciples of Jesus, with everyone performing various functions. The function of the hierarchy is to make sure that what is being taught within the Church is in harmony with God's Revelation. That doesn't mean the hierarchy is the only one to know the Revelation, or even know it best. St Francis knew more about the meaning of 'Blessed are the poor' than all the theologians and bishops, and Mother Teresa shames us all with the authority of the charismatic. But the hierarchy's authority is absolute in the sense that it is where the buck stops."

Then what of the authority of the Bible?

"Roman Catholics accept it as authoritative, but not as isolated," Ambrozic replied. "The Bible is always read within the tradition of the Church. The tradition isn't above the Bible, but it does develop certain insights, makes the message clearer, gives depth over time. It shows a continuity in battling the same basic intellectual and moral temptations over 2,000 years. Tradition can become a cage, when it takes my ability to think for myself, but without tradition I become the victim of present thinking. I need tradition to protect me from the omnipotence of the present."

What about the individual conscience?

"It has always been recognized. But conscience isn't the law-giver: it's the law-discerner. God did not give the Ten Commandments on a 'take it or leave it' basis. They were to be obeyed. In certain situations, however, disobedience is not sinful in the eyes of the person. The Church can't be the judge of that person's conscience, his relationship to God, but it can judge what he says. If he says that adultery is all right, the Church can say he's wrong. The Church can't force a person to act against his conscience, or even prevent him from propagating an error. It can say what is or isn't Catholic, and prevent him from preaching error in the name of the Church."

These complex and philosophical ideas are not just the stuff of seminaries and pulpits. Put into plainer words, they penetrate into areas no less intimate than the conjugal bed. Many Catholics had to confront them seriously in 1968, when Pope Paul VI came out against artificial birth control. In essence *Humanae vitae* argued that the only purpose of sex is to generate new life and the only acceptable method of limiting children is to abstain from intercourse during the periods of fertility. This encyclical seemed to fall from the sky like a bomb upon an overpopulated world in which the Pill had become available, women were moving into the workforce, and sex was being promoted as a healthy communication rather than a wicked decadence. Suddenly people who considered themselves good Catholics had to decide between the opinions of a celibate old man and the hardships of unplanned parenthood.

"It is to be expected that not all will find this doctrine easy to accept," the Pope wrote. "Too many voices, magnified by the mass media, are now clashing with the voice of the Church. However, the Church sees no cause for wonderment in being lifted up, like her divine Founder, as 'a sign to be contradicted.' Not on this account may she neglect her duty of humbly proclaiming the entire moral law, of nature and of the gospel. It is not the Church which made the law, in either of its aspects, and hence she cannot deal with it as she pleases. She can act only as its guardian and interpreter."

Perhaps, many Catholics thought, but this was the same Church that had persecuted Galileo for suggesting that the earth revolved around the sun. More recently, as a result of Vatican II, it had thrown out all sorts of regulations that once defined obedient Catholics. So why obey this one now? This liberty seemed to be condoned a few months later when, in an effort to mollify the outrage and rebellion among laity, priests, and theologians, the Canadian bishops issued a statement at Winnipeg with an emphasis on conscience.

"Since they are not denying any point of divine and Catholic faith nor rejecting the teaching authority of the Church," it said of those who could not accept the arguments of the encyclical, "these Catholics should not be considered, or consider themselves, shut off from the body of the faithful. But they should remember that their good faith will be dependent on a sincere self-examination to determine the true motives and grounds for such suspension of assent and on continued effort to understand and deepen their knowledge of the teaching of the Church."

The press played up the first part, not the second, and so many Canadian Catholics thought they were off the hook that the bishops had to issue a corrective less than a year later. "It is false and dangerous to maintain that because this encyclical has not demanded 'the absolute assent of faith,' any Catholic may put it aside as if it had never appeared. On the contrary, such teaching in some ways imposes a great burden of responsibility on the individual conscience. The Catholic knows that he may not dissent from infallible teaching. In the presence of such teaching he can only seek to understand, to appreciate, to deepen his insights. In the presence of other authoritative teaching, exercised either by the Holy Father or by the collectivity of bishops, he must listen with respect, with openness, and with the firm conviction that his personal opinion, or even the opinion of a number of theologians, ranks very much below the level of such teaching. His attitude must be one of desire to assent, a respectful acceptance of truth that has upon it the seal of God's Church."

With or without that attitude, multitudes rejected the Pope's opinion for their own, and that had implications which stretched far beyond the length of a condom. Whether people felt damned by their presumption or freed from damnation by the fact God did not strike them dead for it, they had made a breakthrough after which it became easier to select or discard their Church's teachings, according to their own judgement.

For the supporters of *Humanae vitae*, such as Archbishop Ambrozic, the general use of artificial birth control conditioned widespread sexual permissiveness. By separating intercourse from procreation, by refusing periods of self-control, by placing personal comfort above human life, modern society gave countenance to extramarital sex, homosexuality, and abortion. "It's like Hitler's sterilization of the unfit," Ambrozic said. "Once the denial of fundamental rights to some people was accepted, the way was opened for the denial of fundamental rights to everybody." In this case, as Bishop Marcel Gervais told a conference celebrating the encyclical's twentieth anniversary, the way was opened for "kinky sex," the abuse of women as "masturbation machines," and an egocentric unwillingness "to live a little more poorly."

Nowhere has the effect been more serious, in the Church's view, than in the legalization of abortion. While the arguments for an abortion are often the same as for birth control – the control by women of their bodies, the unnecessary responsibility of unwanted children, personal choice based on individual conscience – the Church sees a terrifying difference. If one is just a prophylactic practice (however important the underlying moral issues), the other is the murder of innocent beings. Thus, while the Church accepts that it should not agitate for a ban on condoms and the Pill in a pluralist country such as Canada, it has marshalled its political strength to oppose the liberalization of abortion.

"This is one of those things where we don't have the right to have opinions. There is a strong and necessary Catholic position," Cardinal Carter told me. "Our strategy is only to say what we believe, loudly, for there's no place to hide here and no room to bargain. We're not dealing with unions or salaries; we're dealing with life and death. Unless you say that morality isn't possible in legislation, then Catholic legislators have to oppose abortion. They have no choice. The pluralist argument just doesn't apply. We can make a practical argument why stores should be closed on Sundays, and there is a good moral argument why capital punishment isn't intrinsically evil, but that's not the same as the killing of innocent people."

Whether they have the right or not, many Catholic women have abortions, many more Catholics sanction freedom of choice, and a large number of Catholic legislators are reluctant to impose their religious principles on the whole society. "The issue of abortion has gone to the Supreme Court and a decision has been made," wrote Mike Lavelle, a Roman Catholic professor of religious studies at the University of Toronto, in a public denunciation of Cardinal Carter's stand in March 1988. "The court has given the population at large the responsibility for making moral decisions based on personal conscience. This is surely the way it should be left."

Unfortunately for the bishops – and the unborn fetus, if they are right – their credibility has been undermined by two other issues: their confined experience as celibate males and their Church's own treatment of women. How glibly did Bishop Gervais speak of living a little more poorly and of the unplanned child as a clear blessing, when neither poverty nor raising a large family was to be his cross. How hollowly did his rhetoric ring about the dignity owed women, when his own institution kept girls from serving at Mass and women from becoming priests. These matters have nothing to do directly with abortion, of course. They are mostly organizational rules, not based upon a divine decree as bold as "Thou shalt not kill!" To many Catholics, however, the authoritarian and legalistic domination by men accounts for the Church's pro-life interpretation of God's Law.

"No one contests the principle of equality," Cardinal Carter once told a delegation of five women from Canadian Catholics for Women's Ordination, a lobby group set up in 1981. "As to the ordination of women, the Church position is not an infallible one. There are theological reasons, which aren't very strong in my opinion, and there are cultural ones, which are very important in a universal Church. Africa, Latin America, Poland just wouldn't go along with it."

Archbishop Ambrozic thought that the answer went much deeper than the cultural reasons. "Man has been a symbol of going out, of not accepting, of pushing ahead. Woman has been a symbol of holding in, of accepting, of nurturing. Man is the symbol of transcendence. Woman is the symbol of immanence. So I think God, because He is transcendent, has to be described symbolically in male terms. Christ then is the Son of God, and the priest is the icon of Christ. All sorts of holes can be shot through this argument as stated, but I think it is valid."

I thought it was Kwanza.

"I just can't convince myself that only some kind of male chauvinism has prevented the ordination of women throughout history," he said, as if reading my thought. "Jesus was a revolutionary, he broke convention by having women with him, so why didn't he break it when he came to choose the apostles? I've just finished a 500-page book in German examining all this, however, and it concludes that it's ultimately a matter of faith that a priest has to be male."

Many men and women have an equal faith that the Spirit may enter either sex. After all, being limitless, God must be both transcendent and immanent, symbolically both mascu-

158

line and feminine. "God created man in his own image," says Genesis, "in the image of God he created him; male and female he created them" – which means that woman is as much in the image of God as man. Pope John Paul II recognized that in his 1988 statement, "On the Dignity and Vocation of Women." But when it came to the issue of their ordination, he returned to the fact that Christ was male, all the apostles were male, no women were at the Last Supper, and the Church had been described in the New Testament as Christ's bride.

"It is the Eucharist above all that expresses the redemptive act of Christ, the bridegroom, toward the Church, his bride," the Pope wrote. "This is clear and unambiguous when the sacramental ministry of the Eucharist, in which the priest acts *in persona Christi*, is performed by a man."

I once heard an Anglican bishop, still unreconciled to the presence of women priests in his church, deliver a variation on this point: if the Church is the bride of Christ, and if priests marry the Church, then priests have to be male or else the relationship smacks of a lesbian marriage! Either way, it seems a case of metaphor running amok. After all, the Church has also been described as the Body of Christ, so what kind of men were marrying that? More seriously, it seems odd that drunken pederasts may represent the person of Christ, but Mother Teresa may not.

Historically the Roman Catholic Church has wavered between putting women up on a pedestal with the Virgin Mary or dismissing them, like Odo of Cluny did, as *saccus stercoris*, a bag of muck. In terms of power, that assured the supremacy of men over women in society. In terms of spirituality, it promulgated the prejudice that women have been the source of man's downfall, pulling him from knowledge of the Truth into the ignorance of earthly delights, since the day Eve offered the apple to Adam. Priestly celibacy is centred on the idea that these men have married the Church, not a woman, in order that they should dedicate their lives to seeking God's male-female unity within themselves rather than through an alliance with an intimate other. It is not a lunatic idea, though

the dangers of that path have no doubt produced more lunatics, neurotics, and sadomasochists than saints.

Today the hierarchy is taking pains to distance itself from
the negative biases against women that have permeated the
Church at least since the teachings of St Augustine. The
Pope's statement absolved Eve of any blame for the Fall not
shared by Adam, for example, and it put a modern spin on
those Biblical passages by which men have lorded over
women. But, he insisted, "even the rightful opposition of
women to what is expressed in the Biblical words, 'he shall
rule over you,' must not under any condition lead to the 'mas-
culinization' of women. In the name of liberation from male
'domination,' women must not appropriate to themselves
male characteristics contrary to their own feminine 'original-
ity.'" In other words, women are equal to men, but their
vocations are different. The most different is also the greatest:
motherhood.

Cardinal Carter suggested to the delegation in his office
some areas where the "womanly gifts" could be applied,
including parish work, pastoral teams, the mandating of lay or
religious ministers in special situations, and more high-level
appointments in the diocesan bureaucracy. But the women
wanted ordination. A vital energy in the Church was not being
tapped, they argued; remote communities were being denied
the Mass because women missionaries could only lead worship sessions; many women would prefer to have spiritual
guidance from other women; women priests would ease the
shortage of clergy and provide fresh insights and leadership.
Carter listened sympathetically, but he knew what they were
asking was impossible at present.

"After the meeting," he told me, "I got a letter from one of
the gals, and she said something about women not feeling
fulfilled in the Church. I wrote back and said that feeling
fulfilled in the Church is not a question of power structure. If
priesthood is just to get power, then forget it, it's not worth it.
That's where many of these ladies are hung up, in the power
structure. And if that's their idea of Christianity, then they're
on the wrong road."

160

The "gals" found this hard to take, especially from an old powermonger such as Emmett Carter. "He wrote back and said that women have always been very important in the Church and you can always be holy," said Ellen Leonard, a Sister of St Joseph and an associate professor of systematic theology at St Michael's College. "Sort of like that's where you belong, in the holiness of the Church but not in the office. Up on a pedestal but not in the pulpit."

At the temporal level the crux is authority, of course. For if the buck stops at the hierarchy, as Ambrozic claimed, then only men can give the ultimate verdict on truth and error, on politics and pensions, because only men can be pope or bishop. Roughly half the "People of God" (Vatican II's definition of the Church) are disqualified from sharing directly in the decisions about God's nature, revelation, law, and plan for His Church on earth. Their vocations, unlike those of men, do not come with that right. So it is not surprising that modern, democratic women wonder if the voice of the Holy Spirit has not been distorted down through the ages by coming always from the mouths of males, who have their own historical interests to protect. Certainly that anomaly has weakened the punch Rome can bring to its convictions about human equality, social justice, birth control, or abortion.

The punch is weakened further by the fact that the males themselves are divided about these convictions. In public as well as in private, bishops, priests, theologians, and lay leaders have been bickering about married clergy, marriage after divorce, homosexuality, women priests, and the entire range of socio-economic issues from nuclear disarmament to Third World revolution. In late 1987, for example, the tensions among American bishops surfaced in the media when a committee of the United States Catholic Conference issued a report on AIDS. Without advocating the use of condoms, it recognized that information about them could help prevent the spread of the disease. As justification it quoted the opinion of Thomas Aquinas that "those who govern rightly tolerate certain evils lest certain goods be impeded or also lest some greater evil obtain." To conservatives such as O'Connor of

New York and Law of Boston, as well as to Vatican spokesmen, even this small concession to the reality of the culture could unshackle the demons of artificial birth control, sexual promiscuity and perversion, abortion, euthanasia, indeed almost any evil, and they engaged in open battle with liberals such as Bernadin of Chicago and May of St Louis to prevent it. (While the fight went on there, the same matter flared up in Toronto when the Church's social agency for street kids was caught handing out free condoms. That practice was halted immediately.)

No one has articulated the internal dissent more savagely than Matthew Fox, the California-based Dominican priest and theologian who has popularized a blend of Catholic mysticism and New Age ideas he has termed "creation spirituality." Its gist is the celebration of all creation by drawing on the awe of science, the traditions of native peoples, the mystical teachings of medieval Christianity, feminism, environmentalism, the arts, animals, children, ecumenism, liberation theology, and aerobics. In this cosmology all religions are one wisdom, Mother Earth is the centre of worship, the Original Sin of humanity is less important than the Original Blessing of the universe, sexuality is the union of body and spirit, joy replaces guilt, and dogs and infants probably have more divinity and knowledge than all the cardinals of Roman history.

"Ours are times – because of the unprecedented crises of Mother Earth, of our youth, of the spiritual vacuity of institutional Christianity in Europe, of the boredom that most worship instils in persons – for holy impatience, disobedience, and discontinuity," he once wrote, citing his conscience as his authority and accusing his own Church leaders of intellectual and spiritual sloth, misogyny and a dysfunctional obsession with sex, fascism, sadomasochism, anthropocentrism, adultism, and moral bankruptcy.

"Bureaucracy and control and making television personalities of popes is not what the Church is meant to be about," he went on, fretting that "today's Catholic Church seems to reward authoritarian personalities who are clearly ill, violent, sexually obsessed, and unable to remember the past." What is needed, in his view, is a complete overhaul of the organization, "so that beauty and justice might become requirements for leadership once again. It is patent hypocrisy for the Church to call for justice in society when it is mired in injustice. The structure as it now stands allows no way to depose the unworthy, the sick, the megalomaniac."

Beyond his *chutzpa* and cleverness, his message has an obvious appeal rooted in the common criticisms many Catholics express (somewhat less viciously) about the power and thinking of Rome. Not only does it cater to current preoccupations with ecology, politics, therapy, and the body, but it challenges the dogmatism, dry intellectuality, liturgical routine, and conservative morality of the Roman Catholic hierarchy. The media give him a lot of coverage because of his confrontational quotes and trendy ideas; his books and tapes sell into the hundreds of thousands; and his seminars in Vancouver and Toronto have been packed.

I was one of some 300 people who filled a high-school auditorium one weekend in Toronto for his programme of lectures, slides, readings, and ritual. ("It's been a long time since I've come to a theological lecture," said a middle-aged man at the door on Friday evening. "This better be worth twenty-five bucks.") All of us, I suppose, showed up as sympathizers: it is hard to be against Mother Earth, dogs, children, freedom of speech, personal conscience, guiltless delight, and a priest who denounces the terrorism of the "christofascists." And certainly Father Fox seemed likeable enough with his folksy plaid shirt, prematurely grey hair, clear and articulate voice, and user-friendly message. Quoting D. H. Lawrence, Walt Whitman, Albert Einstein as well as the Bible, he joined science and religion in the great mysteries, reunited all faiths around the Divine Light within everyone, and sang the wonderful gifts of the Cosmic Christ: sex, child-like awe, art and creativity, worship, and the supreme and terrible wisdom of oneness.

"How can we gaze out on seventeen billion galaxies with nineteen billion years of life rolling out behind us and be bored – and bore our young – to the point of suicide?" he asked.

Out to prevent boredom and possible suicide, he crowded his audience on to the stage for a circle dance. For about half an hour we spun around slowly, sometimes lifting our hands to the ceiling, sometimes bowing our bodies to the floor, singing hypnotically to the beauty above and below us. I cannot report that the sight of a couple of hundred disenchanted Catholics, mostly overweight and over forty, had the grace and reverence of a Dene drum dance. From one angle it was comic, but the overall impression was pathos: they were trying so sincerely and hopefully, they were seeking so seriously and obediently, they looked so gullible and wounded.

The wounded are the main clientele of religions as well as hospitals, of course, and Father Fox made much of the wounded child within us, the wounded earth around us, and the wounded Cosmic Christ. In fact, we had to go to the basement cafeteria – where we were arranged into small groups and given crayons and paper like kindergarten children – in order to draw and discuss images of our wounded and healthy selves. Beside me a woman was drawing black hail killing green grass. Then we were lifted out of these lower regions, however, to swoop around the auditorium like eagles and do t'ai-chi exercises to the music of Hildegard of Bingen and pray by means of a Greek folk dance. A man wandered into the hall looking for boxing lessons and saw our embarrassed, awkward, unconvincing mob trying to wheel and bob like Zorba, and he said, "What the hell is going on here?"

What was going on, I assumed, was another exercise by Catholics to find expression for their beliefs and powers as the "People of God." More conventionally, some join activities such as the Catholic Network for Women's Equality, the Canadian Association of Separated and Divorced Catholics, Dignity (for gay Catholics), the Jesuit Centre for Social Faith and Justice, or the Coalition of Concerned Canadian Catholics. Some speak up for free choice regarding abortion; some press for more power in the parish, the diocese, and the Vatican; some take up a collection for guns; some work quietly for the unemployed or the mentally handicapped. Underlying most of this is an emphasis on individual conscience as the best judge of Truth.

"I believe that one has to define one's personal faith and then try to fit that definition into the institution, instead of trying to adopt a preconceived image of what the Church perceives as a good practising Catholic – or, alternately, leaving the Church altogether," Lucinda Vardey, a Toronto literary agent, stated baldly as a questioning lay Catholic. "The Church cannot offer this personal definition. It can only come from within the individual."

This credo is not exactly that of the apostles, but it finds support among theologians, priests, and even bishops. "As long as we're open to discernment, to weigh the pros and cons in light of our traditions with experience and common sense, the Spirit will guide us," said Remi De Roo, the radical Bishop of Victoria. "Our lay people are educating themselves, and some are better versed than some of the clergy. Rather than trying to control the emerging forces, we should let life move without worrying about the power struggles. After all, what's called orthodoxy is only the perspective of certain powerful people in the Vatican. There's no monolithic interpretation of what orthodoxy means. We might as well settle down for a couple of rough decades ahead, without getting lost in fear or anxiety. That fear betrays a lack of faith in the laity. It presumes a super-class of ordained ministers and an ordinary class who can't be trusted. But where is the Spirit? Isn't it here today, working around and through us? We should be prudent, we have to listen to tradition, but we must trust in the Spirit and go forward."

Certainly Vatican II encouraged the laity to participate more in the affairs of the Church and to test their faith by reason and intellect (what St Augustine called *fides quaerens intellectum*, faith searching for understanding); and the critical shortage of priests, already older and grumpier than ever before, promised further power and prestige to lay Catholics. Synods of laity and clergy arose to challenge the bishops and the curia; "base communities" of parishioners formed to pursue their own political objectives and theological tangents; the strength of the democratic ideal reinforced the call for an elected hierarchy and responsible decision-making; and the triumph of secularism contributed to the notion that Truth was relative, debatable, and personal.

"Surely Jesus did not intend a fascist institution, did he?" asked Father Fox.

Perhaps not, the Vatican began to argue back, but nobody ever elected him the Messiah either. If left unchecked, this type of thinking would open the door to Protestantism, selective beliefs and practices, and the collapse of the universal Church. Confusion would replace conviction; error would compete with truth; anarchy would threaten tradition; and the gullible masses would fall victim to the latest craze and their own sinful delusions. As Vice-pope Eric said in a Monty Python book, "Look, when you're propagating a creed of tolerance, poverty, and humility, you need a very rich, powerful, authoritarian organization to do it." Increasingly, under John Paul II, Roman centralism has been flexing its muscles again around the world. Progressive bishops in Europe, Brazil, Africa, and the United States have been disciplined; prominent theologians such as Küng, Boff, Schillebeeckx, and Curran have been silenced as Church teachers; nuns who signed a pro-choice statement have been pushed to retract or resign; gay Catholics using Church facilities have been forced to go elsewhere; a new universal catechism has been drafted with a reactionary tilt; and theological conservatives – including Aloysius Ambrozic – have been placed systematically in crucial dioceses around the globe.

"The problem of selecting beliefs and practices *à la carte* is the criterion of selection," Ambrozic told me. "It can't just be my own likes and likes. Ultimately it ought to be divine authority. I may not follow it, but at least I should accept it as the Truth and feel some guilt for disobeying it. *À la carte* religion allows for disobedience without any sense of guilt."

On the level of maintenance, all organizations require some deference to their regulations by their employees. Even in democratic states the civil servants are not entitled to majority rule on the policies of their departments, nor are they allowed to dissent publicly without some danger of reprisal. The alternative would be chaos. Nor do such restrictions infringe upon their democratic rights: they can quit, they can pay the penalty, or they can be tolerated. "There are situations in which a priest will just have to be suspended or transferred, though most know where the limits are," Ambrozic said. "I'll do anything to avoid that, by dialogue or by not pushing unless I have to, but ultimately there are some areas where the priest must stand with the house. That still leaves a fair area for opinions and disagreements."

Much more problematic and significant is authority on the level of mission. At the centre, let's say, there is the Truth – God or no God or even both. Seekers go looking for the Truth. Usually, admitting their ignorance, they come upon a person, an institution, an object they believe to have some insight or way to the Truth. Therefore, they put themselves under the authority of this wisdom for as long as they continue to believe in the wisdom of him, her, or it. But obedience does not necessarily mean a lack of self-reliance. The moment that belief dies, the authority dies. For why should any seekers dwell there if they believe they know more or better than the authority? And what good can come of staying to fight the authority in which they no longer believe? The only reasons can be power and martyrdom.

In 1988, after four years of investigation by the Vatican, Matthew Fox was ordered to cease lecturing and preaching for a year. The order came from the Master General of the Dominicans, acting under pressure from Joseph Cardinal Ratzinger, who is in charge of weeding out heresy as head of the Vatican's Sacred Congregation for the Doctrine of Faith. Though a committee of three Dominican scholars had found no heresy in Fox's writings, Ratzinger was bothered by his "exaggerated and erroneous positions" on such issues as Original Sin, God as Mother, homosexuality, and the employment of a witch at the Institute in Culture and Creation Spirituality "to teach in what is supposed to be a Catholic college." He concluded that Fox's "personal, gratuitous, and subjective interpretation of Christian spirituality" was both "dangerous and deviant."

Father Fox's Toronto workshop was one of the last before his silence was to begin, and his audience shared his contempt for Cardinal Ratzinger. I, however, became uncomfortable with it. I did not mind his eclectic scavenging of religious traditions or his unconditional optimism or his selective interpretation of history and theology – he could make a good case for them, at least – but I noted an intellectual arrogance, a physical stiffness, and a psychological defensiveness not unlike those for which he condemned the Vatican. And when he got on to his pet peeve, Ratzinger, his grasp on wisdom looked less and less sure.

For Father Fox clearly claimed to know more or better than the Pope and Cardinal Ratzinger. So why did he remain within an institution that honours their special authority as divinely appointed guardians of the insight and the way? By now he had his own institution, his own followers, his own texts, and his own sources of revenue. So why was he wasting his time and energy ranting against Rome? I sensed a deep and bitter need to take on a patriarch figure such as Ratzinger, some twisted psychological mess in which love had turned to hate, some distorted Catholic neurosis that longed for punishment and crucifixion. When I suggested this to Fox, the audience hissed. "I'm not into martyrdom," he said. "Creation spirituality is conscious of throwing off the temptations to masochism." Moments later, however, he told of a dream in which Cardinal Ratzinger – "Mr Rat himself" – had tried to kill him with a gun.

Putting aside the possibility that a decade of circle dances and crayon drawings had taught him little about his real nature (or basic Freudianism), I was left with the only other explanation, power. Even if he did not desire to become pope, he definitely wanted his ideas to reign as broadly as possible. Their best chance was through the established mechanisms of the Church. If Fox quit, he would lose his power as a public attraction. No longer a dissenting priest engaged in single combat with tyrants on behalf of democracy and Mother Earth, he would become what he in fact is: just another New

Age philosopher competing for press attention with Shirley MacLaine. If he is expelled, he would enjoy at least the cachet which has done so much for the careers of Hans Küng and Charles Curran.

It is not surprising that the first split in more than a century came not from the liberation theologians or the pick-and-choose priests but from the pro-Latin, pro-tradition, anti-Vatican II fanatics under Archbishop Marcel Lefebvre. The lukewarm believers, the political activists, and the comfortably agnostic generally have stayed put in the underworld of the Church. It is ironic that the strongest force of cohesion in the Roman Catholic Church may be the flimsiness with which most of its members hold their beliefs. "The problem today isn't schism. The problem today is agnosticism," Archbishop Ambrozic said. "Religion has less and less influence on the lives of people. They may call themselves Christians, but their grandchildren probably won't. Autonomous man is declaring himself to be self-sufficient. He thinks he doesn't need God. That is the real problem."

The Roman Catholic Church has an episcopal tradition that places ultimate authority regarding the preservation and interpretation of Truth with the bishops, especially the Bishop of Rome, not with a congregation or a priest or an individual. To belong to that Church must mean to have some faith that the bishops, as custodians of the teachings and the tradition, know what they are talking about. Without such faith they would have no authority. When Catholics choose to follow their own thoughts about birth control or transubstantiation, it is precisely because that faith has been eroded. Part of the erosion is due to the deep confusion between the Church as a social and political institution and the Church as a spiritual director.

"Some people really believe that we can vote on the Truth," Ambrozic said. "But there is a core of Truth that cannot be voted on. Either Jesus is God or not God, for example, and if you say he isn't God, you're not a Catholic."

Thus, when Christ preached from the mountain, he was speaking his truth, not seeking office or consensus. No doubt some among the multitudes dismissed him as a crank, but most were "astonished at his doctrine: for he taught them as one having authority, and not as the scribes."

"And not as the scribes" – there is the rub. For many may have faith in Christ and his way to the Truth, but no longer trust the Church leaders to lead them correctly to either. For these Catholics the Church's authority has been undermined by corrupt popes, misguided theologians, political ambitions, historical circumstances, and all the sins to which human beings are vulnerable. In other words, ignorance, compromise, and downright wickedness have made the Vatican version of the Truth highly questionable. Nor is all the evidence drawn from medieval decadence or the wars of the papal states. Modern feminists point to Rome's sexism as a sign of its errancy; liberation theologians point to its wealth and European bias; the media point to charges of financial hanky-panky and dogmatic intolerance.

Nowhere in recent years has this disillusionment been played out more dramatically than in Newfoundland. Because of the province's physical isolation, its relative lack of industrialization and urbanization, and the pious Irish traditionalism of most of the island's 200,000 Roman Catholics (more than a third of the population, concentrated mostly in specific communities), there has been preserved a level of attendance at Mass, moral obedience, and respect for the clergy equal to what existed in Quebec before the Quiet Revolution and seldom seen in the Western world since the Second Vatican Council. In the small towns and outports especially, the parish priest has maintained his old-fashioned status as local chieftain, welfare officer, and family counsellor as well as spiritual adviser. As Wayne Johnston described him in *The Story of Bobby O'Malley*, his wonderfully comic novel about growing up Catholic in such a town, "Our priest was of the old school. He asked nothing of his congregation but absolute subservience, to him, and, where those few were concerned who recognized the distinction, to God."

Father James Hickey may not have been of the old school, but he was popular, trusted, and placed upon a pedestal by his parishioners in Portugal Cove, a picturesque village of colourful clapboard houses set on the rocky coast not far from St John's and overseen by the elegant white tower of Holy Rosary Church. In the fall of 1988 Father Hickey pleaded guilty to twenty charges involving sexual assault and gross indecency with adolescent boys, some being the children of Portugal Cove, over a period of more than fifteen years. His trial was accompanied by lurid details in the press about groin areas, unseemly wrestlings with the priest in sacred precincts, and Father Hickey's waterbed in the rectory.

The shock across Newfoundland was tremendous, but mild compared to those to come as more and more priests, former priests, and lay brothers faced similar charges in the following months. By June 1989 sixteen men had been hauled into court, tales of sexual and physical abuse in a Catholic orphanage in the 1970s were being investigated by the government, and a Church commission was holding public hearings into cover-ups and incompetence at the highest level. In Portugal Cove one woman told the commission that her son had become suicidal as a result of Father Hickey's molestations; couples who had been married by Hickey wanted to be remarried and parents whose children had been baptized by him wanted them rebaptized; kids asked their teachers if it was all right to shake hands with a priest; and voices in parishes, Catholic organizations, and the media called on Archbishop Alphonsus Penney to resign.

"A lot of the problem is that we have a weak master," one man said to the commission. "I consider the Archbishop, and I've known him since I was a boy, to be a weak man. He should not be archbishop."

"He was the man at the helm of the ship when it went down," said the Knights of Columbus of Pouch Cove, whose priest had been sentenced to five years for manhandling the altar boys. "For the good of the Church, the Archbishop should resign."

These denunciations, it must be remembered, were applauded by people who had been raised to believe that women saying bad things about a priest would bear deformed

171

children. Now they did not suppress their anger and hurt. Whether Archbishop Penney knew or did not know about the immoral antics of some of his priests, whether he protected them or sent them to new parishes or merely gave their lies more weight than the cries of young boys, ordinary Catholics felt betrayed by the fact that he never even visited the traumatized parishes at the time.

"What does it take to tell this man he has lost our faith?" an old man asked.

Sitting through Mass at Holy Rosary one Sunday, as the fog rolled in and out of Portugal Cove amid fresh revelations in the weekend newspapers and a report Father Hickey was seeking early parole from Dorchester Penitentiary, I could not help wondering about the reaction. Why now and why in Newfoundland? Certainly these were not the first instances of sexual deviancy among clergy in the province or the country, to say the least. Of course, the secular media were finding pleasure and profit in doing for their priests what others had done for Jimmy Swaggart and Jim Bakker; but that hardly explained why Bob Nutbeem would moan in "Dogberries and Cream," his column in the St John's *Evening Telegram*, "The society which has been nurtured, and of which we have been inordinately proud, over 500 years, is in peril."

Looking around the church – at the faces of the families and every generation from infants to the elderly, at the six cherubic altar boys in white robes, at the old priest administering the prayers of hope and comfort – I realized it was this very scene that was in peril. It seemed an anachronism, a Norman Rockwell painting evoking a North American illusion no longer permitted by nuclear missiles, acid rain, AIDS, technology, and the Third World debt. Post-modern reality had been hovering like lightning over Newfoundland, ready to strike almost anything, and the conflagration it ignited spread far beyond the careers of the priests and bishop.

The squalid facts were forcing this community to look again at their traditional verities, some of which had been discarded by the Church itself a quarter of a century before: What is a priest? Must faith be blinded by secrecy and obedience? What is the basis of authority? What is the responsibility of the People of God? To be confronted by such mighty issues in the guise of paedophilia and buggery was to acknowledge the impact of contemporary society. Suddenly people touched by the values of secularism had a reason for their doubts and anxieties; kids who would rather be playing computer games had an excuse to write off the priests as hypocrites and scoundrels; and the obsolete social structure was rocked to its foundations to make way for the new order. When one priest announced from the pulpit that he had a girlfriend, the congregation applauded with relief!

As happened in Quebec, this new order has to be constructed on an intelligent faith, lay participation, dialogue, social action, and a necessary amount of uncertainty and discomfort. If people give up confession and Mass just because of the evil in one priest or the ineptitude of one bishop, they probably never understood their Church very well. "Holiness is not a case of being perfect," Cardinal Carter once explained to me. "The definition of a saint is one who keeps on picking himself up. There was no saint who wasn't hurt, who didn't make a lot of mistakes, but saints keep trying and gradually they purify themselves. The only person I ever met who was beatified was Brother André, and God knows he was a pretty irascible little old guy. It's fallacious to think of priests as floating above humanity. Jesus himself was a man. And an incarnational Church has to be a Church of sinners. It is a divine institution run by miserable sinners."

This is quite subtle, and the Church itself can be accused of sending out mixed signals. On the one hand, it separates the priest from the congregation, cloaks him in mystery and sanctity, allows him to absolve sins and distribute the Eucharist, and trains him to be an inspirational guide. On the other hand, it says he is only human. Have faith, the Church seems to be saying, that the Barque of St Peter is heading toward Truth by God's direction, even if the captain is bewildered, the crew is drunk, and the cliff is looming ahead. For ultimately, once more, only faith can make a person stay on board and not abandon the ship as I did.

Many of the present tensions within Catholicism are rooted in this thorny question of authority. If the passengers also have a function as crew, if God has been known to chart Truth's course through some of them, then why should they not be heard with louder (perhaps even equal) voice? "As an American theologian once put it," Gregory Baum said, "of course we can make religion uniform – if we take the mystery out of it. In the end religion isn't in the hands of the hierarchy or any human being. It's the vitality that opens itself up in people, and you can't get that too tidy. I think even Ambrozic would agree with that."

If Archbishop Ambrozic does not agree with that, every Catholic in Toronto has the same options people have always had. Some will defer to his teachings and may even find peace, strength, and greater faith by doing so. Some will seek other teachers, within or outside the Church. Some will find an agreeable niche inside the institution where they will organize attacks against him or merely ride out the storm. Most, I suspect, will carry on with their lives in their own way without giving a fig for his opinions.

The great puzzle is this: Ambrozic may tame his priests and parishioners, his Church may continue to grow in numbers and power, yet the stability and success may be built on neither faith nor Truth. On the other hand, Ambrozic may be hounded and humiliated by almost everyone, his Church may crumble under the impact of North American secularism and a lack of clergy, yet the chaos and failure may be a sign of its faith and Truth. When the popes were at their greatest, with states and fortunes and armies, they were furthest from Christ. When Christ was at his lowest, betrayed and tortured and murdered, he was closest to God.

"I can't get romantic about an oppressed Church, a remnant Church," Ambrozic said. "Sure, you get rid of some problems, but you pick up others, including agnosticism and a loss of idealism. If you have a thousand sinners, you might get one saint. If you have a hundred sinners, you probably won't get any saints at all. But sometimes we may have no choice. We're already a minority in an agnostic and materialist culture. To paraphrase Thomas More, the University of Toronto and Bay Street would have snored through the Sermon on the Mount, and *The Globe* would have sent a cub reporter. So we have to struggle hard, to make it clear where we disagree with certain ideologies that animate modern man. Though we may antagonize modern man, that fight must go on."

EIGHT

This Too Shall Pass

"I cried for a year," one woman confessed, not about the death of her guru (as I assumed for a moment) but about the city of Halifax. "When I got into Tibetan Buddhism almost twenty years ago, I knew it would be a hard path. I knew the practice would be long and difficult, I knew there would be setbacks and surprises. But never, never did I think I'd have to live in Halifax!"

She was not alone. In fact, she is one of several hundred people – Americans, by and large – who had been shocked to discover that the road to enlightenment apparently passed through Nova Scotia. They had been settled happily in Boulder, Colorado, which certainly seemed closer to Nirvana (or Tibet at least) with its mountain scenery and fresh air and spiritual enthusiasms. There they had assembled over the years, from New York and California, from England and Canada, from almost anywhere, drawn by their teacher, Chogyam Trungpa, Rinpoche, the Eleventh Trungpa Tulku, whom they usually refer to as Trungpa Rinpoche or simply Rinpoche, a title like Eminence or Right Reverend meaning "precious jewel." There, since 1970, they had helped establish a meditation centre called Karma Dzong, retreat facilities in Colorado and Vermont, an expanding network of urban branches known as Dharmadhatus, national and international organizations under the name of Vajradhatu, and (perhaps most famous of all) the Naropa Institute, a college of Eastern and Western studies founded in 1974, which attracted thousands to courses by scholars such as Gregory Bateson and Herbert Guenther, poets such as Allen Ginsberg and Gregory Corso, and counterculture heroes such as Ram Dass (alias Richard Alpert, the Harvard LSD wizard turned Hindu preacher) and Trungpa Rinpoche himself.

To hear them tell of it, Boulder is a lost Eden, a garden of earthly delights and heavenly auras, where the yuppie comforts of good restaurants and decent shopping meet the sacred fundamentals of positive vibrations and t'ai-chi lessons. If there were problems with Boulder, if it had become too commercial and too distracting and too much a "scene," they seemed to fade in memory as the seldom-absent rain and fog of the North Atlantic coast depressed the spirits of the exiled and the general talk shifted to the bad winters, the short summers, the limited job opportunities, the high cost of houses, the poor food, and the coldness of the people in Halifax. Even devoted Haligonians have admitted to me that their society is not easily accessible to outsiders at the best of times, so what were the prospects for a horde of middle-aged, Yankee Buddhists blowing into town to bow and scrape around some mysterious Tibetan?

"Mummy, I'm still not used to this place," a nine-year-old girl said a year after being uprooted from her friends, her school, and her culture.

"Neither am I," her mother replied.

Even when the sun shone, the Buddhists often found the place a downer after Boulder. They noticed the number of eerie cemeteries and monuments to the dead in the city centre. They observed the warships in the harbour and the military vainglory on the hill. They encountered the intransigent and unimaginative mentality of the bureaucracy in a government town. They saw the squalor and decay of decades of economic recession, the enervation and pallor of welfarism, the alienation and handicaps of immigrants without contacts or resources. They experienced strong but subtle class prejudices, evident in whether they wore suits or jeans downtown. The Jews among them picked up on an atmosphere of anti-Semitism; the others knew they were suspected of being cultists. Even without all that, of course, they faced the loneliness and tensions of abandoning their nation, their loved ones, their careers, their customs, to start anew in an unfamiliar environment. Here clearly was authority and discipline that even the Pope might envy.

On the other hand, if Halifax did not throw a party for them, it did not throw many rocks either; and few of these immigrants were without advantages. On the whole, they were white, they spoke English, they were educated, they had social and economic skills, they had entrepreneurial energy, they had each other, and they had their guru. It was not long before they recreated bits of Boulder in this unlikely setting – a trendy cafe, a metaphysical bookshop, a quaint hotel, renovated houses, the Karma Dzong Buddhist Church of Halifax, the world headquarters of Vajradhatu International, and the Naropa Institute of Canada (offering Haligonians an opportunity to study flower arranging, tea ceremonies, creativity in business writing, and mime). As well, they founded a monastic centre, Gampo Abbey, on a savage promontory at the northern tip of Cape Breton. Each year since 1983 a little more of the administration moved from Boulder, including Trungpa Rinpoche and his family, key directors, and the central offices and archives; and each year the community grew, from 100 to 250 to 375 to 500, as Boulder became an outpost managed from Halifax.

Why Halifax?

I was not the only one asking that question, it seemed. When snow turned to rain, and rain turned to fog, it arose like a cry from Job at Vajrayogini Feasts and Karma Dzong Library Benefit dances. It was even on the lips of the burghers of the city. And such was the unfathomable silence and opaque ways of Trungpa Rinpoche in his final years that even his confidants are not certain of the answer. The most thorough explanation came from David Rome.

Rome grew up outside New York City, in a Conservative Jewish family, the grandson of the founder of Schocken Books, Kafka's American publisher. (While denying that there is a preponderance of Jews among the leadership or membership of the movement, he agreed there are many. He thought that the attraction is the rigorous intellectual tradition, based on texts and commentaries, that Tibetan Buddhism shares with Judaism, but another Jew suggested that Jews are drawn by their immediate grasp of the first law of Buddhism, that all is suffering. "Next life in Jerusalem!" they cry.) Without really rejecting the faith of his father, Rome slid away from the practice of it while at Harvard in the 1960s, and like many of his generation he picked up a marginal interest in Eastern religions via the hippies and the Beatles. ("Religions are like games of backgammon and checkers," Voltaire once remarked. "They come to us from the East.") He went to Kenya with the Peace Corps for two years, he worked at Schocken for a while, he hitchhiked around Europe, and there a friend "dragged" him along to a Tibetan monastery in Scotland. He found the teachings fascinating and he found himself infused with "an intangible feeling of rightness," so he read more and practised more and, back in America in 1971, went on a retreat to the Tail of the Tiger, the Vermont centre recently opened by "the really crazy guy" Rome had heard of in Scotland, Trungpa Rinpoche.

"So my original connection was the practice, not his personality," Rome said. "He came for a day when I was there, and I thought him very simple, very modest. It was a pretty bohemian scene then, and he just seemed to blend into it. He advised me to stay in New York – he called it a good place to practise – and far from attempting to seduce me, his advice had more the quality of a rejection."

Rome returned to Manhattan and publishing, but the next summer he drove to Colorado to study with Rinpoche – and he stayed there from 1972 to 1983. In 1974 he became Rinpoche's private secretary. Hence, if anyone knew the answer to "Why Halifax?" (I was told), David Rome would.

"Rinpoche's decision was based on his *vision*," Rome explained over lunch in a downtown restaurant one day, "so it's hard to say precisely, except that in the long term he saw that this is where we ought to be. I think there were several factors. One, because of reactionary developments in the United States, that may not have been the most accommodating environment for us in the future. Two, according to the Tibetan sense of geographical identity, he wanted a place with its own geographic integrity. Boulder was a good place to get started, because it had a Tibetan quality up in the mountains, but it's right in the middle of the American continent, whereas Nova Scotia is a peninsula on the edge of things. Three – and this may have been the most important factor – he expected our group to be very influential wherever it was put, so it's better to be in a place where that influence can be exerted as time goes on, where it can be felt for the benefit of the society at large. Four, though he had mixed feelings about his years in Britain between India and the United States, he appreciated the wealth of British tradition, how society worked there, and he found some of that here. Five, while he characterized the prevailing neurosis of the United States as aggression, he characterized that of Canada as ignorance, and an environment of ignorance is more appropriate to the practice of meditation and the development of Buddhism than an environment of aggression. Basically we're more likely to practise here than in the heart of yuppie materialism. There's a kind of simplicity and spaciousness here."

"Boredom and emptiness" were the more usual descriptions, applied negatively as in "There's no good movie theatre here" or "It's impossible to get decent French bread." But Trungpa Rinpoche used to stress the virtues of both. In his lectures on *The Myth of Freedom*, he even stated that "there is no other way to reach the depths of meditation practice except through boredom," and when one reaches those depths, one discovers a perfect emptiness.

From that angle, apparently, Halifax is a useful station on the way. Rinpoche first discovered it on a visit in 1977. He returned each year after 1979, and chose to pass his year-long

180

personal retreat between 1984 and 1985 in Mill Village, Nova Scotia. In 1986 he came to stay, moving into a white mansion on fashionable Young Avenue. This house was named the Kalapa Court, and its Old Halifax neighbours took to watching with guarded but amused curiosity the comings and goings that centred around it – much as their grandparents had kept a close eye on the pageantry and shenanigans of the British garrison.

That hundreds of followers quit their homeland, their jobs, and their Elysium to trek after him was testimony to his charisma and the authority of the guru in Tibetan Buddhism. Almost none was a salaried employee; almost all had to find new work for themselves and new schools for the kids; and though few even understood the reasons David Rome enumerated, they were used to accepting the enigmatic instructions of their teacher. "My father's always after me about why I had to come here, why I have to stay," said one member. "He still doesn't understand that this is my life's work – and maybe the work of my future lives too."

Generally they represent another manifestation of the New Age. Others journeyed back to Christianity by turning Jesus into the perfect freak or reviving the Gnostic heresy; others returned to their Jewish roots by dancing insanely with the Torah or studying the mystical cabbala; but, for many, Christ's message and God's command failed to penetrate through the boring sermons, the dull ceremonies, the irrelevant scholars, the uninspiring priests, the worldly hierarchies, the corporate institutions, and all the guilt and repression surrounding sex and pleasure and human freedom. Instead, through travel and books and word of mouth, reports circulated of wondrous techniques and wise saints from exotic traditions in remote places – the more exotic and remote, the more wondrous and wise, it seemed – and there grew a rage for Sufi sages, Zen roshis, Navaho shamans, African witch doctors, Hindu gurus, Peruvian sorcerers, Tao masters, and Tibetan lamas.

These traditions had been alive in various parts of the world for centuries, of course, and many of them had been practised by immigrants and converts in Europe and North America for

decades upon decades. But the 1960s glamorized and popularized them throughout Christendom as never before. I myself
knew people who started worshipping Allah and Krishna in a
fanatic way, who hunted for Don Juan in Mexico and Bhagwan
Shree Rajneesh in India, who got a mantra from Maharishi
Mahesh Yogi and a koan from Suzuki-roshi, who studied every
word of Krishnamurti and Trungpa Rinpoche.

Each tradition had its charms, but few arrived with more
charms than Tibetan Buddhism. Tibet! Just to say it was to
conjure up ancient monasteries amid the snow-capped peaks
of the Forbidden Kingdom, the magic and mystery of Shangri-
la, the colourful mandalas of kaleidoscopic beauty, the hum of
chants and the blast of horns and the bang of gongs, the
demonic masks and embroidered costumes of the extravagant
rituals, the countless monks in maroon robes studying the
sacred texts, the reincarnated lamas brimming over with wisdom and powers! Tibet has long captured the mystical imagination of Western travellers and novelists, and it captured
mine when I was twelve and won as a school prize Heinrich
Harrer's account of his seven years there. I do not know who
chose that book, or why, but it instilled a deep romance about
the people and the place that culminated a dozen years later
when I travelled to Dharamsala to see the Dalai Lama.

Behind the baroque romance of Tibetan culture I found the
ascetic tale of Siddhartha Gautama, who became the Buddha,
the Enlightened One. Born to wealth and position in a kingdom on the modern India-Nepal frontier in the sixth century,
BC, he was raised in perfect pleasure and comfort, had a wife
and son, and apparently knew nothing of misery and pain
until he was twenty-nine. Then, by chance, seeing old age and
illness and death for the first time, he perceived that such
suffering is the fate of every being. He also saw a wandering
monk, and that inspired him to leave his family, his fortune,
and his palace in order to find – for everyone – the path out of
suffering. For six years he journeyed from sage to sage to seek
the Truth; he practised their meditations and the severest
forms of physical austerity, until his mind was fully concentrated and his body was on the edge of death. Pulling back

from these extremes toward a middle and more balanced way, he sat one May night beneath a peepul tree near present-day Bodh Gaya and, taking on the most powerful forces of illusion, his mind penetrated down to the root of existence. When he emerged, he had seen all, he had understood all, he was the latest of a line of enlightened teachers, he was the Buddha.

"I have gone round in vain the cycles of many lives ever striving to find the builder of the house of life and death. How great is the sorrow of life that must die!" he is said to have proclaimed. "But now I have seen thee, housebuilder. Never more shalt thou build this house. The rafters of sin are broken, the ridge-pole of ignorance is destroyed. The fever of craving is past. For my mortal mind is gone to the joy of the immortal Nirvana."

Rather than dwelling in that indescribable bliss, a condition of "not-becoming" beyond the wheel of birth and death and rebirth, the Buddha's mind was filled with compassion, and he set forth to teach the world what he had rediscovered and what anyone could attain by following his teachings. These teachings, which he gave constantly until his tranquil death at the age of eighty, are summed up by the Four Noble Truths. The first truth is that all existence is suffering, meaning emptiness, impermanence, disappointment, frustration, illusion, as well as pain. Pleasure exists, but only as a subtle form of suffering, because it is founded on illusion and must pass away. The second truth is that suffering is caused most directly by craving, clinging, hatred, fear, the relentless effort to grasp pleasure and flee pain. This selfish pursuit is related to the illusion that there is a self (or even a soul) to enjoy the pleasure and be spared the pain. The third truth is that there is liberation from suffering in the extinction of craving and hatred and illusion, in the "going out" which is Nirvana. The fourth truth is the way to that extinction, the Noble Eightfold Path.

Of the eight aspects of the practice, three concern ethics: right speech (not to lie or slander, for example), right actions (not to kill or steal, for example), and right livelihood (not to make weapons or sell drugs, for example). On this moral foundation come three that concern mental discipline: right effort, right awareness, and right concentration. The trained and purified mind is applied then to wisdom: right thought (such as selflessness and universal love) and right understanding (which takes an intellectual knowledge of the Four Noble Truths to a total experience of them).

"According to Buddhism," Walpola Rahula wrote in *What the Buddha Taught*, "the Absolute Truth is that there is nothing absolute in the world, that everything is relative, conditioned and impermanent, and that there is no unchanging, everlasting, absolute substance like Self, Soul, or *Atman* within or without." Nor is there an omnipotent and omniscient God. Therefore, devotions, prayers, priests, even beliefs are of little or no account. Instead, each person must establish the ethical base, develop the mind through a variety of techniques, and attain enlightenment by individual effort.

"What we are today comes from our thoughts of yesterday, and our present thoughts build our life of tomorrow: our life is the creation of our mind," the Buddha said. "If a man speaks or acts with an impure mind, suffering follows him as the wheel of the cart follows the beast that draws the cart. If a man speaks or acts with a pure mind, joy follows him as his own shadow."

As he himself predicted, upon his death divisions and corruptions evolved from his teachings. Disputes arose over the interpretation of his words; factions quarrelled over the practice of his techniques; different times and cultures demanded different organizational rules and ethical standards. Increasingly the rigorous mental disciplines were overwhelmed by the popular trappings of conventional religion: the Buddha became as God, meditation deteriorated into empty rites and vain prayers, and monks made pacts with social and political power as Buddhism spread across India, out to Sri Lanka and Burma and Thailand, down to Cambodia and Vietnam and Korea, on to China and Japan, and up into Tibet.

It entered Tibet in fits and starts over some 500 years, primarily because it ran into furious opposition from the entrenched native religion known as Bon, a faith full of shamans and demons and magical powers. Through the patronage of certain kings and the effectiveness of certain teachers, the Buddhists broke the Bon hegemony in the eighth century and conquered it by the eleventh century. Even today, however, there is a controversy about whether Tibetan Buddhism absorbed the forms and symbols of Bon for its own purposes or were absorbed by their gods, their devils, and their sorcerers. On the one hand, Tibetan Buddhism looks and sounds like no other Buddhism, with its heavy overlay of Tibetan culture and popular devotions. On the other hand, this uniqueness is ascribed to the special qualities of Tibetan Buddhism, which claims to have preserved not only the public teachings of the Buddha but also the secret teachings he gave to select students. In this explanation Tibetan Buddhism incorporates both the basic techniques of the orthodox or Hinayana tradition and the compassionate exercises of the reform or Mahayana tradition, and then it adds to them the esoteric practices of the mystical or Vajrayana tradition.

Since the Buddha taught a wide range of techniques, exercises, and practices, depending on the propensities and capacities of his students, each tradition asserts its legitimacy from his authority; and since his authority is up for grabs, each tradition has its schools, its sects, and its particularities. In Tibet four main orders emerged – Nyingma, Sakya, Kagyu, Geluk – from separate gurus, doctrinal nuances, and practical variations, and their spiritual divergences were aggravated by their political history. Because of the social and economic power of the monasteries, kings and conquerors and local chieftains sought alliances with high lamas that set sect against sect. The Mongolians let the Sakya order rule in the thirteenth century, for example, until a rebellion put the Kagyu order into government. In 1642 the Mongolians returned and put into power the Fifth Dalai Lama, the head of the Geluk order, which ironically had begun almost 200 years before as a purist reaction against the politics and corruption of the older orders. His successors (all chosen by finding the young boy into whose body each deceased leader had reincarnated himself) reigned as priest-king of a theocracy until

185

1959, when China invaded Tibet and the Fourteenth Dalai Lama fled into exile in India.

This business of reincarnation explains Trungpa Rinpoche's title, Eleventh Trungpa Tulku. A "tulku" is an enlightened being who voluntarily returns to human form in order to teach others the path out of suffering. Found usually through a combination of written clues, explicit visions, and tricky tests, he often is taught as a boy by monks he had taught as an adult, and thus the lineage of knowledge is both perpetuated and made hallow. In this way a boy born in 1939 to a farming couple in northeastern Tibet was discovered to be the heir of the abbot of Surmang, the Tenth Trungpa Tulku, who had died the year before, and he was whisked off to be trained to resume his position. In the same way Elijah Ary, born in 1972 to a Montreal couple, was recognized by the Dalai Lama in 1980 as the reincarnation of Geshe Jatse, a great scholar-monk who had died in the 1950s, and at fourteen moved to a Tibetan monastery under the name of Tensin Sherab, as he put it, "to gather everything that I had in my past life, and more."

That is how Trungpa Rinpoche spent his youth too, preparing to take charge of the Surmang monasteries, part of the Kagyu order and the Karma Kagyu sub-order that trace their origins back to Gampopa, an eleventh-century student of the great poet and holy man Milarepa, himself the chief disciple of the famous translator and scholar Marpa, who in turn had studied under the renowned Indian Buddhist and tantric master Naropa at the magnificent university of Nalanda in India. But the Chinese invasion intervened, and at the age of nineteen Trungpa Rinpoche had to escape his homeland. He learned English in India, won a scholarship to Oxford in 1963, studied Western philosophy and art, co-founded a meditation centre in Scotland, and became a British citizen – "in fact," he liked to boast, "the first Tibetan ever to become Her Majesty's British subject."

He had no sooner settled than everything proved "relative, conditioned and impermanent" once more. "Driving one day in Northumberland," he wrote in his autobiography, "I blacked out at the wheel of my car, ran off the road and smashed through the front of a joke shop."

Though the accident left a side of his body paralysed, his mind experienced a kind of epiphany that produced "a sense of relief and even humour." Before it he had been struggling with the problems of bringing Tibetan Buddhism into Western culture. After it he saw a solution in giving up his monastic vows. "I should not hide behind the robes of a monk," he perceived, "creating an impression of inscrutability which, for me, turned out to be only an obstacle." It was a subtle argument, made more subtle for his students and colleagues in Scotland by the fact that this desire to transcend cultural boundaries coincided with his decision to marry a pretty, sixteen-year-old English girl named Diana Pybus, now known as Lady Diana Mukpo. ("It's a *Tibetan* title," the Old Haligonians always hasten to add.)

"In Scotland he was trying to represent the teachings in a completely Tibetan way, but he wasn't able to penetrate the Western mind with it," explained Lady Diana, still a youthful and attractive blonde in her mid-thirties, when I met her at the Court. "He wasn't sure how far he should plunge into Western ways. The car accident served as a message. It was a big shock, and it woke him up to the necessity of going forward."

By his account the marriage caused "consternation" in his young wife's family and "conflict" in the Scottish centre (where "jealousy and resentment" led to an "atmosphere of turmoil and neurosis" verging on the "demonic," in which he was denounced as a "renegade" and "neurotic criminal"), until the newlyweds decided to follow the advice of the *I Ching* and "cross the great water." In early 1970 they spent six weeks in abject circumstances in Montreal before being allowed to enter the United States, where Rinpoche began to teach in Vermont and Colorado. There he found "an undisciplined atmosphere," "free-style people indulging themselves in confused spiritual pursuits," and the special dangers of dilettantism, "spiritual shopping," and what he termed "spiritual materialism" intended to inflate the ego rather than dissolve it.

"In those early years," Lady Diana said, "the hippies and students were exploring beyond the conventional, but their behaviour was wild and their minds were untamed. Rinpoche came down to the level they were at, in order to make communication and work up from there."

If that was the method behind his madness, it was effective for many. It shattered the self-deception of the macrobiotic vegetarians and the mantra-mumblers, while it opened a line to those who had been turned off by guilt and commandments. Among his first students in Colorado were a bunch of communal dopeheads known as the Pygmies; celebrity acidheads such as Ginsberg and Ram Dass adopted him; and word spread from Boston to Los Angeles about this far-out Tibetan teacher who drank, smoked, ate meat, tried LSD, bore a son from a "situation" in Tibet, eloped with a sixteen-year-old, and still held out the possibility of enlightenment in this life. Of course, he had other qualities – his lectures could be brilliant when he was not drunk, his personality could be charming when he was not sullen, his meditation courses could be deep when they were not disturbed by loud parties – but what set him apart from almost all other Tibetan, Buddhist, or Eastern gurus was his unapologetic outrageousness.

"His behaviour – then and later – was controversial among Tibetans and Westerners," David Rome said, "and for a few years he was really on his own. To me there was a heroic quality to his journey, as he continually left behind his connections and reference points for periods of isolation and rejection. Having shed everything and joined into the hippie lifestyle for a while, he began to create a structure from a clean slate and draw on a combination of Tibetan heritage and Western resources. We had revelled in his outrageousness and unusualness, and we were shocked to discover that he represented an establishment and tradition, though in an anti-establishment and non-traditional way."

The shock came in September 1974 in the form of a heavy, moon-faced, smiling man named Rangjung Rigpe Dorje, His

Holiness the Sixteenth Karmapa, the head of the Karma Kagyu order. He showed up in the United States for the first time from India and was received by his wayward disciple, Trungpa Rinpoche. The visit had amazing consequences. To those who had doubts about Rinpoche's wisdom and authority based on his behaviour, the Karmapa reassured them by proclaiming Rinpoche a Vajra Holder and Possessor of the Ultimate Lineage Victory Banner of the Practice Lineage Teachings of the Karma Kagyu. Meanwhile, Rinpoche's behaviour and instruction took unexpected turns. He wept and shook at meeting His Holiness again; he went to extravagant lengths to welcome the Karmapa in Vermont and Colorado with exquisite brocades, fine china and silver, elaborate thrones and quarters, indeed all the pomp and ceremony usually bestowed upon the Queen or the Pope; and he badgered his motley students on how to dress properly, how to serve table, and the infinite details of social grace, personal respect, and spiritual devotion.

It was an astonishing – and not altogether pleasant – change for the dharma bums of Boulder. "The shrine room had been redone in brilliant reds and golds and banners hung from the walls," wrote Rick Fields in his superb history of Buddhism in America. "Ritual became more evident, especially in the advanced practices, and the suits and ties and shining shoes that people had worn for their audiences with His Holiness were now worn to dinner parties and seminars. Rinpoche's annual birthday party, which had been a rather wild affair in the old days, now included formal toasts and ballroom dancing."

Though it looked from the outside as if the Karmapa had got Rinpoche to clean up his act, in fact the visit served as a catalytic excuse for a transformation Rinpoche had begun in 1973, when he moved from basic lectures and meditation techniques to the intense study and practice of three-month Vajradhatu retreats and initiated a few students into the vajrayana teachings. If the first steps of developing discipline by learning to sit in silence and developing compassion through exercises of humility and service were relatively

189

straightforward, the third step was exceedingly complex, constantly demanding, and full of perils. Essentially, instead of working to overcome the illusion of existence by withdrawing from it, the student works to penetrate it by embracing its energy and directing that toward enlightenment. It means entering into the force of emotions, evil, and ignorance to break through to the truth of reality through a complicated process of mental efforts, psychological perceptions, and symbolic devices.

If that is too hard to grasp, I guess you had to be there – and getting there is not much easier. First, there is an introductory lecture, then an all-day lesson in sitting meditation, then thirty days of practising that. Later comes the three-month seminary, and beyond that comes Ngondro, the prelude exercises: 100,000 prostrations from standing to flat on the floor, 100,000 recitations of a mantra, 100,000 creations and destructions of a mandala as an offering of yourself, 100,000 respects to the lineage of the teacher. All going well, you are ready for Abhisheka, the initiation into the tantric way, the transmission of power to the student from the teacher, in which the student submits totally to the mind of the teacher while the teacher gives the student a deity (representing an appropriate psychological state such as anger, lust, or pride, and accompanied by an associated mandala and mantra) to visualize to the point of complete identification. That living and potent imagination is then used to cut through to the truth of the Buddha.

"A problem with many religious traditions is that they make a point of condemning us," Rinpoche taught. "They talk about how wicked we are or how terrible we are and how we have to pull ourselves together. And if we do so, they promise us some candy or reward. But the vajrayana is an entirely different approach. The tantric tradition builds us up so we do not have to relate at the level of a donkey reaching for a carrot any more. The donkey has the carrot already, so the donkey should feel good."

The dangers in that – in going into the senses, the emotions, the ego – are obvious: we may not come out again. "Working with the energy of vajrayana is like dealing with a live electric wire," he warned. As a result, "many students get into trouble. They can't take it. They simply can't take it. They end up destroying themselves. They end up playing with the energy until it becomes a spiritual atomic bomb."

"The tantric style is to deal with neuroses by seizing them by the throat and transmuting their poison into medicine," David Rome explained. "And because it uses powerful methods that are designed to accelerate the path, to deliver enlightenment in one lifetime, you are always in danger of perverting it, putting it at the service of your ego, or going crazy."

That is why the vajrayana is a guru-centred path. Its teachers are more than wise men or benevolent guides: they are empowering masters, "capable of transmitting the vajra spiritual energy to us," Rinpoche once said, but "also capable of destroying us if our direction is completely wrong." Because of the dangers, they demand perfect obedience to their instructions, and perfect obedience therefore requires perfect devotion and perfect trust. That was the great lesson Rinpoche demonstrated in 1974 by means of his own submission to the Karmapa.

Not that he ever made obedience, devotion, and trust especially easy. Even after the new formality of business suits and ballroom dancing, he boozed constantly, philandered openly, and behaved unpredictably. In 1975, to cite the most notorious example, during a debauched Halloween party two-thirds through a seminary retreat, he commanded his bodyguards to fetch a couple from their room. After a nasty brawl, they were dragged back to the scene, where some men and women had stripped naked and Rinpoche was reported "apparently drunk and not particularly coherent," and he ordered his guards to remove the couple's clothes as punches flew and the music was cranked up. In the aftermath all the students received a stern and angry letter from their teacher: vajrayana was no game, it permitted no fooling and no secrets, and anyone not ready to hand over the self should leave at once. No one left.

Then there was his private regiment. It was an unarmed corps that grew from the support staff around the Karmapa's visit into a spiritual practice of discipline and service. It had uniforms imported from England, it was drilled in security and first-aid and domestic service, and it was marched about in training camps. "Part of it was a pragmatic need to protect him," Rome said, after admitting it was odd for a New York Jewish intellectual of the 1960s to find himself on military parade, "but it also reflected the tradition of a mandala. It is symbolic but also real, an actualization of spiritual matters in reality. The community itself becomes a physical mandala, with Rinpoche occupying the Court at the centre as a kind of monarch, his government around him, and the protection forces on the outside. Most of us were unlikely candidates for uniforms and regimentation. It was strange, we had no sympathy for it, but we had to confront doing something we didn't want to do and why we didn't want to be there. We had to look at our aggression and our evasions of it."

The most common rationale for Rinpoche's outlandish ways was the tantric tradition of "crazy wisdom." Like the tricksters of native religion and perhaps the International Clowns for Christ, the guru of crazy wisdom uses unsettling and unconventional actions to snap the minds and egos of his students from their rigid illusions of normality, much as the Zen masters use logic-breaking riddles. "So crazy wisdom is absolute perceptiveness, with fearlessness and bluntness," Rinpoche once said. "Fundamentally it is being wise, but not holding to particular doctrines or disciplines or formats. There aren't any books to follow. Rather, there is endless spontaneity taking place."

"I was married to him for seventeen years, and I still never knew what happened in his mind," Lady Diana said. "He always had a bigger view, which went far beyond how people should act. He wanted people to understand their mind and take command of their life. We never had a conventional marriage, so I never had bad feelings about his unpredictability, because it was based on sanity and was never vicious. He never ever hurt anybody: he made you look at your own mind. Actually I never thought he was unpredictable, because he had trained me to have no reference point of predictability."

It came down to a matter of faith again, and not everyone made the leap. On Saltspring Island in British Columbia, for instance, I met students who had fled the antics of Boulder for the more austere and traditional three-year retreats on top of Mount Tuam begun by another Kagyu guru, Kalu Rinpoche. I knew of women who were turned off by Trungpa Rinpoche's sleeping with students and keeping a number of semi-permanent "consorts." Some found his advances terrifying – for if the guru begged and sent his guards with entreaties, was a refusal a lack of perfect obedience? – while others could be crushed equally by his lack of interest in them. More alarmingly, however often he cautioned his students to follow what he said instead of what he did, he created a community rife with alcoholism, promiscuity, and infidelity.

The most damning words I heard came from Herbert Guenther, the very distinguished Buddhist scholar whose translations of Tibetan texts are classics of the tradition in English. A student of Chinese, Sanskrit, and Pali in Austria and Germany before the war, he went to India in 1950 and by chance got caught up in Tibetan studies. From 1964 until his retirement he headed Far Eastern Studies at the University of Saskatchewan in Saskatoon, where I visited him in 1988 in his modest bungalow full of Tibetan treasures. He had known Trungpa Rinpoche since 1972 and had lectured at the Naropa Institute, and he had his doubts about both.

"The Karmapa and I were good friends," he said in his thick German accent, "and he came to visit me here in Saskatoon. We had a long talk in which he told me that Trungpa should not have come out to the West, he had not finished his education. In England he got into all sorts of strange things and had to leave, but in America, it seems the more you get into a scandal, the higher you are. With enlightenment, however, certain temptations and behaviours fall away: it becomes impossible to think of them. We are sexual beings, naturally, but we reduce our sexuality to the biological level. The more enlightened we become, the less genital our sexuality becomes, as we realize the erotic nature of perception. Trungpa at least drew attention that there was more than

Christianity, but now people want substance, and there he failed."

So why did the Karmapa proclaim him Possessor of the Ultimate Lineage Victory Banner?

"Pure politics," Dr Guenther replied. "One crow doesn't pick out the eyes of another crow, and you can't go against your own party."

Sex, liquor, and a taste for luxury were not unique to Trungpa Rinpoche, of course, and at least he was less hypocritical than others in trying to hide them. Since the 1960s numerous high-profile Zen monks, Hindu swamis, Tibetan lamas, and other imported teachers have been found in all sorts of tangled webs, whether from loneliness, ample opportunity, or the culture shock of being dunked into the Land of the Free at the dawn of Do Your Own Thing. In some respects they were no different from the home-grown Pentecostal preachers, native shamans, Catholic priests, and New Age cultists who came out of poverty and guilt to discover what money, power, and fame could buy. At a deeper level, as illustrated by Christ in the wilderness and the Buddha under the tree, the purer one becomes, the closer to the Truth one gets, the greater and subtler are the temptations and the illusions. To think oneself wise and liberated is infinitely more dangerous than to think oneself rich and beautiful. When a spiritual leader falls, it is not always because he was a fraud. It is often because he indeed had flown too high with wings of wax, and so his fall is all the more tragic.

"It is possible that by following the tantric path we could develop vajra indestructibility and a sudden realization of enlightenment," Trungpa himself warned over and over. "But it is equally possible that we could develop an indestructible ego and find ourselves burnt up, as if we were an overcooked steak." Nor did he exempt the gurus. "If teachers feel that they can go outside the law, so to speak, outside the boundaries, or if they feel that they no longer need to commit themselves to the practice, they can be punished along with their students." And again he sounded the terrible tantric cry, "Be careful;

think twice; pay respect; don't just take this carelessly – *be careful.*"

To his enemies, for all his qualities and intelligence, he had lost his bearings. To his followers, for all his defects and incomprehensibility, he was still on track. And when the track took him to Halifax, theirs was not to reason why, theirs was but to do and emigrate. One year he was obsessed by teaching his Americans how to speak the Queen's English, and everyone had to suffer through elocution lessons. Then, as if progressing from content to form to emptiness, he lapsed into impenetrable silences, and everyone had to suffer through hours of intent stares. In retrospect this was interpreted as preparation, as letting go, as weaning his students from himself. For, soon after settling in Halifax in the fall of 1986, Trungpa Rinpoche had a cardiac arrest – and after months of excruciating illness, compounded by his history of alcohol and work, he died the following April. Some saw the very ugliness of his death as another lesson.

"It was his last great Fuck You," one of his oldest students said of the man they called Mr Pleasure-Mr Pain. "He brought us here, then he left us here."

"He took the easy way out," another joked, meaning out of Halifax. "He used to say he was tired of being a Tibetan, that he wanted to reincarnate to Japan because of its culture and food and simple precision, so maybe he just took off."

"He told me five years before his death that it was coming," Lady Diana said. "He knew exactly when, but he didn't feel badly about it. Look at what he had done in his forty-seven years of life. Look at what he had created in seventeen years in North America. He had given us his complete teachings."

He also had planned for his succession. In addition to the Court and the government of directors, he had empowered a spiritual heir in 1976, a young and personable Italian-American named Thomas Rich from New Jersey via Los Angeles, where he had been known as Narayana, a student of the Hindu swami Satchidananda. From their first meeting in 1971 they had what Rinpoche called "some definite sense of connection," and soon afterwards he recognized that this new student would develop into the Vajra Regent, Karma Moon of Dharma Excellent Intellect Radiant Holder of the Teachings Victorious in All Directions, no longer Tom Rich from Passaic, no longer Narayana the baker, but now Osel Tendzin the guru-in-training.

The appointment took some students by surprise, to put it mildly. It was one thing to surrender your self to a reincarnated abbot from Tibet; it was another thing to submit to the first Western lineage-holder and a guy you had known since the hippie days. So what that Rinpoche had elevated him? So what that the Karmapa had blessed him? "Regent, schmegent, who cares?" said some of his closest friends. "When Rinpoche goes, the whole thing's finished."

In the event, it was not nearly as bad as that. The Halifax community continued to grow, the Boulder seminars and the Dharmadhatu centres continued to attract students, Gampo Abbey continued to expand, and after a tough year of feeling abandoned in limbo, "some kind of organic happening occurred," Lady Diana said. "After being babied for seventeen years, we realized we had to take responsibility. We had the teachings, we had the people and the organization, we had all that we need." Perhaps, but on my first visit to the Halifax Buddhists in 1988, tensions were already apparent.

For one thing, money seemed scarcer. "No one knew how to spend money like Rinpoche," I was told, "but no one knew how to raise it like him either." When resources become tight, their allocation becomes more significant, and allocation always comes down to power. Power appeared to rest with the Regent and the directors, but there was another power centre at the Court around Rinpoche's widow, his sons, and their faction. The Court was still the core of the mandala, after all; a couple of his sons (plus one whom Lady Diana had by Rinpoche's doctor) were recognized as tulkus; and the faction claimed to be the guardians of a second set of teachings, the Shambhala training, which Rinpoche had introduced in 1977. Named after a mystical kingdom and designed for people who had neither the time, capacity, nor religious interest to pursue the Buddhist path, it was established as a secular programme of mental discipline, social service, and personal development based on the notion of warriorship.

"The Shambhala training has the same principles as the Buddhist training – how to work with your energy and fear, how to be gentle and compassionate, and so on – but it's not just a translation of Buddhism into a different language," David Rome said. "It has its own roots, from the cultural tradition of Tibet and all human wisdom, and Rinpoche wanted it kept separate. He had inherited it as a separate teaching, and though Shambhala people have become interested in Buddhism, it's been successful in its own right."

Though the Regent has been described as the co-founder of the Shambhala training, Lady Diana saw its lineage passing to Rinpoche's eldest son, the Sawang, with herself as the bridge between him and the Regent. Since the Shambhala programme still shared quarters on Tower Road with the vajrayana programme and the Naropa Institute, the line of authority over organizational and financial matters was somewhat fuzzy. More particularly, in pinched circumstances, what should go to the Buddhist church and what should go to the Court? For the riches and luxuries of the Court, its elegant dinner parties and domestic servants and ambassadorial grandeur, were integral aspects of the Shambhala discipline of respect and celebration. By 1989 Lady Diana expressed her fear that the mansion on Young Avenue might have to be sold because of its bills.

Against this background I encountered a fair bit of sniping between church and court (an old story in every religion). Around the Court they spoke with contempt about how the Regent's recent statement regarding psychiatry flew in the face of Rinpoche's thoughts; and they wrote off many of the directors as smug and obnoxious, odious even to Rinpoche in his final years. Around the Church they talked of the adolescent boy who had just jumped out of a window at the Court, apparently on LSD, while at a birthday party for Gesar, Rinpoche's wild teenaged son; and they wondered at Lady Diana's spiritual qualifications, given her self-confessed laziness about practising the disciplines. And this was the background against which the major scandal broke bit by bit.

The first I heard was that Osel Tendzin, the Vajra Regent, had been separated for a while from his wife and four children. Nothing too odd about that, I thought, given the lack of conventional "reference points" in the community's personal relationships. Then I picked up that the Regent was gay. Another "live electric wire" to seize, I assumed, and not one that seemed to bother the inner circle who had known for years. Then, in December 1988, I learned that he had contracted AIDS. A heavy karma for a guru, I believed, but one deserving of infinite compassion. Then the news came out that, knowing of his illness since 1985, he had infected one of his male students, who unknowingly had infected a female friend. For me, and many others, this definitely was not crazy wisdom or guru transmission. It was against the basic Buddhist code never to hurt another being.

In February 1989, the story hit *The New York Times*, *Time*, and the Halifax *Chronicle-Herald*, and the board of directors asked for the Regent to resign. He refused, on the grounds that a Karma Moon of Dharma Excellent Intellect Radiant Holder of the Teachings Victorious in All Directions does not hold authority at the discretion of a board. Meanwhile, back at the Court, Lady Diana told friends that she never wanted to see the Regent again, and there were some who thought the directors themselves should resign for not having confronted the problem a lot earlier and a lot more forthrightly. Since no appeal was possible to His Holiness the Karmapa, who had died in Zion, Illinois, in 1981 (and will not be in a position presumably to arbitrate for years after his reincarnation is found and trained), the matter was sent up to various Tibetan leaders in India for advice. A year later, however, the situation was still a standoff, though the Regent had handed over his responsibilities to representatives while he entered a strict retreat. By that time it certainly looked as if the board was in control, not least because Lady Diana had sold her house, closed down the Court, and gone to live in Hawaii.

Some old students, in need of a living guru and dissatisfied with the community's politics, moved on to other teachers and paths or pulled back to wait for the dust to settle; most others stayed to carry on Rinpoche's instructions and find their guru inside themselves; and some new students, with no connection to either Rinpoche or the Regent, moved in, drawn by the power of the teachings alone. "The events had serious implications and caused lots of reflection," Rome said, "but it was remarkable how little it slowed the momentum of our work." For, despite its controversial methods and personalities, Tibetan Buddhism is recognized as an ancient and effective tradition, capable of taking its practitioners to the Truth. In that sense, its claims are no greater or less than those of the Roman Catholic Church. Popes may be libertines and priests may be pederasts, goes the argument, but the Church is holy and incorruptible. "Thank God for those Newfoundland priests," one Buddhist said lightly, for if the crimes of the Christian Brothers did not excuse those of the Regent, they did create a context and a diversion in which it was harder to single out him or his church.

(Despite a few shocking headlines and much wagging of tongues, Halifax did not seem particularly agitated about the scandal, in fact. When I asked a Haligonian why, he said, "Because we didn't expect anything else from those people. We always assumed they were deviant cultists, so we weren't as surprised as we were with those Catholics.")

Personally, though I found the Halifax Buddhists very likeable in their candour and even admirable in their dedication, I found myself questioning their path for many of the same reasons I had questioned Roman Catholicism. I was no more drawn to a drunken guru than to the drunken bishops I have known, for all their learning and charms; and devotions to deities, mantras, complicated rituals, lavish ceremonies, dense texts in Tibetan and Sanskrit, and total submission to a master seemed no more efficacious than worship of the Virgin Mary, rosary prayers, the rites of the Mass, bells and incense, Aramaic and Latin commentaries, and obedience to an infallible pope. When I ask directions to Kansas, let alone Nirvana, I tend to discount them if they come from a guy with booze on his breath; and I would certainly have doubts about the sure path or fast cut to Saskatoon, let alone Heaven, if I found myself no further ahead after twenty years of walking.

"For whatsoever a man soweth," Christians and Buddhists agree, "that shall he also reap" – not just in some future Heaven or Nirvana but in this here and now. So what was I to make of Catholic monks and Buddhist students who, after all their prayers and mantras, after all their humilities and prostrations, still had to go to Alcoholics Anonymous? What was I to think of a Christian Brother and a Buddhist teacher who, despite the training and blessing of their ordination, abused their offices for sexual pleasures? What opinion should I hold of Catholic bishops and Shambhala warriors who, steeped in the glories of service and compassion, pulled away from the poor and oppressed into luxury and spiritual self-satisfaction? Not all do so, of course – there are no doubt more saints and sages walking those paths than walking the path of greed and ignorance – but I had to conclude that ancient forms and long lineages are not enough to assure the right direction. Each step of every tradition must be tested constantly against the actions from which it comes and to which it goes.

"A fool who thinks he is wise goes through life with himself as an enemy, and he ever does wrong deeds which in the end bear bitter fruit," the Buddha said. "For that deed is not well done when being done one has to repent and reap with tears the bitter fruits of the wrong deed."

NINE

The Raggedy Band

This was no Vatican Council. Instead of being in a cathedral resplendent with marble carvings and stained glass, I found myself in an auditorium at the University of Victoria – in the very heart of apostasy, as it were. Instead of mingling with august bishops in embroidered vestments, I was surrounded by a chatty crowd dressed for a British Columbia August in light and casual wear. And instead of having a pope pontificating on the last word from God (or the curia) on moral and theological points of contention, I witnessed 388 delegates to the 1988 General Council of the United Church of Canada struggling to decide among themselves what is right and wrong.

To traditional Catholic eyes the ludicrousness of that was evident in the ludicrousness of that summer's hottest issue: whether or not the United Church should permit self-declared, practising homosexuals to be ordained as ministers. Rome's response, based on the Bible and tradition and probably delivered in Latin, would be an unequivocal "Are you out of your minds?" Though the Canadian Catholic hierarchy has had ample cause in recent years to know some priests are gay, its conviction remains that they are also sinners. Even to consider otherwise is to demonstrate once more to many bishops the wacky consequences of spiritual democracy.

Many conservative Protestants, within and without the United Church, were wondering about those consequences too. When the Protestant Reformation rejected the authority of the Vatican because of the vice and politics of the leadership, it went back to the "paper pope" as guide and guru and sought to anchor the congregations and clergy to the authority of the Bible. Translating the Scriptures into the vernacular, putting them into the hands of ordinary people, and often leaving their interpretation to each community and individual moved power downwards. On the positive side, that made everyone more responsible for his or her faith. On the negative side, it encouraged endless divisions and feuds based on any number of interpretations with no strong and central arbiter. This lengthy and dramatic dispute in the United Church of Canada, with all its theological arguments and schismatic threats, was simply the most recent expression of Protestantism's positive and negative faces.

I have beside my desk almost three feet of documents, press clippings, and discussion material related to this quarrel, and they represent just a fraction of the trees that died to become study kits, petitions, virulent letters, editorial opinion, background papers, and tissues to wipe away the tears in this battle of words. Reviewing all the verbal outrage and learned exegesis of those who oppose the ordination of gays, however, I found at the centre just a few sentences – drawn, as might be expected, from the Bible. From Leviticus in the Old Testament, the twenty-second verse of the eighteenth chapter: "Thou shalt not lie with mankind, as with womankind: it *is* abomination." From the New Testament, the ninth and tenth verses of the sixth chapter of First Corinthians: "Be not deceived: neither fornicators, nor idolaters, nor adulterers, nor effeminate, nor abusers of themselves with mankind, nor thieves, nor covetous, nor drunkards, nor revilers, nor extortioners, shall inherit the kingdom of God."

There it is in black and white, dictated by God and confirmed by Christ's apostles: homosexuality is a sin. Like all sins, it may be viewed with compassion and cleansed by faith, but nothing will ever convince conservative Christians that homosexuality is anything less than a sin. Ultimately that is all they ask their churches to declare.

The star spokesman for this conviction became a slight, soft-spoken United Church minister named John Howard. Born in Calgary in 1947, looking younger than his years despite a beard and a family of three children, Howard gained prominence both as a dissenting member of the National Coordinating Group for the Programme of Study and Dialogue on Sexual Orientations, Lifestyles and Ministry (NCG) and as the most public representative of the "ex-gay movement." As he admitted to me when I interviewed him in his office at Collier Street United in Barrie, north of Toronto, God had given an unlikely role to someone who had always seen himself as shy, inferior, and unconfident.

"I struggled with my homosexuality for more than twenty years and never had the courage to talk about it with anyone, not even my wife," he said. "Except for one adult encounter in 1974, I didn't get involved sexually with other guys. But, by 1983, I reached a point in my fantasy life where it was out of control. I felt driven toward acting out my feelings. God seemed to be saying that I was at a crossroads: either I reach out to receive help or I carry on down to the park scene, the washroom scene, the scene of getting caught and losing my family and job."

One day two women in his church realized he was wrestling with something, and they asked if he wanted to talk. "That scared me, because I thought I was hiding it. But then I saw them as God saying, 'I'm offering you help. Go for it!' So we met and loved and cried and prayed. It was a gradual process of inner healing, to get control of my thoughts and feelings."

From there he connected with ex-gay associations, such as Love in Action in California and Metanoia in Seattle, and in 1985 he went to Vancouver for a training seminar in Homosexuals Anonymous, a spiritual and psychological programme that proved to him that homosexuality is a learned behaviour rather than a God-given condition. "Around the same time," he said, "one morning in the shower I heard a radio report about some men being picked up in an Ontario town on homosexual charges. One was a Sunday-school teacher with the United Church. After his arrest he went home, kissed his wife and kids, and killed himself. I was struck by a sense of grief. That could have been me. So I said, 'Hey, Lord, if you want me to go public about my own healing, I'm willing for that to happen.'"

God did want it, apparently, because Howard's personal crisis coincided with his Church's obsession with exactly the same questions of gay sin, gay healing, and gay ordination. Given the clarity of the Biblical text and the weight of traditional Christian morality, the real conundrum may be how officials, theologians, and stalwarts of the United Church could do other than elevate John Howard to the Protestant equivalent of Mother Teresa.

By most accounts the story began in January 1981, when a young candidate for the ministry told the ordination committee of the Waterloo Presbytery of the Hamilton Conference that she was a lesbian. Susan Mabey had not intended to make a big fuss about it. She just assumed the committee deserved to know why her marriage had broken down. But in the general atmosphere of gay liberation her declaration sparked the firestorm most liberal churches had been expecting sooner or later. Following the presbytery's advice that she not be ordained, the conference's executive committee announced that it would not ordain any self-declared homosexuals, and in 1982 the biennial meeting of the Hamilton Conference petitioned the General Council being held that year in Montreal to give guidelines to the entire Church on this matter.

The first result was a report on human sexuality, "Gift, Dilemma and Promise," presented to the 1984 General Council in Morden, Manitoba. The delegates rejected its recommendation that sexual *orientation* (as distinct from sexual *behaviour*) not be a barrier to ordination, but they did agree to more study and dialogue as a way to cool the heat and anger generated. That agreement led to the formation of the National Coordinating Group in November 1984, consisting of a chairperson (Betty Jean Klassen), a staff official (David Ewart), and ten members chosen equally by the head office's

Division of Mission in Canada and Division of Ministry Personnel and Education drawing on nominations from the Church's regional conferences.

"The selection of the group was the key thing, and it was tragic," said Duncan White, the NCG's other dissenting member and a minister from Port Hope, Ontario. At the group's first meeting in April 1985, he found three homosexuals, no one from the conservative United Church Renewal Fellowship, and only himself likely to oppose the ordination of gays. "The die was cast right from the start. I thought we had an exciting opportunity to reshape our theology by listening to our congregations, not just to theologians way over the hills and out of sight. But, regardless of what came in and was heard technically, the NCG wrote recommendations most of which could have been written the first day it met. Its report reflected the dream world we were living in."

"It may be fair to say that most of the group were more open to the final recommendations than Duncan White," David Ewart replied, "but it's not accurate to say that the report could have been written in the first meeting. Thinking did change, positions did shift."

The most immediate change was the addition of John Howard as a voice for ex-gays and the Renewal Fellowship. That did little, however, to dispel the pervasive conviction that the liberals in the national headquarters – known as "85 St Clair" after its Toronto address – had stacked the cards deliberately in their favour. For the issue of gay ordination was only the latest and most shocking focus for the suspicion, hostility, and alienation that had been developing between the leadership and the grassroots over twenty-five years. A great part of the issue's fury had less to do with homosexuality than with other, more subtle issues such as political leftism, radical feminism, cultural relativism, and moral anarchy; and everyone who ever had a quarrel with 85 St Clair seemed to be using this excuse to tame the beast.

"It seems to be if you aren't of the extreme feminist, extreme liberal ilk, you don't get a chance to be nominated or appointed to the significant positions," White told me in his

Port Hope office one afternoon. Though born in Canada, he was raised in Scotland and still speaks with a heavy brogue thirty-five years after his return. Ordained in the Church of Scotland, he once found the United Church a comfortable home with its mix of religious evangelism and social service, but now he is not so sure. "The Church's structure is very susceptible to manipulation. Whoever controls the process can pretty well control the outcome."

Rev. John Tweedie, the executive director of the Renewal Fellowship and a minister in Brantford before he quit the Church in 1988, agreed with White. "Homosexuals like to talk about isolation and persecution. Well, I can tell them all about that as an evangelical in the United Church," he said when I spoke to him before his resignation. "That is what I have experienced in stares, in comments, and in what has happened to some of our ministers."

The United Church Renewal Fellowship (UCRF) had been formed in 1965 by a dozen people in Barrie, Ontario, as a reaction to the growing liberalism. The year before, their Church had released its "New Curriculum" for use in Sunday schools, and its modern slant on the Scriptures shook the beliefs of the grassroots to the foundations. Of course, the notion of applying historical criticism and scientific method to the Bible went back at least a hundred years, since the days when Darwin suggested the world was not created in seven days and European scholars began reading the text in the context of its times; but generally the leaders of the United Church had preferred to make their adjustments and compromises in moderate ways that did not disturb the old-fashioned cosmology of the faithful.

This seemed particularly important for the United Church because it began as a merger, in 1925, of three denominations: the Methodists, the Congregationalists, and about two-thirds of the Presbyterians. (The Evangelical United Brethren joined in 1968.) Doctrinal disputes, theological divisions, and their implications for Biblical interpretation therefore tended to be played down for the sake of unity. Good works and good behaviour were all that most people needed to understand of the Good Book, and a bottle of beer was looked upon as a graver sin than loss of belief in the Trinity.

"The New Curriculum was an effort to make the Church more modern in order to keep faith more intellectually agreeable to what people had learned in other parts of their lives," said George Hermanson, an ordained theologian who was one of the NCG's strongest members. "But many people were upset to be confronted by the fact that Adam and Eve weren't real. It showed that the clergy hadn't been passing on to the laity what they had learned in school. They were afraid to engage people on that level."

Once the anchor of a literal and inerrant Bible had been cast aside in the nineteenth century, Truth floated away with the historical and social context, which was both liberal and democratic in direction. As early as 1936, for example, despite St Paul's instructions to the Corinthians that their "women keep silence in the churches," the United Church allowed the ordination of women; and in 1962, despite Christ's own warning that whoever "shall put away his wife, and marry another, committeth adultery," the United Church recognized divorce and remarriage. Instead of hanging on to specific passages, the Church tended to apply the spirit of the entire New Testament to the conditions of the day.

The conditions of the 1960s challenged the Church on two fronts. The political and social turmoil (particularly the American civil-rights movement, the demonstrations against the Vietnam war, and the emergence of the developing nations) reinforced the political and social meaning of the Gospels, in terms of Christ as the champion of the poor and oppressed, and that caused the further radicalization of the Church leadership. In effect, it moved from the "Social Gospel" and the Liberal Party to liberation theology and the New Democratic Party. At the same time, the mounting suspicion that God may in fact have died, the disenchantment with organized religious forms, the loss of the young to drugs and cults and communes, and the general search for meaning in a world of nuclear weapons and corporate technology provoked deep reassessments of the Church's message, government, and relevance. Among the consequences was a shift in power from a small group of men at the top to the active laity.

The main beneficiaries, in practice, were women. Even by 1960 there were very few women in the ministry and fewer yet in the national office. With the rise of the feminist movement the Church opened its bureaucratic doors, and large numbers of women responded. The ministry was on the way to becoming a women's profession, and the lay men who used to run the Church like feudal barons became an endangered species. Furthermore, most of the new blood was sympathetic to the emergence of a feminist theology, which raised even more questions about the Bible, the liturgy, and the Church structures. It attacked the very concept of God as male, the patriarchal language and laws of the Scriptures, the hierarchical order of the universe and the institution, and the dualistic divisions of male and female. Though its full impact has yet to be felt throughout the Church, it has already transformed much of the language and assumptions at the upper levels and in the theological schools.

It set the stage, for example, for the NCG's report. By confronting traditional authority and calcified laws, by joining the rhetoric of oppressed peoples to the issues of human sexuality, feminist theology naturally prepared the grounds for gay ordination. Biblical verses lost their apparent meaning because they had been written in the context of male biases; masculinity and femininity became cultural patterns rather than eternal givens; and the qualities of love and justice overrode anachronistic judgements and legalistic codes.

"We have understood that we are addressed by God through the Bible, and it is inspired of God," the report stated at the outset. "At the same time, we have understood that the Bible itself and all of our traditions of the interpretation of the Bible are culturally and historically conditioned."

Then how is Truth – or right and wrong – to be discerned in the absence of fixed criteria?

"Because we affirm that God is currently active, and that God speaks to us through reason," the report answered, "we can use contemporary knowledge, as it has been tested through rigorous examination, to discern what is true and to inform our understanding of the Bible."

Applying the device known as the Wesley Quadrilateral, named after the founder of Methodism, the NCG tackled its questions through a combination of Scripture, tradition, reason, and experience. Of these, however, experience became the dominant factor. The group's first meeting consisted of sharing each member's stories and attitudes regarding homosexuality. Needless to say the accounts of pain and persecution told by gay members such as Charles Bidwell and Christine Waymark carried particular impact. Bidwell, an associate professor at the University of Alberta, told of his early sexual crises, of the effect his acknowledgement of his gayness had on his wife and two children, of his search for a church where he could worship God without denying his own nature, and of his care for his young lover who was dying of AIDS.

"Do people have the right to impose their standards when we have no more choice over our sexual orientation than they have over theirs, just because theirs happens to be the normal, the predominant?" he repeated to me when I visited him in Edmonton. It was a sunny spring day and he had just brought Patrick home from the hospital so that they could enjoy an afternoon in the garden. "It's uncompassionate and unjust to say if we're going to be homosexual, then we can't have sex. If we understood homosexual acts to be abusive, then we'd be against them as we're against rape. But I have yet to have anyone tell me what is sinful about my love for Patrick, about my ability to be a lifemate to him and support him through his illness right to death."

From the testimony of Christian gays, as well as from medical and psychological studies, the report made its most controversial leap. "Sexual orientation is like being left-handed or right-handed or ambidextrous," it asserted, after refusing to view it in terms of sin or alcoholism or birth defect. "Some people are one way; some another. We don't know why this happens. Nor does it matter. What does matter is what one does with whatever 'handedness' one has. There are a variety of orientations: homosexual, bisexual, heterosexual. These ought to be seen as natural and as a gift of God."

"We were faced with the question of whether homosexual behaviour is *always* immoral and irresponsible – or, like heterosexual behaviour, is it only sometimes immoral and irresponsible?" David Ewart said. "If the latter, then what are the grounds for moral and responsible behaviour? The same, we answered, as all sexual behaviour: when our actions are 'faithful to God's call to be just, loving, health-giving, healing, and sustaining of community.' There have been significant changes in the understanding of ourselves as sexual beings, and the Church has to be informed by that, just as it was informed by Darwin and had to adjust its understanding of Genesis. That doesn't mean we can do what we want. It means that rigid rules and automatic responses have to be challenged by our experience of what is actually happening in each situation."

It was on this crucial point that John Howard and Duncan White lost their screaming matches with the rest of the group. White saw himself as a moderate, torn between compassion for gays and his adherence to moral tradition. "The one time I tried to control the process, I dumped a load of Scriptural references on them, and they got very angry," he said. "They thought themselves disempowered by all that stuff, because it wasn't based on experience. But the experiential process disempowers people just as much. So the report became purely and simply an advocacy report for the homosexual position. At root was a desire to see it as good. Since people want to be good, they redefine what is good when they can't be good in the old terms."

Certainly the NCG treated the Bible with a lot more suspicion than it treated experience, and certainly it opened the door to all kinds of sexual relationships outside heterosexual marriage. Despite being warned that Duncan White represented the general membership of the United Church, the majority of the group preferred to be "prophetic" and speak the truth as they saw it regardless of the immediate reaction. Except for tinkering with some of the unnecessarily provocative phrases in order to make the package more saleable, about 100 members of the two divisions from the national office and the regional conferences voted to approve the report's major recommendations at the end of a twelve-hour meeting in February 1988. Those included the understanding of truth as "provisional, conditional, and contextual," the possibility of gay behaviour that is morally responsible, and the affirmation that sexual orientation not be a barrier to ordination.

As soon as the report and recommendations were released in March, the reaction against them was ferocious. Groups of ministers and laity sprung up across the country to fight gay ordination; hundreds rallied in different cities to protest against their national leadership; and a movement began to withhold contributions to the Mission and Service Fund because it had financed the NCG. "Holding the Church to ransom is far more sinful than anything the gays are doing," said Anne Squire, the grandmotherly moderator at the time who was deluged by hate letters, including some from Christians wishing she would get AIDS. The Renewal Fellowship saw the whole business as the ultimate proof of what it had been arguing against for twenty-five years. More significant was the emergence of the Community of Concern. Unlike the UCRF, which represents less than 2 per cent of the Church's 850,000 members, the Community of Concern attracted the mainstream. Though plentiful with UCRF names and chaired by William Fritz, John Howard's colleague at Collier Street United in Barrie, it garnered the signatures of over 1,000 ministers and 32,000 supporters.

"Some of the report's assumptions and recommendations are far too accommodating to popular idols of contemporary culture – hedonism, narcissism, and relativism," argued Angus James MacQueen, one of the four ex-moderators who signed the Declaration of Dissent. "Despite its many references to God, to Jesus, to the Holy Spirit, and to scripture, the report is a *Te Deum* to personal happiness, physical gratification, conformism, and fashion. It takes little notice of historic religious and moral values such as self-control, abstinence, fidelity, and spiritual growth."

211

Most of the signatories were probably like Duncan White: they were not Biblical literalists, they were not without compassion, but they believed that homosexuality and sex outside marriage had to be judged as sins. "I must admit I was surprised by the Community of Concern," said George Hermanson. "It's an important indicator of where the United Church is – moving to the right – and I just hadn't realized so many were that traditional. They want to make Scriptural interpretation supreme above reason and tradition and experience, not just first among equals, and their theological method demands certainty in an age of complexity. But I come out of a theological method that sees uncertainty and complexity as part of God's experiment, that welcomes diversity and pluralism."

"A lot of people who aren't fundamentalist become fundamentalist when you talk about sexuality, because it is so powerful, so emotional, so irrational," David Ewart said. "Like in the abortion debate, we were coming at each other with completely different principles, so we ended up just name-calling. The opposition seemed to be a volcanic 'No!' rather than a constructive process of examining how truth is known or how moral behaviour is discerned."

The opposition mobilized to prevent approval of the NCG report and the divisions' recommendations at the General Council in August. That meant beginning at the congregation level and working up through the Church's democratic maze of four "courts" to send delegates, petitions, and a strong message to Victoria. I decided to track their struggle during the spring and summer of 1988 in the Ottawa area, which contained a number of high-profile factions, including Community of Concern leaders, UCRF supporters, gay activists, and report advocates. Neither as liberal as Toronto or Winnipeg nor as conservative as Hamilton or Halifax, it encapsulated the white, Anglo-Saxon, middle-class, middle-of-the-road personality of the United Church. That was a perfect description of the hundred people who gathered after dinner on March 30 in the church hall beside Hawthorne United in an Ottawa suburb. They represented a sixth of the membership of the two congregations in the pastoral charge of Bethany-Hawthorne, one of 2,400 such charges in the first court, each led by a minister and governed by a board. Everyone seemed rather perplexed. There had been just one copy of the report floating around both congregations, there was no time now even to read it, and Rev. Thomas Simms was pressing his flock to vote to send a petition against it in time for the upcoming presbytery meeting, the second court that meets regularly to administer the local charges.

"Why do I have the terrible feeling we're being stampeded?" one woman asked as the crowd was broken into discussion groups of ten for half an hour.

With nothing specific to discuss, the one I joined fell into general complaints about the system and personal attitudes about the issue. Apparently ordinary United Church members are no happier with their democracy than ordinary Roman Catholics are with their bishops. Despite the Church's decentralization into an unwieldy and expensive structure, most people in the pews still feel powerless. Power invariably tends toward a few hands in all human organizations; Methodism brought into the union a centralist tradition that still causes tensions with the congregationalists; and the professionals of every institution often arrive at judgements that differ from the more superficial opinions of amateurs. (The professionals may not always be right, but they are probably on stronger ground for being wrong.) On the other hand, I was moved to see these earnest and decent people wrestling with what they believe and why. One woman had a gay nephew. Another was worried about gay teachers. One man quoted the Bible; a young woman replied that the Bible could not always be taken literally; and everyone dropped the matter.

"How do we know that the people who go to Victoria will vote our way?" the minister was asked when we reassembled.

"They vote by secret ballot according to themselves," he replied, "not according to their congregations."

"Then we're wasting our time, aren't we?"

They voted anyway: eighty-seven against the report, fifteen for it, with four abstentions. It was all over by nine o'clock.

"Right across the Church there were a lot of angry, agitated clergy who wanted to control their congregations and the direction the Church should go in," B. J. Klassen, the NCG's chairperson, complained. "They didn't allow for dialogue and debate and education." While some congregations may have had more study and deeper discussion, however, the lopsided vote at Hawthorne United was typical. Nor could it be attributed even largely to the machinations of the minister. All the polls and surveys showed that, at the congregational level, the gut hostility against gay ordination was extremely high.

About two weeks later, on April 12, I returned for the monthly meeting of the Ottawa Presbytery, one of ninety-eight across Canada. Over 150 representatives from its fifty-nine charges, including all the clergy as well as selected lay members, met at Rideau Park United to debate the report, with B. J. Klassen and Duncan White present as experts. At supper (shepherd's pie served on paper plates) the buzz was rumour and opinion: Was it true that the Montreal Presbytery had elected a majority of delegates to Victoria in favour of the report, though its congregations had been overwhelmingly against it? Why didn't homosexuals just go away and leave the United Church alone? Who had given some local ministers the right to sow dissension and shame by urging the withholding of money to the Church? Then everyone went into the church to pray.

"I may speak in tongues of men or of angels," they heard from St Paul, "but if I am without love, I am a sounding gong or a clanging cymbal." They heard a prayer for the Church that is "confused about its message, uncertain about its role, undisciplined and unimaginative." Then they sang together:

And we, shall we be faithless?
Shall hearts fail, hands hang down?
Shall we evade the conflict,
And cast away our crown?
Not so: in God's deep counsels
Some better thing is stored;
We shall maintain unflinching
One church, one faith, one Lord.

Back in the hall, where the supper tables had been replaced by rows of chairs, they did not evade the conflict, though not unflinchingly. The debate went on till midnight. There were some notable differences in this second court. Everyone seemed to have studied the report; the number of ministers both for and against it lifted the quality from unread prejudice to theological knowledge; and the crowd actually encountered the human stories from gays and lesbians present. The most emotional moment came when Alyson Huntly, a pretty and popular young woman who was serving as a diaconal minister, revealed for the first time publicly that she was a lesbian and begged for justice, compassion, and even celebration. When she finished, still shaking with nerves, her friends embraced her in a circle.

"Whenever people could put a face or a story to what we were talking about," said B. J. Klassen of that meeting, "it became a totally different thing than when they just received a theoretical statement or Biblical quotation."

Oddly enough, perhaps, most of the eighteen ministers who had been engineering the opposition in the Ottawa area deliberately kept silent. They knew they had the petitions from the congregations and they knew the presbytery's vote whether to agree or not with those petitions would not come till the May meeting, so there was little point to forcing a confrontation now. Indeed, when the presbytery met again on May 10 in Shawville, Quebec, it voted to reject categorically the main thrusts of the report despite the conciliatory tone set during the April debate. Significantly, however, the opposition vote in this court was closer to 65 per cent than 90 per cent. As the proportion of clergy increased, as the amount of study increased, as the degree of complexity increased, support for the report increased.

This pattern was repeated when lay and ministerial delegates for all five presbyteries got together as the third court for the annual meeting of the Montreal and Ottawa Conference over the last weekend of May. More than 300 people showed up at Carleton University to deal with regional business and almost 200 petitions, ten times more than usual because of

215

the report. Each of the twelve conferences (a thirteenth has been created since) handled the overload differently. Here the petitions were grouped into seven categories based on their point of view, from full acceptance of the report to full rejection. When even that proved too unwieldy a process for determining the wish of the conference, the debate narrowed down to three crucial resolutions moved by members of the meeting. The crunch came over the distinction between sexual orientation and sexual behaviour. It was an attempt to find a compromise, in which understanding was shown toward homosexual tendencies while monogamous heterosexual marriage was reaffirmed. Though the gays and the conservatives both thought it absurd to separate gay orientation from gay practice, the conference voted to tolerate the first and condemn the second. Such toleration represented a shift from the attitude of the congregations and presbyteries, and that shift was confirmed by the numbers. In this court the opposition to the report won by a bare majority rather than by two-thirds of the votes.

Finally, for just over a week in August, the General Council gathered in Victoria to decide (amid other Church affairs) what to do with more than 1,800 petitions relating to the report. This fourth court convenes every two years to elect a new moderator, govern the work of the national executive, and set Church policy. A committee of some two dozen commissioners, chosen to reflect a variety of opinions, studied the petitions (98 per cent of which were from congregations) and found 60 per cent of them against the entire report, 11 per cent wanting more study, 8 per cent wanting a referendum on the question, and only 6 per cent approving of the report. The committee also found the same discrepancy between the views of the congregations and those of the conferences as I had. Though no conference supported full acceptance of the report, only three of the twelve supported full rejection. Most agreed that sexual orientation alone should not prevent ordination. In light of that discrepancy, the committee proposed to replace the divisions' recommendations with its own, in hope of getting a consensus from the Council.

However, when the first draft was presented Thursday evening, August 18, by the committee's warm and intelligent chairperson, Marion Best from British Columbia, it admitted to a lack of consensus on the key matter of orientation. The committee had split, nineteen for and five against, on the recommendation that sexual orientation should not be a barrier to ordination. After hearing questions and criticisms from the delegates, it went back to work, and in the afternoon of the following Monday it returned with a second draft and unanimous endorsement. Confessing to "a history of injustice and persecution against gay and lesbian persons in violation of the Gospel of Jesus Christ" as well as to an inability to agree upon "a Christian understanding of human sexuality, including homosexuality," the committee resolved that "all persons regardless of their sexual orientation, who profess faith in Jesus Christ and obedience to him, are welcome to be or become full members of the Church. All members of the Church are eligible to be considered for Ordered Ministry."

"The committee wasn't prepared to say that homosexuality is a gift of God or no different than being left-handed," Marion Best explained to the media, "but we weren't prepared to say it is a sin either. We want gays and lesbians to walk with us, and we left their eligibility for the ministry to the appropriate bodies of the Church that decide anyone's suitability."

Significantly, too, the committee was not prepared to define orientation in any way that excluded practice. That became the heart of the debate during two hot and muggy afternoons. If the General Council did not condemn specifically homosexual acts, the opposition contended, sexual orientation would be taken to mean behaviour as well as inclination. Perhaps, the proponents conceded, but would practice mean dancing, holding hands, cohabiting, even worshipping together? ("Besides, I don't need practice," said one gay minister. "I'm already perfect.") Both sides knew that insisting on celibacy by homosexuals would destroy the fragile compact, but the opposition wanted it broken. Into the evening and into the night, speakers went to the microphones to argue for and against this key point. There were procedural wrangles, amendments and sub-amendments to the committee's statement, tearful confessions, bitter words, and lofty rhetoric, and gradually the direction of the majority of commissioners became obvious. They defeated a motion to state clearly that orientation did not include practice; they refused to confine sex to marriage; they hissed at the suggestion that paedophiles and rapists are also persecuted but hardly deserve an apology for that; and they refused to brake the momentum by putting off the inevitable to another day.

"I plead for a morsel to take back to the congregations," said Jim Somerville, an Ottawa minister. "We must send them a signal that we have listened to them. In the name of justice we are doing a greater injustice to those in the pews, who will vote with their feet and their dollars, because they will interpret our action as approval for the ordination of self-declared gays and lesbians."

"This is indeed a miraculous moment," Eilert Frerichs said as the next speaker. A chaplain at the University of Toronto, he had been one of the major advocates for AFFIRM, the organization of United Church homosexuals. "Probably this won't affect the ordination of gays at the presbytery level for ten or fifteen years, but finally we are being offered an opportunity to share this 'home.'"

At last, at midnight, the vote was taken on this crucial section amid tension and exhaustion, and it carried by almost 55 per cent. Though the debate to consider the rest of the statement would go on for most of the next day, the real battle was over. The gradual move away from the adamant convictions of most of the congregations now was complete. The process up to the highest court had led from outright rejection of gays and lesbians to at least acceptance in principle, though all ordinations still had to be approved by presbytery and conference committees.

"The United Church is about as democratic as any conciliar system can be," Anne Squire explained. Between 1986 and 1988, she had been the second female moderator and the first lay woman to head the Church. "But it is a representative democracy, not a direct democracy, and it differs from other democracies in that its promises are made before God as well as the people. Delegates to General Council don't have to vote the way their presbyteries or conferences want. They have to vote the way they feel God wants. I've seen that happen, when a solution or a prophetic word suddenly catches fire and the Spirit moves through the crowd. Sometimes I feel we make a wrong decision, but for the most part I have trust in our Church."

Not all her opponents, who accused her of exercising her prejudice toward gay ordination despite her supposed neutrality, shared that trust. Where she saw the Spirit, they saw head-office manipulation and back-room lobbying. "They've rubbed our faces in it and given us nothing," Jim Somerville told me. "They were just better organized, I guess. It makes you wonder what our people have to do to get heard by their Church. We've petitioned, we've worked to get elected as commissioners, we've warned about a financial squeeze, we mobilized the Community of Concern, but it didn't make any difference. My own congregation is safe – it had been burned by an experience of boys in the manse and it won't let that happen again – but our Church has redefined sin in a way that makes it permissible."

"The only new thing is our welcome, but we can't legislate that," Marion Best concluded. "Our Church is a raggedy band, led by Jesus Christ, standing on the bank of the Jordan River and seeing the Promised Land. Some don't know how to swim, some are just getting their feet wet, and some are wishing they had never left the fleshpots of Egypt, but I believe that most will stay together."

Some chose not to, however. Despite the prosaic pressure that ministers would lose their handsome pensions and congregations would lose their valuable buildings, about three dozen ministers and congregations pulled out in the aftermath of the General Council, including John Tweedie and most of his Brantford congregation. (I remembered the words on a poster in his office: "It's hard to soar with eagles when you work with turkeys." To which a poster in George Hermanson's office seemed to reply: "Great spirits have always encountered opposition from mediocre minds.") An estimated 2,500 members left the Church because of the controversy; there was a significant drop in donations from almost all the conferences, with the Mission and Service Fund experiencing one of its worst years since the Depression; and there were ongoing rallies and manoeuvres by the Community of Concern and the UCRF.

Though they lost their demand for a referendum to overturn the Council's work, they succeeded in forcing the issue back on the agenda of the next Council in London in 1990 for reconsideration; and though time and power might be on the side of the liberals in control of the national organization, the conservatives are no longer a minority fringe confined to the Renewal Fellowship. The Community of Concern has become a dynamic, respected, and reasonable network for the aggravated majority, and its potential effect goes far beyond the issue of homosexuals. It is bent on redefining the Church's structure, the teachings at the theological schools, the authority and interpretation of the Scriptures, and the huge question of the relation of Truth to culture and society.

"As we struggle to understand the issues, we realize that the question underlying every other question is one of power," Anne Squire had told the General Council in her last speech as Moderator. "We are locked in a power struggle that is often too easily labelled liberal versus conservative. It might better be termed 'culture-affirming and culture-denying.' Do we as a church acknowledge a changing world and celebrate it as God's doing, or do we call a halt to change and stand over against culture, challenging it as opposing God's will?"

Essentially it was the same power struggle I had seen between Roman Catholicism and native spirituality, between the Vatican authorities and the local churches of Africa and Asia and the Americas, among New Age movements and transplanted Oriental traditions. If cultures are affirmed and celebrated as God's doing, is everything included? If not, then what should not be condoned, who judges, and with what criteria? The United Church does not celebrate racism and nuclear submarines, for example, but on questions of human sexuality, it has responded with a resounding, "Don't know!" That does not make it an agnostic church, as some have claimed, for it still has faith and hope in God and Jesus Christ. However, it is a bewildered church, lost so deeply in the culture that it no longer knows the way to Truth. In the end, for all the petitions and reports, God might have spoken clearer if the General Council had just flipped a coin.

There seem to be two churches warring in the bosom of a single institution. The conservative one, always there, has risen to prominence as a response to the change and anxiety of the age. Older, more rural, more centred in the traditions of the congregations, it is seeking security in familiar codes and customs, in simple laws and family standards and basic beliefs. Because faith is more important to it than reason or experience, it is not bothered greatly by its contradictions and inadequacies. While it ignores the Bible on issues from slavery to the eating of shellfish, it clings to the text when that is comforting; and while it is proud to be prophetic vis-à-vis the moral laxity of the times, it does not want its leadership to play prophet with it. If the rest of the world must be tormented by darkness and strife, these people want their Church to be a haven of certainty and peace.

To the liberals, that is understandable but ultimately ignorant, cowardly, and in vain. Because the Church is in and of this world, they argue, it cannot be excused from change and anxiety. Everything is evolving with creation, perhaps even God, so nothing can be fixed and absolute. In this vision there are no rigid laws, no easy answers, no presumptuous dogmas, and therefore little certainty and peace. Truth must be discerned by each mind and heart in the crucible of each situation. Instead of knowledge, there is a dangerous journey through the wilderness, fraught with temptations, delusions, and ignorance. Infinite ambiguity may be all there is.

"The Canadian religious story of the 1990s will be the break-up of the United Church," an evangelist leader once told me, and I imagined him licking his lips at the thought of the Community of Concern dropping into his paws.

221

Perhaps, but in the wake of what had been billed as the worst crisis since the Church's union, the exodus has not been so great. People generally treat their religious affiliation as a family heirloom to be passed down rather than a used car to be traded in. Passions die down, reactionaries die off, and the General Council's compromise virtually assured that self-declared homosexuals will be found more in the nightmares than in the pulpits of most congregations. As with the Roman Catholics, indifference will work to keep the United Church united, while secularism will likely do more damage than schism. Already less than a quarter of the four million Canadians who call themselves United Church on the census bother to be members; the membership has been falling about 1 per cent a year since 1965, when it reached above one million; and a 1988 poll estimated that half the members are over 60, with few young people coming in to replace them. In other words, if few are likely to be driven out, few are likely to be drawn in.

The United Church is the most Canadian of churches, and like Canada, its strengths may be the same as its weaknesses: diversity, tolerance, compromise, humility, practicality, and niceness. Truth gets written by committee, mystery gets lost in the negotiation, decency gets translated into dullness, and the spirit gets hamstrung by the bureaucracy. (Some jocularly call it the "Church of Christ, Sociologist.") "The United Church has an amazing ability to avoid doing the thing that will screw up the works," a Vancouver theologian explained to me. "It may not do the best thing, but it can be counted on not to do the worst."

That may have been a reassuring idea for him, but it did not strike me as much of a rock upon which to build a church.

TEN

___

Among Those Dark
Satanic Mills

To call what happened a "brawl" would be to exaggerate. These were Anglicans, after all, civilized and polite and unruffled. Indeed, if the heat and glare of Victoria's summer had been fitting for the United Church's arguments, the grey and damp fog that settled about a year later over St John's, Newfoundland, seemed well suited to the deliberations of the Anglican Church of Canada. At one point a bishop even asked for the air conditioning to be turned off, "since our debates have failed to raise the temperature of the room." Church officials had appeared proud that almost nothing of controversy was on the agenda of the triennial meeting of the General Synod, held at Memorial University for nine days in June 1989. So they were rather taken aback by the quarrel that broke out the evening before the closing ceremonies.

It was about a resolution to oppose NATO's low-flying tests over lands claimed by Indians and Inuit in Labrador. This relatively innocuous proposal had followed other resolutions supporting aboriginal rights; it had followed a sentimental educational event dedicated to the World Council of Churches' current reflections on "Justice, Peace, and the Integrity of Creation"; it had followed a strong and emotional speech by a young black woman from South Africa; and, in case anyone could miss the obvious implications of this background for a debate pitting native interests against NATO bombers, this poignant woman intervened to remind the delegates that justice, peace, and the integrity of creation begin at home. But, it appeared, it is one thing to support remote struggles in the Arctic and the Orange Free State or pray with moral rectitude for disarmament and jobs and clean air. It is another thing when those struggles and prayers impinge upon local economic interests and national defence policy.

"The prime concern behind this motion is opposition to NATO, not concern for the natives," said Bishop Martin Mate of the diocese of Eastern Newfoundland and Labrador. "The natives are being used. I deplore the politicking and manipulation around this issue here. The other side has not been allowed to be heard."

Up popped a chaplain to the Canadian Forces (which have their own bishop and synod delegates) to lecture about the military superiority of the Soviet Union and Canada's commitments to its European allies. Up jumped a young Indian from the Yukon to beg his Church for help for his people as the caretakers of the earth and animals. Up stood a Saskatchewan layman to appeal to the W.W. II veterans in the room not to jeopardize the lives of the brave young airman – who, like the lads during the Battle of Britain, were defending the freedom to speak so openly – by denying them the ability to train effectively "just so we won't be disturbed on our patios." Up rose an Inuit delegate to express his confusion as to why his Church would condemn the oppressors of everywhere else and yet sympathize with them here.

The answer to that was unpleasant but obvious: so many of the Church are the "oppressors" here, as corporation executives who gain profit from exploiting the resources of the North, as government officials who write the laws and judges who interpret them, as white and middle-class Anglo-Saxons who feel a claim to Canada for their own kind. As the heir of the church of the British establishment, the Anglican Church of Canada is still burdened by its social position. Its pews are still filled with the fine old families and the ambitious new ones; its periodicals are still fascinated by the doings of the Royal Family; its cathedrals are still draped with regimental colours; and if the Primate is an honorary chief of the Nishga, he is also an honorary chaplain of the RCMP detachment in Regina. (The introduction of the "sign of the peace" into the service caused a terrific brouhaha, which I never understood until one Sunday in Montreal's Christ Church Cathedral when I caught the expression of utter disgust on the face of a Westmount patrician as he realized he had to shake hands with a filthy drunk in the pew behind.) Furthermore, though the Church inherited a large number of native peoples from the missionaries and blacks from former British colonies, and has made some inroads among Asian and European immigrants and even among Quebec francophones, it remains as much an ethnic church as the Greek Orthodox or the Sikh.

Yet when the resolution came to a vote – two votes, actually, since the bishops always vote separately from the clergy and laity – the majority of the 300 delegates in all three orders chose to support the native peoples against NATO. The losers were good sports, of course, safe in the assumption that the federal government would not give a tinker's damn about the General Synod's advice, but that did not prevent their muttering in the corridors against the liberals in charge of Church House, the national headquarters in Toronto.

The Anglican leadership does not revel in going to the barricades as the United Church moderators appear to, nor does it share the Catholics' style of coming down on the flock like a ton of rocks. It lets the United Church take the heat on the left for being the avant-garde of social and political transformation; it lets the Roman Catholics take the heat on the right for being the rearguard of authority and tradition; and, when the heat dies down, it comes down the middle looking composed and conciliatory. Thus, while the Canadian Church is among the few of the twenty-eight autonomous churches belonging to the world-wide Anglican Communion that have allowed the ordination of women as priests, its approach since 1976 has been to avoid pushing anyone too fast or too hard, by leaving the unsympathetic diocesan bishops and the parishes with plenty of room to manoeuvre, so that women still make up barely 10 per cent of the clergy and no woman has yet been elected a bishop in Canada. And what could be a more Anglican solution to the explosive question of the liturgical revision than the introduction of a voluntary alternative? In 1985 *The Book of Alternative Services* (BAS) was presented as an option to the traditional *Book of Common Prayer* (usually referred to as the Prayer Book), produced in England in 1662 and last revised in Canada in 1959. Both or either could be used, according to the preferences of the parishes.

Even power and authority seem hard to pinpoint in the Anglican Church of Canada. On one hand, it has the Archbishop of Canterbury as head of the Church of England, the Lambeth Conference at which more than 500 bishops of the Anglican Communion meet every ten years, and bishops in charge of dioceses – *but* the Archbishop of Canterbury is more a symbol than an authority, the Lambeth Conference cannot legislate or compel its churches to do anything, and the Canadian bishops are elected locally by the clergy and lay representatives of the diocesan parishes. On the other hand, it has national and regional and diocesan synods, a bureaucracy headed by the Primate and run by the National Executive Council, and parish councils – *but* the synods are organized to allow the bishops a veto power, the bureaucracy includes a "House of Bishops" that behaves much like the Canadian Conference of Catholic Bishops as an influential national body, and more day-to-day clout rests with the diocesan bishop than with the congregations.

"Anglican authority is both episcopal and synodical, and there's constant balance and tension between them," said Michael Peers, the Church's Primate since his election in 1986. Born in 1934 in Vancouver and eligible to hold office until he is seventy, Peers is a dynamic, unpretentious, politically astute man who speaks French, German, and Russian, as well as English. "The Roman Catholics have their bishops. The United Church has its Council. We have both. Often that works against precipitate action – or any action at all – but in the end we get there. However, in a voluntary association like

226

our Church, if the national organization makes decisions not acceptable to the parishes and dioceses, then they just don't happen."

Nevertheless, the grumblings against Church House are loud. Generally they are voiced by three varieties of Anglicans: the Anglo-Catholics whose teachings and traditions have much in common with Rome's, the evangelicals whose Biblical emphasis and old-fashioned morality have much in common with the United Church Renewal Fellowship, and the charismatics whose emotional experience and born-again fervour have much in common with Pentecostal enthusiasm. All three have their own constituency within the Anglican Church; often they have sympathetic bishops, like-minded priests, pet parishes, and organizations such as the Anglican Renewal Ministries; and though they have a tremendous diversity of views, they frequently ally to bash the fourth major strand, Anglican liberalism, which accentuates reason, science and psychology, history, social and political action, and the immanence of God in the world and its cultures. For example, the Anglo-Catholic intellectuals of King's College in Halifax have been making common cause with the Bible-thumping Anglican evangelicals to oppose the BAS, which they see as a sly device to insinuate liberal doctrine and language into the Church gradually, even though Catholic tradition has never had much truck with Scriptural literalism and the evangelicals could never abide the "bells and smells" of the High Church.

"The debate over liturgical reform is really about the principle of change," Peers explained to me. "Those who feel that our society has moved away from its roots in Christian, family values see the BAS as an acceptance by their Church of this new society. They see it as the Church taking a positive view of some of that society's insights, which they cannot view positively. Where people are anxious about the future, change is seen as an abandonment of principle and of the things that are particularly Anglican."

In another form, therefore, it is the same debate that the United Church has been holding. If the focus is about a prayer

227

book rather than gay ordination, it is because the Prayer Book has been the touchstone of Anglican belief and Anglican identity. To tamper with its poetry and doctrines is equivalent to tampering with the Mass or Biblical interpretation. As science and history tore apart the Bible, as reason and education ripped into faith, liberals in all denominations turned their attention from some implausible Up There to some sensible Down Here. Since they believed Christ to be both God and man, the transcendent made flesh, if the road to understanding God was blocked by ignorance and doubt, why not take the road to understanding man? If God was lost to the point of having no definition, why not seek Truth in creation, on the planet, within culture, through politics and relationships and the human body? If Heaven and Hell may not exist beyond this earth, if good and bad may be relative and contextual, why not simply fall back on Christ's certain spirit of love, forgiveness, and justice? In other words, deeds began to replace creeds.

Doing good has always been an important part of the Christian path, but there have been periods of history – and of every individual's spiritual development – when service and charity have been set aside for worship, prayer, study, contemplation, otherworldly mysticism, and private absorption. With the transcendent out of fashion, however, the trend has been growing the other way for at least 100 years. As the historian Ramsay Cook argued in his award-winning book, *The Regenerators*, "the religious crisis provoked by Darwinian science and historical criticism of the Bible led religious people to attempt to salvage Christianity by transforming it into an essentially social religion. The orthodox Christian preoccupation with man's salvation was gradually replaced by a concern with social salvation; the traditional Christian emphasis on man's relationship with God shifted to a focus on man's relationship with man."

Drawing on Christ's inspiration as friend to the poor and oppressed, expanding upon Christian traditions of loving one's neighbour and hating wickedness, this movement picked up the liberal and socialist critiques of nineteenth-century industrialization and applied them to faith. From feeding the hungry and freeing the slaves, Christians of all denominations began to ask why hunger and slavery existed. This was particularly true at first among Protestants, because of Rome's aversion to liberal and socialist ideas and because of the Reformation's inherent *protest* against hierarchical authority. Though some Protestants grew very rich, very powerful, very established, and hence very conservative, the ethos of their religion was basically liberal; so their wealth and sway were always being confronted by guilt, responsibility, conscience, and more radical voices.

This was especially the case in Canada, where the early efforts by the Anglican Church to set itself up as the one official church failed. Most of the Anglicans who arrived in the wake of the conquering British army or on the run from the American Revolution brought with them an orderly view of the world, imperial pretensions, and the example of the style and position of the Church of England. They succeeded in getting special privileges for their Church as early as the Constitutional Act of 1791, but those privileges came under attack almost as quickly. The unique situation of the Roman Catholic Church in controlling the French-speaking population of Lower Canada demanded concessions that, in effect, made it a quasi-official religion. Then the immediate presence of Scottish Presbyterians challenged the sole establishment of the Anglicans, since the Church of Scotland was also a state institution and therefore felt entitled to any benefits the Church of England received in the Canadian colonies. Finally, the political and social ambitions of both the Anglicans and the Presbyterians were undermined by the size and impact of other denominations and sects.

Much of the politics of British North America in the first half of the nineteenth century had a religious character because the self-serving conservatives of the Family Compact tended to be Anglicans and the reform-minded liberals tended to be anti-establishmentarians. The latter included almost all the groups that had broken with the Church of England and the Church of Scotland, either in the homeland or in the American colonies, for political or theological reasons: the

Baptists, the Congregationalists, the "Free Kirk" Presbyterians, the Methodists, and so forth. It was as if those who were not going to be told what to think about God also were not going to be told what to think about the lieutenant governor. Religion and politics became deeply entwined over land, education, favours, public money, and the party system; quarrels over the grants known as "the clergy reserves" were a major cause of the rebellion of 1837; and the link between religious belief and social policy was strengthened.

"There would be no established church, but neither would the churches be private organizations catering merely to the spiritual needs of their individual members," John Webster Grant concluded in *A Profusion of Spires*, his book on religion in nineteenth-century Ontario. "Despite the existence of an unreconstructed minority of outright voluntarists, the major churches would parcel out among themselves the functions of an unofficial moral and educational establishment."

The prevailing tone was set by the Methodists, it seems, who had emerged out of the Church of England in the middle of the eighteenth century after an Anglican priest named John Wesley felt his heart "strangely warmed." This conversion experience led him out of the formal rites and intellectual rules of the established Church toward a system of populist meetings and itinerant preachers, designed to inspire the grace Wesley had found. The system was a blend of central direction and local spontaneity, of personal evangelism and social activism, of clergy and laity, and it proved extremely effective in the isolated conditions of the North American frontier. Moving among ordinary people and touching their emotions, the circuit riders taught about spiritual nourishment and learned about social problems. Though the tug between personal salvation and political radicalism was a constant tension, exacerbated by disputes within the British and American organizations, Canadian Methodism overcame a history of divisions by an acceptable balance. Its great war against liquor, for example, was both to gain Heaven and improve the lot of the working class. Even when the Methodists got rich and powerful – particularly in Toronto by the turn of the century, as exemplified by such dynasties as the Eatons, the Masseys, and the Flavelles – they were not allowed to forget their debt to society. Money and influence meant hard work, sober example, generous giving, civic duty, and pious devotion.

If the nineteenth century had conditioned all the churches to look for good to do, the twentieth century offered plenty of opportunities. In city slums and immigrant ghettos, amid the debris of war and depression, existed new miseries and enormous hardships. The causes shifted from individual sin to social evil; the focus moved from booze and Sunday observance to unions and just legislation; the solution went from Jesus Christ to political reformers. What emerged became known as the Social Gospel, particularly among liberal Methodists and Presbyterians, an interpretation of Christianity that put less emphasis on saving individual souls than constructing the Kingdom of God on earth. "What doth it profit, my brethren, though a man say he hath faith, and have not works?" they quoted from the epistle of James. "Can faith save him?"

That question pushed Methodist ministers such as J. S. Woodsworth and Stanley Knowles into the Co-operative Commonwealth Federation (CCF, the forerunner of the New Democratic Party), where they met the Presbyterian minister King Gordon, the Baptist minister T. C. Douglas, and F. R. Scott whose father was a well-known Anglican priest. It coloured the liberalism of William Lyon Mackenzie King and Lester Pearson, the one a devout Presbyterian and the other the son of a Methodist pastor; and it inspired the Marxism of Norman Bethune and Herbert Norman, sons of Presbyterian and Methodist manses respectively.

"It wasn't enough to talk about pie in the sky; it wasn't enough to talk to people about some afterlife with no misery and sorrow and tears," Tommy Douglas once said, explaining why he left the pulpit for politics in the 1930s, eventually becoming the first socialist premier of Saskatchewan and leader of the federal NDP. "We had to concern ourselves with the problems people had here and now."

To some degree the Social Gospel affected every church, from Anglican bishops influenced by William Temple and English Christian Socialism to the Roman Catholic co-operative movement at Antigonish in Nova Scotia inspired by social Catholicism. Its motives and rhetoric gave leftism in Canada a spiritual aura, a Christian heritage, a moral potency, and therefore a broader acceptability not granted to godless communism or selfish unionism. Even Christians who were not persuaded by its programme were influenced by its philosophy of egoless service, fairness, compassion, peace, hope, and good will. Unlike radicalism in the United States (at least until the Southern Baptist dynamic of the civil-rights movement), Canadian social democracy inherited the mantle of God's work, of Christ's message, and many of its marching songs were familiar and stirring hymns:

> I will not cease from mental fight,
> Nor shall my sword sleep in my hand
> Till we have built Jerusalem
> In England's green and pleasant land.

It was a disturbing philosophy. It asked for more sacrifice and saintliness than most devout tycoons, politicians, and bourgeois citizens could provide. Shortly before his death in 1989, King Gordon told me of the ire he and other social democrats had aroused among prominent ministers and laity of Montreal's Presbyterian community in the early 1930s. The result was his dismissal from teaching Christian ethics at the United Theological College, though Gordon went on to work for the Fellowship for a Christian Social Order, an association formed in 1934, dedicated "to the belief that the capitalist economic system is fundamentally at variance with Christian principles," and closely allied to the League for Social Reconstruction and the CCF.

At least since the fourth century, when Constantine converted to Christianity and Augustine laid the doctrinal and organizational bases for it to become a state religion, there has been tension between the revolutionary and oppressed faith of Jesus Christ and the evolution of his churches as stabilizing and persecuting institutions in partnership with political and financial power. On the one hand, there is no doubt that the faith's alliance with power – especially imperial power, from Rome to the United States of America – produced the authority and resources to take Christ's teachings to every corner of the globe down through the centuries. If they are the Truth, if they bring wisdom and peace to humanity, then the compromises and preoccupations with Caesar's things have been worthy. On the other hand, if those cultural and political purposes have corrupted the faith to the point where it is not the Truth any longer, then they are hateful.

"The contrast is always between the *institutional* concept of the church, as priest or building, and the *prophetic* concept of the church, as critic or community," King Gordon said. "That has big implications. If a church identifies itself as an institution, then the support of that institution becomes all important. Inevitably such a church becomes the religious expression of the social and political establishment, because its welfare is dependent upon the establishment, and its ethics become the ethics of the business community. It will say, for example, that its clergy should leave economics to the economists, as if there is no moral dimension to economics."

If the Depression bestowed unusual authority on the prophetic element, the Second World War gave it back to the institutional element. Woodsworth's pacifism cost him his leadership of the CCF, for instance, and God was clearly on the side of freedom and democracy. The churches were full of prayers for the boys overseas, the priests and ministers were busy blessing tanks and bombers, and unemployment had vanished with the munitions factories and conscripted battalions. "Onward, Christian Soldiers" was the new marching hymn.

Nor did the survivors come home desiring socialist sermons. They wanted peace, they wanted prosperity, they wanted normality. Moving into modern bungalows in the new suburbs, pursuing the Canadian version of the American Dream, Mom and Pop wanted a local church, the standard tunes, an uplifting message, and traditional values for their kids as a restful prelude to Sunday lunch. The churches went on a building spree, the collection plates overflowed, attendance may never have been greater, and charity took care of conscience at home and in the Third World. Faith was held to be a private matter again, with little public dimension – except, of course, to affirm the virtues of the status quo, rail against communism and heathenism, and officiate at social events.

"Institutional Christianity, in short, has become a comfortable creed," wrote Pierre Berton in his provocative and best-selling book, *The Comfortable Pew*, about Canada's Protestant churches in the early 1960s, "a useful tool for Peace of Mind and Positive Thinking, a kind of sugar-coated pill that soothes those who fear to face the traditional Christian concerns of evil, suffering, and death – concerns, be it said, that have been miraculously minimized and glossed over by the religious establishment."

Because it was a cardboard castle, built on nostalgia and custom rather than intellect and conviction, it could not withstand the storms of the 1960s. Vatican II and then political liberation movements provoked self-criticism in every church; the civil-rights movement and the peace movement reawakened the responsibility of Christianity to be in the vanguard of justice and love; the material success of science and humanism reinforced scepticism about mystics and gods; and the kids who had been dragged off to Sunday school to learn wholesome values were on the road to Woodstock and India. Those left behind in the buildings and organizations, faced with dwindling flocks and mounting debts and social irrelevance, had to review both their faith and how to communicate it. Some of them brought in guitars and dancers to enliven their ceremonies. Some of them took their message out to the streets and the picnic grounds. Some of them became "Jesus freaks" and competed with the Krishna acolytes for the minds of airport travellers. But many of them, affected by the radicalism of the period, looked for meaning and expression in secular activism again.

The Social Gospel had not died altogether. It lived in the post-war agenda of the World Council of Churches, founded in 1949 amid the physical and spiritual rubble of Europe. It lived in the ban-the-bomb demonstrations of the Student Christian Movement. It lived in the pulpits of Alabama. By 1970, however, it had returned to the forefront, stronger and more revolutionary than ever, particularly when Catholic liberation theology pushed the old Protestant reformism toward Marxist analysis. It marched against the war in Vietnam, it boycotted Californian grapes, it rallied against apartheid in South Africa, it supported women's liberation, it agitated against Third World hunger and colonialism. Radicals and liberals, such as Robert McClure in the United Church and Edward Scott with the Anglicans, moved into many senior positions; social activism captured the imaginations of the bureaucracies and theological schools, which elevated and trained more of their own kind; and, most significantly, churches began to ally across denominations on political and social issues. Archbishop Peers, for example, remembered being particularly affected by the words of a Jesuit from Brazil in the early 1970s: "It is not that you are rich and we are poor. It is that you are rich *because* we are poor." (As one Jesuit remarked at the time, "I seem to be the only one around who doesn't think the purpose of our order is to guarantee the victory of Marxism in South America.")

Ecumenism and church unity were two of the hottest topics of the 1960s. Though union usually did not get past the discussion stage, whether between the Roman Catholics and the Anglicans or the Anglicans and the United Church, it did cause Christian leaders to meet more systematically and to talk more about their agreements than their differences. At the same time, their paths kept crossing on the same side of the barricades. As believers in Christ among so many nonbelievers, concerned with identical questions about the role of their institutions and the nature of their faith, they naturally discovered a host of mutual sympathies and obvious reasons to pool their efforts on a continuing or ad hoc basis. "It's particularly characteristic of the Canadian churches that we do things, by and large, ecumenically," said Peers.

Thus, denominational agencies such as the Canadian Catholic Organization for Development and Peace, Canadian Lutheran World Relief, and the Mennonite Central Committee were supplemented by a score of inter-denominational bodies such as the Inter-church Committee for Refugees, the Church Council on Justice and Corrections, GATT-fly, and the Task Force on the Churches and Corporate Responsibility; and there are a score of other groups in which churches have joined with non-religious associations for causes such as peace (Project Ploughshares), native rights (Project North), and Third World development (Canadian Council for International Cooperation).

In recent years, for example, twelve church leaders (including Michael Peers) signed a letter to the Prime Minister denouncing Ottawa's defence proposals as "a dangerous and provocative maritime strategy that would increase the likelihood of nuclear war," while the social-affairs committees of six major churches distributed a pamphlet through the Ecumenical Forum on Economic Justice raising serious questions for Canadian Christians about free trade with the United States. Then, at yet another level, the Canadian Catholic bishops and the United Church worked with representatives of unions, farmers, women, and the poor to produce a booklet of social and economic policy directions entitled *A Time to Stand Together, A Time for Social Solidarity*.

"There is a pressing need today to develop alternative economic and social policies based on social solidarity rather than market-oriented priorities," it said. "This means converting to a people-oriented economy and society that puts top priority on serving people's basic needs, enhancing the value and dignity of human work, achieving a more equitable distribution of wealth and power among peoples and regions, and creating a more vital and participatory democracy."

This statement, issued in the fall of 1987, may not have been the official position of either church, but it did describe the general attitude of their Canadian leadership. While most

Canadians had come to expect nothing less from the United Church, they were still adjusting to the politics of the Roman Catholics. Because Rome and the bishops held to the traditional line on so many social issues, from premarital sex to women's rights, people assumed they were also holding to the conservative posture toward state and economic issues. In fact, of course, they had come a very long way from the *Syllabus of Errors* of 1864. Developing upon the "social Catholicism" of *Rerum novarum* (1891), *Quadragesimo anno* (1931), and subsequent papal statements, the Second Vatican Council affirmed the worldly duties of the Church in the 1965 decree usually known as *Gaudium et spes*, which began: "The joys and the hopes, the griefs and the anxieties of the men and women of our age, especially those who are poor or in any way afflicted, these too are the joys and the hopes, the griefs and the anxieties of the followers of Christ."

That document is considered the springboard from which later popes launched their attacks on inequitable world trade, technocratic capitalism, and nuclear arms. It lent legitimacy to the Latin American bishops who edged closer to liberation theology's "preferential option for the poor" and recognition of the justice of class struggle at Medellin, Colombia, in 1968 and at Puebla, Mexico, in 1979. It marked Pope John Paul II's 1981 encyclical *On Human Work*, which celebrated the ninetieth anniversary of *Rerum novarum* by declaring again the priority of labour over capital, the primacy of man over things, and the subordination of the right to private property to the right to common use. Just a month after the booklet on social solidarity created its fuss in Canada, the Pope released his more controversial *Encyclical on Social Concerns*, in which he surveyed the human condition from Third World debt to arms production and judged the liberal capitalism of the West as "sinful" as the Marxist collectivism of the East for their tendencies toward imperialism and war.

Individually and collectively Canadian bishops have been bringing this message home since the 1960s. A collection of their social teachings from 1945 to 1986 shows their progression from moral platitudes each Labour Day to global concerns about poverty and human rights, hard-edged analyses of wealth and power, macro-economic critiques, and unabashed partiality toward Third World liberation, native peoples, nuclear disarmament, the environment, workers and farmers and fishermen, and the unemployed.

"Many people agree that there is something wrong with the present social and economic order," they stated in 1976. "It fails to meet the human needs of the majority of people. The present economic order results in the very uneven distribution of wealth and the control of resources by a small minority." Christians had to get out of the comfortable pew. "The challenge of living the Gospel of justice in this way is a disturbing experience for all of us. Some who have committed themselves to this new way of life have been misunderstood and criticized, particularly by the more affluent and powerful sectors of their communities. But the message of Christ crucified is not a comforting message."

To judge by the press and the fury, however, the new message was not really heard until December 1982, when the bishops' social-affairs commission under Remi De Roo produced its *Ethical Reflections on the Economic Crisis*. The storm over its radical rhetoric and interventionist solutions demonstrated their novelty to much of the public, and much of the debate had less to do with unemployment or inflation than with the appropriateness of a Church statement on economics or the intrusion of the bishops into politics. The idea that economics could be separated from ethics proved to the bishops just how unethical liberal capitalism had become.

"As bishops, we do not claim to be technical experts in economic matters," they said in their defence. "Our primary role is to be moral teachers in society. In this capacity, we attempt to view economic and social realities primarily from the perspective of the Gospel message of Jesus Christ and his concern for the poor, the marginalized, and the oppressed."

It was the same defence used by the primates of the Anglican Church and the moderators of the Presbyterian Church when the general public eventually realized how radical their politics had become, despite the image of their churches as staid and conservative institutions. In 1973, for example, their leaders joined those of the United Church, the Roman Catholics, and the Lutherans in an appeal about trade and aid to the Third World (*Development Demands Justice*), and in 1976 the same alliance confronted the Prime Minister on a wide range of social problems involving the distribution of wealth and power at home and abroad (*Justice Demands Action*). "We stand in the biblical tradition of the prophets," all of them proclaimed, "where to know God is to seek justice for the poor and the oppressed."

I got the clear impression from many church leaders and thinkers that they were actually enjoying their new role as political gadflies and social critics. Not only are they often political animals by nature, they seemed to find personal relief in biting the hands that had been feeding them at the banquets they had had to bless. Though they still live well, at least their words can undercut the unsettling contradiction between their bourgeois habits and Christ's example of humbleness and crucifixion; and, in a time of doubt and ambiguity, what pleasure there is to have conviction and clarity again! God may be a woman and Jesus may never have turned the water into wine, but it no longer matters really, for they *know* that apartheid and nuclear holocaust are bad, that housing and food are good, and that even industrial strategies are easier to conceive than the Holy Trinity. Their faith could be firmer, their actions could be purer, their sermons could be full of righteousness, and instead of worrying about dwindling numbers, they would lead a remnant of true believers.

"A church in diaspora, in the sense of going out and getting involved in the suffering of the world, will always be a minority," said Douglas Hall, a United Church theologian at McGill University. "The few exist for the sake of the many, as the yeast or the salt or the light of their society. They don't want the old conditions of Christendom, producing only stained-glass versions of the values entertained by everyone. If you live in the king's house, you don't have vigilance for the king's poorest subjects or for the victims of his empire. What is the price of that influence, and isn't the influence of the minority likely to be more prophetic and creative?"

Weighing the benefits of majority against the virtues of minority is fast becoming a useless exercise anyway, as Archbishop Ambrozic pointed out, because the days of Western Christendom have passed and are never likely to return with the same degree of power and uniformity. Jesus has become just another voice crying to be heard in the wilderness of television. But, as the leadership gets more and more carried away by the idea of being prophet to society, it seems to get more and more carried away from the spiritual needs of its own diminishing band of faithful – which helps explain why the evangelical movement is on the rise in the Anglican Church and among Protestants generally. A common complaint in all the major churches is that the leaders have taken off on their own agendas, pushing through radical reforms, promoting extremist causes on behalf of everyone, and hammering the congregations over the head Sunday after Sunday with one-sided rants about El Salvador and South Africa.

"We are aware that some among our church membership will resist some of the changes we have advocated," the church leaders admitted to the Prime Minister in 1976, "but we are prepared to inform them continually of the grounds for these positions."

For many members, to be informed continually is to be aggravated continually. Nor do they place much hope in getting the tune changed through their organizations. In practice the liberals and radicals appear to control the process and the votes (or, in the case of the Roman Catholics, the management of the Canadian Conference of Catholic Bishops), and it is a rare day that any conservative resolution can get through without abuse, derision, and defeat. When not preoccupied with homosexual ordination or the authority of the Bible, for instance, the United Church's 1988 General Council was asked to deal with free trade, uranium mining, the ozone layer, AIDS, breast-milk substitutes, pornography, racism, refugees, abortion, the postal service, Korea, the Philippines, the Middle East, nuclear submarines, South Africa, genetic engineering, and the destabilization of Mozambique – and one had only to know the topic in order to guess correctly which view the commissioners would support, often unanimously without a debate.

That is not to say there is no debate. That famous Catholic convert, Conrad Black, quickly took up the cudgels on behalf of capitalism by denouncing his bishops as "trendy, biased, misleading, and reckless" on social and economic issues. Conservative Anglicans, Presbyterians, Lutherans, and United Church members have argued that their ministers should pontificate on religious matters, not political questions, or at least should recognize that Christianity does not necessitate support for socialist policies and the African National Congress. The Fraser Institute, the right-wing Vancouver think-tank, even founded the Centre for the Study of Economics and Religion to combat the leftist assumptions rampant in the major denominations.

For those concerned with the Truth rather than with the institutions, social activism carries risks far greater than any numerical or political effect. To get to God by seeking justice means to confront the Devil directly in his own playground, the secular world of power and illusion. Instead of making the mundane more sacred, the forays into politics and economics may only make the sacred more mundane. The transcendental side of Truth gets lost in the incarnate aspect; magic and miracle get lost in reason and science; prayer and ritual get lost in petitions and rallies; love and inclusiveness get lost in animosity and exclusion. God created Conrad Black, after all, but my encounters with him showed me the extent to which the ego and greed of some entrepreneurs produce a particular sort of human misery. To set up him and his kind as the enemy may be to miss the real target, for even if they are conquered, the greater sufferings of death and ignorance will remain.

In Ramsay Cook's judgement, Christianity's effort to regenerate itself by shifting to social salvation and human relationships backfired. "By urging Christians to emphasize social utility and to downplay or ignore doctrine, these advocates of the social gospel were in fact making the church irrelevant in a

241

world where other institutions were better equipped to perform the socially useful roles once fulfilled by the church." In other words, by moving from theology to sociology, by striving to build God's kingdom on earth rather than to find God in Heaven, the churches ironically contributed to the secularization of Canada and their own marginalization.

It is a well-argued thesis. Certainly many of the clergy who moved into politics did so because their faith in God had been shaken as badly as their faith in their conservative churches. Certainly the rough and tumble of political struggle drew attention from the mystic to the material, spent reflection's time on revolution, and pulled the activists from their knees to the smoke-filled rooms.

"I would never want to be heard saying that social action isn't where it's at – there are far too few active in the world, far too many yuppies, far too many people in churches being led into middle-class existence – but I worry about a community of faith that stops exploring the *why*," Douglas Hall said. "Christianity has become an issue-oriented faith, but why can't we combine this with a depth of insight and the search for wisdom? The churches at their best have always tried to get to the bottom of the witches' brew. If they don't think, then what have they got to bring to the analysis as well as the cure?"

It may be too simple to dismiss the liberation theologists, the United Church, or the Anglicans as the Marxists, the NDP, or the Liberal Party at prayer respectively. At their gatherings I have always been impressed by the fact, more astounding in this era, that these politically conscious individuals of all ages and regions had not abandoned their religion completely for party conventions or partisan committees. It is a constant puzzle whether their faith had brought them to radicalism or whether their radicalism had made them redirect their faith, but the combination makes a difference. It is the difference between "What's in it for me? and "What does God expect of me?"

That spiritual basis in prayer and Scripture still gives the churches a fervour and authority unavailable to self-interested allies such as political parties or unions. Just as Mahatma Gandhi and Martin Luther King were able to mobilize the masses by their spiritual authority, so Archbishop Desmond Tutu in South Africa and Catholic prelates from Poland to El Salvador to the Philippines have emerged as central figures in struggles for political and social justice. The American Catholic bishops were among the few loud voices heard in opposition to Ronald Reagan's military strategy, and the Canadian church leaders were among the few credible critics to speak up for compassionate policies in a time of conservative economics, deregulation, consumerism, and corporate domination.

"There is a certain risk in becoming deeply involved in secular affairs, but there's also a risk in engaging in piety, which can make you hardhearted and unmoved by suffering," Gregory Baum said. "People complain about the Roman Catholic Church becoming political only when it criticizes the society. When it blesses the existing order – 'God Save the Queen' – no one notices that that too is political. Religion always has a political role, either to stabilize the existing order or to raise critical questions. God's judgement is not only 'How many times do you masturbate?' but also 'How many unemployed are there?'"

As usual, however, God seems to be asking a question to which He provides no clear solution. If He has ordained Jesse Jackson and Desmond Tutu to speak for the poor and oppressed, He apparently has also ordained Pat Robertson and the Dutch Reformed Church to speak for the mighty and established. If His will was misinterpreted when the bishops and priests of French Canada tried to protect their people against materialism and greed by sending them to the bush instead of the boardrooms at the start of the twentieth century, why are the bishops and priests correct in pushing the same line at the end of it? And what is the essential difference between a church agitating to ban NATO flights – to defend the weak, to exalt the spiritual – and a church agitating to ban liquor or books or native tongues for the same holy reasons? Moreover, because absolutes are rarely practical in a relative world, because moral and religious conviction are rarely compatible with a pluralist society, it is uncertain whether a theocracy of the left would be any more agreeable to tolerance and liberty than the terrible theocracies of the right. As the histories of Rome, Geneva, Jerusalem, and Teheran have shown, nothing corrupts the seekers and guardians of Truth faster than earthly power. "Again, the Devil taketh him up into an exceedingly high mountain," Matthew wrote of Christ's ultimate temptation in the wilderness, "and shewed him all the kingdoms of the world, and the glory of them; and saith unto him, 'All these things will I give thee, if thou wilt fall down and worship me.'"

"We aren't into theocracy," Michael Peers protested. "We're into the validity of our voice on issues that have moral and ethical implications – and few don't – particularly those issues such as race, environment, and peace in which groups are having a hard time making themselves heard. Not that the government takes much notice of what we say or think. We're not instant opinion-shapers like the media, but we can cause things to move (against capital punishment or investment in South Africa, for example) when we find allies in the society. And we have a great advantage in terms of long-term attitudes: unlike government and the marketplace, we're in for the long haul. But if the liberal tradition ever gets uprooted from some sense of reality and the awesomeness of God, it will become just chatter. Those three elements have to live together as part of the same thing."

ELEVEN

Saint-Soldiers

However furious Anglicans may be with Anglicans about politics, their disagreements rarely result in an iron bar to the
head or a gift-wrapped parcel of shit in the mail. "Be careful," I
was warned about Sikh factionalism. "It's a jungle of complexity."

The warning did not come from someone who had bought
the widespread image of the Sikhs as terrorists and fanatics. It
came from a very sympathetic observer who was merely cau-
tioning me about what I already knew: many Sikhs have
become particularly sensitive to misrepresentations because
of the negative image, while true representations have become
harder to obtain because of the contradictory information in
India and Canada alike. Most Sikhs are concerned about the
fate of their people in the land of their origin; few Sikhs are
immune to the reality of racism in the country of their dispersion. Little seems certain beyond that – including whether to
pronounce them "seeks" or "sicks" – because it is so difficult
to find much upon which all Sikhs agree.

I had arrived among the Sikhs of Vancouver with what I
hoped was a fair attitude. I assumed they were human rather
than perfect, diverse rather than uniform, and neither as bad
as their press nor as good as their Guru. To their credit I could

recall the generous hospitality they provided at their temples when I was a young man hitchhiking through East Africa; I could recall the magical hours I spent sitting in the Golden Temple in Amritsar, India, listening to the chanting of the Granth Sahib; and, because of the extraordinary beauty of their songs, I had two Sikh musicians play through my wedding. On the debit side, though I am cognizant of the violence and human-rights violations perpetrated by the government of India upon Sikhs in recent years, I still resist the call for an independent Sikh state, Khalistan, for most of the reasons I resist the call for Quebec independence and worry about the future of democracy in Israel. The division of the world into states based on one ethnicity – or, far worse, one religion – can only be a backward step for peace, tolerance, and democratic freedoms. More troublesome than the ends are the means. Though pro-Khalistan violence in Canada or the Punjab is usually the work of a few extremists and hotheads (or perhaps Indian agents in some cases), I found too many Sikhs willing to excuse it, ignore it, or deny it.

I had gone into the Sikh community because I wanted to get another perspective on religion and politics. I might have looked into the Muslim or Hindu communities. The former is the fastest-growing religion in the world, with enormous wealth and political sway in the Middle East and Asia and vigorous appeal from Africa to the black ghettos of the United States; the latter is considered the oldest and most complex religion in the world, with hundreds of millions of followers from India to Trinidad and a fascinating array of beliefs and practices. In Canadian terms, however, neither has had the impact – for better or for worse – of the Sikhs, though they are among the world's smallest and youngest faiths. While their global population is a mere fifteen million, they make up, for historical reasons, one of the largest minority groups in Canada – over 120,000 at the best guess – particularly in British Columbia. They constitute about 18 per cent of Williams Lake, for example. Also Vancouver has a special role in world Sikhism, not unlike the role Montreal has had in world Jewry, and that will only increase as the Vancouver region becomes more and more an "Asian city." Finally, their beards, their turbans, and their politics have called more attention toward the Sikhs than most other immigrants either claim or wish to possess.

Sikhism began theologically as well as geographically between the great traditions of Hinduism and Islam. It originated (where Muslim Pakistan and Hindu India now border) at the end of the fifteenth century, when a thirty-year-old man who had been born a Hindu and raised among Muslims had a transforming spiritual experience. He vanished for three days, to the court of God apparently, and his first words after his return were, "There is neither Hindu nor Muslim, so whose path shall I follow? I shall follow God's path. God is neither Hindu nor Muslim and the path which I follow is God's."

Guru Nanak had had a glimpse of the Truth, "the One without a second," and it left him unimpressed with the divisions of organized religion, rituals and prayers that had lost their meaning, and such social consequences as the caste system and the degradation of women. He taught a mystical, pietist message in order to get back to the Truth behind the bureaucratic structures and empty rites by pure and simple methods, including meditation, devotional hymns, service to others, and basic morality. Whether or not he set out to articulate the common ground beneath Islam and Hinduism, he drew on ideas, practices, and forms from both of them; and whether or not he meant to establish a new religion, he promoted it by attracting disciples ("sikhs" in Punjabi), asserting the authority of the guru as teacher, and appointing a successor.

There were nine successors between Guru Nanak's death in 1539 and Guru Gobind Singh's in 1708, and they seemed to have undergone the ups and downs of the early popes as they moved to consolidate the mystical vision of a holy man into a social organization with political implications. Some were inspirational, some were temporal, some were crucial, some were marginal – which may be explained by the fact that, from the fourth on, they were chosen as much for their heredity as for their piety. Taken together, they created Sikhism by instituting management, building temples, making deals with the Mogul emperors, getting the teachings down in writing, and developing the devotions.

Needless to say, a lot changed within two hundred years, and the heart of many controversies centres on what Guru Nanak would have thought of the result. Would he have dismissed it as another empty form that contradicted the Truth he had seen or would he have embraced it as the faithful continuation of his teachings? (In this respect Guru Nanak is in the same boat as Jesus Christ, the Buddha, and Lao Tzu.) The main controversy concerns the shift – in tone, at least – from pacifism to militancy. If Guru Nanak was not an absolute pacifist, he certainly advocated the path of love, compassion, and forgiveness. Though he denounced injustice, he was more concerned with spirituality than politics. "Sweetness and humility are the essence of all virtues," he said. But, it is argued, he lived in a period of relative peace and tolerance, so he never had to address directly the proper response to aggression and persecution. That was the unfortunate duty of later gurus, who faced increasing campaigns by the emperors to convert everyone to Islam. The fifth guru, Arjan, was executed by Emperor Jehangir, as a result of which his son, Guru Hargobind, equipped himself with an army and two swords, which represented temporal and spiritual power. The ninth guru, Tegh Bahadur ("brave sword"), was beheaded by Emperor Aurangzeb for refusing to become a Muslim, as a result of which his son, Guru Gobind Singh, uttered the immortal lesson, "When all efforts to restore peace prove useless and no words avail, lawful is the flash of steel, it is right to draw the sword."

He did more than talk. In 1699, two hundred years after Guru Nanak's transcendental experience, the tenth guru met with his followers. "He reminded them of the perilous time in which they were living and spoke of a plan to replace their weakness by strength and unity," Owen Cole and Piara Singh Sambhi wrote in their very useful book on the Sikhs. "It would demand supreme loyalty to the Guru. He then asked for men to come forward who would give their heads to him. He made the request in a spectacular manner with drawn sword. No one responded for some time, save with a hushed and fearful silence. At last one Sikh came forward and was led into the Guru's tent. The Guru reappeared alone, with a blood-stained sword. Four more men followed, though in the time it took the volunteers to come forward many other Sikhs departed from Anandpur." That certainly has the ring of truth, but those who left missed the best part: a moment later the Guru led all five out, alive and well. "Some Sikhs say that he had raised them to life, others that the blood was that of a goat, but all agree on their fearless devotion to the Guru and his ideals."

These "beloved five" became the first members of the Khalsa, "the pure ones." They were initiated, given a code of discipline, and required to wear five symbols (unshorn hair, comb, steel bracelet, short breeches, and sword). They also took to wearing a turban and changing their names to Singh ("lion") or – in the case of women who joined – Kaur ("princess"). The baptism, the vows, and the distinctiveness of the Khalsa were intended to set them apart from Hindus and Muslims, reinforce their devotion to the guru's teachings, and make them instruments "of spreading the faith, saving the saints, and extirpating all tyrants," as Guru Gobind Singh himself put it.

Given fresh direction as a defence force against oppression, and assisted in that direction by the influx of landowning Jats with their own quarrels with the Moguls, Sikhism went to war in the eighteenth century. By the end of it a Sikh named Ranjit Singh had carved out an independent kingdom in the Punjab, though he did not make Sikhism its official religion. Fifty years later, in 1849, the kingdom fell to the British and was annexed into their Indian empire. But many Sikhs quickly became invaluable allies to the British, particularly around the time of the Mutiny of 1857, and their support elevated them into important positions of trust in government and the military. Some argue that it was the British who turned the Sikhs into a martial community, more than the tenth guru, though the British may only have rewarded elements that history had woven into the faith. Either way the effect was evident in the formidable bearing of Sikh men, the glorious history of Sikh regiments, and the fact that about 2 per cent of the Indian population made up about 20 per cent of Britain's Indian armed forces.

The secular achievements of the nineteenth century were offset by religious problems. As today, when less than a third of the world's Sikhs are thought to be baptized, not all the followers of the gurus took on the style and disciplines of the Khalsa. Once the persecution lifted, many drifted back toward the customs and beliefs of their Hindu cousins; some were even tempted toward Christianity by the British missionaries. There was at the top a decentralization of authority, conditioned by the second great reform of Guru Gobind Singh. As he lay dying from an assassin's knife in 1708, he overrode the conflicts of succession by appointing no man or woman as guru. Instead, he designated a book, the Adi Granth ("First Book") or commonly revered as the Guru Granth Sahib, the collection of sacred poetry by the gurus and a few Hindu and Muslim mystics. While a book can radiate as much wisdom and receive as much devotion as a living master, it cannot as easily settle disputes of interpretation, regulate the legitimate adaptations to change, or instil the awe and fear of human touch.

Sikhism seems to have suffered the same kind of diffusion that Bible-centred Protestants and Torah-true Jews were experiencing around the same time; and, as with Protestantism and Judaism, there arose a traditionalist reaction. In 1873 the Singh Sabha movement developed in Amritsar, where the Golden Temple sits as the holiest shrine of the Guru Granth Sahib, in order to bring Sikhs back to the original teachings and the Khalsa. Its educational and political work resulted by 1920 in a central temple management committee to order Hindu influences out of the gurdwaras in India, as well as a volunteer army (Akali Dal) to carry out the orders. In time this committee became the leading authority over Sikh congregations and the Akali Dal became a Punjabi political party.

Knowing this history, I was not startled to hear Vancouver Sikhs say over and over again that there is no difference between religion and politics; nor, as a veteran of United Church sermons about South Africa and Jewish prayers for Israel, was I shocked to hear long harangues about Khalistan when the music stopped in the Ross Street temple. Designed by Arthur Erickson as a rather formidable chunk of white marble topped by a square tower and abstract crown, it was built in 1970 by the Khalsa Diwan Society to replace the West 2nd Avenue gurdwara that had been founded in 1908. It claims to be the largest Sikh temple in North America, with some 20,000 members, and it is certainly one of the richest and most prestigious in the world. Its huge square and spartan hall, lit by skylights and warmed by the red carpet on which everyone sits, can hold 2,000 people – men on one side, women on the other – and its basement is an active warren of offices, library, kitchens, and dining space for 400 at a time.

It reminded me of some of the Orthodox synagogues I have visited: modern and expensive but with traditional and garish bits, the separation of sexes, the constant comings and goings, the family atmosphere, the buzz of chatter, the fuss of priests, and front and centre under an extravagant and protected sanctuary the holy book they worship. The music was not the same, the languages were different, but they both evoked deep beauty and feeling, remote kingdoms and times. And in the sermons of gurdwara and synagogue I heard similar themes: accounts of oppression and genocide, the distant land of the people under siege, discrimination in the place of their exile, and a dislike of Joe Clark.

Sikhs themselves make the parallel, though the Jews have become accepted as a kind of third national religion along with the Roman Catholics and the Protestants. The arrival of large numbers of Hindus, Muslims, Sikhs, Buddhists, Jains, Taoists, Zoroastrians, and Rastafarians has changed the dynamic since the days when a Jew was the most exotic person in town. By all estimates it is only a matter of time before Canada has more Muslims than Jews and more Hindus than

Presbyterians. Some Sikhs speak with rhetorical looseness about *their* Diaspora and *their* Holocaust, though their history in India cannot match the history of the Jews in the world. More to the point, many Canadian Sikhs use the Jews as a model for their aspirations: to be fully accepted within their new society through education and hard work, with power and influence in government and finance and the media, but without loss and compromise of their religious identity, family heritage, and links to their ancient home. In this, they might have an easier time than the Jews had, in part because of those Jews who battled against prejudice and racism, broke the hegemony of the Christians in every major institution in Canada, advanced the cause of multiculturalism and tolerance in public prayers and faith symbols, and proved that loyalty to the here and now did not require betrayal of the then and there.

All minority faiths in Canada are enjoying the fruits of world ecumenism, Canadian multicultural policies, and the spiritual eclecticism of the age. Frankly, however, much of the tolerance strikes me as apathy and ignorance. Intolerance was often the result when religion mattered. Now that God does not really matter for most Canadians, all religions can be respected – or dismissed – equally. The movement to open stores on Sundays or remove prayers from the classrooms rarely comes from a new sensitivity toward the growing presence of citizens who honour other holy days or deities; it usually comes from indifferent Christians who want to consume seven days a week or spare their children an indoctrination into fear and guilt. If the discrimination against Jews had its origins in the killing of Christ, the discrimination against Sikhs has its origins in their colour. As evidence I could cite the slogans I saw painted on a fence in a Sikh neighbourhood in Burnaby: "Go away, you fucking Hindus forever and ever" and (more concisely) "Kill Hindus." Clearly the authors were not preoccupied by the manifold theological points that distinguish Sikhs from Hindus – unless, of course, the authors themselves were Sikhs.

Neither the Sikhs nor the prejudice against them are new to British Columbia. They arrived together in the early years of this century. Though there are reports of Sikhs in Field and Golden twenty-five years before, the first significant numbers came between 1904 and 1908, when some 6,000 men seized the short opportunity before the barriers to immigration were raised as suddenly as they had been lowered. Between a hostile reception and the economic hardship many opted to go on to California or return to the Punjab, so that only 1,000 remained by 1921. Only three of them were women. As small and isolated groups, the Sikh men worked in sawmills or on farms, travelled back and forth to India every few years to marry or see their families, sent money home or saved it to bring out the sons to earn more, worked hard and kept to themselves. As they prospered and as the regulations changed, they began to come back with their wives and small children. It was not until 1960, however, that their population again reached the mark it had had briefly more than fifty years earlier.

Wherever these "pioneer" Sikhs landed, they soon formed a religious society and built a gurdwara. The Khalsa Diwan Society, founded in Vancouver in 1906, built more than the precursor to the Ross Street temple: it built branches in Abbotsford, Victoria, Port Alberni, and five other towns. Though all but one of British Columbia's thirty-two gurdwaras function as autonomous congregations now, with their boards elected by their members, the history and wealth of the K.D.S. and the Ross Street gurdwara effectively make them *primus inter pares*. Control of them brings community-wide clout, prestige, assets over $10 million, and a budget above $650,000 a year.

At least until the construction of the Ross Street temple, control of the K.D.S. was indisputably in the hands of the more successful pioneer families. Established as businessmen, potent as go-betweens to the majority culture, serving as godfathers to numerous kin and recent arrivals, they oversaw the cosy world of West Coast Sikhs. By most accounts these men were not a very devout lot. Not only were most of them willing to shave their beards and shed their turbans if that helped them get ahead, they seemed delighted to leave the prayers and the rituals to their women. Many of them tended to look upon the temples as social centres more than places of worship, an excuse to get together for a couple of hours once a week, a hall for a wedding or a party, a diversion for the lonely wives and a playground for the assimilated kids, a sop to civic duty and good conscience – and if it got too tedious or archaic, they could always slip out to the parking lot for a drink with their old buddies. Still, like their counterparts at St Michael's Cathedral in Toronto or Shaar Hashomayim Synagogue in Montreal, they took objection to any suggestion that they were not good practitioners of their faith.

The first suggestion to that effect occurred in 1953, when the more traditional members argued that the temple's executive, at least, should be bearded and baptized. They lost, and they left to form a new society and gurdwara based on that principle. The Akali Singh temple, on 11th Avenue at first, was much smaller and poorer, but it grew quickly in the late 1960s as more Sikh immigrants arrived with more attachment to their ways. The temple was packed every Sunday, with people standing pressed to the walls, until a large and modern building was erected on Skeena Street in 1983. Those crowded conditions, in such dramatic contrast to the new Ross Street gurdwara, made some of the more energetic and ambitious immigrants think about "cracking" the Khalsa Diwan Society, as one of them was to express it.

The Sikh community of Vancouver – and Canada – underwent a qualitative and quantitative transformation between 1960 and 1980, as the immigration doors opened after 1967 wider than ever before for Indians. Not only did the Sikh population multiply by ten, it now included large numbers of professionals, families, and elderly who were not beholden for their entry to the old-timers. On the contrary, fresh from the cities and villages of the Punjab, numerous enough to retain their language and customs in the new place, many of them tended to regard the pioneers with shame. And at no time was that shame felt more deeply than on their first visit to Ross

Street. Going there to worship as at home, to be among their own, to bolster their faith and culture in this alien land, they were shocked to find so many clean-shaven, to see the men wearing gold bracelets (rather than the steel ones that were supposed to symbolize equality), to feel the looseness of the rules and devotions. The epitome of the degeneracy was the sight of bare heads in the gurdwara.

It is an issue that has tormented other religions (whether women should cover their heads in Roman Catholic churches, for example, or men in Jewish synagogues), pitting those who revere the sign of respect against those who disregard archaic gestures. Certainly the general etiquette for men at Sikh temples is to remove one's shoes, don a kerchief provided at the door for those who are not wearing turbans, walk down the centre aisle and bow on one's knees to the Guru Granth Sahib under its ornate canopy, leave a small donation, and receive in cupped hands a bit of sweet food as a symbol of universal brotherhood, before taking one's seat on the floor for the singing and prayers. (One of the great mysteries of religion is how dignified men of the faith look in such headgear, while someone such as myself appears totally ridiculous in turban, kerchief, feathered bonnet, mitre, or skullcap.)

There is a question about how bare heads came to be tolerated at the Ross Street gurdwara. Some point to the possibility that such customs had been less defined and enforced even in India before the authority of the temple management committee after 1920, so that the early Canadian Sikhs had come with looser standards; some point to the possibility that the more orthodox had been drawn back to India to fight for its independence, so that only the "opportunists" and "money-mad" remained; others just point to the inevitable pressures on a small minority cut off from its traditions to adapt to the new and forget about the old. Until the wave of the 1970s the pioneers set the tone, and the tone was modern, secular, and assimilative. In fact, one old-timer suggested to me that bare heads came about because of the constant flow of non-Sikh visitors, invited to the gurdwara as part of the old process of seeking immigration favours. Since they removed their hats as they would in their own church, no one took it as an insult, and some Sikhs picked up the habit.

For the newcomers bare heads were shocking in a way that shaved faces, gold bracelets, and alcohol were not. God knows they saw enough of the latter three among Sikhs in Amritsar or Delhi, but the former was something new. Therefore, it became the cause around which many could rally, and they did rally because it served the purpose of those who wanted to take over the K.D.S. for religious, social, or personal reasons.

As the number of newcomers increased, opposition to the lax ways of the old-timers increased, and it began to express itself in the biennial election of the temple executive. In 1973 an opposition slate was elected with a show of hands by the congregation, but the outgoing president abruptly overruled the vote on technical grounds and staged another by secret ballot a couple of weeks later, open only to the few members who had been registered officially. This second meeting, of course, elected a second executive, controlled by the old guard. For months both executives claimed authority, administered over different followers, kept separate books, until a compromise team was agreed upon for the sake of the temple. Unfortunately for the old-timers, even these moderates kept requesting them to cover their heads, backed by an instruction from the committee in Amritsar. So, in 1975, the pioneers mobilized their forces to recover the executive at the next election, and then introduced membership rules and fees to consolidate their hold.

They made some concessions to the traditionalists, but they also could not afford to alienate the established families who were their chief financial sources. Bare heads continued to be permitted, resulting in arguments, scuffles, and even fist-fights in the gurdwara. Meanwhile, some of the opposition leaders formed the Sikh Sewak Society specifically to organize members and funds to fight the temple elections – each side was spending tens of thousands of dollars each campaign by now – and in 1979 they succeeded. "They had the numbers and they had more time on their hands for this kind of thing," said one old-timer. "There were some close votes, but they became impossible to beat. So the temple was taken over by people we didn't know." Volunteer work was not worth this amount of hassle and abuse, the pioneers concluded, and after 1983 they went off to build a new temple on No. 5 Road in Richmond. They made sure this one would be as tightly controlled as a private club.

All these shenanigans would have been without broader significance, just another example of the human foibles that plague organized religion from parish scandals in Newfoundland to Pentecostal politics in Edmonton, if they had not become entwined with developments in the Punjab. Throughout their history the Sikhs have been concerned with creating a space for themselves as a religion and then as a people between the Muslims and the Hindus, and at least since the glory days of Ranjit Singh's kingdom that concern has been translated occasionally into the idea of an independent Sikh state. It surfaced in the 1940s on the eve of Indian independence, for example, when the Akali Dal wanted the British to carve out "Sikhistan" when they were carving out Pakistan for the Muslims. Instead, the traditional territory of the Punjab was split into two, with the larger and richer portion being given to Pakistan. Perhaps as many as two million Sikhs abandoned their land and homes to escape Muslim domination by moving to the Indian side of the border, and hundreds of thousands lost their lives as well.

They soon had reason to wonder if the trek to religious freedom had been worth the enormous costs, for they found themselves forced to share an Indian state with an equal number of Hindus. In effect, their language and identity were threatened by the arrangement. In the 1950s and 1960s, led by Tara Singh of the Akali Dal, agitation kept up for a Sikh state either within the Indian federation or independent of it. The former was granted by Indira Gandhi in 1966, when the Punjab was divided once more and one of its parts was made a state governed by Punjabi, the language of the Sikhs. That was not the ultimate solution, however. There was still a very large Hindu component, whose language and religion were supported by the sea of Hindus around the new Punjab; the Sikhs' political force was broken now between the Akali Dal and Gandhi's Congress Party; there were scores of major and minor disputes between Punjab and its neighbours or the central government in Delhi; and Sikhism itself was in jeopardy from both the growing number of Hindus attracted to the increasingly prosperous state *and* the growing number of Hindus converting to Sikhism in order to get a job or escape their caste. (If growth by conversion seems a plus rather than a minus, just ask an Orthodox Jew in Israel how he would feel about half a million Palestinian Muslims converting to Judaism through non-Orthodox procedures in order to get a vote.)

The prosperity of the 1960s – in which the "green revolution" with wheat and rice met the entrepreneurial zeal, hard work, and educational ambition of Sikhs – brought other kinds of problems. It aroused envy and covetousness among the less advantaged, leading to more disputes about money and resources, while it shook Sikh society into the modern, secular world of cities and possessions. The Sikh percentage dropped as more had the means and desire to move to even greener fields (Canada being high on the list), and the impact of change, alienation, and other contemporary tensions dealt further blows to those who remained. Out of this turmoil rose two predictable movements – political nationalism and religious traditionalism – and equally predictable, given Sikh history, was that they would ally.

This is not the place to detail the Byzantine course of Punjabi politics since 1970. Suffice it to say that the vision of Khalistan as a separate Sikh country emerged around that time, that it found its (few) early advocates among older traditionalists and disgruntled youths who had been harmed in one way or another by the changes, and that it received an infusion of energy and purpose once it was joined to the Sikh ideals of the Khalsa as an army of saint-soldiers educated to waging a holy war against oppression. The strongest link was made by a charismatic priest named Jarnail Singh Brindranwale, who turned his religious fundamentalism into violence against "heretical" Sikhs, Punjabi Hindus, and eventually the government of India. His end came in June

1984 when Indira Gandhi sent her army to storm the Golden Temple, which Brindranwale and his followers had been using as their base of operations.

If few Sikhs had bothered about Khalistan before that, Operation Blue Star (as the army attack was called) gave it unprecedented legitimacy and broad acceptance. Even the most secular Sikhs could be horrified by the killing and destruction within their holiest shrine. Even the most apolitical Sikhs could respond to the image of martyrs dying for their faith and their people at the hands of imperial forces. In India and around the world Sikhs called for justice, for revenge, for the defence against tyranny that had inspired the tenth guru to create the Khalsa in the first place. When Indira Gandhi was assassinated four months later by her Sikh bodyguards, Sikhs danced in the streets of London, New York, and Vancouver. When almost 3,000 Sikhs were murdered in India in the immediate aftermath of the assassination, with the active or passive assistance of the Indian government, Sikhs had new cause to believe the charge of systematic Hindu persecution aiming toward genocide.

These traumatic events coincided with the total victory of the newcomers over the old-timers at the Ross Street gurdwara. It does not seem as if the takeover had been engineered for political reasons, but the tragedies in Amritsar and Delhi instantly radicalized people already sensitive to religious tradition and Sikh identity. The new temple executive coalesced behind the flag of Khalistan, and because of their temple's direct or indirect influence upon the congregation, the other British Columbia gurdwaras, and almost every Sikh organization, support for Khalistan was advanced throughout the community. Speakers advocated it in the temple services, money was directed toward it through temple channels, and organizations sprang up to defend it out of temple connections.

These leaders took pride and inspiration from the fact that the Khalsa Diwan Society in Vancouver had been a branch of the Ghadar movement in the first quarter of this century, when Sikh expatriates in Canada and California formed a political movement to support the struggle against the British Raj in India by propaganda, arms, and even soldiers. Historians have suggested that the expatriates were more militant than those back home, not necessarily because they had less to lose in terms of life or property, but because their anti-colonial nationalism was their way of reacting to the fear, alienation, assimilation, and racism they were experiencing in North America. That suggestion seems as appropriate now as seventy years before. Though the opinions of the silent majority of Canadian Sikhs are extremely hard to verify, it seems fair to say that a greater percentage of them are in favour of Khalistan than Sikhs in the Punjab are; and certainly the religious and political leadership of the Canadian community is less divided about full independence than that of Indian Sikhs.

"Sikh leadership in Canada basically means the temple executives," said Ujjal Dosanjh, a clean-shaven Sikh lawyer who has not let death threats and a severe assault stifle his liberal and secular statements. "They aren't spiritual leaders, they're elected managers, and they're not elected to represent Sikhs beyond such objectives as faith, culture, language, and social activities. Only the more religious and more orthodox go to the temples, obviously, so for the media and the politicians to make them the spokesmen for the whole community is b.s. We have industrialists, intellectuals, engineers, doctors. How many do you see leading the Khalistan movement in Canada? They don't want to be associated with this kind of nonsense, but they don't want to fight it publicly either. Why get bashed over the head? The stakes aren't here. The stakes are in India, and the people in India will decide what will happen. Even among the recent influx there are many who want nothing to do with this medieval fanaticism. They're happy-go-lucky, like the rest of us.

"The temple attracts those who are more insecure and who haven't been able to make a place for themselves in Canadian society, by and large, or those few and far between who are truly religiously oriented," he went on. "The leadership of many temples is in the hands of people with mediocre intelligence and capabilities and education. Some are totally illiter-

260

ate. Their biggest qualification is the turban and the beard. Being outwardly religious is their way of finding security among their peers. It gives them something to do, it gives them status, and now it's given them a cause that they never found in this society."

Those are fighting words to someone like Joginder Singh Sidhu, who came to Canada in 1970 after a career in the Indian army, rose to middle-class prosperity in the lumber industry, and got involved in the Ross Street temple, first as part of the compromise team in 1974, then as president from 1985 to 1987. He has also been active in the World Sikh Organization, an international lobby group founded in New York in 1984 in response to Operation Blue Star. "In my opinion," he told me, "Dosanjh is not as good a Sikh as I am, though he may think he is. I may have no right to judge what kind of Sikh someone is, but I can know what a Sikh is supposed to do or not do. If I follow the directions as laid out in the scriptures, then I'm a practising Sikh. It's clear that a Sikh shouldn't shave. If some shave, I have to educate them, love them, tell them in a gentle manner that this is a requirement of the religion. There's more teaching of the traditions here and in India now, more people (especially young people) are coming back to them, and most of the credit has to go to Brindranwale. People have woken up. The average Sikh is not detached from his past, though many are silent, and emotions have been particularly high since 1984. When your house is on fire, you ask what you can do."

Among those who asked that question was Ripuduman Singh Malik, a clever and determined businessman who has made millions since coming to Vancouver in 1972. Though he never wanted a temple position, he has been instrumental in supporting the Khalsa Credit Union, the Khalsa school and summer camps, and (more controversially) Talwinder Singh Parmar and the Babbar Khalsa. Parmar, a militant and fundamentalist priest sometimes nicknamed "Canada's Brindranwale," had moved to Canada in 1970, found God in 1973, discovered Khalistan shortly afterwards, and formed the "Tigers of the True Faith" by 1979 to battle for his religion and his nation. Parmar's battles have brought him on several occasions under the suspicion and surveillance of the police in both India and Canada, especially after the bombing of the Air India jet from Toronto to Bombay that killed 329 innocent people in June 1985.

"Anyone who isn't baptized, anyone who cuts his hair, isn't a Sikh," Malik asserted. "I was baptized in 1979. Before that, I had kept my beard and turban but I wasn't very religious. Then, when I made a lot of money easily and figured it didn't matter if I died with $2 million or $100 million, I decided it was time to do something for my community. God brought me to that, I believe, and I'm not a halfway kind of person. I want Western technology and Sikh culture – that's the best mix – and if you're positive, God will give you what you need. The Khalsa are saint-soldiers. We have to be saints before we are soldiers. We fight against bad actions, we fight for rights, and though that might mean killing, I have to protect my house if a crowd is coming to destroy it. Remember, Jesus Christ and Gobind Singh were found guilty by the law, so I'll have to make up my own mind about true guilt. Sometimes bad news is best news. We've had billions of dollars of free publicity since the attack on the Golden Temple. In 1972 we were afraid to go out at night in Vancouver because of the Klu Klux Klan. Now we aren't afraid, even though some may think we're terrorists. Best of all, they don't think we're Hindus!"

"I'm no less a Sikh for not being baptized or not practising," Dosanjh countered. "Sikhism has a broader definition. The Khalsa have always been a minority, even in the Punjab, and they never excluded the non-baptized from worshipping at the temples. In fact, before 1984 there were probably more Punjabi Hindus worshipping at the Golden Temple on any given day than Sikhs. Without the tenth guru we'd be no different from Hindus, and he gave Sikhs their martial shape to protect their Hindu kith and kin too. He even called a Muslim who was distributing water one of his Sikhs. Now these Sikhs are afraid of losing their identity, so they're trying to rewrite history; nor is their religious influence progressive like it was in the 1920s when it opposed the British and purged evils within Sikhism. Theirs is based on the most decadent elements of our ritual."

As for his own credentials, Dosanjh said, "My great-grandfather went back to India from Canada to fight for liberation and was hanged in 1916. My grandfather spent eighteen years in British jails as part of the progressive movement against temple corruption and religious communalism. My father was a baptized Sikh who never smoked or drank, but he remained a progressive. When I speak, I speak with all that emotion in me. They didn't struggle and die for these few crazies to divvy up India into little states. These guys mouth all kinds of platitudes about peace and nonviolence, but they acquiesce implicitly or by silence in all kinds of militant and violent acts perpetrated by a tiny minority. Unfortunately, many Sikhs have been raised never to utter a word against anyone of their faith talking about its welfare, so they find it difficult to condemn violence committed in the name of religion. But I want to preserve the good image of my community for my children. I don't want to be led by buffoons."

That is how I left the Sikhs of Vancouver, hurling charges and countercharges among themselves: that Dosanjh, the pioneer families, and their sort were friends of the Indian government; that the Akali Singh gurdwara, the Nanaksar Gursikh temple in Richmond, and others were dupes of India for trying to keep Khalistan politics out of their religious devotions; even that Parmar, Malik, and such activists were *agents provocateurs* manipulated by India to discredit Sikhs around the world. And though everyone agreed that Sikhism and Sikh culture would prosper in Canada in the future, no one seemed to agree whether prosperity would come with beards and turbans, with Khalistan and the World Sikh Organization, or with inevitable acculturation to the ways of Canadian society in the twenty-first century.

On the one hand, there is no doubt that in recent years, particularly since Operation Blue Star, many young and old Canadian Sikhs have rediscovered their traditions. This has been assisted by the numbers and vitality of the community, the subsequent reinforcement of its language and customs, increased communication with the Punjab, the rise of educational and social institutions supported by increased wealth, and the active direction of the temple leadership, as well as by the Canadian government's support of multiculturalism, Ottawa's financial help, and the changes in law and attitude toward Sikh symbols such as the turban in the RCMP and the sword in the school yard. Professionally and socially it became easier for young Sikhs to keep their identity, just when the politics of India and their families were encouraging them to do so. Because the Sikhs have passed the threshold of survival with their institutions, they are likely to remain a significant piece of the Canadian mosaic.

On the other hand, there is no doubt that many of them will feel the pressure to conform in the long run. The children are still teased at school; their parents still meet racism in the workplace; the elderly will take many of the traditional bonds when they die. As the custom of arranged marriages fades, the issue of intermarriage looms large. As the meaning of sacred formalities diminishes, the authority of modern secularism gains strength. And whether or not Khalistan remains a hot cause for Sikhs in India and the world, it has not got the historical and religious power that has made Israel the definition of Jewish unity. Just as likely as the survival of the Sikh community, therefore, is the subtle adaptation of their religion and culture – and their politics – to Canadian norms and the withdrawal of many individual Sikhs from their traditions.

That does not mean an end to the religious conflicts between the orthodox and the liberal. There has been no end to them among the Christians or Jews, after all, nor will there be an end to them among the Muslims or Hindus. In every religion faith has been entwined with politics; and millions have been slaughtered in the name of just or holy wars. In fact, it is difficult for anyone to read in the newspapers these days about Israel, Iran, South Africa, Northern Ireland, or the United States of America and *not* know that reality.

Some situations may seem simpler than others, sometimes justice and righteousness may seem more evident, but the concept of a holy war is always complex and delusive. There may be all sorts of political, social, personal, or even ethical grounds for killing Adolf Hitler and Indira Gandhi – or Salman Rushdie and Oscar Romero. Certainly priests and theologians have posited excellent religious reasons to butcher infidels, heretics, witches, and imperialist oppressors, based on the judgement of God, Christ's assault on the moneylenders, the will of Allah, the destructive aspect of Shiva, or the instructions of Guru Gobind Singh. Nature itself teaches that death is a necessary component of life, as if to confirm the sages' assumption that the Truth must incorporate evil as well as good. But that is far from assuming that the Truth is evil (as we humans know it) or that we can lie, cheat, steal, drink, fornicate, and murder our way to the Truth.

Most – perhaps all – great religions have made satanic pacts to achieve their power and numbers, always arguing that brutal dictators, appropriate tortures, or class struggles are God's instruments for His inscrutable plan. Indeed, they are usually by definition great because they have made those pacts with politics. History is littered with brilliant seers and insightful sects that would not or could not do so. The victors attribute their success to their proximity to God, naturally, but no true prophet has articulated the Truth as hatred, anger, revenge, or selfishness. Though great religions may harbour great seers and insights, to take up the sword in defence of them is no closer to the Truth than to drop bombs in defence of an ideology, homeland, or possession.

In an age when religion and spirituality seem to have no other purpose than to assure individual health and happiness, even the diminishing numbers in the churches and cults do not want to know about sacrifice, compassion, and the total abnegation of ego. In other words, they would rather not face the Truth as taught by their spiritual masters. If the Truth is to be found in love and oneness beyond the illusions of self and other, at some point each seeker has to deal with the realities of pain and death, if only to realize them as unrealities. To confront them takes tremendous strength and courage. Often, consequently, metaphors of war have been used to describe or inspire the resolve required – whether Christian soldiers marching as to war, Krishna persuading Arjuna to go into battle, Buddha defeating the armies of Mara, or Mohammed calling for holy struggle – and all too often, unfortunately, the metaphors have been misinterpreted as literal commands. No doubt Jesus Christ would have been horrified to see crusaders fighting under the cross, his most powerful symbol of peace, self-sacrifice, and the insignificance of death; and what would the Sikhs' ninth guru, who embraced martyrdom for his faith, have made of the murder of Indira Gandhi?

"It is a great act to exercise forgiveness," said Guru Tegh Bahadur, who preferred to be called Degh Bahadur, "brave cooking pot" instead of "brave sword," generous to the poor instead of skilled in arms. "To forgive is to give alms. It is equal to bathing at all places of pilgrimage. Forgiveness ensures man's liberation. There is no virtue equal to forgiveness." Nor does it seem irrelevant that when his son, Guru Gobind Singh, came to create the Khalsa, he invented a test that called on Sikhs to die for their faith, not kill for it. If his challenge had been to slay someone else, more than five might have responded. The beloved five became the pure ones because they were willing to be slain.

"He alone can win merit who has accepted death in life," wrote Guru Nanak in a hymn, "who has put down his lower nature and lives hourly in the spirit, and who, moment by moment, loves, serves, and remembers God."

TWELVE

The Lord's Song in a
Strange Land

It was a dreadful evening, wet, cold, and dark. The rain was torrential. It soaked into my overcoat and shoes; it created wide pools at the curbs and made the fallen leaves on the sidewalks treacherous underfoot. The wind pulled at the umbrellas of the old couples who were clinging to each other for shelter and support as they walked from their cars or nearby apartments. The young ran for cover. At the door of Shearith Israel, generally known as the Spanish and Portuguese Synagogue, the crowd pressed toward the warmth and the light, anxious not to be late for the 7:30 meeting, eager to get dry and grab a good seat.

The weather suited the occasion: a commemoration of the fiftieth anniversary of Kristallnacht, the Night of Broken Glass, when the National Socialist government of Germany orchestrated a violent attack on Jews, their synagogues, and their businesses with the intent to drive them out or destroy them. That night of vandalism, arrests, and flames – November 9, 1938 – is considered the beginning of the Holocaust, the systematic extermination of six million Jews in Nazi death camps during the Second World War. Now, fifty years later and far away, Montreal's Jewish community was gathering to remember the terror and the dead and say never again. The rain, as heavy as the tears these people had known, symbolized their sorrow and increased their dolefulness. At the same time, it attacked them, caused them to huddle up and scurry, exposed their vulnerability and haplessness. It was a night from a horror film, full of spectres conjured from a night more horrible than any fiction; and whether from my own imagination or from the memories in the minds of those around me, I felt sinister forces in the wind in the trees and the sound of tires splashing in the streets.

It was a relief, therefore, to enter the synagogue, an elegant and warmly lit building put up in 1960. I was touched again by the simple power of a sanctuary from life's literal and figurative storms – a power that enhances the psychological meaning of religion as well as the physical beauty of sacred places – and I was struck at once by how much more powerful this sanctuary was to those around me. I was a visitor, still unsure where to fetch a skullcap or how to keep it on my head. They were at home, even though they were drawn this evening from fourteen congregations, eighteen associations ranging from the Holocaust Remembrance Committee to the Labour Zionist Alliance, and the general public out to hear the reminiscences and reflections of the distinguished philosopher, Emil Fackenheim, who had been living in Israel since his retirement from the University of Toronto in 1983. With a few exceptions, all of them were Jews, and the comfort of being among themselves was almost palpable.

I already knew better than to mistake this comfort for uniformity or unanimity. Like Sikhs, Jews can be extremely hard on each other. I have witnessed verbal brawls that would give Yassar Arafat pause. But, underneath the abuse and the shouting, I always sensed the common blood. Indeed, like the demands and disputes of a large and fractious family, the pressures and quarrels of Jew against Jew seem to be permitted a vehemence and severity *because* of the underlying and permanent bonds. As proof, I used to watch with amazement the speed and fury with which Jews would rally to the defence of one of their own who had been attacked by non-Jews with softer blows and gentler words than they themselves had used.

268

"Please let's not wash our dirty linen in public" was a popular refrain when they caught someone like me overhearing their battles, as if their synagogues and conferences and newspapers were private spaces.

This notion of family accounted for the well-being I felt beneath the diversity of ages, of experiences, of opinions, even of cultures and languages gathered that night in Montreal. It also helped me over a hurdle I had faced very quickly in my contact with this community. I had approached it as a religion, yet I soon met many Jews who do not believe in God and never go near a synagogue. Are they an ethnic group then, like the Italians or the Chinese? Not really, because they include members of many ethnic groups, Poles and Iraqis and British, Italians and Chinese too, and they are open to converts. Perhaps they could be defined as a culture, with shared customs and attitudes, with history and a couple of particular languages? Closer, but again they include so many cultures, so many different customs and attitudes, and though history tends to unite them, many no longer know Hebrew or Yiddish. Often they bring together religion and ethnicity and culture to describe themselves as a nation, but that is a loaded word these days that does not convey the Jewish reality of geographical dispersion. I was baffled until an old man said, "Think of us as a family. By and large we all stem from one family. We have a traditional family religion, a language that is dear to us, a family history that we pass on and cherish. We may vary greatly, we may be joined by others, but basically think of us as a *tribe*." In that light, this commemoration was another tribal event, to honour the ancestors, to repeat the stories, to reinforce the continuity.

One of the great strengths of Judaism has been its ability to maintain the intimacy of history for almost 4,000 years. Given the mythic dimensions to which some dynasties inflate themselves merely because a patriarch plundered a fortress nine or ten generations back, it is not unreasonable that the Jews should have recorded and revered their life and times since God apparently singled out Abraham's tribe as the Chosen People, "a kingdom of priests and an holy nation." It was a revelation witnessed not by one person, as in Christianity and Islam, but by thousands. Through that divine covenant the gods became one God – Yahweh, Jehovah, I AM THAT I AM – and as such entered the affairs of the Jews.

Their judges, their kings, their ups and downs became pregnant with religious import, while many of their religious festivals centre around political events such as the exodus from Egypt and the destructions of the temple at Jerusalem. "Why is this night different from all other nights?" the youngest member of the family asks the father at the dinner table each Passover, and in similar ways are the traditions, the teachings, the magnificent songs, and the wonderful stories bequeathed as patrimony. In similar ways, too, have the Holocaust and the founding of Israel taken their place with the Babylonian captivity and the revelation to Moses on Mount Sinai as both fact and symbol of God's unique involvement with this extended family, to be remembered and recounted to the children.

That divine covenant has been an awesome burden as well as a splendid grace, and there have been occasions when it seemed more a curse than a blessing. It brought laws and duties, it brought trials and punishments, it brought exile and persecution. "I will scatter them also among the heathen, whom neither they nor their fathers have known," said the Lord to Jeremiah in response to their disobedience, "and I will send a sword after them, till I have consumed them." History seemed to sit on the shoulders of these people in the synagogue like an oppressive weight: how high the standards of morality and learning to sustain, how horrible the consequences of failure, how long and devastating the road from Canaan to this foreign place! Like Funes the Memorious in the Borges story, for whom the ability to remember absolutely everything becomes a debilitating illness, these men and women were condemned – and had condemned themselves – to suffer memory.

That was part of their responsibility to God and to the tribe. Certainly it was part of their responsibility to those friends and family who perished in Auschwitz and Buchenwald. It brought them out, fifty years later almost to the day, on a night

270

such as this, to go over once more in their hearts and their heads the broken windows, the burnt synagogues, the mass arrests, and the unburied bodies. Those hellish images were alive again in the eyes of the survivors and in the cantata performed by their grandchildren.

The Montreal and Canadian Jewish communities are marked by a particularly high proportion of Holocaust survivors and their descendants. Their experience permeated the psychology of the whole tribe; the languages and cultures they brought from Europe checked the trend toward assimilation that had existed before the war; and the renewed resolve never to forget thee, O Jerusalem, lest the right hand forget her cunning and the tongue cleave to the roof of the mouth, coincided with the encouragement of multiculturalism in Canada. As well, they found in Montreal an existing community that was older, better organized, and more traditional than almost any other in North America. The vibrancy of its schools and associations, its library and scholars and Yiddish poets, even its place in the tension between two linguistic and religious powers reminded many of Vilna as an important centre of world Jewish heritage.

Until recently Montreal was without doubt the most important Jewish centre in the country, and though there are now more Jews in Toronto, with as much or more clout in Canadian and Jewish affairs, Montreal is still regarded as "the capital of Jewish Canada." It still has the national headquarters of the Canadian Jewish Congress; it still has some of the country's most influential and generous Jewish leaders; it still has an extraordinary abundance of religious institutions, social services, educational facilities, and cultural centres. Most of all, it still has the radiance of its past. Here Canada's first Jewish congregation was founded in 1768 and its first synagogue was built in 1777 – both of which continue to exist in modern guise where we had come for the commemoration of Kristallnacht. Here arose great business families, from the Harts at the end of the eighteenth century to the Bronfmans two hundred years later; important political figures, from Ezekiel Hart (first elected to the assembly in 1807) to David Lewis

271

(who became leader of the NDP in 1971); prominent religious teachers, from Abraham de Sola to Harry Stern; and a host of English and Yiddish writers, poets, and academics, the better known of whom include A. M. Klein, Irving Layton, Leonard Cohen, and Mordecai Richler. Through here passed most of the Jewish immigrants to the West, often assisted by agencies such as the Baron de Hirsch Institute or the Friendly League of Jewish Women. From here developed national organizations such as the Canadian Jewish Congress as "the parliament of Canadian Jewry" and the earliest Zionist groups.

As the historian Benjamin Sack wrote of Montreal, "the history of the Jews in that city until the end of the last century is by and large also the history of the Jews in the entire Dominion," because their numbers were so small and so concentrated there. In this century Toronto competed with Montreal in attracting the overwhelming majority of Jewish immigrants and finally surpassed Montreal's declining Jewish population during the 1970s. These two cities account almost equally for more than three-quarters of Canada's 300,000 Jews, a fact which gives them the power and wealth to dominate the much smaller communities in Winnipeg, Edmonton, or Vancouver. (Many people seem startled to learn there are so few Jews in Canada. Not long ago a federal cabinet minister congratulated an official of the Canadian Jewish Congress for the magnificent contribution "*just a million* Jews" have made to Canadian politics, business, public service, learning, and the arts.)

The Montreal segment of the tale began soon after the British conquest of New France, since non-Catholics had not been permitted in the colony – unless one wants to begin with the bizarre story of Esther Brandeau, the young Jewish girl who sneaked into Quebec in 1738 disguised as a boy named Jacques La Fargue. Since she was hustled back to France as soon as all the efforts of "zealous ecclesiastics" proved unable to convert her "flighty" mind, the honour of the first Jew in the region is traditionally shared by Aaron Hart and the small band of merchants and traders who came from England or the American colonies in the wake of the victorious army. Not all stayed, not all were alike, but they established an enduring community.

Most of them were Ashkenazim, Jews of German or Eastern European origin, but they did not follow the Ashkenazic forms of worship. Instead, they joined with Sephardim, of Spanish or Portuguese origin, to practise the Sephardic rite that had come to Spain from ancient Babylon and then had spread across Europe and the world with the expulsion of the Jews from Spain in 1492. Both the largest synagogue in London, England, and the oldest congregation in North America in New York were Sephardic, and since the two or three dozen Jews in Montreal had come largely from those cities, they continued that tradition. Not only did they name Shearith Israel ("Remnant of Israel") after the New York synagogue, for most of its first sixty years they had to depend on visits from New York rabbis for certain ceremonies – an early example of the extraordinary social, cultural, and religious ties that exist between the Jews of Montreal and New York. Indeed, the synagogue's current rabbi, Howard Joseph, was invited from New York in 1970. Like about 85 per cent of his members at the time, he is an Ashkenazi who had to learn the Sephardic melodies, customs, folklore, and mentality.

By 1846 there were enough Ashkenazim who wanted their own rite to form a breakaway congregation, and in 1859 they built Canada's second permanent synagogue, Shaar Hashomayim ("Gate of Heaven"). "I regret to say," said an early observer, probably understating the matter, "that the feeling between the two congregations was not that of brotherly love – caused by each congregation trying to get any new member that arrived in Canada to their synagogue." Since most of the new arrivals came from Germany or Poland and then from Russia or Eastern Europe, Shaar Hashomayim had the advantage, and it passed the Spanish and Portuguese congregation in power and prestige by the turn of the century. Because it was identified with German and Polish Jews – as well as with the more established, the richer, and perhaps the more assimilated – it soon got competition from synagogues built by new arrivals from Romania, Russia, and Austria; but Shaar Hasho-mayim has remained the wealthiest and most influential syn-agogue in Montreal, mostly because of the wealth and influence of the families who trek down the slopes of West-mount each Yom Kippur and grace the boards of the major Jewish agencies from generation to generation.

Though Jews lived in relative harmony amid the English and French societies for their first century in Montreal, they fared worse for most of the next hundred years, partly because of their greater numbers and visibility, partly because of the anti-Semitic implications of the First Vatican Council, which renewed the old Christian animosity toward the Jews as the "killers of Christ" in need of conversion. That attitude soon showed up in the Catholic nationalism that developed in Que-bec from the last quarter of the nineteenth century until the end of the Second World War. Though it seldom got translated into legislation, it was prominent in the rhetoric of the Catho-lic politicians and intellectuals who considered Jews an eco-nomic, radical, or racial threat to their utopia on the St Lawrence. Henri Bourassa once called them "vampires"; Abbé Groulx saw them as impurities in the blood of French Canada; Adrian Arcand and his fascists wanted them deported to Hudson Bay.

Such overtness virtually disappeared with the growth of Quebec liberalism during the 1950s, the influence of the Sec-ond Vatican Council during the 1960s, and the laws to pro-mote human rights and ban hate-mongering. However, with the Quiet Revolution and the not-so-quiet movement for a leftist and independent Quebec, Jews found themselves again a target of attack, not explicitly for being Jews but for being a perceptible part of the English-speaking minority that was seen as the colonizer. There were a few ironies in that. In this century Jews themselves had been the victims of social ostra-cism, university quotas, and other humiliations by the Anglo-Saxon community that controlled Montreal's economy and élites. They had become affiliated with that community pri-marily because the Roman Catholic authorities forced the Jews to operate their schools within the Protestant, English-speaking school system, thus throwing the "heretics" together. As a result, though Jews had begun in close physical and social proximity to French Canadians and were more likely to speak French than the average Anglo-Saxon, education and ambition directed them into the camp of the linguistic majority of Canada and North America.

The significant exceptions were the French-speaking Sephardim who came in numbers during the 1950s and 1960s, many from North Africa as a result of the independence of Morocco, Tunisia, and Algeria. Not all the Sephardim who arrived in Montreal were francophones, nor were all French-speaking Jews Sephardim, but the influx did give the Jewish community two new elements at once. Montreal had a substantial Sephardic presence for the first time (which gave the Spanish and Portuguese Synagogue an overwhelmingly Sephardic congregation at last); and there were now whole groups of Jews who gravitated naturally toward the francophone society.

Too naturally, in the opinion of some of the old groups. They did not like the high rate of intermarriage between the North African Jews and French-Canadian Catholics. They did not like the demands of French-speaking Sephardim for their own schools and social institutions, because the established ones seemed too English, too European, and too Ashkenazic. They did not like the idea that the francophone Jews might be the means by which the entire community would be absorbed into the French majority or the preferred ones with whom the Quebec government would insist on consulting and negotiating. There were disputes about the allocation of money, organizational power, and whether the Sephardim were contributing enough of either to the whole community. There were different attitudes toward the Arabs in the Middle East and the nationalists in Quebec.

"We tended to smile at the extremist views among Jews here," one former Moroccan told me, "because we had lived as a minority with the Arabs, we had worked with them, we had even liked them. And the October Crisis seemed amusing after the real issues and problems we had faced. In fact after our battles with the Ashkenazic establishment there, some of us were even sympathetic to the French-Canadian demand for sovereignty-association!"

Also, to be frank, there was not a little racism involved between the European Jews and those from the Middle East and North Africa. "We used to have a nice little community here," I was told one day, "before those goddamn Moroccans came."

With time, however, ethnic traditions faded into a North American style closer to the community norm, and intermarriages between the two groups increased. New Sephardic synagogues, schools, and cultural activities worked to discourage the assimilation of their immigrants. The Centre Communautaire Juif moved into the Jewish "Y" on Westbury Avenue, and in 1977 the Communauté Sépharade du Québec joined the Allied Jewish Community Services as a constituent member. Meanwhile, the rise of the Parti Québécois convinced the anglophone Jews that it might be politically prudent to use the francophone Jews, who now made up about 25 per cent of the community, as a kind of symbolic and practical bridge. That did not work out especially well, however. The bilingual leadership preferred to speak for itself, the francophone Jews did not necessarily represent the others, and the French-Canadian nationalists were not that impressed.

"If you speak French but don't have the right name, you still have a problem," said Julien Bauer, an Ashkenazi who came from France more than twenty years ago. "I'm not considered a true Québécois, I'm a neo-Québécois, and I would be only a little bit worse if I only spoke English. At first the Sephardim believed they were *in*. Then they found they were no more *in* than the rest of the Jews."

"The Sephardim did make contact with the French Canadians on every level, and the educated ones have been particularly successful in penetrating that world," said David Rome, not the Tibetan Buddhist in Halifax but an octogenarian historian who may know more about the Jews in Montreal than anyone alive. "But they found there were limits to the closeness. They felt a deep anti-Semitism. So, despite some progress, their integration became neither possible nor desirable."

With the rise of Quebec nationalism, many in the Montreal Jewish Community became sensitive to the least signals of anti-Semitism in the air. Every unwelcoming noise and gesture provoked a reaction based on centuries of tribal memory, especially among the victims of twentieth-century European nationalism. From fear or for peace of mind, from the inconvenience of learning French or for better job prospects, an estimated 15,000 Jews left Quebec during the 1970s for Toronto or the West or the United States, and many of them were the young and well-educated hope for the community's future. By the end of the 1980s 20 per cent of Montreal Jews were over 65; by 2000 the largest growth will be with those over 75; and by 2010 the city's Jewish population could be down to 75,000 if the low birth rate, the high proportion of elderly, and the trend of emigration over immigration continue.

Among those who remained, said one observer with only some exaggeration, the mood was set by the Holocaust survivors: "tough, bitchy, hysterical, and *screw you!*" They raged when Premier Robert Bourassa suspended their freedom of expression under the Charter of Rights in order to advance the use of French on outdoor signs. "Particularly as Jews," wrote Rabbi Allan Nadler of Shaar Hashomayim in a call to protest, "we are obliged to speak out against insidious forms of draconian legislation which instruct minorities to become invisible." Many registered their anger in the provincial election by voting for the Equality Party, whose Jewish leader won his riding by a large margin. When a francophone Sephardic rabbi attacked him in *La Presse* in March 1990 for making "noisy and inconsiderate declarations" not representative of the positive Sephardic attitudes toward the "affirmation of the French fact in Quebec," Rabbi Moise Ohana himself was attacked by another rabbi for seeking to break "the consensus of the Jewish community" and setting up "good" Jews versus "bad" Jews in the eyes of French Quebeckers.

For the most part the community's approach has been one of moderation, conciliation, negotiation, and an appreciation of the valid concerns of Quebec, though occasionally stronger feelings have slipped out – most sensationally, for example, when Charles Bronfman succumbed to the paranoia on the eve of the 1976 election by publicly calling the Parti Québécois "a bunch of bastards who are trying to kill us." Anti-Semitic incidents tend to get downplayed as mere incidents, not indications of general hostility. In fact, say many Jewish leaders, anti-Semitism may be less prevalent in French Canada than English Canada – not to mention Eastern or Western Europe. Look at Goldwin Smith or Mackenzie King in the past; look at the cases of Jim Keegstra in Alberta, Ernst Zundel in Ontario, or Malcolm Ross in New Brunswick now; look at the vandalism against synagogues in Toronto and Saskatoon and Vancouver recently. If the Jewish community really wants to see racism, they suggest, it should look at the treatment of blacks and Sikhs and native people across Canada.

That is small comfort for people who are visited by "language police" for using English or Hebrew in their shop windows, who heard the Jewish names in the FLQ manifesto's hit list in 1970, who had grown up to the jeers and street battles of the French kids around St Urbain Street and St Laurent Boulevard, who have seen their cemeteries desecrated, and who are never allowed to forget the dark side of ethnic nationalism (unless, of course, it is the dark side of Zionism). That is not simply paranoia, they respond, and they point to the fire set at the Poale Zedec Synagogue in September 1988, and to the swastikas and slogans that defaced Beth Zion just a week before the Kristallnacht anniversary that November. "Kill the Jews!" someone had scrawled in French. "Kiss Mr Hitler!"

At the Spanish and Portuguese Synagogue before the Fackenheim lecture, two men had been whispering behind me about their leadership's reaction. "They're hushing it up again," said one with contempt. "All their effort is to keep it out of the media."

The official attitude toward the fire, as expressed by the Quebec Region of the CJC, was to describe it as an act of arson not necessarily anti-Semitic in intent. As for the graffiti, the policy was not to arouse overreaction and fear among Jews for what was probably the work of a few kids and, at the same time, not to inspire more by giving the incident wide publicity. Going to the barricades for every minor event, the leadership argues, only weakens the community's effectiveness in fighting the serious threats.

"But the silence was worse," Bauer replied. "It made our people feel that no one cared because no one was speaking up. You can't tell a little old lady who can't sleep at night remembering Poland sixty years ago that, at the bureaucratic level, there's no problem."

The fire and the slogans happened in the midst of a more unsettling and public controversy – the so-called "l'affaire d'Outremont" – and both sides used it as a vindication of their stance. To the leaders it was exactly the kind of serious threat they could overcome only because they had maintained their level-headedness and credibility; to the grassroots it meant the exposure of the anti-Semitism they always insisted was real and present.

The controversy had its origins in a very petty matter, a petition to the Montreal suburb of Outremont for a zoning change to allow the construction of a new Hassidic synagogue on a vacant lot. Nothing could have been simpler on the surface; little could have had more nuance underneath. Outremont is a particularly pleasant and prosperous municipality, tucked along the north slope of Mount Royal and home to generations of French Canada's élites. In recent years it has become the favoured quarter of upwardly mobile Quebec nationalists, intellectuals, artists, and professionals who wanted trees, services, and proximity to the downtown without the treachery of moving into the English-speaking enclaves of Westmount, Town of Mount Royal, or Hampstead. Its mayor in 1988 was Jérôme Choquette, who had been Quebec's Minister of Justice during the FLQ crisis in October 1970. Its opposition leader in 1988 was Gérard Pelletier, not the former federal cabinet minister but the former member of the FLQ, who had been jailed when Choquette was minister!

Pelletier opposed the zoning change, perhaps only to undermine Choquette by playing to the disquiet some of their fellow-citizens were feeling about the increasing number of ultra-Orthodox Jews living on the town's eastern edge. While the declining birth rate among French Canadians had contributed to a drop in Outremont's population by 7,000 in the last twenty years to around 23,000, the Hassidim had multiplied to over 2,500. Always highly visible because of their traditional dress and customs, deliberately uncommunicative with strangers and isolated from the modern world around them, they now began to impinge on the majority's sensibilities. In 1985, for example, their influence was seen behind an unpopular bylaw banning bikinis in the parks, and in 1986 a visit by one of their New York gurus stirred local complaints of noise and inconvenience. Such incidents fuelled the loud debate instigated by Pelletier, who succeeded in getting the synagogue application refused. (In 1989 he again stoked the flames by denouncing a parade in honour of a visiting Hassidic leader as an insult to French Canadians, because it was to be held on the St Jean Baptiste holiday. This time three of his party members on the council resigned in protest to sit as independents.)

"Very soon Outremont won't belong to us any more," a woman wrote to the community newspaper at the time. "It's the children of these Jews who will buy your houses within a few years. It's these Jews who have money." And a sticker appeared on Jewish buildings, declaring in French, "Outremont is not the West Bank where Israelis do what they want in defiance of the opinion of the whole world. Outremont owes nothing to the Jews, just the contrary!"

The council vote, a couple of racist remarks, and a few bad attitudes might have blown away if *La Presse* had not chosen to report the story in September with the front-page headline, "*Outremont se découvre un 'problème juif.'*" Besides using the Nazi euphemism, "Jewish problem," the article caused further insult by characterizing the Hassidim as a "bizarre minority," with its bearded men all in black "like bogeymen" and its kerchiefed women and children done up "like onions." Though the newspaper apologized for any inadvertent offence, it stoked the indignation of the Jewish community by printing even sharper comments by a columnist, an editorial cartoonist, and a reader about a week later on Yom Kippur, the Day of Atonement, Judaism's most sacred holiday. Their gist was that the Hassidim – and, by extension, all Jews – were the authors of their own misfortune by failing to integrate into the French-Canadian majority and, worse, by coming to identify with the English-speaking minority.

As the "Outremont affair" became the "*La Presse* affair," the issue moved from a specific business with the Hassidim to a general question of toleration. More sinister than the phrase, "Jewish problem," was the echo of the argument by which the Nazis had turned the victims into the victimizer. The Nazis had attempted to legitimize their persecution of the Jews by just such an intellectual inversion: the Jews were responsible for what happened to them because they had not made the necessary effort to strip themselves of their values and customs in order to put on those of the majority culture. "Congress thus interpreted the *La Presse* coverage as an unambiguous and dangerously provocative example of anti-Semitism with potential ramifications that reached far beyond the Poale Zedec incident," wrote Michael Crelinsten and Jack Jebwab, two CJC officials, in a report on their public rebukes and private meetings to undo the damage.

Though Julien Bauer was not alone in judging their response neither quick enough nor tough enough, it certainly seemed a demonstration of Jewish unity. I was intrigued, therefore, to discover that it only patched over a deep fissure that exists between most Montreal Jews and the dozen Hassidic groups. "The real problem for the Hassidim isn't with the French Canadians," I was told. "It's with the rest of the Jewish community. There were a lot of Jews around the time of the Outremont thing who said that if the Hassidim don't want us on Tuesday, they shouldn't count on our help on Thursday."

The story goes back to Poland in the eighteenth century, with the modern emergence of a mystical and emotional revival movement in Judaism. With caution it could be compared to Pentecostal or charismatic revivalism, with its emphasis on fervent prayer, its protest against dry intellect, and its literal approach to Biblical law. Both promise an *expe-*

rience, both exalt ego-crushing faith, both turn inward for the Truth, both call for preparation for the coming Messiah, and both moved from the radical fringe of their traditions to the conservative edge of orthodox interpretation. That said, the differences are as deep as the gulf between a WASP family singing "Saved! Saved! My sins are all forgiv'n!" in a suburban church and a Hassidic family dancing with the Torah and shouting during the festival of Purim.

The mystical strand, coming down from ancient Jewish saints through the esoteric theories and practices of the cabbalists, meant that Hassidism would be more than an emotional lift once a week and a psychological comfort in between. It sought to infuse every moment of living with sanctity, wisdom, and delight by study, stories, music, demonstrative prayer, submissive faith, and strict adherence to the laws of the Torah – all under the guidance of a master teacher. As different masters arose in different places with different emphases, Hassidic sects arose around them (Belzers from Belz, Tashers from Tash, Satmarers from Satmar, and about three dozen other extant "courts," big and little), often continuing with an hereditary leadership. If at first the exuberance, the accessibility, and the powerful personalities of the path attracted as many as half the Jews in Eastern Europe within a century, persecution, rivalry, and modernity pushed the movement back to the margins. As more and more Jews gave up or modified the laws about dress or diet or the Sabbath, the Hassidim were set apart increasingly as an ultra-Orthodox, even heretical minority within Judaism – somewhat as the Amish and Hutterites have been set apart within Christianity – and, in accordance with their devotional beliefs and practices, that suited them fine. "I am the Lord your God," they read in Leviticus. "I have made a clear separation between you and the nations."

"In the world but not of the world," few Hassidim have chosen to follow their Christian counterparts to the isolation of Pennsylvania or Alberta, though the Tashers founded a secluded community in 1964 near Ste Thérèse, north of Montreal. An estimated 80 per cent of their quarter of a million people live in the United States, and half of those are said to live in Brooklyn, New York. The old link between the Jewish communities of New York and Montreal is one reason for the liveliness of the Hassidic presence in Outremont and other areas, though the first significant arrival of Hassidim came from Poland in 1941 as refugees. They were nine Lubavitcher students who quickly looked around, saw nothing for them in the relatively loose standards of North American Judaism, and immediately set about establishing their own school. Synagogues, camps, and other religious or social institutions were to follow as the numbers grew by birth and immigration.

Apparently such devout and independent spirit was not greeted enthusiastically by the more settled and assimilated community. It threatened the tightness and the control. Worse, it undermined the general strategy that is still known as "the culture of appeasement" vis-à-vis the dominant society. Suddenly and all too visibly there were these stereotypical Jews with sidelocks and fur hats, clinging to their medieval costumes and Yiddish tongue and "backward" superstitions. If there were Jews who looked upon them as "dirty," "lazy," and "fanatic," then what would the English and the French think – of all Jews? From some angles the piety and discipline of the Hassidim were seen as the pride and tradition of the Jewish people, what all good Jews should do. From other angles they were seen as an embarrassment and an anachronism.

Nor did the Hassidim appear to have much respect for the Jews around them. When most Jews moved from the eastern side of Outremont to the western outskirts – from the working-class "Second Settlement" around St Urbain and Fairmount to the middle-class "Third Settlement" around Queen Mary and Côte Ste-Catherine – most Hassidim preferred to stay put, opting to live amid a sea of Greeks and Portuguese and French Canadians than risk more insidious corruption by secular Jews. One day a modern Jew was walking past a Hassidic school when one of the kids called him a Gentile. A rabbi overheard and said, "No, you're not a Gentile – but neither are you a Jew."

The tensions only mounted when the population explosion of the Hassidim (who are encouraged to have large families) pushed them westward during the 1960s into the mainstream neighbourhood dense with synagogues, schools, recreational and cultural centres, and the "town hall" housing the Allied Jewish Community Services, the Jewish Public Library, and the Holocaust museum. In 1962, when the Lubavitchers transplanted their synagogue and yeshiva from Park Avenue to Westbury Avenue (not far from where the Spanish and Portuguese congregation had been established since 1946), they met local opposition using many of the same arguments the Vishnizers were to encounter in Outremont in 1988: what about the noise, the large families, the rudeness, the property values?

The Lubavitchers pose a particular problem for many Jews – including the other Hassidic sects. Founded in Lithuania in 1773 by Rabbi Schneur Zalman, they are generally considered more moderate, more modern, more worldly, and more intellectual than most Hassidim. Whether those attributes are good or bad depends on who is considering them, but both sides seem hostile toward the Lubavitchers' unique enthusiasm for recruiting new members. "And you shall spread far and wide," said the Lord, and this became like a commandment to Rabbi Menachem Mendel Schneerson, the sect's seventh leader, an octogenarian who has lived in New York since he fled Warsaw in 1941 to join his father-in-law, the sixth "rebbe." From 1950 he has inspired a vast and relentless outreach programme from schools to social services to missionaries, primarily intended to bring Jews back to their faith and the Torah, and he has succeeded in making the Lubavitchers the largest Hassidic group in the world, as well as the most controversial.

Attentive to reason and education, supportive of Israel and Jewish causes, open to personal problems and social concerns, the Lubavitchers have had enormous appeal to men and women seeking a reaffirmation of their Jewish identity, college kids seeking an intelligent mysticism, and children who have been exposed to their day-care centres and summer camps. To many outsiders, however, they might as well be the Moonies because of the guru-like authority of the Rebbe, the

intensive indoctrination techniques, the well-financed prose-
lytization on campuses and street corners, and the reactionary
values about the role of women or the coming of the Messiah.
Yes, it is derived from the best of Jewish tradition, not the
worst of New Age corruption; yes, no one is either initiated by
actual brainwashing or forbidden from leaving; but the average
Jewish father probably would be no more delighted to hear
that his son was hanging around the Chabat Lubavitch centre
at McGill than the average Christian father would be to hear
his daughter has become a devotee of Elizabeth Clare Prophet.
As for the other Hassidim, whether from competitive jealousy
or from theological conviction, they suggest that the Lubavitchers have lost the way. Some accuse the Rebbe of becoming
the false Messiah; some denounce his incursions into the
contemporary world and Israeli politics; others see weakness
in the tendency toward intellect over passion.

The expansion of the Lubavitchers in particular, the
increase among the Hassidim in general, and even perhaps the
unembarrassed energy with which the CJC sprung to their
assistance point to an important dynamic within Judaism
today. If most Jews, like most Christians, have been lured into
the secular materialism of the age – neither sure nor unduly
concerned about the existence of God, seldom obedient to the
traditional laws and practices, casual toward their religious
institutions except on certain holidays and personal occasions
– there has occurred among those who have remained more or
less involved in their tribal faith a marked shift toward tradition and Orthodoxy.

Part of this could be ascribed to uniquely Jewish factors.
Israel revitalized Jewish identity, Jewish history, and Jewish
unity, to the benefit of the synagogues that became the functional focus for pro-Israel sentiment and activity. More subtly,
the threats to Israel stirred the spiritual essence beneath the
meaning of Israel, why it should exist and what it must preserve. While Christian parents are returning to church on
Sunday not because of rediscovered beliefs but in order to give
their children an exposure to traditional values and teachings,
many Jewish parents are doing exactly the same thing, but

with even more dedication brought on by the obligation of every family never to forget the tribe's past. "In the 1950s Orthodoxy was expected to expire in North America within a decade," said Rabbi Reuben Poupko, a young and extremely active participant in religious and secular Jewish life in Montreal. "Instead, while everyone else is stagnating or declining, Orthodoxy has become the most vibrant part of Judaism since the 1960s. We have the babies, we have less attrition and assimilation, and we get the returnees. There are now kids at Harvard and on Wall Street wearing yarmulkes! They've discovered that being observant – keeping the Sabbath and the holy days, keeping kosher, keeping the family purity laws – isn't nuts. It's an attractive lifestyle."

"The real factor has been the impact of the North American cultural revolution and the failure of that culture to live up to the anticipations of those who adapted to it, especially to the anxiety-ridden, post-Pill forms of marriage and sexuality," said Rabbi Jordan Pearlson, who has a Reform congregation in Toronto. "Traditionalism offers role models and structures to men and women who are uncertain of who they are. Women don't have to be centrefolds with a staple in their navels for the rest of their lives, dressing not to entice men but to defend themselves against other women. Men don't have to do the sex act with a manual in one hand. Kids don't have to lose themselves in the collectivity of rock concerts as a way of expression because of the absence of a constructive and anchoring mythos in which to retreat from the artificiality of their world. Modern man is so damned lonely. In that loneliness there has to be another way of asserting individuality beyond spending $5,000 on clothes and make-up. People are looking to religious forms to give them back their manhood and womanhood, their sense of purpose and meaning. That's not a rampant return to classic mysticism; it's only a retreat from the pathological individualism of our society.

"Take the question of homosexuality," he went on. "I have a pet thesis. In the past girls wore tight sweaters with low necklines. Now fashion has de-emphasized their breasts and covered their necks, but their backsides are highlighted. By drawing attention to that cleavage, the insane subliminal signal of a crazy culture is: since sex is non-procreative anyway, whichever set of buns turns you on is your option." (I began to feel I was in a Woody Allen movie, I must admit.) "But what began as a controllable option has become an uncontrollable obsession – and it hasn't created happy people. The tasks of liberals are, one, not to reject the traditional forms without creating alternate forms and, two, not to abdicate the capacity for autonomous judgement. All of us have been given our cards. God can't be blamed for them, but they are our challenge. Without that challenge there is only disaster and bleakness and existential despair."

At this level the return to religion seems a matter of personal or social utility. It is not connected necessarily with the Truth. Proof that God and the Torah are fantasies would not make people feel any better, while proof that God and the Torah are facts would not make them feel very comfortable. "Judaism doesn't know a distinction between the secular and the sacred, but its 'civil religion' aspect is stronger now than its quest for the transcendental," Rabbi Dow Marmur of Toronto's Holy Blossom Temple agreed. "The emphasis too often is on maintenance rather than mission, because mission has to speak about God – and many people find that embarrassing. It is that absence of the transcendental that drives away so many of our most sensitive young people to cults or the extreme Orthodox. True religion is always a minority pursuit, like classical music. That minority may be growing, though it may also be exaggerated at times since people go in and out, whenever they're defeated by their mortgage or the bourgeois lifestyle."

The ultimate principle of Judaism, Emil Fackenheim wrote, is *"the intimacy of the divine infinity."* In history, at least, that has meant that God and his people were as close as lovers. So what would happen if God's people refuse to be the people of God? "A Jew would have to stay at his post even if he were a remnant of one," Fackenheim replied to the awful question he had posed. "He would have to stay at his post lest God, left by His people, become 'as it were, not God.'"

THIRTEEN

The Bonds Are Strong

Just hours before going to the Kristallnacht commemoration at the Spanish and Portuguese Synagogue, I witnessed another graphic demonstration of what happens when a religion abandons God for politics. All that day the Quebec Region of the Canadian Jewish Congress had been holding a series of workshops at the Holiday Inn, and in the speeches and in the corridors most of the "community dialogue" was about Israel. It is always a hot topic among Jews, made hotter now by the luncheon speech of Leon Wieseltier, the literary editor of the American magazine, *The New Republic*.

Wieseltier personified liberal Jews who have had increasing problems with Israel's firm response to the *intifada*, the populist Palestinian uprising that began in December 1987. In fact, his arguments went deeper than last night's TV news by challenging some key assumptions, particularly that Jews must support Israel right or wrong and that Israel is the highest (if not the only) expression of contemporary Jewish life. Since Jews have no natural cause to behave better than other people and since their state is not immune to the corruptions of power, he argued, there could be times when no Jew should support Israel – for example, if it ever acted on the demand of some of its citizens for the mass "transfer" of Palestinians out of Israel and the occupied territories. Moreover, he contended, Jews in the Diaspora (especially in the United States) have been evolving indigenous forms of Jewish thought and culture that are different from – but not less valid than – Israel's. Welcoming that pluralism, he concluded that Israel should not have as much impact on North American Jews as it does.

"It is an independent state with its own work," he said, "while we have our work to do here."

It was not exactly the pep talk to which Montreal Jews had been accustomed, and many in the crowd could hardly wait to jump on Wieseltier at a panel discussion following the lunch. "The bottom line is the security of Israel," he was told, to applause. "The Arabs want to destroy us, period." Given that, the rest followed: criticism of Israel serves the enemies of Jews here and there, the intellectuals should look instead at human rights in the Arab countries, those who do not live in Israel have no right to tell Israel what to do, crisis requires individuals to hold their tongues and temper the truth for the sake of the community, war is war and not an intellectual debate. "So where was Woody Allen when Israel was threatened in 1967?" one woman shouted angrily, as a way of dismissing all bleeding-heart Jewish smarty-pants, including Leon Wieseltier.

At times he seemed taken aback by the reactions, some of which he confessed were so outdated and out of touch that he had not heard their kind among American Jewish circles for more than ten years. The reason became evident when a young man stood up and declared his pleasant surprise. "This is almost the first time I have been able to talk about these things in public," he said.

Though Jews and Zionists number among Israel's harshest critics, much of the Montreal community sees any abuse of the Jewish state by the media or the politicians or the Christian churches as merely another manifestation of the persecution of the Jewish people. Indeed, the universal history of anti-Semitism is the main defence for why Jews should be allowed a state of their own at last, even if Palestinian Arabs or democratic principles must take second place to assure it. In that light, the 1975 declaration of the General Assembly of the United Nations that Zionism is a form of racism seems no different than all the discriminatory laws that accused the Jewish ghettos of being the cause of their own grief.

The identification with Israel is as deep in Montreal as the memory of the Holocaust. A Zionist society had been formed in the city within a year of the famous meeting at Basel in 1897 to promote the idea, and within two years there was a federation of Zionist societies in cities across Canada. Ever since then Zionism moved progressively toward the centre of almost all Jewish communal activity in Canada. Israeli politics were often the meat and potatoes of the sermons I heard at the Spanish and Portuguese Synagogue and Shaar Hashomayim; the Canadian Zionist Federation is made up of twenty-two Israel-related organizations and itself is a partner with the Canadian Jewish Congress and Canadian B'nai B'rith in the Canada-Israel Committee; there are seven associations in Montreal to help universities in Israel and no end to the number of committees, foundations, projects, clubs, campaigns, gala dinners, tributes, and bazaars to sell Israeli bonds or plant a tree in the desert.

"Israel might seem an artificial way of propping up our identity, *except* that Israel has never been allowed to exist in peace," said Ruth Wisse of McGill's Jewish Studies department. "I hate 'crisis Judaism,' I wish Israel wasn't at the centre, but Israel does put a legitimate claim on all Jews, including the pressure to move there."

Jewish unity had been strengthened by the vision of poor, small Israel struggling to build a civilization out of sand, making extraordinary sacrifices to become the one haven for Jews in a hostile world, fulfilling the promise made to its people by God, and under constant threat and actual attack by numerous and powerful enemies. That vision was never as intense as during the Six-Day War in 1967. On the one hand, the image of solitary David going into combat against formidable Goliaths rallied Jews and the friends of Israel to a unanimity not seen before or since. On the other hand, Israel's swift victory both punctured the notion of its vulnerability and created circumstances that were to sow more and more animosity and discord over the next twenty years.

The circumstances involved Israel's capture of East Jerusalem, the West Bank, and the Gaza Strip (as well as other Arab territory subsequently given up), because with the occupation came some three-quarters of a million Arabs, now estimated to be more than twice that number. What is Israel to do with them? They could be integrated as full citizens, but not without their booming population inevitably undermining Israel's constitutional existence as a Jewish state; they could be given what they seem to want, their own Palestinian state, but not without risk to Israel's security and serious political opposition among many Jews; or they could be left as they are, under military control and without full democratic rights. Because none of the alternatives is ideal for Israel, all now have their vehement proponents and opponents among Jews and non-Jews everywhere. Television reports of Israeli soldiers shooting at stone-throwing children or bulldozing Arab homes were added to previous controversies about the democratic nature of Zionism, Israel's invasion of Lebanon in 1982, and the rise of an extremist and militant Jewish right.

Whatever their own doubts and upset, most Montreal Jews insist that disunity will only jeopardize the very survival of Israel, give ammunition to the Palestine Liberation Organization (PLO) and the enemy states, and play into the forces of global anti-Semitism. Though the Montreal community is considered rather more united around a hardline policy for Israel than the larger, younger, newer, and more liberal Toronto community, both are considered a great deal less conciliatory and open-minded than the American community.

"It's disgusting!" Ruth Wisse said. "Do you know any other community that divides when it's under attack?" (I refrained from telling her about the Sikhs.)

In the face of exile and persecution, unity has always been a particular obsession of Jews everywhere. They often take pains, for example, to assert that the three major movements within Judaism do not represent the same rigid divisions that describe Christian denominations. Because the practical congregationalism of Judaism leaves ultimate authority for rituals, morals, and legal interpretation with the rabbi and board of each synagogue, goes the argument, the variations are more like one spectrum of views than three separate boxes with their own beliefs, rites, and central authorities. Moreover, as Emil Fackenheim pointed out in *What Is Judaism?*, Orthodox Judaism is a misnomer we are stuck with because of common usage. Orthodoxy technically refers to belief, but the differences among religious Jews are not usually about that. Almost all would agree – boiling the famous thirteen principles of Maimonides down to three fundamentals – that there is only one God as supreme and incorporeal Creator, that God gave Moses the first five books of the Bible (the Torah or the Pentateuch) as teachings and laws of divine will, and that God rewards and punishes people according to their actions. In addition, most believe in the deliverance of the Jewish people and all nations from oppression and suffering on this earth through the eventual coming of a Messiah or messianic time.

On the other hand, there are a multitude of differences about orthopraxy, the correct practice. They stem at the root from the Torah, which included not only the Ten Commandments but 603 more *mitzvot* ranging from the ban on eating pork to the requirement of circumcision. In time, naturally, interpretations and debates developed (orally and then in writing) about "the Law" and its role in normal life. By the sixth century these discussions, decisions, and moral stories had been collected to form the Talmud, "the teaching," a compendium so important to Judaism that it is sometimes included in a broad definition of the Torah as a divine revelation. Further interpretations and adaptations of both the Torah and the Talmud produced further applications of the Law and the teachings, to the point where today Orthodoxy can mean a strict and literal "ultra-Orthodox" approach to the 613 commandments, a liberal and modern "neo-Orthodox" view of them, and a range of practices in between.

Orthodoxy stands as one, however, when set against the nineteenth-century movement known as Reform Judaism. Though it can be misleading to draw close comparisons,

Reform Judaism has many notable similarities to Protestant Christianity. Both were liberal phenomena, geared to change, progress, reason, science, and individual conscience; both applied historical criticism to the Bible and moved from the letter of the law to its spirit; both transformed their worship, by the use of the vernacular or by the emphasis on the sermon, to make it more meaningful and relevant for the faithful. In essence, Fackenheim wrote, Reform Judaism "springs from the conflict between the claim of past authority, that of a revealed canon included, and the modern claim of the free, 'autonomous' moral and religious conscience" – which puts it precisely where radical Catholics and liberal Protestants are to be found.

Arising out of Germany (where Luther had nailed his ninety-five theses to a door and "higher criticism" was beginning to put Adam and Eve under investigation), it quickly had its greatest impact in the United States, where its liberalism met the liberalism of the prevailing culture, the uncongealed nature of a diverse and scattered Jewish community, and the organizational enthusiasm of Rabbi Isaac Mayer Wise of Cincinnati, who was instrumental in founding the Union of American Hebrew Congregations, still the key association of Reform synagogues, in which Canada is one region. By 1885, when the "Pittsburgh Platform" elevated "only the moral laws" above "all such Mosaic and rabbinical laws as regulate diet, priestly purity, and dress" conjured from "ideas altogether foreign to our present mental and spiritual state," Reform Judaism was the Judaism of choice for the quarter of a million Jews in the United States. Under its dynamic sway two Reform temples were built in Canada, in Hamilton and Montreal. In the 1920s they were joined by Holy Blossom, Toronto's oldest and most prestigious synagogue, which had been liberalized gradually since its beginnings in 1856.

That was about the extent of the Reform movement in Canada until the 1950s, however. It had trouble penetrating a community that was so small (barely a tenth of the U.S. Jewish population in 1881), so concentrated (almost half in Montreal alone), and so firmly rooted in tradition and ethnicity –

nor did Rabbi Wise help his cause by delivering a controversial speech against Zionism in Montreal in 1897. Even in the United States, after Reform's initial impact, the huge migrations of Jews from Eastern Europe and Russia around the turn of the century strengthened Orthodox customs and institutions, though perhaps more for the sake of cultural preservation than religious fervour.

Moreover, Reform met a new challenge in the growth of Conservative Judaism, another nineteenth-century movement with intellectual roots in Germany. It swept through the United States as a centrist compromise between the radical changes of Reform and the outdated traditions of the Orthodox. "You can think of it like the Anglicans," I was told, "running between the United Church and the Roman Catholics" – open to many modern modifications in ritual and thought, but anxious to safeguard the heritage and identity of the Jewish people. By 1887 it had its own training school, the Jewish Theological Seminary in New York; and by 1913 it had its own organization, the United Synagogue of America, to which Canadian Conservative congregations belong. Conservatism obviously made sense to those Jews who wanted to fit into a new time and place without being assimilated totally, and it attracted many of the older, more acculturated congregations – including Shaar Hashomayim in Montreal, which kept the custom of separate seating for men and women, however.

While new immigrants continued to reinforce Orthodox Judaism, which had organized itself into the Union of Orthodox Jewish Congregations of America, Reform in effect had to wait for its second wind until the 1950s, when second- or third-generation North American Jews were ready to leave behind more and more traditions as they moved up the social ladder or into the suburbs. Even then, whether because of the Holocaust or Israel or the religious identity stressed by Protestants and Catholics in post-war America, the pressure was on Reform to shift closer to the blend of modernity and tradition that was the great advantage of the Conservative movement. By 1970 half the Jews who were affiliated with a synagogue in the United States belonged to the Conservative movement, 30 per cent were Reform, and 20 per cent were Orthodox. At the same time, Toronto had slightly fewer Conservative (44 per cent), but 38 per cent Orthodox and only 18 per cent Reform. In remarkable contrast, Montreal had 60 per cent Orthodox, 30 per cent Conservative, and a mere 10 per cent Reform. In fact, the city's once-renowned Reform synagogue, Temple Emanu-el in Westmount, has been suffering declining membership and a turnover of rabbis in recent years.

"Montreal is a very traditional Jewish city," said Rabbi Joseph, a bright and amiable man who looks like a sober Groucho Marx, when I visited him in his cluttered study at the Spanish and Portuguese Synagogue. "Even those who aren't very traditional in practice often belong to the traditional synagogue where their parents went. That's very Montreal. If they moved to the United States – or even Toronto, which has a more American style – they might join a Conservative or even Reform congregation. Here they stay with what they grew up in, and they want their synagogues and rites to be in the Orthodox tradition. That's their communal standard, even if it isn't their personal standard."

"That makes Montreal very different from the rest of North American," Rabbi Poupko agreed. "Here centrist Orthodoxy feels closer ideologically and socially, even geographically, to Conservative and Reform Jews than to ultra-Orthodox Jews. So, while our Conservative and Reform may be more traditional than in other cities, our Orthodox are more wishy-washy."

Whether genuine or a wish, this general religious togetherness has been dramatically fractured in recent years by the intense debate within Israel and throughout the Diaspora over the question of who is a Jew. Traditionally a Jew has been defined as someone born of a Jewish mother or someone who has converted according to Orthodox law and custom (such as male circumcision or immersion in a bath known as a *mikvah*). Both strike many modern Jews as being too narrow, particularly given the diminishing numbers who fit that definition because of a declining birth rate, intermarriage, and assimilation. Almost all Reform rabbis and a large number of Conservative ones have moved to make conversion easier, and Reform's Central Conference of American Rabbis has extended the definition in 1983 to recognize the children of Jewish fathers – a recognition rejected, by the way, by Toronto's Reform rabbis for the sake of communal harmony. As a consequence, Orthodoxy has refused to consider as Jews those who were converted by non-Orthodox procedures, as well as those who think of themselves as Jews by virtue of their paternity and upbringing alone, and it is not too sure about the children of Jews who were married or divorced by the non-Orthodox either.

This is not the first such feud – the Conservative movement developed out of the refusal of American Orthodox leaders to accept the rabbis trained by the Jewish Theological Seminary, for instance – but it has become the most serious. Its implications are that hundreds of thousands of Reform and Conservative Jews might be judged as non-Jews in the eyes of the Orthodox, producing a schism not seen since some Jews decided Jesus Christ was the Messiah. In 1984 Rabbi Reuven Bulka of Ottawa published a book on the rift, ominously called *The Coming Cataclysm*.

"With no meaningful communication between the Orthodox and the Reform, with the two sectors diverging radically on the ever-critical social interaction level," he wrote, "each will go its own way – the Orthodox toward more intensive actualization of commandments, the Reform toward a new, autonomous existence. In time, marriage with a member of the Reform community may become as catastrophic for Orthodox Jews as mixed-marriage (marriage without conversion) is now." Looking at the overall scene, Rabbi Bulka foresaw for Judaism a dynamic, expanding, and prolific right wing bound to a literal interpretation of the Bible and the law that would even be at odds with the compromises of modern Orthodoxy, a confused and secularized left wing picking and choosing its way through folkloric customs and beliefs, and a weak centre being pulled to the extremes. "The saga that is unfolding is one of more rupture, more civil strife, less coherence, less unity."

Already there are signs of a shake-up. When Conservative's Jewish Theological Seminary moved to accept women rabbis in 1987 and women cantors a year later, a group of dissenting rabbis – including many Canadians – created the Union of Traditional Conservative Judaism. More recently, when the Union of Orthodox Jewish Congregations moved to enforce the separation of sexes in its synagogues, several dozen of its more modern rabbis – including Allan Nadler of Shaar Hashomayim – started the Fellowship of Traditional Orthodox Rabbis in opposition to the regressive step. In these two new organizations, some see the seeds of a new movement, which will pull together the Conservative right and the Orthodox left to create a new centre. In this scenario Reform will either move to the right or become totally secularized, and right-wing Orthodoxy will make up a bigger piece of a smaller pie throughout North America.

A minor indication of the potential strife occurred in Toronto in July 1988, when non-Orthodox conversions were barred from using the ritual bath managed by the Orthodox. It was just one skirmish in the global war that flared up later that year around the policies of the three ultra-Orthodox religious parties competing in Israel's November election, including a Hassidic party heavily influenced by the Lubavitcher Rebbe in Brooklyn. Although they were divided among themselves, they shared the goal of reinforcing the religious character of the Jewish state by applying the laws of the Torah to the whole society: no women in the cabinet, for instance, or no sports and entertainment on the Sabbath. The three parties won no more than 11 per cent of the vote in 1988 and gained only 13 seats in the 120-seat parliament, but that was enough to give the government to either the Likud Party (with forty seats) or the Labor Party (with thirty-nine). This time the price for their support was high: they wanted an amendment to the Law of Return.

The Law of Return is an Israeli law, adopted in 1950 and altered in 1970, that grants full citizenship to any Jew migrating there. A Jew was defined subsequently as "one born of a Jewish mother or converted to Judaism," leaving unresolved the controversy surrounding conversion. The amendment would have added the qualification, "according to Jewish law," to freeze out non-Orthodox converts. The words were simple and the numbers affected were small, but the outrage that followed was neither.

Reform rabbis accused the religious parties of being "Jewish ayatollahs" bent on establishing an ultra-Orthodox theocracy based on "stale repression, fossilized tradition, and ethical corruption." Conservative rabbis urged their followers not to give money to the Lubavitchers, who want to turn Israel from a "state into a shtetl." Even some Orthodox rabbis in favour of proper conversions argued that it was not democratic for religious leaders to compel a government to enforce a religious law. And since most North American Jews are non-Orthodox, they saw the amendment as a delegitimization of their own rabbis and traditions. They sent stern warnings to Tel Aviv through their official agencies, including Montreal's Allied Jewish Community Services, not to change the law. According to one source, the AJCS was going to stay out of the issue because of the city's Orthodox majority, until "some big-money people whose children had married into Conservative and Reform put the pressure on."

"As an Orthodox rabbi," said Reuben Poupko, "I have the 'sick' idea that Orthodoxy is the authentic version of our faith. Reform has broken the rules to the point that we don't even know if they're Jewish, and since their Wonder Bread Judaism is failing, they have to scream and yell from their pulpits about religious pluralism. But Orthodoxy has been keeping the rules for 3,500 years, and the conversion rules are like an initiation into a fraternity: if you want to join, you have to walk around the roof drunk."

Though Poupko refuses to sit with non-Orthodox rabbis on the Board of Jewish Ministers of Greater Montreal, "for the same reason that surgeons don't recognize chiropractors," the atmosphere in Montreal is still relatively cordial. The Lubavitchers control a *mikvah*, for example, but they have not denied use of it to the non-Orthodox here as they did in Winnipeg. "There have been some small incidents," Rabbi Joseph said, "but no public issue. It's a close-knit community, and because ethnic groups stick together in Quebec, we define ourselves more as Montreal Jews than as Orthodox or Conservative or Reform. That may change, of course, but for now there's a sense of harmony."

Ultimately Yitzhak Shamir preferred harmony too, and he made his deal with Labor rather than with the religious right. It was no time to jeopardize support for Israel in the Diaspora, and the wish of the American Jewish Congress and B'nai B'rith was heard louder than any will of God. That retreat seemed to confirm the view of cooler heads who argue that, even if Rabbi Bulka's cataclysm comes to pass, Jews will continue to be united by other forces. Judaism, they repeat, is only one element of the tribe. For evidence they point to the so-called "secular Jews," some coming out of a coherent philosophy that a Jew is still a Jew without any religion (because of blood or history or culture), many coming out of an incoherent scepticism about God and the transcendental. The former would make no bones about their atheism, choosing instead to concentrate their energies on this world through radical politics or Yiddish literature or the building of Israel. The latter would be more agnostic, influenced by the secular materialism of the times yet not averse to attending a synagogue on the High Holidays or observing the dietary laws from time to time. Whether secular by commission or omission, the crucial fact is that the vast majority of them would still define themselves as Jews and still be so defined by most of the Jewish community.

Some of that is due to the vague boundaries that Judaism has always drawn between the sacred and the secular; some is due to the stories and traditions learned on a mother's knee or in a grandfather's study; some is due to the pressures on a small and persecuted minority never to abandon the tribe or alienate its own kind; some is merely the result of Jews never being allowed to forget they are Jews by the hostile societies that surround them. Indeed, I have a friend in Montreal whose only link to his Jewish heritage seems to be the constancy with which non-Jews remind him of it.

If the presence of the sceptical sort can be presumed for as long as there have been Jews in Canada, intermarrying and assimilating and munching pork sausages, the ideological variety really came in the wave at the end of the nineteenth century. They brought socialism and ethnic clubs instead of rabbis and synagogues to Montreal, creating a vital and challenging element between the religious faithful who arrived with them and the acculturated traditionalists who were already established. Largely because of them, Jews began to clash with Jews over issues of class, unions, Canadian politics, Zionism, social services, and education, often because the working-class "downtowners" laboured in the factories and businesses of the upwardly-mobile "uptowners." "Where formerly the principal divisions in the community had been denominational – with Sephardic, Ashkenazic and Reform Jews all vying for supremacy," wrote Benjamin Sack, "now religious divergencies were almost wholly overshadowed by a deeper and more significant social cleavage."

Socialists, communists, and bundists (such as David Lewis and Fred Rose) took on capitalists, religionists, and Zionists in public battles, but their intensity was often the ferocious intensity of a family fight. That became most obvious when the community as a whole was attacked by French-Canadian fascists or English-Canadian racists; and the high number of radical Jewish leaders who ended their lives with Orthodox funeral services was no more remarkable than the high number of devout Jewish tycoons who dedicated their fortunes to social causes. By the end of the Second World War most of the conflict and nastiness had evaporated, as the Holocaust forged Jews into a more cohesive and less assimilable people, as anti-Zionism became an untenable idea for Jews, and as the Jewish working class moved almost entirely into the bourgeoisie.

As the ideological secularist faded to the edge of extinction, the sceptical one loomed larger and larger. With the important exception of the post-war refugees who clung understandably to the traditions and beliefs of their decimated homelands, the Jewish patterns in the 1950s and 1960s were not unlike those of Christian North America. On the surface, there was a significant movement toward the synagogue for the sake of family, values, and identify. Underneath the expansion, however, there were ominous signals. The synagogues became community centres, recreation halls, learning facilities, as much as places of worship. The prestige and authority of the rabbis passed increasingly to the officials and patrons of the national and local Jewish agencies. The rate of intermarriage began to climb until it reached crisis proportions. (Even though the Canadian rate is about two-thirds the American rate of 40 per cent, its long-term effect is considered a nightmare. "What anti-Semitism doesn't erode from without," Rabbi Marmur once told me, "assimilation will erode from within.") In the turmoil of the 1960s a noteworthy number of young Jews turned from the God of their fathers to political activism, oriental meditation, cult gurus, even to Jesus Christ. Synagogue affiliation dropped to no more than half the Jews in Canada and the United States. In 1971, for the first time, more Canadian Jews described themselves in the census as Jews by ethnicity rather than Jews by religion. I was told of one woman, as an example, who was extremely active in Jewish education and Yiddish culture and who thought of God as her personal friend, yet never went to synagogue and only abstained from ham during Passover.

Such sceptics would be offended to be called "lapsed Jews," however, in the way their counterparts are called lapsed Catholics and Protestants. In fact, many would argue, their Jewish identity has never been stronger. The reason is Israel. "God, Torah, and Israel are one," says the Zohar, a thirteenth-century mystical work – with Israel meaning the people of God, or what I was told to consider the *tribe*. From the earliest times that community was linked to the land of Abraham and Isaac and Jacob – *Eretz Israel*, the land of Israel – to the degree that those people became as one with that land. It was part of God's covenant with them; it was where God promised to return them from their slavery in Egypt and their captivity in Babylon; it was the place they longed to call their own again since their exile from it by the Romans. "Next year in Jerusalem," they had wished every Passover for centuries.

The spiritual prayer became a political platform during the nineteenth century, when the renewed persecution of Jews in Europe and Russia produced a cry for a safe and independent homeland in their ancient territory, then known as Palestine. Zionism grew as a worldwide idea among secular and religious Jews (though the political left used to attack it as an irrelevant utopianism and the religious right still harbours those who condemn it as a blasphemous misjudgement of God's true will); it got powerful support from the British government in 1917; and it succeeded in establishing the state of Israel in 1948 out of the ashes and exodus of the Holocaust. Increasingly since then, and especially since each military threat by Israel's Arab neighbours "to push the Jews into the sea," Israel has been defined less as the whole people and more as the specific state. More significantly perhaps, as Jews quarrelled and divided over the existence of God and the authority of the Torah, the existence of the state of Israel became the most effective expression of Jewish unity and hence of Jewish identity.

"Canada's Jews remain Jews and wish to invest that identity with some transcendent, or religious, legitimacy and meaning," Jack Lightstone and David Rome observed in their essay on Judaism in the *Canadian Encyclopedia*. "In all the retained ritual activity, Jewish peoplehood and its constituent unit, the Jewish family, are endowed with ultimacy. God and Torah seem either conspicuously absent or carefully hidden."

Just as many modern Christians have given up on a distant God and literal Bible for political and social expressions of their faith, so many Jews are focusing their spiritual aspect in history and current affairs. Thus, the Holocaust and the state of Israel are sanctified as religious myths as well as secular realities, so that they have come (as Lightstone and Rome wrote) "to constitute powerful symbols to Canadian Jewry of the 'eternity' of the people, guaranteed by a deity of whom few Jews will speak."

"Israel is a symbol that we are part of a distinct nation," said Rabbi Joseph, "and the national sense of destiny has reawakened many Jews to the spiritual dimension of Judaism as well.

And, at the gut level, Israel has given us a strong sense of identity. Giving back three inches of land becomes like diminishing my identity by three inches. In the Diaspora, every Jew knows that if things go bad, we can go to Israel. So Israel becomes too precious, on a spiritual level, to be threatened."

But the decision to invite Leon Wieseltier to promote his provocative views in Montreal indicated that there were important elements within the Jewish leadership who thought it was time to reconsider Israel right or wrong. As Wieseltier himself stated, his criticisms were not out of hatred for Israel, but out of love, and his love required him to warn Jews about what he understood as Israel's greater dangers. With the collapse of the status quo as a viable option, and in light of alternatives fraught with peril, neither clinging to outworn cant nor burying one's head in the sands of Zion seemed to him in the long-term interest of the Jewish people. More and more were agreeing with that, and speaking out.

Just three weeks before, for example, to celebrate the seventy-fifth anniversary of the Jewish People's Schools and Peretz Schools, the huge crowd of students and parents squashed into the gymnasium of Bialik High heard much the same message from Arthur Hertzberg, a former president of the American Jewish Congress and a distinguished scholar. His distinction and scholarship did not prevent him from being feisty and controversial. He too saw only three ways out of the current uprising: "a Palestinian entity of some sort," "Belfast forever," or a mass expulsion "that would horrify me, because it would be so reminiscent of what happened to us." Considering the political and psychological damage to Jews of either putting down a permanent rebellion or shipping people out on trucks, he stressed the necessity of looking for negotiated alternatives, "even if they're bad ones."

"The hidden premise of the minority extremists is the notion that we don't need rational answers for politics and religion: *we're going to be bailed out by living in messianic times,*" he said. "Well, I've got news for them. The Messiah isn't coming in this generation! If he didn't show up in Auschwitz, he's not going to show up now. We're going to have only our human wisdom and human decency to rely upon."

When he was asked how Israel could negotiate a peace with Arabs who do not want peace, Hertzberg was even blunter. "That question's an old ploy. If you say that Arabs are terrible people, et cetera, then the question becomes whether we can shoot enough of them. Shall I give you some plain and dirty talk? They're outbreeding your possibility of shooting them all!"

If such plain and dirty talk was supposed to shake the Montreal Jewish community into understanding the new dynamics in the Middle East, to bring it around to some moderate proposal of exchanging territory for peace, it was a failure. The immediate effect was a sharp increase in criticism of the regional and national leadership, for inadequately combatting the anti-Israel propagandists at work within world opinion, the Canadian government, the universities, and the media and for failing to maintain the hard line that the Diaspora's only role is to give unqualified support for whatever Israel decides it must do for the sake of its security.

"The leadership is cut off from the grassroots," said Julien Bauer, a professor at the University of Quebec at Montreal. He characterized most of the leaders as rich, in favour of Israel's Labor Party, uncomfortable about the emphasis on the Holocaust, and ignorant of the religious parties. "They have a tendency to organize everything behind the scenes, which is O.K. as long as it works. When it doesn't work, they can't relate to their people because they're not used to relating. Even well-to-do, wishy-washy, don't-rock-the-boat types don't defend them, except maybe to say, 'They're not too bright.' They totally failed the test of the uprising. Since they themselves didn't know or understand, how could they explain it? So people felt let down, they got no help from their leadership."

As proof, Bauer cited the furore that erupted in 1988 after reports that fifteen prominent Canadian Jews (including the presidents of the Canadian Jewish Congress and B'nai B'rith Canada and two Reform rabbis from Toronto) had met secretly in April with fifteen leading Canadian Arabs at Montebello, Quebec, for a dialogue on the Middle East, organized by External Affairs and the Canadian Institute for International Peace and Security. Many Jews suspect External Affairs of pro-Arab bias, especially since Joe Clark delivered a speech critical of some Israeli actions to the Canada-Israel Committee that March; and many were enraged by the very idea of a bunch of people sitting in a lodge near Ottawa to discuss Israel's future.

"The purpose of Montebello is, clearly, to neuter Jewish public opinion by driving a wedge between a small and willingly co-opted minority and a Jewish majority left without a coherent voice," declared an open letter signed by 121 Jewish officials, academics, professionals, and rabbis, assembled by the Canadian Institute for Jewish Research, a Montreal-based group set up in response to the pro-Palestinian current following the *intifada*. Calling the Jewish participants "deliberately not representative" and accusing External Affairs of "manipulative tactics" designed to tilt Canadian foreign policy toward the Arabs and the PLO, it demanded – and eventually obtained – the cancellation of a second proposed meeting in August.

"For the first time," said Bauer, one of the letter's signatories and an active member of the new institute, "the leadership had to change its mind because their people were screaming."

Nor was it the last time, it seemed. Despite his own well-publicized support for the Labor Party, Charles Bronfman initiated a committee of Jewish leaders to explore the community's failure to manage the crisis produced in public opinion, the educational system, government circles, and the media by the uprising on the West Bank and to recommend organizational changes for future crises. Even by the time of the Canadian Jewish Congress's national meeting in May 1989 – also in Montreal – the influence of the protest was evident. No Wieseltier or Hertzberg had been asked to provoke the delegates, even as just one voice on a panel. Now there was no complexity, no nuance, no division, no pluralism, as the Israeli ambassador to Canada and two hardline Americans hammered home the theme of Jewish unity.

"I've never been forgiven since I took up the cudgels against the invasion of Lebanon," said Rabbi Reuben Slonim, a provocative Toronto writer. "Now Israel is God, and the Torah comes from the Prime Minister. Anyone who says differently is beyond the pale. Because the Holocaust survivors dominate here, and because the rest of the Jews are afraid to oppose them, Holocaust psychology colours much of our Jewish opinion. Israel backs up that attitude by saying it has to be strong militarily so that there will be no more Holocaust. Originally Zionism was peoplehood, a state devoted to spiritual values, with freedom for everyone – even Arabs. But Zionism has been perverted, Judaism has been perverted."

In what way?

"For example, the Bible says that the West Bank shall belong to the descendants of Abraham. The Bible also says that we should love our neighbour as thyself, which means we shouldn't be doing to the Palestinians what we are doing. So which governs, the literal heritage or the spiritual obligation? The spiritual always takes precedence. My colleagues are very fine citizens, but they have no courage at all in their spiritual persuasion. Jews lived for 4,000 years in uninterrupted tradition with no army or air force, while empires fell around them, because of their reliance on the spiritual conviction that the essence of Judaism is to serve humankind. Militarism has the seeds of its own destruction, but the spiritual dimension will continue as long as there is a minority to support it."

It was much the same argument I had heard from the Christians who feared their involvement in politics and social affairs would absorb their faith instead of being absorbed by it. Israel had gone from being Heaven on earth, "the land of milk and honey," to being a temporal state, complete with ambitious politicians and back-room deals and competing interests. It had gone from myth into history, and Jews were having a rough time integrating its spiritual ideals with its secular realities. Many Jews required of it higher standards of behaviour, befitting its sacred mandate. Some Jews wished it would disappear, lest its imperfections and presumptions incur the wrath of God once more.

In the end, as generations move away from the experience of the Holocaust and as Israel sinks deeper into the mire of politics, is the largely negative obsession with survival enough on which to build hope, define ethics, and bear the Truth? As one Jewish friend told me, "If being a Jew means Holocaust and Israeli wars all the time, who wants to be a Jew?"

"Israel as a state is in more danger than Judaism as a religion, so I don't try to downplay Israel," said Allan Nadler, the young, Harvard-educated rabbi recently installed at Shaar Hashomayim. "Besides, Jewish identity is so weak in America, whatever ignites the passion of a Jew is all right. Living in a secular world, most Jews generally aren't turned on to a purely spiritual message, if there's no political or social action involved."

"Israel has become the Golden Calf of the Jewish People," Rabbi Poupko said. "I get the unaffiliated Jew back to Judaism by Israel and the Holocaust, but to the affiliated, I say, 'Before all comes God and Torah.' If the Holocaust recedes into memory, if Israel becomes less fun to identify with, then we will drop off the edge if we don't push the old message. For 2,000 years we survived without a land, because we understood that land is less important than our ideas. Ideas can't be burnt in gas chambers. The survival of our people has always depended on putting more importance on what no man can touch or see. Zion reborn is the greatest proof of God's existence and the chosenness of the Jewish people in this century. But the central focus of our faith and people has to be God and Torah."

FOURTEEN

The Circulation
of the Saints

I was staying in Leduc, just south of Edmonton, one weekend, when I happened to pass the Family Worship Centre on Black Gold Drive. A bright white building shaped like a horizontal cross, it was advertising for that evening a free dramatic production called "Heaven's Gates and Hell's Flames." Call it divine inspiration, call it utter boredom, but I decided to go.

"Thank you so much for visiting with us today. We trust that this service will minister to you and that you will find yourself reaching out to our Father God in a personal way," said Pastors Peter and Lilly Hubert in a pamphlet I picked up at the door. "Obviously, the empty gods of our society have shattered all around us, and I believe that within the hearts of people all over is a cry for fulfilment, security, and purpose. Many folk are re-evaluating their priorities. Many are trying to deal with the void in their lives, and only He can fill that void."

To help folk fill that void, the pamphlet announced, the Family Worship Centre was offering weekly services, Bible study classes, "children's church," sports events, orchestra and choir ministries, "family nite" activities, men's and ladies' intercessory prayer, the Leduc Christian Academy, indeed "something for everyone" – including this road show brought into town for a few days. These are merely the vehicles, of course, for the beliefs the church affirms as a self-governing affiliate of the Pentecostal Assemblies of Canada: Christ as Saviour and Healer, the Bible as infallible and absolutely supreme, and "the distinctive position that speaking in tongues is the initial evidence when Christ baptizes in the Holy Spirit."

All my doubts were referred to the Holy Scriptures. Why the use of musical instruments? Psalm 150. Why the lifting of hands in praise? Psalm 6. Why the gift of tongues? First Corinthians 14. Why the invitation of people to the altar? Matthew 10. Why the need for tithes and offerings? Malachi 3. "We were born physically once, and we must be born spiritually (salvation) to become alive in God. See John 3:1-8," I read, waiting for the performance to begin. "Salvation is by faith in Jesus Christ and not by human works. But, if we are truly in love with the Lord, then we will want to obey Him and live lives pleasing to God. See Romans 10:9-10 and John 1:12."

The church was no Notre-Dame. It was a bare, white amphitheatre, temporarily made glitzy by yards of aluminium foil as backdrop to the stage. When Pastor Hubert bounced on to the set, with thunder from the organ and a microphone in his hand, to lead the full house in "When the Roll Is Called Up Yonder" (why hymns? Ephesians 5), the words were projected on to a blank wall. "Thank you, Jesus. Thank you, Jesus, " we sang and clapped (see Psalm 47). "Thank you, Lord, for loving me." Pausing only to tell how as a boy in Lethbridge he had sung Calgary for Calvary, he introduced his colleague, all the way from St Catharines, Ontario, the host of tonight's presentation brought to us by Reality Outreach – Larry Booth!

Out came Larry Booth, with a pleasant smile but with a serious message. He was still under forty but he had the suit and paunch of a salesman past his prime. In fact, he had the look and voice of someone pitching things that slice and dice – not least when he announced his wife would be in the lobby to sell souvenir tapes or mentioned "financial needs" in a prayer just before inviting donations (Deuteronomy 16) from the audience. He was, in essence, a travelling showman for Christ, on the road in a camper most months (except for the "down time" of mid-summer and Christmas) with his wife and their two adolescent children, taking the show and the Gospel to about three dozen towns a year from Fort Smith to Minneapolis, wherever he was invited and the Lord sent him.

Born in 1950 in Napanee, Ontario, he lived there almost all his life, married there, worked there, and probably would have stayed there but for a call to do God's work on a full-time basis. "It was nothing dramatic," he told me the next day, as we sat on the edge of the stage in the empty auditorium. "It was a passion to share the Gospel which became an ultimatum: make a move or give up the idea. My wife and I waited five years for the right opportunity."

The right opportunity turned out to be Reality Outreach Ministries Inc., a very small outfit founded in St Catharines in 1979 by Rudy Krulik and Allan Grubb. Their vision was to spread the message by means of a drama, which would involve local congregations in an affirmation of their faith and reach out to the unsaved too. Thus, three teams equipped with aluminum foil, masking tape, and a sound system wander the continent like medieval players. In this case, the Booths breezed into Leduc on Friday. That evening Larry "indoctrinated" (his word) the four dozen volunteers gathered from the centre's members, and the next morning they all began to put the performance together. The set was assembled, the parts were assigned, the Booth kids arranged the sound, and the simple lines were memorized. The script had been recycled from the 1950s, when it was written and used by an American named Bruce Thumb, who also toured and sang with his family in something called "The Sunshine Indian Party."

If one day and a couple of rehearsals seem inadequate preparation for amateurs, it must be realized that this was not exactly Shakespeare. It began with a compressed version of Christ's death: he carried the cross, he was assaulted by some nasty punks, he was crucified by the Devil, and amid angels and rejoicing he rose from the tomb. This established the general scene: on the audience's right the Devil and demons and make-believe flames and red lights on the foil, to the left Christ and saints and golden gates and blue lights on the foil, and in the centre a podium ringed by angels in white and topped by the Book of Life.

There followed a long series of episodes, none very concise or subtle: two young girls died of a drug overdose ("I don't believe in that Jesus stuff, do you?"), two men died in a plane crash (one an ordinary churchgoer, the other a born-again Christian), two families died in a car crash (one a bunch of happy Christians, the other into money and success), two construction workers were killed in an industrial accident (just after the believer convinced the doubter to accept Christ), and so on and on. The dead all were hauled before the Book of Life, in which an angel wearing a glittering crown then looked for their names. The results were both invariable and predictable. Those who were born again were ushered into Heaven while bright lights flash and the "Hallelujah Chorus" blasted over the speakers. Those who were not are dragged off to Hell while the Devil laughed devilishly and a fan caused red streamers to flutter like fire.

"And where will you spend eternity?" Larry Booth asked us after the grand finale, in which a woman had belted out on tape, "It's your life and you can lose it." Larry prayed for God to sweep across the crowd *right now* to call us to Jesus. "The message will never be as clear," he said.

Too clear, in my opinion. On one side, he dangled our greed for eternal youth and happiness. As in the case of the doubting construction worker, who seemed to have spent a life drinking and whoring, all we had to do was say the magic words and we too would hear Handel forever. On the other side, he stoked our fear of eternal pain and misery. No matter what our good deeds, no matter how innocent our children, no matter our intentions or circumstances, if we did not say the magic words we would be condemned without forgiveness or sorrow. What a vain and perverse deity, I thought.

Others must have thought so too, because only six people raised their hands when Larry asked for those who wanted Christ in their life. *No one* stepped forward when he asked for a demonstration of their desire. As a piano played poignantly in the background, Larry persevered. "If I could force you, I

would, but even God can't force you. I *beg* you to come down."
A couple of people went to him, weeping. "Give up the struggle! Give up the battle!" Larry yelled. Most of us were struggling to stay in the room. Two hours of mediocre acting and
inane theology, with no bathroom break, were taking their
toll on the old and the young who had come to see their
relatives or enjoy a night out in Leduc. "I know I'm pushing it
tonight," Larry admitted as his pitch passed the quarter-hour
mark. "If you think I like standing here begging and pleading,
you're wrong." He mopped the sweat from his forehead. "I
know there's someone out there. O Lord, release that one!"

"Pardon me, sir," said a handsome young man, tapping me
unexpectedly on the shoulder. His pretty blonde wife stood
beside him and grinned. "Do you know Jesus Christ?" I could
not say that I did.

"The road will get rough," Larry said, after suggesting we
might be killed on our way home, "but Jesus Christ will get
you through." At last, after those who had been called were
herded through the black hole of a backstage door for a booklet
and five minutes of "sharing" while the rest of us sang "Amazing Grace," we were released. We staggered into the cool air as
if from an airplane in which we had been hijacked by a fundamentalist fanatic. I felt slightly sorry for those we had left
behind, but there seemed no use in everybody getting taken.

"I wouldn't take a million bucks to do what I do – or *not* to
do it," Larry told me about the altar call, which he had picked
up from experience and through the correspondence course he
was taking for full ordination. "Spiritual warfare, that's what
takes place out there. My only strategy is to say, 'Lord help
me.' My role is to stir the pot. I leave the follow-up to the
churches. This is the age of accountability, to make a decision
for Christ. I look at the wars, the famines, the cults, drugs,
AIDS, satanic rock and roll, and I know that world sin is
adding up to the end. We are living in the season of Christ's
coming, and the Scriptures are clear: narrow is the way that
leads to God, there is no other mediator than Christ. That
means we have to have a personal relationship to Christ
through the Spirit. Religion as an institution will send as

many people to Hell as killing and stealing. I believe many members of the Pentecostal Assemblies will go to Hell because they think being a member of a church is enough. But when Christ said, 'Upon this rock I will build my church,' he meant upon our personal acceptance of him in our lives."

His words and procedures cannot be foreign to many North Americans these days. They fill our television sets on Sunday morning and in the middle of the night. They penetrate the political process. They leap out at us on street corners. They beam from the car radio. They capture the attention of the press in demonstrations against abortion and no end of sexual or financial scandals. They are prominent in every small town and suburb. Some preachers may preach better, some may make more money, some may be better known, but Larry Booth comes out of an old tradition. Emotions are more important than intellect, experience is more important than understanding, and there is little place for nuance or ambiguity.

Since the Great Commission, when the disciples went forth to preach the Gospel and gather as many as possible to Jesus Christ, their faith has been linked to evangelism. Missionaries headed out across Europe and Asia and the Americas in that spirit, and divines forayed into slums and brothels for that reason. Not surprisingly they learned a few tricks over time about how to get a crowd of souls in need of saving, how to hold it, how to move it, and how to sign it up – by hymns or oratory, by schools or legislation, by army bands or Christmas entertainments, by threats or punishments, by free food or selfless help. Sometimes that meant converting a king, sometimes that meant conducting a crusade, sometimes that meant coercing a heathen. "I would rather have a man know less Latin and more Horse," said James Robertson, the influential nineteenth-century Presbyterian superintendent of missions in Canada.

Getting the clergy away from their cosy dens, books, and complicated theories, out into the real world of farms and factories and family life, was not a new idea, but it proved especially well suited to the frontier conditions of Canada. In the early years that was no place for purposeless sophistry or unenergetic routine. When Henry Alline brought Newlightism to Nova Scotia at the time of the American Revolution by his relentless travels on horse and boat, the mystical enthusiasm of the Great Awakening established the Baptists in the Maritimes. The success of Methodism over Anglicanism in Upper Canada and the West is attributed to the circuit riders getting out to the bush, the emotional rather than doctrinal pitch of their preaching, and the "strangely warmed" feelings of the camp meetings. It was an activist approach based on Wesley's own disenchantment with the dry and cerebral religion he knew at Oxford, and its activism was a blend of evangelistic fervour and social concern.

Increasingly, the blend became separated. The Social Gospel moved away from Biblical emphasis and personal salvation toward political issues and social sin. It left behind in all denominations those "evangelicals" who were not ready to accept the implications of historical criticism of the Bible, scientific humanism, political liberalism, worldly progress, and cultural affirmation to some degree or another. Against modern reason they stuck to the familiar interpretation of the Scriptures, whether regarding creation or morals. Against public involvement they emphasized the private quest for wisdom and peace by personal conversion through Jesus Christ. From having been the mainstream of nineteenth-century Protestantism, these conservatives now slipped into a backwater beside which the current of contemporary history rushed.

While every major church continues to have a conservative wing, sometimes organized into factions such as the Anglican Renewal Ministries or the United Church Renewal Fellowship, most of the dedication to Biblical inerrancy and personal conversion shifted to the plethora of sects that sprang up between the eighteenth-century revival and the turn of the twentieth century, from the Nazarenes to the Salvation Army, from all sorts of Baptists to the Pentecostals. Often breaking from the institutional sterility and doctrinal confusion of the main churches, often appealing to the victims of modern change, they urged a return to the *fundamentals* of their faith

– to use a term that was introduced in the United States by a series of booklets written between 1910 and 1915 under that title.

The birth of Christian fundamentalism did not mean that everyone agreed on the fundamentals. Since the relationship to Truth was supposed to be personal, authority was to rest either with the individual or with the congregation of like-minded individuals. There was often an inherent instability in the organizations, as a result, as people drifted in and out. Apparently, like sex, schism gets easier after the first time. With no strong, central authority to impose uniformity and discipline, the tendency is to keep splintering. That happened when Protestants split from Rome's monolithic authority and divided into numerous churches and sects. It happened again when Protestants split from each other over doctrine, the interpretation of the Bible, politics, personalities, or in-house squabbles. Those who believed Christ would return *before* the thousand years of peace promised in Revelation 20 split from those who believed he would return *afterwards*. Those who believed in predestination split from those who believed in salvation by good works. Those who believed in pacifism split from those who believed in holy wars. Any spin put on any verse was enough to prompt a walkout, especially if there was an articulate (and ambitious) dissident to lead it.

If the underlying dynamic of Catholicism is to stay within the bosom of the universal Mother, the underlying dynamic of Protestantism in the face of feuds is to get the hell out. A glance at a list of religious bodies in Canada shows the effect. There are, to mention a few, the Associated Gospel Churches, the Bible Holiness Movement, the Christian Congregation Inc., the Church of God (Anderson, Indiana), the Church of God (Cleveland, Tennessee), the Evangelical Covenant Church of Canada, the Independent Holiness Church, the Plymouth Brethren, the Seventh-day Adventist Church in Canada, and the Standard Church of America (Canadian Section). Then there are the subdivisions: four kinds of Methodist churches outside the United Church, seven kinds of Lutherans, thirteen kinds of Mennonites, two kinds of Latter

Day Saints, and seven general associations of Baptists (most of them having sub-subdivisions and even sub-sub-subdivisions based on region, doctrine, and specific rules of baptism).

I picked one at random, the Brethren in Christ Church, Canadian Conference (world headquarters: 301 North Elm Street, Nappanee, Indiana; Canadian headquarters: bishop's office, Stevensville, Ontario). "The Brethren in Christ, formerly known as Tunkers in Canada, arose out of a religious awakening in Lancaster County, Pa., late in the eighteenth century," read its blurb. "Representatives of the new denomination reached Ontario in 1788 and established the church in the southern part of the present province. Presently the conference has congregations in Ontario, Alberta, and Saskatchewan. In doctrine the body is evangelical, Arminian, holiness, and premillennial."

One of the more significant subdivisions was the split between the evangelicals and the Pentecostals. Pentecostalism arose in the first part of this century, in Kansas apparently, more from Wesleyan ecstasy than from the Calvinist pessimism of most fundamentalists. While both groups are born-again Christians who believe in a literal Bible, the Pentecostals revel in the frenzy of being touched by the Spirit, in screams and glossolalia and shakes and cures, much to the disdain and suspicion of many evangelicals. The best known of Canadian Pentecostals was Aimée Semple McPherson, whose Foursquare Gospel Church spread across North America in the 1920s and still exists. It is just one of a dozen Pentecostal groups in Canada, such as the Church of God of Prophecy, the Italian Pentecostal Church, the Open Bible Standard Churches of Canada, and the Pentecostal Assemblies of Canada. Founded in 1919 and now gathering together about 175,000 members in over 1,000 churches (including the Family Worship Centre in Leduc) into a loose alliance, the PAOC has emerged as a major national organization, though its clout is in operations and overseas missions rather than doctrine. Its prosperity is indicative of the growth in numbers and social acceptability of the movement since the 1960s, when the charismatic phenomenon took the style of Pentecostalism into the major churches and the preachers brought their rhetoric and healing to television. Indeed, Pentecostalism has become the fastest-growing part of Christianity around the world, from native leaders in Northern Canada to African villagers to Latin American ex-Catholics, by adding emotional impact to a simple message. It even has its own schools in Newfoundland.

Waking late on Sunday morning in Leduc, I found one of those preachers on my TV set, broadcast from Edmonton out of Central Tabernacle, another self-governing church aligned with the PAOC. Since I had taken to scanning the religion page of the weekend papers as I used to scan their movie listings, looking for an interesting sermon or an unusual entertainment, I already knew that Central was both old (est. 1917) and profitable. I decided to dash into town for its eleven-o'clock worship. Painted on a grain elevator by the side of the highway were the huge words: "Jesus said: 'Shall it profit a man, if he gain the whole world, and lose his own soul?' Mark 8." I had cause to remember those words during the next couple of days.

Central Pentecostal Tabernacle turned out to be a rich and impressive place up on 107 Avenue, one part a new three-storey block of offices and meeting rooms (the Christian Education Building), the other part the main sanctuary (resembling a three-sided pyramid with one corner pulled out far to create a vast triangular floorspace). The church's interior is a bright and spacious amphitheatre, with elegant wooden walls and pews and a gigantic copper globe over the stage, which was filled with a choir of four dozen in white robes by the time I arrived. Led by a mighty organ and an enthusiastic musical director, they aroused the large, well-heeled crowd into a lusty rendition of "All hail the pow'r of Jesus' name!"

The room glowed with middle-class success, and I had to admire the ingredients of that success – beyond the movement of the Holy Spirit, that is – from the ample parking to the television broadcasts. There were nursery facilities for "sleepers" and "leapers"; there was a special "children's church" for preschoolers; there was even "Wee College" to teach four- and five-year-olds "the Scriptures and fundamentals of our faith." There were ministries for older girls (Crusaders, a "character-building" programme of Bible instruction, service to others, and badge work), older boys (Christian Service Brigade, divided into Tree Climbers, Stockade Builders, Stockade Sentinels, and the Battalion), young adults, singles, young married, women, the deaf, and seniors. There were the music ministries, from ear training to TV sound systems, from the Singing Christmas Tree to the King's Kids' current production of "We Like Sheep." The Central Lay Institute prepared God's People as leaders and cell-group organizers. The Birch Bay Ranch was available for retreats and summer camps. The Pastoral Care Department offered counselling and visitations.

Then there was the service itself: a bit of melodic sing-along ("The greatest thing in all of life is loving You") with hands in the air and bodies swaying, a couple of soft and easy-listening numbers from the choir, and a few prayers from the request sheet – for Vivian whose daughter is about to marry a non-Christian, for Jean whose daughter in Toronto needs deliverance from drugs, for Muriette who is depressed, for Kathleen who is losing her sight, for Edith who has a sore throat, for Wilma whose husband has just filed for a divorce, for Dean who needs a job, for Daniel whose mother can't reach him in Mexico, for Betty-Lou "that she may have peace in her heart regarding family situations." To pick us up from life's swamp, a pretty young woman in a pink dress showed up on stage, a microphone in one hand, and belted out in torch-song fashion, "If the ship of your life is tossing on the sea of strife, you need someone." We applauded when she finished.

We applauded again when we were introduced to a young man who was about to go off for two months to teach English at the National University of Defence Technology in Changsha, China. "Just don't fall in love over there, ha, ha," he was told.

The highlight was the sermon, based on a reading from Luke 24 and delivered by a visiting preacher, "Brother" Bill Griffin, the PAOC's executive director of overseas missions, a tubby chap with strands of hair combed over a bald patch. Though his message was plain enough, to put our sorrows and illnesses into faith in Christ through the Spirit and the Word, his presentation was dramatic. By the end, with the organ moaning in the background and tears running from his eyes and pity quivering in his voice, he beseeched God to focus our faltering faith. He skipped the altar call, but his effect was evident in the raised hands and loud sobs and murmured amens. Seventeen years of Bible-college work had given him an edge over Larry Booth.

Good as Brother Bill was, I was disappointed not to witness the resident pastor at the time, Robert Johnson. He had been on the radio in Montreal when I was a youngster, and he was the star of "60 Minutes with Central" on TV every Sunday, so it felt somewhat like being in the audience when Johnny Carson is on vacation. Moreover, something fishy was going on and I was curious. In the "Central Times," the church's weekly schedule of its many events (a video series on cults, a get-acquainted class, a "couples in action" Bible-study meeting, a water baptismal service, a strawberry tea for seniors, a car rally for senior highs, a puppet show for junior highs), there was a notice for a special business meeting the following Tuesday night to address "the problems of disunity within the body of Christ" and to go over "events leading up to the Senior Pastor's Resignation."

Though the meeting was billed for members and adherents only, I could not stay away. Nor could hundreds of other people, all of whom seemed equally curious and equally in the dark. There appeared to have been a power struggle between Pastor Johnson and Central's elected board. "What did he do?" a man ahead of me grumbled. Some said the board was not happy with the pastor's general management ability; some said there were fights over the pastor's priorities and his allocation of funds; some said the board was jealous of the pastor's fame and the autonomy that gave him. Clearly the issues had been about administration, not doctrine, but the details were never divulged. For Pastor Johnson finessed his opponents by resigning before they could get him fired. "This is the Devil's win," he told the packed hall. "There have been witches out in the cemetery working for the collapse of Central!"

Perhaps, but the actual trouble was with humans in the boardroom. "You don't have a spiritual board, you have a political board," he said. "Three or four people on the board run this church. They were chosen for their success in secular life, not their spiritual qualities. Well, maybe you should look for spiritual qualities the next time. I'm tired of the political intrigue. We haven't agreed on anything in two years. We've been a disgrace! I'm sorry to say it, but that's the reality behind the doors."

Things had become so bad, behind the Sunday scenes of love and peace, that one board member was heard to say of his opponent, "I'd like to throw acid in his face."

In a brilliant manoeuvre, Pastor Johnson then called on the scandalized members to fire the entire board as well as accept his resignation. The debate raged long past midnight. Often it looked like a cross between an Alcoholics Anonymous meeting, with weepy confessions and personal entreaties, and a Chinese re-education session, with bitter denunciations and doctrinal critiques. For about half an hour it was sidetracked completely by a woman in white who read a seemingly irrelevant prophecy from God, but not even Pastor Johnson had the nerve to keep her (or was it Him?) to the point.

"I'd rather worship in a warehouse full of the Spirit than in a resplendent church where it has gone," said one man, raising the quote from Mark in my mind. "The Spirit has gone from Central."

Pastor Johnson was gone, anyway, and slightly more than two-thirds of the 400 voting members agreed to get rid of the board too. It may have been just a nasty little squabble, "full of sound and fury, signifying nothing," but it did show that questions of authority are not always solved by congregational control or a strong laity. Where there are prestige and power and money, sin gets a playing field. That is no surprise for anyone who has followed the soap opera of Jimmy Swaggart in the United States or the "indiscretions involving morals" of Ralph Rutledge of Queensway Cathedral in Toronto.

Generally, however, congregational control does have two advantages: it allows extraordinary variety on the outside and it encourages extraordinary uniformity on the inside. Evangelicalism can range in style and doctrine from sober Baptist services barely distinguishable in pomp and participants from Anglicanism to wild Pentecostal happenings full of mad shouts and holy rolling. Some churches have dominant preachers who can pull in the crowds or get on the media; some have ethnic identifications; some are even engaged in liberal political action. But because of that very independence, once a church has shaped its character, there tends to be little conflict about it. Since like attracts like and repels the opposite, people either toe the line or leave. Thus, most of the mess around the interpretation of the Scriptures is avoided, as well as any subsequent disagreements about sexual morality or political action or theories of creation. Because everyone agrees, everything is clear and simple; because everything is clear and simple, more and more agree.

Those advantages explain much of the growth of the evangelical movement throughout Christianity in this century. On the one hand, it could construct spiritual packages to suit every need and taste. They were entrepreneurial, local, both understanding and understandable. They offered a personal experience, a good feeling, the transmission of normal values, a sense of community, social activities, some food for thought, Christmas and Easter pageants, the easy-listening idiom of popular culture, and free parking. On the other hand, it could present a coherent alternative to the confusion and stress of modern life. In the face of divorce and drugs and gay liberation and computer technology, it offered some Old-Time Religion.

"Why the growth?" I asked Brian Stiller, the peppy and youthful executive director of the Evangelical Fellowship of Canada (EFC), an umbrella organization founded in 1965 and now representing an estimated two million evangelicals and more than two dozen denominations, including the PAOC.

"Secularism generates disbelief," he answered, "and, as C. S. Lewis said, 'When people believe in nothing, they'll believe in *anything*.'" He must have caught how startled I was by this blunt confession, because he quickly added, "I mean, there's a vacuum for people to find something that's true and affirming and that works."

Why labour, why love, why suffer, why bear children if there is no plan or purpose or point? Given the damage science and reason have done to God and faith, people have two options: to struggle intellectually and emotionally to adapt their understanding of Truth to the lessons of science and reason or to damn both the present and the future and fall back on the truisms of the past. Most people will choose the easier and irrational course, according to the world-wide wave of evangelicalism, especially if it provides a cure for arthritis, peace of mind, pleasant feelings, or something to keep the kids off crack. Catholic cardinals have become charismatics, Anglican bishops are searching for "renewal," businessmen and bureaucrats and members of Parliament meet regularly for prayer and Bible study, new Bible colleges such as Regent in Vancouver are springing up and old ones such as the Prairie Bible Institute in Three Hills (Alberta) are thriving, and the major exception to the general decline in church-building and church-going has come from that direction.

In Calgary, for example, I stumbled upon a 39-page guide to evangelical and renewal organizations there. As well as listing 188 churches, the *Christian Info Directory* listed 8 Bible colleges, 11 stores for Christian books and tapes, 13 Christian schools, and 108 various missions and ministries. There were special ministries for Jehovah's Witnesses, Muslims, natives, truckers, airline travellers, bikers, financial executives, dentists, college students, prisoners, Mormons, and technical professionals. There were Bible clubs, a Christian ski club, a pregnancy centre, an adoption agency, an anti-abortion society, a counter-cult institute, an association to promote "creation science," the Fellowship of Christian Firefighters, the International Clowns for Christ Society, the "To You . . . With

Love" Television Ministry, the Traditional Value Advocates, and the Wycliffe Bible Translators of Canada.

"When people are hurting, they will go to where they can find help," said David Mainse, the host of "100 Huntley Street," the renowned Canadian televangelist who has been on air weekly since 1962 and daily since 1977, drawing an audience of a quarter of a million viewers. "Many churches were just a few little old ladies hanging on to several million dollars' worth of downtown property and a minister being paid from a bequest left fifty years before. There's no evidence that they were impacting upon a significant number of people. But I've seen lives and souls *transformed* by our television ministry: families reunited, alcoholics healed, the daughter of a senior police official turning away from prostitution. God is in charge; his Spirit draws people to Jesus; Jesus leads them to the Father; and that's done through us."

Television has been called "the best fishing hole" available to those who fish after souls, because such a large net can be cast through it. By divine will or random chance it picks up the lonely at three in the morning, the desperate in the throes of their despair, and the weak at the instant of greatest vulnerability. Faith then works its miracles, and the miracles then draw more to faith.

But the hype must be balanced by Reginald Bibby's figures in *Fragmented Gods*. In 1985 he found that only 4 per cent of Canadians watched religious television programmes on a regular basis, and 80 per cent of those people were also regular churchgoers and over fifty-five years old. As for the evangelical churches generally, they form only about 7 per cent of the population. Though the Pentecostals and the Salvation Army had increased, the Baptists had declined. More importantly, over 80 per cent of new members had transferred from other evangelical churches or were the children of evangelicals. In a specific study conducted in Calgary, he concluded that their "church growth is largely internal, related to a birth rate higher than the national average and greater success in holding on to children and geographically mobile members." In other words, the odds are against an International Clown for Christ having been raised Roman Catholic, Jewish, or agnostic. Bibby called this the "circulation of the saints."

If these saints seemed to have been making greater inroads into modern culture than the figures suggest, it is mostly because they have had a lot of press in recent years – too often as sinners. The scandals aside, much of the attention has been about politics. Though evangelicals had been engaged in political action and social work in the nineteenth century, as founders of the Liberal Party or of temperance societies, in reaction to the Social Gospel they began to withdraw into themselves: to worship, to pray, to follow the Bible, and to stay out of Hell. While a few like Tommy Douglas went off to fight the good fight in society, most remained to do God's work in their hearts. Their faith was a personal and private transformation by Christ; and while it did not preclude acts of Christian charity or the sending forth of missions, it was rooted in individual sin and individual salvation.

The most obvious exception was William Aberhart, the Calgary evangelist who parlayed his fame as a radio preacher into his election in 1935 as the first Social Credit premier of Alberta. Raised a Presbyterian, he moved first to the Baptists and then toward the Pentecostals as he became increasingly fundamentalist, not to say eccentric, full of conviction about the coming Rapture, the seven years of Tribulation under the Antichrist, and Christ's ultimate victory at the Battle of Armageddon. During the same time he moved from teaching in school to preaching in church to lecturing at Bible classes that filled a theatre to delivering radio sermons that reached hundreds of thousands. When the Depression hit, he met a solution in an economic theory known as Social Credit, and soon its monetary ideas were woven into the Aberhart's prophecies from Revelation and broadcast across the province. "Bible Bill" and his student, Ernest Manning, were on their way to more than thirty years of power.

"But Aberhart's political success came at considerable religious cost," John Stackhouse has argued in his thesis on Canadian evangelicalism since the Great War. Like other historians,

Stackhouse emphasizes how Aberhart left the mainstream of his faith once he entered the mainstream of his society. As evidence there is Aberhart's feud with the leaders of the Prairie Bible Institute. "Like most evangelicals," Stackhouse writes, "the Prairie people believed the Depression to be a judgement of God on a civilization that had rejected him. They thought that Christians should vote intelligently and prayerfully, to be sure, but also that Christians had no business trying directly to bring about social reform. The real problem was personal sinfulness, and the real solution was evangelism."

This path was strengthened once the Second World War and the prosperity of the 1950s lulled all the churches away from political priorities. "The evangelical movements let the mainstream churches run the society," Brian Stiller explained to me. "We were smaller and poorer, we weren't 'worldly,' and we felt more spiritual. We were comfortable because they would affirm a Biblical view of morality, even if it wasn't our brand of fundamentalism, and we trusted them to manage society on the basis of Judeo-Christian assumptions."

That comfort and trust came apart during the 1960s. Secular humanism, based on the belief that religion should have nothing to do with the management of public affairs, took charge of the state, as seen in "permissive" legislation on divorce and abortion and homosexuality. Yet, in response, the main churches either rushed to ride that tide, turned to liberal and radical alternatives, or fell into a kind of paralytic irrelevance. "We were shocked," Stiller said. "The glue that held us together – that Biblical morality is best for society – came unstuck. By the mid-1970s we began to realize that social issues like pornography and abortion were affecting our lives and were destructive of our society. Before, I think, we had been preoccupied with the return of Christ. Now we were building bigger churches, putting down roots for our families, so we became more concerned with social issues and we felt politically marginalized and rejected. We began to ask what we should be doing as Christians to assert our Biblical faith in social matters as well as individual matters. We began to ask about the structure of society and the sin it generates."

As Stiller suggested, the external changes had coincided with internal changes, which he and others date back to a book, *The Uneasy Conscience of Modern Fundamentalism*, written in 1947 by Carl Henry. It called on evangelicals to think Biblically, but with a broader mind, and it became a catalyst for better Bible colleges, better schools, and less anti-intellectualism. As a result of that and other sociological factors, evangelicals became more mainstream, more professional, and less blue-collar. In turn, their churches grew, their funding improved, and the whole movement moved up the social ladder into the middle class. Whereas the Social Gospel and liberation theology came to social sin from the left by identifying with the poor and oppressed, therefore, evangelicals came to social sin from the right by identifying with their own middle class.

Inspired by the rise of the American religious right, though generally more liberal than it, Canadian evangelicals started to organize and agitate for their beliefs. They demonstrated on behalf of the rights of the fetus. They lobbied successfully to get "the supremacy of God" recognized in the constitutional changes of 1983. In the same year they mobilized the Evangelical Fellowship of Canada by giving it a paid staff and a social action committee. "Most evangelicals have sat on the sidelines watching society buy into unbiblical ideas," an EFC report told its members. "Just because many are waking up to this reality doesn't mean that we can simply rush in and take over. It will take first an understanding of the issues and systems, making a commitment to involvement, and then a determination to work at it on the long term. The operative word is *incrementalism*."

Incrementalism is a dirty word to Ken Campbell, however. The Ontario Baptist preacher, founder of Renaissance International and friend of Jerry Falwell, delights in being extreme and confrontational, whether fighting sex education or abortion, whether taking on Pierre Trudeau or gay ordination. "Even the EFC, as an umbrella group, can't be the cutting edge. That's my calling," he told me during an interview held at 5:30 in the morning at the studios of "100 Huntley Street" in Toronto. He had just come off the air from the night shift, but was eager to talk for almost two hours. "I'd rather be an authentic Christian than a successful evangelist. Whatever the cost, I can't be restrained by the fear of the social, economic, or ecclesiastic consequences of really following Christ."

The son of a Baptist minister, Campbell attended William Jennings Bryan Christian College in Tennessee (home of the famous "Monkey Trial" against Darwinian science) and was ordained by the Fellowship of Evangelical Baptists. While pastor in Milton, Ontario, he first came to notice by withholding a portion of his property tax to protest the "smut" handed out in the local high school (*Rabbit Redux* by John Updike, for example) and a visit by four gays to the students. "As a parent and a citizen I affirmed the Lordship of Jesus Christ," he said, "and I was liberated from the shackling of North American evangelicalism to the gods of affluence and ease. I am compelled to speak the prophetic note. But, like Jeremiah, I'm a realist. The likelihood is that we won't be heard or responded to. We must be there anyway. Things can be turned around. Abraham came with 318 servants to bring back the whole of Sodom's civilization, because among them was his nephew Lot. The remnant can provide an opportunity for a response that could turn the whole tide. We have to be the salting, saving influence on secular society."

In 1986, he was joined on the barricades by the Christian Heritage Party of Canada, founded in Vancouver to "provide true Christian leadership and to defend, promote, and uphold Biblical principles in federal legislation." Among its policies were the sanctity of life from conception, a strong national defence, responsible free enterprise under God, the restoration of capital punishment, common-sense bilingualism, tax reduction, Senate reform, a national day of rest, wholesome human relationships, and a balanced federal budget. In the 1988 federal election the party ran sixty-three candidates, boasted 14,000 members, and collected 150,000 votes.

Among the great mysteries of the universe is why so many people, having been touched by Christ and the Holy Spirit, immediately want tougher immigration laws, deficit reduction, nuclear submarines, and English only on their government forms. "If English was good enough for Jesus Christ," goes the old joke, "it should be good enough for us." Perhaps clear and simple answers attract those who have clear and simple questions. Perhaps the experience of Truth puts a glint in the eye and a resolve in the heart that brook no dissent or compromise. Or perhaps that glint and resolve have been put there not by the genuine and unsettling experience, but by the church leaders who explain it in terms of their own self-serving political agenda, based on traditional authority, conservative values, and individual deference. While the religious right usually proclaims its belief in democracy and toleration, its values often come to clash with pluralism. Should Christian prayers and teachings be allowed in public institutions which non-Christians support and use? Should particular interpretations of Christian ethics, whether about alcohol or homosexuality or abortion, be forced upon those who do not accept them? Often the answer is, "Yes, because this is a Christian country." Even when that is not a code for a white Anglo-Saxon country, it presumes a Christian uniformity that does not exist and it ignores a multi-faith dimension that does.

As they move into the process, modern and moderate evangelicals have had to avoid the absolutism that has given fundamentalism such a bad name in the past decade throughout the world, whether in Christianity, Judaism, Islam, Hinduism, or Buddhism. In fact, they have tried to distance themselves from the very word, fundamentalist, leaving it to their right-wing militants. Evangelicalism, some of them say, includes the civil-rights protests of Martin Luther King and Jesse Jackson, the liberalism of Jimmy Carter and the Mennonite Central Committee, as well as the Moral Majority and Renaissance International; and though it may be individualistic and against many elements of modern culture, its help to the poor and the distressed proves that it is not without compassion.

"Because our theology is conservative, we tend to be conservative in our politics, our economics, and our social analysis,"

Brian Stiller said. "But there isn't really a Moral Majority here. Canadians pride themselves on being fair, we don't let our leaders embarrass us, and we don't respond to the nationalist rhetoric coming out of the United States. A political party with a narrow theological base just won't work here. One religion can no longer build a social convention. But we have to be at the table debating with the others, to convince them that Christian values can construct laws that are good for them for their own reasons."

"Political theology doesn't work." David Mainse said, harking back to the old evangelical suspicion of the temporal world as the Devil's workshop. "Those churches that jumped on the liberation bandwagon 'to get with it' may or may not have been of any assistance. Sometimes the result was death and bloodshed and families torn apart, the exact opposite of what Jesus came to do. Where's the Biblical precedent of the church belonging to a political pressure group? Where are the examples of Christ's attempts to overthrow the despot Caesar? The means have to be just as holy as the ends. The church is here to transform individuals, and as a result society will be transformed. Our influence isn't in numbers. It's in each individual's strength of conviction, how that's articulated, and how that's lived out."

Was the recent evangelical interest in politics and social salvation a signal, then, that evangelicalism was going the way of the Social Gospel and liberation theology, drawn from the mystical Out There to the secular Down Here, lured by education and status and the bottom line from getting the soul into Heaven to getting some bodies into Parliament or the White House?

"The mistake of the Social Gospel was to move completely from personal sin to societal sin," Brian Stiller replied. "It developed a romantic view of the individual, while it stripped Christ of his deity by making him nothing more than a good man. We have to hold that sin is in both the frightfully wicked hearts of men and in society. There is a residue of concern among evangelicals that we are going too far into society, that we should withdraw again, but generally they will allow us to

329

experiment as long as they know there's no basic deviation from our Biblical roots and our classic Protestant understanding of sin and salvation."

Stiller does have another concern, however. It stems from fear that evangelicalism has peaked. In fact, there are projections that as many as half the saints may stop circulating in the next decade, as their third generation loses interest and the whole movement itself gets sucked toward secular materialism. Many of its most successful American preachers have already been pushing a "prosperity theology," based on health and wealth as God's favours. As evangelicals become more comfortable with who they are, less reactionary and less alienated, they are likely to move toward the centre of things social and political.

"Evangelicals in the 1970s were reading their own press releases, and the hype that predicted a new awakening was born more out of hope than of reality," Stiller said. "In some ways modern evangelicalism is a reflection of the materialistic culture of the 1980s. Coming up from nothing, like all *nouveaux riches* we have been preoccupied with symbols, like having respect or the nicest and biggest churches in our communities. As someone said, 'It is a tragedy of things spiritual that we languish if disorganized, yet we're destroyed by the material means of our organization.' Our Achilles heel isn't liberalism or the Social Gospel. It's materialism. Moving into the middle class threatens to be spiritually neutralizing, as our people become as satisfied as everyone else. It will be tough to maintain our energy and momentum over the next ten years. Perhaps the great renewal will only come through divine interaction, by which God intersects Himself with the life of the culture."

FIFTEEN

In the Vestibule of Heaven

The Hutterites of Crystal Spring, forty-five minutes south of Winnipeg, are also Christian fundamentalists, but they have carried their argument with society to the point of withdrawing almost entirely from it; and they have found a simple, effective, and not unpleasant solution to the problem of future numbers: they breed new members.

The efficacy of the method is evident in the results. In the 1870s there were about 400 Hutterites in colonies in North America; now their population reaches toward 30,000, two-thirds of whom are in Canada. Some studies have estimated the average family as more than ten children, and though the guess at Crystal Spring was closer to eight, the place was swarming with kids. Almost a half of the seventy-seven residents at the time were under sixteen; more than a dozen were in their late teens; and another baby was born in the five days I was there.

Being born is just the first step, of course, to the long and intricate process of becoming a Hutterite. At age three every child is taken from the family home to spend most of the day at the colony kindergarten, and from six to fifteen every child attends the colony school. Besides the basics, they get intensive training in the theology and behaviour of their people, a training that has been refined into an art of carrots and sticks. Essentially they learn to submit their egos – "their headstrong will and carnal practice," as a sixteenth-century leader put it – to God and the community. The same lesson is reinforced by their parents, their elders, and their isolation from contradictory influences. They have no radios or televisions, they meet few strangers, and though some colonies have to hire teachers from outside to comply with provincial regulations, Crystal Spring prefers to send one or two men out to get the necessary certification.

"We feel that our children need more than an outside teacher can give," said Eli Kleinsasser, who taught for twelve years before becoming the colony steward (general manager) in March 1987. "We could tell an outside teacher to keep quiet about religion, that that's our business, but for five and a half hours a day for ten years our boys and girls would be in the hands of someone else. Some of his ideas would rub off. Besides, our values are within the full curriculum. In science, for example, we don't go along with the theory of evolution, and in health we don't believe that sex education belongs in the school. Our education has proved to be successful. We have survived and we're happy with how we are."

I was cautioned again and again at Crystal Spring not to mistake the structure or the operation for the essence of the colony. The teasing I received usually concerned my presumption in trying to grasp that essence within a week. A month, even a year, would not be sufficient, or so I was told. "You will see only the outside, because you can't see my conviction," Eli said. "You may make excellent descriptions of our homes or our schedule, but you can't describe fully the reason for them. Once a writer came here and the ladies in the kitchen asked me who he was. When I told them that he wanted to know why we are living here, one lady said, 'What an idiot! We're living here because we believe that this is the Way!' We're not just following a bunch of rules and traditions. The rules and traditions are only practices we've tried that work. They aren't the reason. The reason is deep down, and it makes it possible for us to follow those rules and traditions."

I asked him to give me a hint anyway.

"We're here to serve our fellow man in the name of Jesus Christ, because he died for us and we owe him that service," he replied. "If you believe there is a hereafter, then this life is a very short time to trade for eternity. You have to start with the conviction that, through Adam's fall, you feel yourself a sinner and you need a redeemer. Then you have to believe that Christ is that redeemer. Then you try to follow his teachings. If you serve anyone out of love, you're serving God. If you believe it's not right to kill another human being, then you don't kill, period, regardless of what you have to suffer here."

So living in community is the way to get to Heaven?

"No. We will get to Heaven only through the blood of Christ. The fact that I live in community is just the fruit of my faith. How can I go around telling the world I believe something and not doing it? If I say I love God but not my brother, I'm a liar. For how can I love God whom I don't see when I can't love my brother whom I do see? Maybe that's easier when you grow up in community, but I can live in a community all my life and if I don't have love, it's all in vain. It's what Paul told the Corinthians: I can give away all my possessions to the poor and let my body burn, but if I haven't love, I'm none the better. That's what we tell our children. Even faith must come from God, but God has no hands but our hands. So we let our children hear the word and hope they will grow up to faith."

The Hutterites have been honing their indoctrination techniques on and off for more than 450 years. They had emerged out of the religious and political upheaval of the Protestant Reformation as part of the Anabaptist movement. Influenced by a direct study of the Bible, some literate peasants and craftsmen of mostly German-speaking Europe turned against the authority of both church and state to form small spiritual groups based on shared tenets such as adult (not infant) baptism, equality, and peace. In doing so, they incurred the wrath of the mainline reformers as well as the Roman Catholic Church, of Protestant princes as well as Catholic monarchs, and their history soon became one of persecution, martyrdom, and expulsion. In 1528 a couple of hundred of these nonconformists, on the run to safety in Moravia in present-day Czechoslovakia, organized the first "Bruderhof" (Society of Brothers) around the principle of communal ownership, inspired by two verses from the Acts of the Apostles: "All whose faith had drawn them together held everything in common: they would sell their property and possessions and make a general distribution as the need of each required."

Ego and greed quickly resurfaced in the colony, however, and the experiment might have died if not for the leadership and discipline of Jacob Hutter. He was not the founder of the colony and he was not there long, but his influence left his name with the sect and his death at the stake symbolized the kind of glorious persecution that has welded together more than one denomination or religion, whether Christianity or Judaism or Sikhism. "Resign yourselves to tribulation and trial," he advised, and they did. When they were prolific and prosperous, as they were in Moravia where their numbers approached today's level in North America, they attracted the hostility and envy of economic rivals. When they were poor and powerless, as they became after their ouster from Moravia in 1622, they were booted from place to place and harried to the edge of extinction. Even when a few score of them found freedom and refuge in Russia after 1770, their Christian communism was undermined by internal and external pressures and lost for some forty years before its revival in 1859.

One of the fathers of the revival of *Gemeinschaft* (mutual assistance) as *Gütergemeinschaft* (community of ownership) was a blacksmith and preacher named Michael Waldner. Prone to visions, one day he saw an angel who showed him the beauty of Heaven and the terror of Hell. When Waldner asked which one was his, the angel answered, "Can you tell me whether any person was saved from the great Flood besides those in the ark? Now you know your place. The ark is the *Gemeinschaft* of the Holy Spirit to which you no longer belong." As Waldner wept, the angel instructed him to build a new ark modelled "after the pattern of Jesus and his disciples." The ark remains a primary metaphor for each Hutterite colony, as it does for the Emissaries at 100 Mile House and other spiritual communities.

Two groups arose from this vision – the Schmiedeleut (*schmied* for blacksmith and *leut* for people) under Waldner and the Dariusleut under another preacher named Darius Walter. Soon afterwards, however, Russian nationalism began to press upon the German colonists, and in 1872 compulsory military service provoked the pacifists to move on once more. In 1874 they headed for the United States, where the Schmiedeleut established the Bon Homme colony in South Dakota and the Dariusleut set up at Wolf Creek in the same state. They were joined after a couple of years by a third group, the Lehrerleut. They were barely settled when the Spanish-American war in 1898 had them looking north of the border for a new escape, and though that proved unnecessary then, it prepared the political and economic grounds for the evacuation that happened as a result of American conscription, anti-German sentiments, and the prison deaths of Hutterite leaders during the First World War. Rapidly almost all the American colonies transferred themselves to Canada, though many re-opened branches in Montana and South Dakota when circumstances changed later.

Six Schmiedeleut colonies were founded in Manitoba in 1918 (with South Dakota names like Bon Homme and Milltown), while Alberta got five Dariusleut and four Lehrerleut ones. Despite the start-up woes, despite the Depression and the Second World War, despite the backlash against their pacifism and the provincial laws aimed at restricting their land expansions, the Hutterites persevered and prospered by their agricultural expertise, their frugality, their joint effort, their hard work, and their abundance of children.

It is one thing to encourage large families and forbid artificial birth-control methods for the sake of community survival. It is another thing to create a social and economic system that makes ten children per family a practical option. The Hutterites have created precisely that by means of communal ownership and an efficient division of labour. Since individuals and families receive neither salaries nor bills, it does not matter in terms of household finances whether they have two children, sixteen children, or none at all. On the other hand, since converts are rare and outside workers are expensive, more children mean more benefits for everyone in terms of productivity levels and old-age care. While there is no doubt a toll on women's bodies, emotions, and energy, the constant assistance of the extended family in the first couple of years after each birth, and the daytime integration of the child into group structures after that, dramatically reduce the burdens experienced by the old Woman Who Lived in a Shoe.

"When I was getting my teaching degree in Winnipeg," Eli Kleinsasser told me, "I used to look at the other students, especially the women, and think, 'Unfortunate people.' Those women had been up at dawn, had fed their husbands and children, had taken the bus to school – they were exhausted by the time they arrived. By the time they left, they were close to weeping, and they still had to go home and cook and clean and all that. Meanwhile, I knew the colony was taking care of my wife and nine children and backing me completely."

While the communal feeding, clothing, and raising of kids solve one major problem, its solution obviously presents a greater one: how to cope with the population explosion? At the average rate of growth it is not long before each colony faces the limits of what food and work its land can provide, as well as the point beyond which there are too many people for intimate harmony and social control. The answer has been continual "branching out" into daughter colonies whenever a colony reaches the optimum of six or seven score. There is continual planning and saving in order to buy enough land, build enough homes, and set up enough communal and economic facilities to meet the inevitable day when the new group has to be up and running on its own. Just about the time a colony has paid off its half of the debt involved in establishing a branch, it is time to start putting money aside for establishing the next one – and so it goes, on and on. Out of Bon Homme in South Dakota, for example, came Milltown, South Dakota, which begat in 1918 Milltown, Manitoba, which begat in 1922 Blumengart, which begat in 1938 Sturgeon

Creek, which begat in 1955 Crystal Spring, which has begat both Suncrest in 1970 and Concord in 1987.

At the time of branching the population of a colony is halved roughly, as one group is selected for transfer according to a formal but not insensitive process of free choice, arbitrary chance, family connections, and a balance of genders, ages, and skills. When Concord was created, for instance, Crystal Spring dropped from 139 to 77. (When one man at Crystal Spring told me, with some pride, "We gave them our turkeys," I thought his attitude somewhat less than Christian, until I realized he really meant they had also given Concord the bird business, because of provincial quotas.) Until the numbers built up again, both colonies had to work "like crazy" to meet the debts and do the jobs usually done by twice as many; other colonies had to lend people to help on the farm and in the kitchen; and half a dozen outsiders had to be hired for a year. Neither the administrative process nor the economic changes can do justice to the impact of being wrenched suddenly from kin, buddies, and often the only place in the world a young person had ever known. As John Hostetler wrote in his superb study of Hutterite society, "Only the will of God is strong enough to separate family members – parents from older children, brother from brother – and break personal and sentimental ties. The individual will must be subordinated to the will of the community."

Since it is not thought advisable to cram one family into one colony, the colonies maintain strong emotional links across hundreds of miles through blood relationships and frequent visits. Rich ones assist poor ones; young men and women are sent back and forth, ostensibly to work but often as fresh prospects for marriage; and the head preachers of each *leut* meet regularly to look over the broad economic and moral scene. Though the three groups of "people" tend to keep a social distance and organizational autonomy from each other, they share enough views and customs to have organized themselves in Canada in 1951 under a single board and chairman as the Hutterian Brethren Church to represent their legal and political interests.

Nevertheless, each colony usually operates with an independence, based on the fact that it owns its own property and manages its own affairs. All have a preacher, a steward, an executive council of six or seven "witness brothers," and an informal operations committee normally made up of the preacher, the steward, and the farm manager. The baptized men of the colony vote on major issues and elect – from among themselves only – all the office-holders except the preacher. As the spiritual head as well as the ultimate managerial authority, he cannot be chosen by mankind alone. So after candidates are nominated and shown to have a modicum of support, the names are placed in a hat and one is pulled out: to give God an opportunity for input. Even then the preacher is on probation for years, both to learn the role and to prove himself worthy. If confirmed, he keeps the position for life, unless he is found to have "sinned" and is removed.

The head preacher at Crystal Spring is Jacob Kleinsasser. Generally known as Jake or Jake-Vetter ("vetter" meaning uncle or cousin, but used to show respect to all older men), he was born in 1922, became a preacher at a remarkably early age in 1946, took charge of the colony when it was founded in 1955, and in 1978 was elected as the senior elder of the Schmiedeleut. (His great-grandfather was Michael Waldner, the *schmied* himself; his father came to Canada in 1919 to dodge the American draft; and Jacob and his eight brothers, including Eli, appear to dominate Crystal Spring and Concord – a reality God must have appreciated when He selected none other than Jacob's son Ed as the assistant preacher in 1987.) A paunchy, pallid man with gloomy black clothes and a grim white beard, he had the stern and rather forbidding demeanour of a Maurice Sendak gnome or Ingmar Bergman pastor; but beneath the gruff voice with its terrifying message of sin and Hell, there lurked a little humour, a certain kindness, and a shrewd intelligence. Some of the severity was just fatigue and overwork; some of the uptightness was just responsibility and spiritual seriousness.

The weight of eternity may have been on his mind, but the weight of the world was on his shoulders – and seems to have been for decades. As well as overseeing the material and religious life of Crystal Spring, he was up to his ears in the directions and details of Hutterite colonies across Western Canada, east and west in the United States, even in England and Germany: a hog operation here, an insurance company there, gas distribution here, branching there, economic trouble here, moral decay there. Sometimes the work kept him away from home for months at a time, and even during my short stay there was a parade of preachers coming for co-ordination and advice, of relatives coming for business and pleasure, of colonists coming for a snack and to chat in the German dialect that has been preserved since the Reformation.

"Jake gets a lot of guests, and it's my duty to serve them," his austere but not unfriendly wife told me one day during a mid-morning break of coffee, licorice, popcorn, a Kit Kat bar, and an orange. We were in their dining-room, bright with the winter light but with little ornamentation beyond an embroidered "Give us this day our daily bread" on the wall and a canary named Spotty in a cage. I was lodged in a separate apartment up at the back of their house, which looked like the original farmhouse plus additions. When Mrs Kleinsasser used to wake me at 7:30 for the communal breakfast – except on Sunday, when families breakfasted in their own homes and I had smoked salmon, boiled eggs, and cheese with these Kleinsassers and their adopted daughter after the four of us got through a German hymn a cappella thanks mostly to Mrs K.'s strong, clear voice – I always had the feeling she had been up for hours. She spent most of every day supervising in the kindergarten. "I'm usually so busy, there's no time for a nap at noon," she said, "even if I sometimes feel like one." That was not a complaint, really. It sounded more like a point of pride, and like many busy people, all her activity seemed a kind of relief from deeper troubles. She hinted at personal tragedy in her past, and she shared with her husband a sense that this life was solitary, poor, nasty, brutish, and short.

"Jake gets very involved in helping the colonies that are down in the dumps," said Eli, more affable, more worldly, and more easy-going than his brother. "If some members write him about a problem or some banks come to him about a bad debt, he'll appoint people to go and check things out. Sometimes he'll have to get rid of the management, sometimes members of this colony will go and manage that place for a while, but every colony gets better results. If a colony is doing poorly, the reason usually has to do with the honesty and integrity of the members. If you have a team of horses pulling in one direction, you will get out of any mess you're stuck in. The mess could be simple incompetence, but Jake always looks for spiritual reasons – selfishness, greed, the abuse of authority."

That was precisely Jake's line of attack against Daniel Hofer, a member of the Lakeside colony who had raised a sizeable revolt against the leadership in 1987. Hofer was excommunicated after accusing the Lakeside and Crystal Spring ministers of "swindle" and "breach of trust" involving the invention of a pig feeder, financial losses, and unjust punishments. The feud resulted in Hofer's going to court to fight both his expulsion and Jake. Though he lost, the public unity of the Hutterites was damaged.

"We always have to fight against selfishness," the preacher himself told me after supper one evening in his study, "whether inside the colony – what work is mine, what machine is mine – or in the ranking of colonies into rich and poor. The Schmiedeleut has a sharing spirit on the whole, and Crystal Spring likes to share its profits as non-interest loans. We don't want to be puffed up."

To an extent, because of Jake-Vetter's position, Crystal Spring cannot help seeming puffed up. It is close to Winnipeg geographically and economically, it is relatively open to the curious (be they potential converts, sociologists, or a lingering journalist), and it is a focus for executive meetings. Its glory is reflected almost immediately in the large new factory that looms to the left after a visitor drives into the colony. Other colonies may have the same 5,000 acres of grain fields or the same clean and modern facilities for hundreds of hogs and thousands of chickens; all may have the neat and functional blocks of housing arranged on three sides of a park-like quad, with a communal building on the fourth side for the adults' and children's dining-rooms, the huge kitchen, and the church; but few can boast a "shop" as technologically sophisticated and financially lucrative as this one. It has mostly to do with the manufacturing, shipping, and selling of the disputed invention, the simple but clever metallic trough for "wet and dry" pig feed. It sells well, partly because of the Hutterites' reputation for quality work, and it has been a major factor in carrying the colony through droughts and poor hog prices.

I got to know rather more about pig feeders than I had imagined, because Jake-Vetter assigned me to the shop as an apprentice welder on the assembly line. "We can't have you wandering around here all week idle," he had said. "You must work." There were hours, I confess, when I wondered why I had come a thousand miles from home in the dead of winter to a cult of medieval German oddballs just in order to bolt another bloody whatsit to another damn whatnot. At least I would finally pick up a decent trade, I used to try to convince myself, and there was nothing else to do anyway because everyone was working too hard to talk.

I did receive some interesting impressions, however. I saw in practice one of the chief characteristics that distinguish the Hutterites from other Anabaptists among the Mennonites and the Amish. Instead of rejecting all technological advances, the Hutterites embrace most of them. Indeed, they seem to revel in having the latest gadgets, from the fax machine in Jake's office to the word processors in the classroom to the computerized sheet-metal puncher in the shop. Many farmers are handy with engines and automated equipment, but these people seemed obsessed by them – despite, or because of, not owning them privately. The drab, utilitarian nature of the colony's communal vehicles, mostly vans and trucks and tractors, provoked a kind of fantasy life around cars. While I received almost no questions about my life in the great world beyond, I was asked many about the car that I had rented and the car that I owned. Their detailed knowledge betrayed intimate dreams, projected desires, and I imagined these guys at night with a light under their covers poring over photographs in *Car & Driver.*

Modern technology, with exceptions such as radio and television, is one of the few points where the outer world is allowed officially to touch upon the lives of individual members, so it comes with a radiance of bright power and dark mystery. It comes with the mixture of fascination and fear that the rest of us might feel if scientific wonders started showing up from an extraterrestrial civilization. While Hutterites appreciate that most of these things would not exist if the whole world lived the Hutterite way and philosophy, that does not prevent them from using those things that do exist, especially for their economic well-being. On the other hand, they are not unaware of the dangers of creeping materialism, collective greed for objects and comforts, and individualization.

"When I was a boy in the horse-and-buggy age," Eli said, "we used to thresh in teams. We'd talk, we'd have our snacks out in the fields, we were never lonely. Now there's a man in the air-conditioned cab of a combine, and he's alone for weeks except for his two-way radio. The boys keep that thing hot, believe me, because they're bored stiff. Same in the kitchen, where the women used to sit in groups and gossip and chat as they peeled the potatoes by hand. Now one girl does it all with a machine. Everyone's working more individually. So differences don't come up and get discussed, and if they don't get discussed, they get exaggerated. And then there's the worry about underemployment too. Our colonies have already become a little smaller for that reason."

If the alienation was apparent in the shop, it was mitigated by the atmosphere of co-operative effort, by the half-hour break for snacks at home in the middle of the morning and afternoon, and by mealtimes in the communal dining-room. Most of these people had known each other (and virtually no one else) since infancy, and since childhood they had been trained to be subdued, so there was not much occasion for boisterous displays of affection and joy. But neither did I see any cantankerous displays of animosity and ambition. The prevailing mood at work and at the table was even-tempered (either positive as calm confidence or negative as dull passivity), and both love and aggression were swathed in the irony of good-natured teasing or double-edged barbs. One morning, after ten men had gone to an agricultural show in Winnipeg and stopped for dinner at the Bonanza restaurant, the whole colony seemed to rib plump Kenny about how he had risen to the challenge of the "all you can eat" deal on shrimp.

The other theme of that day was money: A pig fetched $6,000 at the fair! Dinner cost $70! An acre went for so much! A salesman earned this amount! Their obsession with prices and incomes was surprising. Usually it was a way of reinforcing how lucky they were to live in a colony. This is very important. Given the impracticality of perfect isolation, as sociologist Karl Peter pointed out, the Hutterites "present to their membership an active, living, and viable lifestyle which stands in contrast to the values and institutions of their host society."

The more I worked in the shop, the more I understood how much their daily living was an expression of their faith. To be assigned a menial chore, to do it well and without complaint, to labour and play in harmony, to exist in this world in an atmosphere of sharing and non-violence were the trials – and the rewards – of their beliefs. This went beyond talking about goodness or even praying for it: it meant living in the "vestibule of heaven." In this sense, Karl Peter wrote, "Hutterite culture has become a culture of work performance." All work is lifted from material necessity to spiritual vocation, while at the same time it becomes "a major source of individual pride and satisfaction."

Every morning the preacher, the steward, and the farm manager meet, if available, to allocate tasks, though specialization has caused less rotation than in the past. "We try to discourage any notion of hierarchy or authority," Eli said. "Every job is a service, and any job can become boring unless it's seen as a service. Women serve where they serve best, men serve where they serve best, and either the whole body helps every part or the whole body suffers."

That made sense enough, but it did not quite justify for me the rigid delineations of labour according to gender. If cooking and cleaning and sewing are as worthy as welding and threshing and feeding the hogs, I was not sure why God or the colony should care whether a man or woman performed the service. Obviously the rationale had to do with religious and social traditions, which were also seen in the separation of men and women by a wide aisle in the church and the dining-hall. What hanky-panky might result from prolonged encounters over the assembling of pig feeders? What female weakness and uncleanliness might break down male strength and rectitude? What burdens would be added to the broad shoulders of men if their meals were not prepared for them automatically, if their socks were not darned, if their homes were not scrubbed? And didn't the women themselves benefit from the absence of sexual pressure, protection from their own human nature, and relief from the need to operate combines, slaughter hogs, and repair engines? Such reasoning might have been more convincing if women were allowed to vote in the colony's meetings or hold a position on the colony's executive. For, underneath the organizational divisions, there lay the old theological premise that God and Christ intended man to be the head of the household and woman to obey him.

"Man may be the head, but woman is the neck," goes the ancient Hutterite joke, "and the neck turns the head." Beyond doubt women have employed all the arts of their sex to overcome the institutional hurdles and exercise their influence for the good of the colony and themselves. They rarely hesitate to speak their minds, and they probably do not hesitate to withhold their favours. I particularly enjoyed a brief exchange I overheard when a bright and attractive young woman expressed envy about the men's dinner at the Bonanza, sighing, "You guys are spoiled and lucky."

To which a young man answered with a defensive sharpness, "We earn your bread and butter."

"Yeah," said the girl's mother, "and then you eat it too."

While I never accepted the political or theological inferiority of Hutterite women, I did come to appreciate the explicit distinctions between the sexes. Perhaps I had spent too much time with the men at the troughs, and certainly the appreciation overtook me unwillingly and by surprise, but as the days passed, I could feel in the children and the adolescents the security and comfort of unambiguous role models that Rabbi Pearlson had desired. The men were burly, bearded, and bearish in black jackets and trousers; the women were discreet, devoted, and determined in long floral skirts and black kerchiefs; and the differences between them seemed of the natural order, of animals and primitives and pastoral eras. In that regard, as in their medieval faith and isolation from modernity, they reminded me of the Hassidim on the streets of Montreal.

Each weekday evening at 5:30 and at 9:30 on Sunday mornings, they gather for worship in a room beside the dining area, a plain room more like a dark church basement than the usual image of a church. Its walls are laminated wood, its floor sports a rather gaudy carpet, and its furnishings are spartan: two sections of wooden pews facing a row of chairs where the preacher and the witness brothers sit. The service is equally as precise and spare. Everyone sings a hymn without music in German; the preacher or his assistant reads in German or English a sermon that has been passed down from the seventeenth century; and everyone kneels on the floor to be led in prayer. There is little place for improvisation or emotion, except perhaps in the austere beauty of the singing, but there is plenty of opportunity to drum in words such as sin, wickedness, evil, repentance, and judgement. The message is as plaintive and grim as the preacher's voice: we are fallen sinners, this world counts for nothing in face of the eternity of Heaven and Hell, the end is near, we must do God's will through meekness and forgiveness in preparation for the Day of Judgement.

"Therefore we have every reason to take care lest by backsliding we forfeit God's grace, bringing his disfavour and wrath upon ourselves and our children," we heard one evening from an epistle written in 1649 by one Andreas Ehrenpreis to the churches at Alwinz and Bodock. Backsliding meant calamity, curses, warfare, captivity, fever, incurable diseases, wretchedness, anguish, wilderness, famine, birds and beasts fled and gone, dead bodies in the streets, and ceaseless damnation. "In the same way," the children who were squirming in the laps of their mothers and fathers heard, "forty-two good-for-nothing boys were torn to pieces by two fierce bears for mocking the man of God and calling him 'baldhead.' Do you not think that the same avenging God still lives and will punish such things in his own time?" I do not know what effect this had on the kids, but it did cause me to wonder if I should have thought Jake paunchy.

The children are allowed here, but they do not get to be a member of the church – to vote, hold office, marry, and perhaps enter Heaven – if they do not get themselves baptized voluntarily, usually in their early twenties. Before that, the colony is wise enough to tolerate a few "foolish" years when mischief, doubt, and illicit radios are not judged too harshly. Then the pressure mounts to assume adulthood, responsibility, and God. Not surprisingly almost all who stay get baptized. More surprisingly almost all stay.

"We haven't done a big survey, but the sociologists say we're still keeping 98 per cent of our people," Eli told me. "We can't force our children to stay. We can only hope and pray and teach and train. Usually those who leave go looking for adventure, and those who remain out tend to be those who got married outside."

In the past decade, however, Crystal Spring was hit by a dozen defections, not for the freedoms and fleshpots of Winnipeg but for more religion. Apparently the source of the remarkable exodus was radio. While turning the dial in secret for a hockey game or baseball broadcast, people began to hear the American evangelists such as Jimmy Swaggart and Oral Roberts, and what they heard was close to the Hutterite message except that it had passion, miracles, tears, and a personal experience of the Holy Spirit. The teachings were no longer dry rites, dreary sermons, sober tunes, gloomy voices: they were spontaneous, emotional, peppy, and in tongues. They were not comatose tradition: they were living grace.

"Or so some say, but I don't believe them," the preacher harrumphed. "Enough have returned and called it all a lie, a cover-up with no true faith underneath. The real problem is too much exposure to the world. Religions come in all colours of the rainbow, and you have to be pretty deeply rooted in one to be firm against the others. Even if you're baptized, if you're not firm when you're exposed to the outside, you have to fight self-will and selfishness or you'll be pulled from your roots. But it's good that those who lost their calling have left. It makes the Church stronger in its faith. It's not hard for the Church; it's hard for those individuals."

Nevertheless, those defections did raise what Jake and Eli both recognized as a critical problem. While they knew their system had an advantage in grabbing the minds of the children so totally, they also knew that it harboured a terrible danger for their souls. For if Hutterites grow up never to have their beliefs challenged by others, they may hold their faith more by habit and convenience than by understanding and commitment. I was aware of Crystal Spring as a very efficient economic arrangement and very comfortable social situation. The work is better than most farm or factory work; the food is excellent and plentiful; the homes are above the standard; families do not have to worry about bills or daycare or old age; and everyone is surrounded by favourite relatives, best friends, and the warmth of community. Of course, there are animosities, disputes, vexations, and claustrophobia too, but rarely as bad as the violence, conflicts, torments, and loneliness of the outside. So if baptism and a daily half-hour lecture about sin are the mere price of admission, it seems a bargain.

"It may be harder for our children than for converts," the preacher admitted. "If they adopt this way of life from habit, if they don't go deep into the difference between the way of righteousness and the way of unrighteousness, then they don't bring out the real motivation of the Spirit. This life is more than just keeping me away from what I am. It's also bringing me toward what I am not. We're all *filthy*, stained by original sin, in need of redemption, unworthy in the eyes of God. That feeling has to be there, to bring on humbleness and humility and genuine love for Jesus as my redeemer. You don't feel it just by growing up to a communal way of life. Like converts, our children have to get free from selfishness, to give up, to commit themselves to the Lord, to see themselves as impure and completely useless until they fall prostrate before God and plead for help. Then the real spirit of redemption takes hold. It makes me happy, it makes me free, it makes me *obedient*."

"Custom or family or comfort would be weak reasons to stay," Eli concurred. "The converts usually have faith first and learn obedience later, while our children usually learn obedience first and have faith later, but both have to arrive at the same understanding. There may be the rare one who just goes through the mill, but I don't believe a person could live this life without a deep conviction."

In other words, the economic and social benefits cannot sustain the operation alone, so if the operation is functioning, at least most of the colony must be sharing something greater than those benefits. As evidence, Eli pointed to the hundreds of famous communal efforts that have come and gone in history. Though the Hutterites too have had their ups and downs, they still survive. In fact, Eli and others have gone to Israel at the invitation of kibbutzim to share the secret of survival past three generations.

"Their young people are taken off to the army for a couple of years, then they travel or get jobs, and half don't go back," he said. "But my surprise was that half do go back! Without a religious base, how can a kibbutz compete with the outside world? When they asked me to sum up the problem in one word, I said, 'Egoism!'"

While the Israeli statistic implies that half a colony could be there for reasons having more to do with socialization and well-being than religion, Eli insisted that faithlessness would reveal itself in disobedience, poor work, bad attitude, and personality tension. These are human traits, of course, and the Hutterites have a procedure to deal with them. Disagreements are talked out, apologies are made in private or public, a recalcitrant offender may suffer temporary exclusion from the life of the colony or even of his own family until he acknowledges his wrong. If all that fails, the church may judge him "not in the circle" and expel him. That is extremely rare, but it does protect the group from any unyielding backsliders – or liberal challengers – like Daniel Hofer.

But if punishments can encourage submissive behaviour even among those of little faith, they cannot heat up lukewarm convictions. That is what those who left to follow Jimmy Swaggart felt; that is what those who yawn and shuffle through the sermons reveal. I found the issue percolating just below the surface of the colony, especially among young people, largely because of the contrast between the old Canadian colonies in the West and the new American ones in the East.

These unique American communities – in New York State and Connecticut and Pennsylvania, plus one in England and one under way in Germany – are primarily the results of the teachings of Eberhard Arnold, a German theologian in the first part of this century. Arnold became interested in born-again Christianity and then communal life, and after visiting the Hutterite colonies in North America in 1930 and 1931, he and his movement were embraced by the tradition and sent to reestablish it in the lands of its origin. Arnold died shortly afterwards, however, and the Nazis put the Bruderhof on the run to England, where anti-German hostility soon moved it on to Paraguay. The Hutterites helped with money and advice, but distance and innovations drew them apart. When a group of the Bruderhof brought their more worldly ways to a North Dakota colony in 1955, the conflicts ended with a formal schism. That did not stop the Bruderhof from shifting from Paraguay to the Eastern United States or from attracting new people to Christian communal life. In 1974, after a decade of negotiations and apologies, the Bruderhof colonies were accepted back into the Hutterite fold as part of the Schmiedeleut.

"I was instrumental in that," Jake said, "so Crystal Spring stays as a kind of contact point to and from them. We exchange members for periods, we visit back and forth, so the whole body has been revitalized a bit. But they haven't changed us as much as we've changed them. Remember, they were the ones who were out of order."

349

But that was not the impression I received from many of the younger Hutterites who had spent time in the East, had brought wives home from the East, or were on an extended stay from the East. "The East" was usually mentioned in a tone of wistful envy, and not just because the winters are less severe, the geography more pleasing, the buildings more contemporary, or the work more creative. Though most aspects of theology, custom, and dress were adapted to conform with the old colonies, the East could not avoid the crucial difference that it is composed mostly of modern and American converts, not traditional and German offspring. Children are allowed to attend local schools from grade nine; women are allowed to participate in colony discussions; men are allowed to use their education and skills beyond agriculture. But such worldly and liberal attitudes do not seem to be the attractions per se. They are appreciated as signs of the vitality and confidence of the faith.

Rather than feeling a paranoid isolation from the spirit of the world, the East is content to test the beliefs of its members and children against the world. If people leave, they leave. In fact, adolescents who are not certain about baptism, or adults who are going through doubt, are shipped out into the outside world at the colonies' expense to try their convictions. With prosperous colonies twice as large as the average in the West, the Bruderhof can afford such risks; but mostly, as first- or second-generation members, their faith is fervent enough to want fervent faith to prevail. And from the atmosphere of fervent faith come other attractions, such as stirring music, joyful prayer, community singing, warmth between women, openness between men, and hundreds of human touches that make visitors homesick in the cold, formal, separated, homogeneous, old-fashioned spirituality of Crystal Spring. The yearning was not for greater freedom, except in so far as greater freedom conditioned deeper faith.

While Eli agreed with Jake that the East has learned more from the traditional Hutterites than it has taught them, he conceded one important exception. "The East is more active in going out and telling people why we're here, and because its third generation is just starting, most of its members have come from the outside with a longing to help their outside brothers and sisters," he said. "Whereas we have been more or less complacent and happy by ourselves; and because we were born and raised in community, we lacked the ability to relate to the outside society like they can. I remember when I was a student teacher during university, it was just before Easter, and I asked the children to bring eggs the next day so that we could paint them. At recess an eight-year-old Indian girl took me by the hand, looked me the eye, and said, 'Eli, I can't bring eggs, because we haven't got any eggs. All we have at home are potatoes.' Meanwhile, we had 12,000 chickens here. That's how I had been living all my life, with the bin full. When I came home and told Jake, we made sure those children had lots of eggs and we packed up boxes of ducks and meats to deliver to that girl's house."

The Eastern colonies have taken their children to hand out food in the slum districts of New York City, in comparison, and they have sent some of their youth to work with the grape-pickers' union in California. In 1988 they organized a conference on social responsibility, with workshops on hunger and homelessness, abortion and drugs, war and racism, as well as repentance and separation. "We need to be salt for present and future generations," they said. "We must be in the world, concerned with problems, complexities, attitudes, values, and solutions. But at the same time, we must not be of the world, succumbing to temptations of power, praise, influence, wealth, and success. Salt that loses its taste is good for nothing."

Ultimately, of course, the salt is neither eggs nor conferences. Though Eberhard Arnold himself was influenced by Christian radicalism and the Student Christian Movement, the greatest quarrel among his successors occurred in the late 1950s when the stability of the new colonies was threatened by a push from American converts toward more liberalism, more democracy, and more social action. The push was halted by a major schism, which left the more traditional elements in charge. Their philosophy is summarized in the sign that hangs in the church at Crystal Spring, a gift from the East: "That we live together in peace and serve each other in love." But, if in the past that sentiment has been interpreted narrowly as peace and service within the community or between communities, now that the Hutterites have reached a certain plateau of stability, affluence, and freedom from persecution, their faith is being pressed to interpret it more widely as long as their way of life is not jeopardized. In the fifteen years since the East joined the West, the older colonies have done more for the outside world than in the fifty years before that, including volunteer visits to prisoners, sponsorship of housing in the Third World, and donations of wheat to the World Food Bank.

"We always felt in the back of our minds that we weren't doing enough for the outside," Eli said, "But we were told that our very existence is the best we can give – to prove that communal living is possible, to prove that we believe in serving God. God's grace has kept us for almost five hundred years. Maybe we have a bigger mission than we realize."

SIXTEEN

Where Late the Sweet
Birds Sang

There is a fish tank in the reception area of St Peter's Abbey, near Muenster, Saskatchewan, and during the days I spent there I often found myself peering into it. The hall serves as a kind of crossroads: it is where visitors arrive and depart, it is the natural gathering place for those on their way into or out of the chapel, and it is the neutral space between the monks' cloistered residence and the quarters of their guests. So that is where I usually arranged to meet one monk or another, and that was where I tended to loiter in the evenings when I got bored with reading in my room. Many times, if the porter's office were shut and everyone were about his business elsewhere, I would be alone, waiting or loitering, and the only sound would be the bubbling of the aquarium. There was no other distraction in that spartan brick hall, unless I wanted to contemplate the carving of the crucified Christ.

It did not take me long to make the association between the fish in the tank and the monks in the abbey. Though fish neither work nor pray (unless swimming is a type of work and waiting for Brother Gerald to drop in the feed is a variety of prayer), there was much in their slow and routine pace within a confined but comfortable milieu to bring to mind the men around me. When especially bored or mischievous, I thought I saw the expressions or personalities of certain monks in certain fish, and I started to name the fish after the monks they resembled. "Idleness is an enemy of the soul," warned St Benedict, the sixth-century founder of Western monasticism in general and the Benedictine order in particular, to which St Peter's Abbey belongs.

However, idleness is the great gift the monks offer their guests – though they do not have much time for it themselves – if idleness means an opportunity to pull back from the hurly-burly of life, to be protected and quiet, to take stock of oneself and ponder the imponderables. "All guests who present themselves are to be welcomed as Christ," was another of Benedict's admonitions, and that seemed to mean to make no demands on them other than to show up at meals on time, to refrain from smoking in bed, and to keep the peace.

Like most others, no doubt, I landed at the doors of the monastery as if tossed up and thrown down by the sea of vicissitude. Winter had come early to the Prairies, first dumping a load of snow, then plunging the temperature to eye-watering lows, and an especially vicious influenza had come with it. I felt even worse than I looked (which was dreadful), I had been on the road too long and working too hard, I was in a terrible funk about the future of the country, my personal life had become extremely complicated (to put it mildly), and if I could not be recuperating at home with the woman I love, I wanted more than anything to be asleep.

Unlike others seeking refuge from a cold and tired universe, on the other hand, there was a difference between my condition and my purpose in coming. I was not there to pamper my wretchedness or catch up on my sleep (though I did indulge shamelessly in both for a couple of days), but to look in on another religious form. So much of what I had seen before had been engaged inextricably in the affairs of the world: the power struggle of bishops, the political and financial management of huge institutions, the theological thrust into liberation wars or nationalist conflicts, the changing morals of contemporary cultures, even the manufacture of pig-feeders at Crystal Spring. But, at the centre of the great spiritual traditions, is a powerful and different lesson: Christ in the wilderness, Moses on Mount Sinai, Mohammed on Mount Hira, the Buddha under the peepul tree, Guru Nanak by the river. It is the lesson of silence and solitude, of sabbaths and retreats, of contemplation and prayer; and though each teacher went back into the world to transform it by his revelation, the Truth had come when each had withdrawn from mundane concerns and madding crowds.

In the East and the West individuals have responded to that lesson by secluding themselves, denying the world as pure illusion or far less than desirable, and practising infinite combinations of physical and mental exercises designed to crack open the self and let in enlightenment. They were natives setting out on vision quests, ascetics sleeping on beds of nails, mendicants surviving on scraps of food, hermits living up on pillars, prophets hallucinating in deserts, yogis twisting their bodies into knots, and filthy old guys shouting on subway platforms about the coming apocalypse. In Western Christianity, in Egypt in the third century, such individuals began to gather into communities under the authority of rules and a wise *abba* or "father," but the communities were as disparate as the local rules and the quirks of the abbots. Around AD 530 an Italian monk named Benedict established a monastery at Monte Cassino, and the charter he wrote for it became the standard of Christian monasticism in the West, partly because of its comprehensiveness and flexibility, partly because of the backing of Pope Gregory the Great and Emperor Charlemagne. Seventy-three chapters long, the Rule of St Benedict covers the gamut from organization to prayer, from recruitment to punishment, all based on the three vows of eternal allegiance to the community, faithful adherence to the monastic way of life (which precludes private property or marriage), and obedience.

St Peter's Abbey traces its history back to the time of Charlemagne and to the Abbey of Metten in Bavaria. More than a thousand years after the founding of Metten one of its monks, Boniface Wimmer, moved to the United States to serve the German immigrants there, and in 1846 he established the first North American Benedictine abbey, St Vincent's, in Pennsylvania. A second, St John's, was built ten years later in Minnesota. In the 1890s some German Catholics in Minnesota resolved to preserve their language and religion by creating a farm colony in Saskatchewan. They were helped directly by St John's Abbey, which sent a monk with their search committee and eventually arranged the transfer of an Illinois priory – which had fallen on hard times, according to one historian, because of a combination of "swamps, snakes, malaria, and Protestants" – to the new settlement. In 1903 Prior Alfred Mayer moved north with thousands of settlers and established St Peter's (which was named, appropriately, after the abbot of St John's at the time), and in 1911 the priory became an abbey under Abbot Bruno Doerfler.

"It's hard to delve into the mystery of why people come and why people stay, but if we really believe in God and the work of the Holy Spirit, then we have to believe that somehow He's behind it," said Abbot Jerome Weber. Born in Muenster in 1915, he is a small, wiry man with a soft voice, strong back, and peppy pace. He reminded me of a very bright squirrel or Tommy Douglas without the hair. Never reluctant to scrub floors or wash dishes if needed, he speeds about the buildings like the star athlete he had been in his youth at St Peter's College, the affiliate school. Indeed, his choice had been between monkhood and professional hockey, and he is still a magnificent skater when he takes to the ice of the monastery's indoor rink. "Few people get a call like Abraham or Paul. They may get a little inspiration, something overheard, an unexpected thought, and that gets nourished by prayer and study and discussion. In my own case, for instance, I had relatives in the community. In the end you just have to make a decision."

In my first encounter with the Abbot, he had given me a single message. "Our main task is prayer, but that's the hardest thing to put into words," he said. "The history, the organization, the routine are easy in comparison. When I was elected in 1960, I consoled myself by trying to emphasize the spiritual, and though I'm amazed by the physical expansion that has occurred since then, my attention has been on our

356

relationship to God, to Christ, and to one another. Our work is important, but the primary purpose of our lives is to seek God through prayer and community."

I remembered that each time I joined the monks in the chapel, for lauds at 6:20 before Mass and breakfast, for midday praise after "dinner" at noon, for vespers at 5:40 before "supper," and at 7:30 for vigils. It was always moving, always mysterious, to watch them gathering from their rooms or their labours, to hear them chanting the psalms, to observe their silence after the readings from the Scriptures. Here was the heart, here was the healing, but they seemed beyond description or explanation. Here was the community, but its essence was in each person.

O God, you are my God, for you I long;
for you my soul is thirsting.
My body pines for you
like a dry, weary land without water.
So I gaze on you in the sanctuary
to see your strength and your glory.

For your love is better than life,
my lips will speak your praise.
So I will bless you all my life,
in your name I will lift up my hands.
My soul shall be filled as with a banquet,
my mouth shall praise you with joy.

"Our monastic tradition is to begin with a reading, then to reflect on it as a kind of meditation about our relationship to God," Abbot Weber explained. "Then we pray, whether with praise or thanks, for a blessing or forgiveness, and if we put our will into it and our heart out, with God's grace prayer can go into the wordless presence of God. It's like admiring a sunset or a painting. That contemplation is a gift God gives. Often it's not long before thoughts start again and the whole process begins back at reading or meditation, but some people can be in God's presence without effort. Most monks find quite a bit of peace."

The more I stayed, the more fascinated and frustrated I became with what was "beyond the visible and the tangible," as the Abbot had phrased it. I toured the neat and efficient farm, I toured the school and the press, I grabbed interviews from the extraordinarily busy schedules of the abbey's officials, I chatted at length with many of the ancients who had more leisure to spend with a visitor. I studied the faces of the monks during chapel, I noted their quirks and relationships, I saw their separate dining-room and the kitchens, I sat in on one of their chapter meetings, and one evening I visited their private quarters during the "recreation period" between supper and vigils. Built in 1962 as a three-storey, brick addition to Michael Hall (the monumental block that had served as the original abbey and school), it is mostly small rooms with a bed and sink, much like student residences everywhere. The top floor has a TV room – not very popular except for sports events – and below it is a lounge cluttered with books, newspapers, magazines, records for the hi-fi, card tables, and armchairs. Most of the monks were lingering, chattering, or playing cribbage here, though some were in another room in the basement playing shuffleboard, pool, or skat, a favourite card game handed down from the German connection. Brother Michael showed me some of his 350 poems – his other hobbies are cake-decorating, candle-making, and ventriloquism – until the bell summoned us to the chapel. Everyone was frank and insightful, but I still felt remote from their experience. Then I remembered something the Abbot had said as an aside. "I must listen to everyone in the community, even the youngest," he had told me, "because God can use the youngest."

The youngest turned out to be Brother Vincent Regnier, a novice who had come to the abbey in January 1988. I was already very familiar with him by sight, and not just because he was one of the very few young men in the place. All of the three under forty years of age seemed intriguing, because they were doing something so rare in their generation and because they were thinking about dedicating all their years ahead to doing it, but Vince seemed a special puzzle. Whereas Brother Randy appeared a very shy, sweet, and slow casualty of alcohol who most likely will spend his life fixed to some other farm if he chooses not to spend it at the monastery, and whereas Brother Demetrius appeared as comfortable as the funeral director he used to be among octogenarian bodies and morbid hopes for the world beyond this one, Brother Vincent appeared high-spirited, streetwise, irreverent, and full of vinegar. Lithe and agile as a skier, he would usually pad into chapel with his hands deep in his habit, a scruffy head of hair, and the expression of a charming rodent. He exuded both fun and anger, strength and fallibility, looseness and tension, honesty and deceit. His eyes were intense and clever, as if clear about the tricks of life and himself while alert to the best opportunities for both.

He was born in 1963 to a French-Canadian father from Manitoba and a mother from England, and as a child of the military he was constantly on the move – to Prince Edward Island, to Regina, to Cold Lake, to Saskatoon. (It is tempting to use that to explain the attraction of never moving anywhere again.) His family was not particularly religious, but the idea of being a priest entered his head during high school, for positive and negative reasons he admitted he never really analysed, and after graduation he entered a seminary. It was not what he wanted, however, so he transferred to university, eventually coming away with a B.Ed. and an alcohol problem. It was then that he decided to try monastic life as "one last religious-vocation shot."

"I became aware that I had a problem with alcohol, and I thought that if I was going to get a grip on the situation, I'd better get my ass into some disciplined lifestyle," he said. "So my motives weren't 100-per-cent religious. I don't have a great sense of God at the best of times, but this was a place where I couldn't lose. The first couple of months were tough. Life sort of comes to a grinding halt in one sense and picks up in another sense. You stop running around, going to movies, seeing a lot of other people; but there's a lot of social processes happening, people testing each other, adjustments to be made."

The long and sophisticated process of becoming a monk begins when a man is attracted to the abbey, for reasons most sacred or most silly, and applies to stay as a postulant. For six months he has a chance to experience monastic life from the inside, while the community uses the opportunity to assess his faith, his motivation, his psychological maturity, and his ability to fit into the group. Since Benedict's only criterion was that the person be truly seeking God, the assessment often comes down to more visible evidence such as whether he sticks to himself or contributes to the work and spirit of the place. If he wishes to remain and if a majority approves by a vote, he enters the novitiate, a one-year period of "formation." Though no vow is taken yet and the novice is free to leave at any point, formation consists of a fairly rigorous routine of classes, duties, testing, and restrictions on personal initiatives. If he still wants to stay and if the majority still wants him, he takes on the temporary or "simple" vows for three years, which often include further study elsewhere. After that, and one more vote, he may take the permanent or "solemn" vows.

"There were six postulants when I began," Vince said. "Two left early, one left just before entering the novitiate, and three of us – Demetrius, Denis, and myself – became novices. Then Denis left suddenly. That was difficult. I was angry at the community for its reaction, which was almost apathy. I suspect the monks have been burnt so often, but it shook me. Next time it will shake me less and less and less. The older monks don't talk that much, and because they've had so many people leave on them, their ability to form bonds has been hardened by the hurt. And sometimes the guys you came in with make things more difficult. Randy had a bitch of a time, because one of them was a real prick – I guess I shouldn't use that kind of language – and some of them are very conservative, especially the young people from Quebec – you know, very obedient, very regimented, very quiet and pious. But I guess I'm competitive by nature, so I take pride that I'm still here while most of the others dropped off one by one. I used to reflect on why they left, but their leaving didn't make me doubt my choice to stay."

"Occasionally mistakes are made, as in all vocations, but there's a lengthy period of trial and testing – five, seven, even nine years – before a permanent commitment," Abbot Weber said. "Recently we had someone who had been here five years and was ready to commit, but we decided not to take him. And we had someone else who had made the commitment but who wasn't working out, so we asked him to leave. The community has to be a united community. Unity is never perfect, but one diseased sheep can infect the whole flock. Once people come into the community, they have to catch the community spirit, they have to come in unconditionally so that God – through the community – will direct them. Seeking God is primary, but they have to be willing for obedience too. To suffer the humiliations and difficulties."

If there was a time when the humiliations and difficulties were deliberate in order to test obedience and dissolve ego, that time seems to have passed. Formation is not a systematic cult technique of isolation, crackup, and brainwashing (though it has some of those elements), and if the postulants and novices usually get menial chores with the pigs and chickens, that is because their temporary status is not conducive to jobs of ongoing responsibility. Artificial humiliations and difficulties are not necessary, actually, because there are enough real ones in having to stay put, having to fit into the community, and having to seek permission for many ordinary adult activities such as driving into town or spending money. On one level, obedience is a basic condition for the smooth functioning of individuals in the group. On another level, it is a key part of the spiritual path.

"Obedience is to submit your will to the one who gives the command, to do so *willingly*, not *unwillingly*," said the Abbot. "We are trying to align our will with the will of God, and we believe the will of God is made known through the superior. We may not understand how, but if our life wasn't based on faith, we couldn't exist."

In other words, the abbot is guru, master teacher, Christ's representative in the monastery, and while he may consult and concur, he is there to be obeyed. He is also there to be an inspiration and a guide, though he shares those roles with each monk's spiritual adviser, the formation director, the prior and subprior, and perhaps every member of the community. "I have to tell monks when their way of doing things isn't acceptable, for their own good and the good of the whole," he said, "but personally I find it hard to interfere in the life of another person. I don't even like correcting students. As I see it, unless you can win their good will to change voluntarily, it's just force. My ultimate punishment is excommunication, to keep the individual away from the common life, but that hasn't much effect nowadays. So I try reasoning and suggesting and admonishing and praying. I'm not always successful, but as Benedict used to say, if the abbot has done everything possible to help to no avail, then the man's on his own."

"In the past and in more conservative monasteries, I've heard that guys would throw pails of rocks down the hall and make the novices and juniors clean up the mess just to test obedience and humility," Vince said. "That doesn't happen here, thank God, or I'd just tell them to fuck off then and there. I'm obedient to everybody, even to guests. I have to listen, I have to respond to their needs, I want to be of service. But I see the monastic community as a community of equals. Obviously, as a novice, I give way to those who've been here a while, but there's no longer the division between brother and priest and I have a choice to say no. I won't wash dishes because I have sensitive skin, for example, and I won't serve at Father Matthew's private Mass because I don't like the theology of private Mass. As a last resort the prior might tell me to do something just because he tells me to do it, but the prior has to be obedient too, which means listening to my needs."

Each hurdle of the course seems very high to most people. One year there were no postulants; five or six a year would be high; the average is probably three. The drop-out rate is usually more than half in the early stages, so there is rarely more than one person out of each class ready or accepted for final vows, if that. The entire community (not including the five hermits, three nuns, resident students, and lay staff who live on the 2,000 acres) only totalled forty-five monks when I visited, twenty-seven of whom had also been trained and ordained as priests. More telling, perhaps, were their ages, which one monk summarized as "one in his nineties, a lot in their eighties, a few in their seventies, some in their sixties, none in his fifties, some in their forties, two in their thirties, and one in his twenties."

"Welcome to the geriatric centre!" said Vince. "I shouldn't say that, because most of these guys are very active, but I have a fair bit of energy and there's not always someone to relate to. Sometimes I'm more aware of the age gap than at other times, and I'm very aware when someone doesn't respect me or my knowledge because I'm younger, but the age difference has become less and less obvious the longer I've been here. A lot of the older monks are very young at heart, and their years don't matter as much."

The explanation for the preponderance of elderly and the gap in the middle lay in the crisis that shook Western monasticism in the 1960s, when a remarkable number of monks joined the remarkable number of priests, nuns, and religious who simply walked out of their permanent vows amid the political, social, and moral turmoil in the culture and the Church. Secluded prayer was denigrated as anti-social self-indulgence; the cry of freedom undermined both authority and structure; the breaking apart of outmoded forms and customs raised doubts about the essentials that remained; and, no longer certain of why they should stay, many decided they could not. More than a dozen, mostly in their thirties and among the brightest and most progressive, abandoned St Peter's, which had numbered above sixty men in the early part of the decade. The general mood among those who remained was bitterness and betrayal.

"The period of renewal produced a dissatisfaction with the very vocation," Abbot Weber said. "Usually it was less a dislike for the community than the greater attraction of some woman or new ideal. Once change and questioning are inaugurated, where do change and questioning stop?"

Though only one has followed them in over a decade, their loss is still felt. "The middle management is missing right now," I was told. "That's why so many of us have to wear two or three hats. If we had those guys, we'd be sitting pretty." Nor was that the only – or even the greatest – effect of the 1960s. After the middle of the decade lay teachers had to be introduced into the school, and in 1972 it was reduced to just a junior college connected to the University of Saskatchewan. Not only did that cause an angry reaction from monks who felt the closing of the boarding school went against the tradition of St Peter's, it cut off a major source of local recruits, so that the fewer novices were also older and less likely to be from the area, of German descent, or with family connections. Moreover, they entered a profoundly different place. Novices were no longer packed into dormitories, "as if we had wanted them to leave," as one monk put it. Brother-monks no longer suffered segregation, humiliation, and second-class conditions at the hands of the priest-monks, who alone had voted for the abbot and been given private quarters (though only a priest may still be abbot). Authority was exercised with more respect for personal responsibility. Where once the abbot appointed all six members of his advisory council, for example, now half were elected by the whole chapter. Like the Jesuits, the Benedictines could be described as "an absolute monarchy, limited by the resistance of its subjects."

"We're living in a more democratic age, so people like to have more say in decision-making, but our various committees on liturgy and the farm and the press and so on don't make decisions," said Abbot Weber. "They present advice to the senior council, , and the abbot then gives the final O.K. It's rare for the abbot not to agree with the council, but this is not a democracy. I have the ultimate authority in all decisions. But I have to answer for everything I'm doing to God, so I have to be fair and give no just cause for *murmuring*. When a monk or a stranger comes in and gives some advice, I'd better listen, because he might have been sent by God for that purpose."

With this attitude Weber steered his monastery through the darkness of the 1960s, willing to throw over the irrelevant but adamant to keep the essentials, among which he included the wearing of habits at chapel and meals, the reading of sacred texts during the noon meal, and the prayer schedule of four times a day plus a Mass (though the prayers were now in

English and somewhat shorter). "In the past," he said, "we weren't always given reasons for the things we were doing, so they got tossed out one after another until we were in limbo and didn't know where we were at. Later we found that there were good reasons for some of those customs, and we added them back over the years and eventually wrote them out in our 'Book of Customs.'" This eight-page statement serves as the chapter's addendum to Benedict's Rule, regarding community life, liturgy, government, formation, and the timetable. It is supplemented by the constitutions of the North American and world Benedictine federations to which St Peter's belongs. "We've agreed to these," Abbot Weber said, "but no one can force an abbot to comply. Benedictine life is strongly grounded in its locality."

"I'd say we're a happy, peaceful community now," said Father Andrew Britz, who came to the abbey as a young man just before the upheaval. "There's little infighting, except perhaps about agriculture. Our farm is in a tight financial squeeze – it'd probably be cheaper to put the whole thing in grass – but we can't get into the cycle of fertilizers and pesticides. There's no consensus on what to do. If someone had asked me in the 1960s what we would be quarrelling about in twenty years, I never would have said our farm!"

"I found the place sort of grows on you," Vince said. "It's no longer just rehab. Rehab can become an excuse to leave: I've sobered up, the philosophical basis of life is clear, why stay? So I had to give up rehab as a purpose and take a serious look at monastic life in and of itself. You can lead a 'double life' here, running to keep fit, reading books, collecting material for some other career, but I got tired of that. It takes energy and it's stupid. About a month and a half ago I caught myself making plans of what I'd do when I leave after the novitiate. But then I thought I'm happy here, so why do I want to leave? (Maybe because I want to make things tougher for myself. This is a comfortable life in many ways. We have some very comfortable monks here.) I was content and more at peace – for the moment anyway – so I just let those ideas about leaving go, and things smoothed out."

Not that the doubts went away entirely. "If you get pressure to do a job you don't want to do, your mind says: I don't need this bullshit," he continued. "But what life isn't like that? The community stresses the idea that problems aren't with other people, but with ourselves. One day I was working in the pig barn with Randy and I got pissed off because I felt he wasn't listening to my opinion about how to do something. Later I realized I hadn't been listening to him either. Service to others is the whole idea of Christian vocation. That's the reason to break down ego."

As Brother Vincent implied, however, there is a fundamental debate surrounding the service, comfort, and isolation of monks and nuns. Is their retreat to prayer really an escape from the toils and troubles of ordinary life? Can Truth be found apart from the joys and sufferings of humanity, and if it can be found, should it be restricted to the peace of a few individuals? Moses, Christ, Mohammed, and the Buddha may have witnessed the Truth in seclusion – goes the argument – but each of them brought it out for the sake of the whole world. And isn't the spirit of renunciation betrayed by the wealth and influence enjoyed by the community, even if its individuals cannot own property or exercise broad authority? These questions have always haunted the proponents of withdrawal, whether the Essenes, the Hutterites, the Emissaries of Divine Light, the Tibetan Buddhists in Cape Breton, or the Tasher Hassidim north of Montreal. They caused the Protestant Reformation to rise up against the superiority and corruption of the great European monasteries, and they caused much of the disillusionment with monasticism in the 1960s.

As an integral part of the colony from the start, drawing most of its members from the regional German-speaking population until recent years, St Peter's Abbey was never isolated from its surrounding community, which numbered almost 10,000 by 1920 in an area of 1,800 square miles. Those monks who were also priests took on typical parish work at once, which caused the abbey to be given in 1921 the rare distinction of being an abbey-nullius, as if it were its own diocese with the abbot as the bishop. In 1904 the monks began producing a

366

local newspaper in German, out of which emerged the *Prairie Messenger*, the renowned and controversial Catholic weekly. In 1921 they started St Peter's College, a boarding school for boys at the high-school level and later a junior college, which provided an above-average education while introducing many students to the Benedictine vocation. And, from its inception, the monastery shared with the colonists the harvests and hardships of farming as subjects of the vagaries of climate, government policy, and world prices.

Though St Peter's has a more intimate involvement with its immediate world than do the other two Benedictine abbeys in Canada (Abbaye Saint-Benoît in Quebec's Eastern Townships and Westminster Abbey in Mission City, B.C.), its connection with parish work, education, printing, and farming is well within the mainstream of the Benedictine tradition. Though the tradition began as a movement of brothers rather than of priests, as a movement of prayer rather than of mission, as a movement of divestment rather of accumulation, it soon became thick with priests, busy with teaching, and fat with prosperity and power. This was an understandable (if not entirely desirable) outcome of the privileges of priesthood, the study of the Scriptures, and the economic and management benefits of cheap, obedient labour. While some Benedictines pulled back toward monkhood, separation, and severity, most have never been completely exempt from the "reality" around them, the politics above them, or the ambitions within them. At St Peter's free trade and abortion are table topics, drought and grain prices are business concerns, and achievement and position are personal secrets. One night a native family came in to ask for food. When the porter went off to make them sandwiches, the children dumped the entire box of fish feed into the tank. Later, when I was helping to drain and clean it, I thought how impossible it was for either the fish or the monks to be totally protected from events. Whether the edict of an angry king, the dropping of an atomic bomb, the demands of sustenance and shelter, or the sudden assault of two children on the glassed enclosure, the connection to the rest of the universe could not be severed.

Not that St Peter's is interested in severing it. There was even a quarrel in the late sixties over whether the abbey should allow hermits to reside there, without any responsibility but prayer. The monks frequently mention the missionary work in Brazil that they began then, as if to balance the ledger. They point with honour to Father Matthew Michel, the oldest monk, born in 1896 and around since 1919, whose political and organizational efforts earned him the title of "father of rural electrification in Saskatchewan." They glory in the radical image of the *Prairie Messenger*, which has taken the line of the Social Gospel since the Depression years, when Wilfred Hergott shaped its editorial thrust under the sway of Woodsworth and the Regina Manifesto.

"Hergott was a very holy man and an exemplary monk who put the paper in the social-action tradition it has maintained," said Father Britz, who has been in charge of it for almost a decade. "Our first monks had tended to be super-active. Many of them were rugged individualists who hadn't made it with their contemplative communities and had volunteered to come with the German colony. But they were quite conservative, and their paper was highly conservative until Father Hergott took over the English edition. He pushed hard for medicare during that provincial crisis, for example, much to the consternation of some of the Church. Nowadays the social encyclicals of the Pope are central to our editorial policy. There's been some crackdown in areas of theology and liturgy – where we have to do some careful dancing – but in the social and political areas we'd have to go a long way to the left to outdo John Paul II. Certainly you can make enemies much easier than friends by publishing a Catholic newspaper in these times, but the community – especially the Abbot – has been very sensitive not to add to the pressure. Usually their support is silent but extremely strong. They know the tradition."

In 1987 the tradition expressed itself further when the Roman Catholic bishops of Saskatchewan gathered at St Peter's and issued their reflections on *Farming – A Vanishing Way of Life?* After examining the economic, social, and eco-

368

logical conditions of Canadian agriculture, they concluded that "present agricultural practices are not in accord with the Christian concept of stewardship," because profit and so-called efficiency have been put before the health of the land and the well-being of its citizens. "The inadequacy of our current system is vividly reflected in the death of small villages, in rural poverty, in the lack of young people interested in farming, in dwindling rural populations, and in the increase in hunger and malnutrition both in the Third World and here in Saskatchewan."

Yet even the most radical monk would not say that political and social action should supersede prayer in the community. "Monastic life always has to be on the periphery," said Father Andrew, "and monks have to be concerned not to get too engrossed in the world personally. The more active they are, the more they need contemplative prayer, though sometimes it's hard to keep the proper balance between work and prayer. I can't say that my years as editor of the paper have been my model years as a monk."

Among the mysteries of faith is the proposition that prayer does more than produce the desire and energy to serve in practical ways. Prayer *by itself* can transform the minds and hearts of humanity. In this cosmology praying for peace and justice may do as much as – even more than – organizing demonstrations and arming peasants, and the force of a few saintly people on their knees may tip the scales against all the deeds of the wicked in history. Whether fact or folly, the precondition is interesting: neither prayer nor the seeking of Truth can be for selfish motives, or else both will remain unfulfilled. As Brother Vincent discovered over nine months, as even I detected in a week, the abbey is not there for rehab from alcohol or influenza. It is there as a functioning symbol of the power of selflessness.

"It's a hell of a lot more difficult to give service to one of the brothers who's done something to you, to live with him day in and day out, than to give service to the world," Vince said. "That really takes a toll. Some days even to sit at the same table with the son of a bitch is tough. Stuff like that makes the apostolic work of a parish priest seem like a joke. It's real easy, it's a privilege and a joy, it's a *relief* to help the people who come in need. The true struggle of service is to do something daily for all the monks. That's one reason why I don't want to be a priest. I think I have the intellectual ability and the social skills, but does a priest serve or is be being served by his status? I like to say that I'd never consider the priesthood until Rome allows women priests and married clergy, but that may just be a way to avoid the important question. I wouldn't want the *stigma* of being a priest, the isolation, the role, the status. There's some stigma in being a monk, of course, but I can put up with that for the benefit of living in a community with Christian ideals. The sense of service comes here. There is the spark of Christ in everyone – I have to believe in the goodness of all people or there's no point in helping them – and here we put ourselves in a situation where we can bring that spark out."

"We are like men condemned to death in the arena, a spectacle to the whole universe – angels as well as men," the monks heard in the chapel from Paul's first letter to the Corinthians. "We are fools for Christ's sake, while you are such sensible Christians."

From one perspective it looks too easy and egocentric to be such a fool. Three meals a day, a roof over your head, a variety of jobs to suit any leaning, and tender loving care until the grave (which usually is not filled till late, as if to prove the ease of the lives); plus the chance to fuss about your soul and the meaning of life free from the temptations of your own weakness and the hassle of personal decision. Both the farm and the *Prairie Messenger* were running small deficits – which would not have been so small if commercial and management changes had not been undertaken in recent years – but the entire operation was slightly ahead because of revenue of close to $2 million from the college, the guest facilities, and the various salaries, pensions, and parish stipends accruing to each monk and because of the savings in producing its own food, supplying much of its own labour, and living with modest demands. (Abbot Weber likes to tell of the car he drove into

370

the ground after nineteen years.) The monks even began building a new chapel in 1989, to replace the current plain and uninspiring room, which looks more like a church basement with its vinyl floor, fluorescent lighting, and two sections of benches facing each other across an empty aisle.

But another perspective is evident from the few who can hack it. Even among those of strong faith, as I found, only a handful show up for six months and most of them cannot last a year. The beginning is supposed to be the worst, but most of the deserters left in their thirties, Father Andrew described the mid-life crisis of the forties as the Hell time, and I was told of at least one monk in his eighties who still had not adjusted to the place. There may be twice as many Hutterites in North America as Benedictines around the world; and the paucity of replacements for the aging monks at St Peter's will become a crisis in another generation.

Obedience and the renunciation of both property and marriage have their trials. ("Chastity will remain a problem as long as we have bodies," Abbot Weber said, and when I asked Brother Vincent if he had come to terms with it, he answered, "Hell, no. I'm an accident waiting to happen.") But authority, lack of possessions, and even celibacy are not so uncommon throughout society. The great trial, it seemed to me, is the vow of stability. I used to feel something like claustrophobic horror in the chapel when I thought of these people having to spend their entire lives more or less in one place. That is the terrible punishment of prison, after all, and walls, bars, and armed guards have to be positioned to check the urge to escape.

It was not the horror of being trapped with the odious and the tedious, nor was it the horror of a permanent commitment. Being stuck in a large family cannot be much easier, and there is something comfortable about the eternal nature of the marriage vow. The horror came in looking at Vincent, Demetrius, or Randy and knowing where they will be in fifty years, what they will be doing at 6:00 in the evening then, if they decide to stay and are not in the cemetery at the end of the walk. The image of their future was sitting around them on the benches, in the wizened shapes of the ancients. That is the fate of everyone, certainly, but the reduction of options was made worse by the elimination of surprises.

"If you look at it like that, it'd be scary," Randy admitted. "If you start looking way down the line, it wouldn't make sense, 'cause it's too far. I looked at the six months as six months. Then I looked at the year as a year. Now I'm looking at the three years as three years. After that, I'll have to look at it one day at a time. Sometimes there's loneliness, probably there will always be doubts, but you have to make a decision and hope to live by it. You keep on by faith. I rely on the divine office a lot for that. I still have trouble getting up in the morning, but I enjoy the work. We never had animals back home, so I find the pigs a challenge. I couldn't stand them at first, but that's turning around. That seems quite a bit for right now."

"When I start having doubts, it's hard to do anything around here," Vince said. "I get real cranky, I get into arguments, or I just sit back fuming. Those doubts aren't resolved by blocking them out and pushing on, but by telling myself that I need to understand this whole business more. A lot of the material we read has a helpful slant to it – oh, how lovely is monastic life, it leads to God, and so on – but my own reason and conscience require that I reflect seriously about those doubts and what I feel in my heart and gut. If the doubts go for good, if I ever get a fixed ideal about monasticism, if I ever stop exploring the possibilities – well, it bugs me, it bugs the hell out of me, when I see people walking in the same pattern, eating at the same table, talking to the same frigging guys day after day, month after month. I tell you, I could draw a chart of the daily course of some of these guys and put X's where they'll stop at a given time every day. That's why we need more younger people and new ideas, as an impetus to grow. Everyone has a tendency to stagnate, and it takes a struggle not to. I'm not saying these people are bad; I'm asking if they can be better."

One bitterly cold afternoon I came across Abbot Weber at the cemetery, a patch of neat gravestones in the snow, surrounded by a tall hedge. Wearing a black coat, black rubbers, and a black hat with ear flaps, the Abbot was on his daily, forty-five-minute constitutional, a rapid hike through the aspen grove with a stop to feed the birds with the seeds in his pocket and "say hello to my friends" with a prayer to the dead. All three of St Peter's abbots are there, and Abbot Weber remembered the day in 1926 when, as a boy, he had gone to congratulate Father Severin on his appointment as abbot. "I guess I'll be joining him before too long," Abbot Weber told me cheerfully, as if amazed by how the time had flown, making him ready for retirement at seventy-five in 1990. And then he said, "You know, now there's as many of us out here as there are inside." It was as if he made no distinction between the living and the dead. Indeed, I reminded myself, in his faith this realm was death and that realm was life: the ultimate stability.

"The best part of life here is the continual sense of regathering my thoughts and strengthening myself," Vince concluded. "It's the chance to stop and read and reflect on what is really important, and then to grow from that. The way I think now is entirely different from how I thought when I was an alcoholic, with different values and emphases and goals. Better too, I hope! I don't think I'm kidding myself when I get a heightened sense of Christ and what it's all about. If it's not seeking Christ and if Christ doesn't really exist, then it's all bullshit – but I don't think it is bullshit. When they talk about the *mystery* of Christ, that's no shit, because some days you really get a sense of why you're here and some days you think there's a lot of crap: this is just an economic organization out to serve itself and run by a bunch of confirmed bachelors. I had a tendency to go off on that tangent a hell of a lot during postulancy. I said I'd just use this place till I got what I wanted and then I'll get the hell out. That happens less and less as I realize that I'm here for a particular reason. I don't need to be here – I'm sober, I've got my degree, I'm reasonably pleasant – but I'm here to seek God in my own way." In 1989 Brother Vincent took the three-year, temporary vows; but by the spring of 1990 the doubts returned. He asked to be released from his commitment, and he left.

"Benedict used to warn not to get scared at the beginning," Abbot Weber once said to me. "Things may be tough, but as time goes on and if you grow in faith and the practice of virtue, you can run along the way of God's path with unspeakable sweetness of delight. You can find that in some of the older monks. It's quite natural."

SEVENTEEN

Amen

I kept remembering "Time Corrected," the beautiful poem by the French-Canadian poet Pierre Trottier. In it he returned his faith to the King of Heaven. He dismissed the twelve Apostles, sent home the shepherds and the Magi, tore down Babel, drank up the water of the Flood, rehung the fruit upon the tree, handed back to Satan the sin of knowledge, and took Eve again into his side.

> *And then,*
> *Nothing remained for me*
> *But to give up the first sigh*
> *In order to blow out the light*
> *And everything returned to darkness*

For I was sitting in an absolute darkness, and I could not have retreated further from Notre-Dame Basilica – or the Roman Catholicism of my boyhood that it represents. That splendid church in Montreal had been reduced to this single cell in India, the size of a deep closet; here the ceiling and walls were white and bare, without any icon for my prayers or baroque ornament for my senses; a small round cushion provided the only comfort on the concrete floor. I sat on it about eleven hours a day, between 4:30 in the morning and 8:00 at night with breaks for meals and rest, for a month. Others were about, in other cells, but I neither spoke to them nor looked them in the eye the entire time; nor did I read or write. Except for the wind chimes on the roof, the gongs to mark each break, the distant whistling and shunting of trains, and the hour-long lecture (part theory, part pep talk) in the assembly hall each evening at eight, there was silence.

The silence and the cell, the lack of objects and of distractions, all were for the same purpose: to leave me alone, to help me turn my attention for this month from the external world to my internal nature. That may seem too attractive a proposition to need help – what could be more delightful than to escape the *sturm und drang* of daily existence, to recuperate amid peace and solitude, to wallow for weeks in self-absorption? – but, in practice, it only takes a few days for most people to start wishing for a diversion, whether a chat or a novel or an idol. It is our lifetime habit, after all, to look out to the views and around the next corner, to look out for love and opportunity, to look out for assurance and falling rocks. Apart from human curiosity, we are usually looking for happiness; failing that, we will settle for an alleviation of misery. We scour the globe for one or the other, looking at expensive cars and Caribbean cruises, physical beauty and political utopias, successful careers and artistic fulfilment, good health and divine salvation, power, sex, and money. Hadn't I just finished scouring Canada for a year for one or another of those desires? It is not our custom to presume that the fault, dear Brutus, is not in our stars, but in ourselves.

Being alone was more than a spatial condition here. It also meant taking responsibility for myself. There were no guards to enforce the silence, check that I was not sleeping all afternoon, or prevent me from leaving in the middle of the night. There was a teacher, who gave the evening lecture and was available if I ran into trouble, but he exacted no extreme submission and brooked no undue devotion. Indeed, because only his old students were considered self-reliant enough for a month's retreat, he saw little need to interfere with us at all: he had already given us what he knew, and now he gave us repeated encouragement, silent inspiration, and a well-organized place to practise what he had preached. And though there were past masters and dedicated guardians of this teaching going back almost 2,500 years, there was no God to worship, no deities to fear, no saviour to summon – or, rather, their possible existence did not excuse me from working toward the Truth.

When I first went to India, for almost a year in the early 1970s, I came across scores of Westerners who were searching for the magic touch of enlightenment. Most of them had dabbled in drugs, which offered fleeting glimpses of cosmic consciousness, and most of them wanted the same instant experience by natural and more lasting means. In squalid lodges from Bombay to Calcutta the talk was of gurus who pulled golden eggs from the ears of their devotees, gurus who could levitate and gurus who could appear in three or four places at the same time, gurus whose mere presence was enough to launch you on an extended high and gurus whose mere word was enough to send you into permanent bliss. Things had to be immediate and easy and induced, of course, because almost all of these seekers were on the lam from authority and discipline and work. Though many did throw themselves at the feet of sages and practise all sorts of mortifications, generally they sought gurus who promoted love ahead of obedience, miracle ahead of labour, and a moral code that did not intrude annoyingly on the enjoyment of casual sex and abundant hashish.

I had not gone to India on a spiritual quest – at least not consciously – and though I found pleasant diversion in the theological discussions and ashram adventures that filled so many starry nights, I felt little motivation to track down Rajneesh, Sai Baba, Sri Aurobindo, or the fat sixteen-year-old who was the rage at the time. A traveller's curiosity drew me to my fair share of Hindu temples, Muslim ruins, Sikh gurdwaras, Christian churches, and Tibetan monasteries, but it took a young Australian woman to get me to a guru. She was an enthusiastic follower of Neem Karoli Baba, a Hindu holy man who had a reputation in the West as the impish wizard responsible for turning Richard Albert, the Harvard professor of LSD, into Baba Ram Dass, the Naropa professor of Be Here Now. Neem Karoli Baba lived in a small temple compound beside a swift river in a lonely valley in the Himalayan foothills, which I reached after arduous days of trains and buses. The long and difficult journey served to increase my anticipation, and all the tales of his unpredictable nature made me wonder how I would be received. I had to wonder a while longer, it turned out, because he had gone away and was not expected back until the next morning. I spent the night in the cottage of an English couple, an engaging pair of spiritual drifters who had settled here for several years to be near their guru. They served him and the community in menial and devotional ways, they chanted and meditated and performed rituals, and in return they were provided with food and shelter. They were happy, and since they could live here for next to nothing, they expected to remain forever. When we woke the next morning, however, we learned that Neem Karoli Baba was dead.

If that was the guru's reception, it was a powerful one. I saw the tears and the anguish, I saw the disorientation and the upheaval, I saw the impermanence and the suffering. Suddenly all the philosophy and ecstasy were gone, all the harmony and expectation were shattered, all the wisdom and strength went up in smoke and ashes with the corpse. Adults wandered around like orphaned children, worrying where to go, what to do, who would protect and provide. When I caught the bus out of the valley a couple of days later, I felt I had had a close escape.

One day, while hiking in Kashmir, two circumstances came together to condition a particularly vivid dream: I was reading a book on Buddhism that someone had given me, and I had just met an American wanderer who mentioned he was off to some sort of course in the hill station of Dalhousie. (Though more resolute than most seekers in my experience, Michael typified them. He had been an engineer with the U.S. space programme in Houston until one acid trip too many sent him on a spiritual odyssey. He vowed to roam the planet for enlightenment or seven years, whichever came first, from the monks of Mount Athos to Krishnamurti in Switzerland, from the yogis of Rishikesh to the aborigines in Australia. When I met him, he was climbing to get Shiva's blessing from a lingam made of ice in a mountain cave.)

I cannot remember all the details of the long dream, but I knew I was in the presence of the Buddha. It was an informal, benign, and immensely fun presence, and we passed the time playing mental games. For example, I was sitting in a garden beside a mountain stream, there was a young boy playing on the bank, I saw him slip and tumble into the cold current. "You have a choice," the Buddha said in my head. "You can rush over and try to save him, you can do nothing and hope someone else will save him, or you can do this – " and it was as if his mind took my mind like a parent's hand might take a child's. Our minds stretched across the lawn and plunged into the water, and we plucked the boy to safety and set him back where he had been. This was followed by tremendous laughter. "All is mind, all is mind!" the Buddha shouted. "That's what's meant by 'All is mind.'"

As the dream faded, door after door began to close, and with each closing my mind was confined into smaller and smaller spaces. I was being pulled further and further from an infinite playing field into the tiny box that was me, I was being taken from my new friend, and I was begging to be allowed to stay out with him. "Go to Dalhousie," he answered. "Go to Dalhousie," he repeated, fainter and fainter as the doors closed and the spaces got smaller. "Go to Dalhousie," I found myself saying when I awoke, clinging to the message as if it were a map to lost treasure.

He might have been advising me to enrol in law school in Halifax, of course, but I interpreted it as telling me to go to Michael's course. If I had been told its details, I had forgotten them. I imagined I was heading to a yoga camp, to be taught how to stand on my head by a bearded swami in magenta robes. When I got there, I discovered it was a ten-day course in meditation, drawn from a Burmese tradition of Theravada Buddhism and taught by a plump and distinguished-looking businessman without beard or robes or equivalent holy frou-frou.

His name was S. N. Goenka. Born into a conservative Hindu family in Burma, he had achieved financial and social success at an early age, but only at the cost of excruciating migraines which incapacitated him every fortnight and almost made him a morphine addict. Though he travelled to the best doctors in Europe, the United States, and Japan, he found no cure until a friend recommended he try a meditation programme given at a centre in Rangoon by U Ba Khin, who was also one of Burma's top civil servants. The headaches went, but their relief was only a by-product of wider consequences, and Goenka continued practising under the close supervision of his teacher while carrying on his business and family life. Fourteen years later, in 1969, he began teaching in India, at the invitation of Indian and Western students who spontaneously organized course after course in tent camps, off-season hotels, and borrowed quarters all over the subcontinent. Thousands were attracted by word of mouth, and eventually they built a permanent centre near a small town in the hills east of Bombay.

That was where I sat in the dark cell more than fifteen years after those monsoon-soaked days in Dalhousie and about two months after leaving St Peter's Abbey. That fact is a wonder to me. Though I emerged from the first course full of interest and admiration, I doubted I would ever attempt anything like it again. It was just too damn hard. I had done some hard things before it – I had hitchhiked across the Sahara Desert, I had climbed in the Himalayas, I had hacked through the jungle of graduate school – but nothing had been as gruelling as those ten days. I did not mind the silence; I got used to the hours; I accepted the temporary vows not to kill or steal or lie or take intoxicants or engage in sex; but I could not bear my own mind.

The first third of the time was devoted to learning and perfecting a simple method of concentration: we had to keep our minds focused on the incoming and outgoing breaths at our nostrils. At first it seemed so simple as to appear an idiotic thing to be doing – this is insane, ergo I might as well leave – but it quickly became a sophisticated and indomitable challenge. Sophisticated because it harboured a number of subtle attributes: the breath is happening in the present moment, it may flow at its natural pace or it may be regulated fast and slow, it is physical yet it is connected to the mental state, it continues even when we do not pay attention to it, it is neither an artificial prop like a mantra nor an imaginative projection like a visualization. And indomitable because it exposed the flightiness of the mind. What a busy little bee my mind turned out to be, speeding from the horrors of the past, zooming to the pleasures of the future, roaring from fear of what is ahead, lingering only to savour delightful memories. Despite my will and effort, it would spend barely five seconds with the breath before it raced away again to countless likes and dislikes past and future. It simply was not used to dwelling contentedly in the present.

Gradually over time, by pulling it back whenever it wandered, I was able to keep my mind on my breath for thirty seconds, sixty seconds, a couple of minutes. Then, for the remaining two-thirds of the retreat, we were taught to apply that concentration to the sensations in all parts of the body. Moving the mind methodically from head to feet, through the trunk and limbs, we were to observe any and every sensation we came upon: heat, cold, tickling, tingling, itching, pulsating, pleasure, pain, whatever we found happening at the present moment. A great deal turned out to be happening. Below our normal awareness the body is an ongoing swirl of sensations, subtle or dense, plain or indescribable, constantly changing – no surprise really, since science tells us that this is the case, but seldom experienced directly at the conscious level unless fear sends a shiver up our backs or love makes a knot in our stomachs.

If that were all, it might be beneficial as an exercise in concentration or relaxation, but it would not be wisdom. Wisdom comes from what is done with the concentration and the observation. A killer directing his mind toward his target is not wise; nor is an observer who reacts to what he sees with desire or hatred. Wisdom is in the equanimity with which we handle whatever rises and passes away.

That is an abstract bit of philosophy, and understanding it rarely helps when we are confronted by greed or grief. Once I tamed my savage mind for a minute and began to look within, for example, I was racked by headaches, backaches, pains in my knees, ants in my pants, emotional storms, psychological terrors, overwhelming fatigue, overpowering doubts about the teacher and the teaching and myself. This meditation was no poetic "emotion recollected in tranquillity." It was more like torture. We were asked to try to sit absolutely still for longer and longer periods, up to an hour at a time. Some days I could not manage ten minutes before the pain, agitation, or enervation would force me to move. Some days I was filled with rage. Some days I was overcome by self-contempt. Some days I was yanked to my feet and propelled out the door at the hands of an involuntary urge to STOP THIS.

This, of course, was me. There was nobody else and nothing external to blame, as we usually do when things go wrong. As it became more obvious that these agonies could not be attributed solely to the long hours, the unfamiliar posture, or old physical injuries, it became more apparent that they were expressions of my mind; and the more I settled into the present, the more my mind tossed up neurotic garbage from the past to fuel the habit of desire and hatred. I could not say that this knee pain or that backache came from this bad action or that wicked thought, but the connection between the sensations and my psychological condition became clearer. As Pascal once remarked, "All human evil comes from this: man's being unable to sit still in a room."

The mind still roved and had to be returned to the sensations, but my major effort shifted from observation to equanimity. Certainly it was not very difficult to stay focused on the equivalent of a knife being twisted in my shoulder; it was more difficult to feel the twisting as a congested frenzy of mere vibration. Yet that was what it was; and once the habitual element of recoiling reaction was removed even for a moment, I was able to see the sensation as nothing but sensation, unworthy of all my fuss and fury. As often as not – and experience may be a prerequisite to believing this – if I could observe the present reality without reacting to it, the pain would dissolve suddenly and permanently. And, more wonderfully, when the physical knot unravelled, at a deep level the psychological knot of which it was a manifestation unravelled too.

There is a theoretical interpretation of why this should be so. It is known among Buddhists as the Chain of Conditioned Arising. It describes life as a cyclical process in which ignorance breeds reaction, which breeds consciousness, which breeds mind-and-matter, which breeds the six senses, which breed contact, which breeds sensation, which breeds becoming, which breeds birth, which breeds death and decay and suffering. The chain can be broken, therefore, at the link of sensation by not reacting with craving or aversion. Moreover, given the lack of reaction, the mind sustains its flow by dredging up past reactions, which come to the surface as sensations. If those are met with equanimity, they too get eradicated, thereby opening the possibility of eradicating all past reactions, halting the flow of consciousness, and ceasing the whole process of suffering – which is Nirvana by any name.

I cannot say I ever grasped the Chain of Conditioned Arising completely, but I never bothered my head about it too much. I could have learned it in Pali and Tibetan, I could have lectured on its most intricate facets, but if I did not *experience* its reality, I would not be a jot closer to the Truth. Conversely, I could have attained all its wisdom through practice even if I had never heard of it. Too much of what passes for wisdom is founded on the delights of intellectual games or the fears of blind authority, and neither of those are well founded in knowledge. As I crossed Canada I met Christian theologians and Jewish scholars who could convince themselves that white is black or prove that God exists, but who could not sit still for three minutes or love their neighbours as themselves. I met devout Sikhs, with portraits of Guru Nanak on their walls, who had disinherited their children for marrying out of caste; I met Pentecostals, with portraits of Christ on their walls, who hated Jews and liberals; I met native elders, with portraits of the Great Spirit on their walls, who refused to talk unless paid; and then there were the drunken Buddhists, the armed priests, the morbid Hutterites, the neurotic rabbis, and the whole horde of believers who thought that Heaven could be stormed by some fast talk, a seminary degree, a few incantations, or a machine gun.

Even by the end of my first ten days of meditation I found my mind slightly quieter, my pains somewhat subdued, my personality somehow lighter, and (as a kind of unexpected bonus) my smoking habit totally eliminated without the least effort or regret. The hardships had been more dramatic than the results, however, and though I was struck by the practical sense and elegant purity of the method, I did not expect that I would be registering for another ten days, six months later near Bodh Gaya. While some students plunged into the courses like fish regaining water, swimming after Goenka from retreat to retreat, I waded into each one shivering and reluctant. On the other hand, while some students lost their enthusiasm once the initial excitements subsided into the drudgery of meditation, either giving up or going on to sample fresher thrills, I persisted over the years, trying to practise an hour a day and taking ten days, twenty days, thirty days a year for deeper work. It still felt like work; there were months when I could not bring myself to make the effort; but any nagging doubts about the efficacy of the technique had been obliterated by the progressive changes obvious to me and those who knew me.

None was more obvious than my sudden distaste for alcohol. Forswearing intoxicants was one of the vows we took for the duration of each retreat, and since I had never had any unusual addiction to the stuff, it was not a tough abstention. In routine life, however, I relished a few cold beers on a summer afternoon, I was fond of a couple of whiskies on a winter evening, and I tended to quaff rather than sip wine on social occasions. I made a happy drunk, and though being drunk was becoming less fun than it seemed when I was twenty, it often came with being a North American in general and a journalist in particular. Like the other four vows, the one regarding intoxicants was less a moral judgement than a practical consideration: it was harder to focus attention and maintain balance when sloshed. What was true for ten days became true for the rest of the time, for where is the peace and wisdom in running around killing, stealing, lying, jumping from bed to bed, and being smashed out of your mind? Thus, my attitude toward Roman Catholic priests who abuse boys or Tibetan Buddhists who abuse alcohol or Sikhs who murder innocent people was not based on some puritanical code. It was based on knowing that genuine practices purify inevitably. If there is no purification, something is wrong somewhere, for sin is less the breaking of commandments than the ignorance of Truth.

Since the retreats offer almost no opportunity to break the vows, keeping them is seldom a problem. But, once outside again, the world presents more than enough opportunities; it presents encouragement and even pressure to break them. When I spoke to Goenka about how difficult it was to stop drinking altogether for personal or social reasons, he advised me not to force it, since force would only increase the craving which was at the core of drinking. Be aware, be moderate, keep meditating – he said – and when that particular habit was ready to surface, as a sensation, it would be erased naturally. And, despite my scepticism, that is what happened. I came out of a twenty-day retreat in 1982 and found, in the weeks and months and years that followed, I had not the least desire for glass of beer or a sip of champagne.

"I'm worried I'm being brainwashed," I said to Goenka in a state of panic midway through my second retreat.

"You are being brainwashed," he answered. "Your brain is being washed!"

It was a matter of faith again, I suppose, but faith tested rigorously, suspiciously, against what it promised and what it delivers. "Do not simply believe whatever you are told, or whatever has been handed down from past generations, or what is common opinion, or whatever the scriptures say," Buddha – is reputed to have – said. "Do not accept something as true merely by deduction or inference, or by considering outward appearances, or by partiality for a certain view, or because of its plausibility, or because your teacher tells you it is so. But when you yourselves directly know that these principles are unwholesome, blameworthy, condemned by the wise – when adopted and carried out they lead to harm and suffering – then you should abandon them. And when you yourselves know that these principles are wholesome, blameless, praised by the wise – when adopted and carried out they lead to welfare and happiness – then you should accept and practise them."

That was the spirit with which I followed this path, however waywardly and tortoise-like, down the years. I set aside, as an agnostic does, questions concerning the existence of God or gods, the divinity of Jesus Christ or the Buddha, the definition of Heaven or Nirvana, the likelihood of eternal damnation or animal reincarnation, because they seem unanswerable, at best a waste of spiritual time and effort, at worst a mammoth delusion. Instead, I observed nature in my breath and sensations, I honed my concentration and equanimity bit by bit, and I watched for positive or negative results in myself and my dealings with others.

Though originally drawn to the technique by irrational circumstances, I was held to it by its reasonableness. It stressed the need for an experienced teacher – especially at the beginning when the foundation has to be established correctly, to avoid errors and even dangers – but it made the teachings the guru. As in the cases of Neem Karoli Baba, Martin Exeter, Trungpa Rinpoche, and even Abbot Weber, a personal guru is too transitory, too human, and there is too great an emotional temptation to let that person's presence substitute for the student's own knowledge and labour. In my first courses I was full of questions for Goenka, until I realized they were more often for comfort and attention than for elucidation. It was not long before I could anticipate his answers within myself, and I stopped pestering him.

Too, I was held by this being a monastic training for householders. Except for the parts of the day and year when I retreat from the world, it allows me to participate actively in it. Becoming a monk may hasten the benefits; certainly the hassles of daily living try both my practice and my equanimity; but the Truth must apply to everyone at any level and not everyone can be a monk. If I had ever had romantic illusions of a monastic vocation, I lost them at St Peter's Abbey. Perhaps I am too in love with travel and too curious about what life will spring around the next corner; probably both that love and that curiosity stem from my ignorance and a lack of resolve; but the permanent isolation from adventure and chance seemed impossible. When I went home from the abbey, for example, I discovered I was going to be a father. (When a doctor told my wife and asked her where the daddy was, she replied, "In a monastery in Saskatchewan.") I did not sympathize with the monks for not having the thrill of fatherhood so much as for not having such an unexpected twist in circumstance.

Furthermore, I was held by the fact that the technique's immediate and long-term benefits were available free of charge to anyone who wanted to practise, regardless of gender or race or creed: man or woman, Easterner or Westerner, Christian or Jew, monk or yogi, scholar or illiterate, rich man or poor man. As Coleridge once noted, "He who begins by loving Christianity better than Truth will proceed by loving his own sect or church better than Christianity, and end by loving himself better than all." And no one can put a price on Truth. The love of money may be the root of all evil; prying cash out of the tightfisted may seem God's work; there may even be monastic or ascetic traditions predicated upon poverty; but as a general rule if you have to pay at the door or hand over your savings for a spiritual teaching, *caveat emptor.* Think of Moses charging fifty dollars for a peek at the book of the covenant; think of Jesus charging admission to hear his sermon on the mount; think of tickets to enter a priest's confessional or a rabbi's study or a yogi's cave. Then think of the fees, far beyond any reasonable operating expense, commanded for a psychic's reading or a cult's seminar or a guru's lecture. Pure teachings usually instil a voluntary urge toward generosity among those who have been helped by them, but no pure teacher could imagine putting a toll on the alleviation of human suffering.

Over the years, as I brought less misery and anxiety to each sitting, I began with less distraction, less fatigue, less discomfort. My mind would stay on the breath or the sensations for longer and longer. I could sit perfectly still for more than an hour. My feeble equanimity grew stronger as I learned not to bear the pains but to observe them. Indeed, there were often periods of neutral sensations when I wanted the pains – partly to break the boredom, partly to uproot another buried neurosis – and I had to learn to accept the lack of pains too. After fifteen years I still considered myself an unsatisfactory student, but I drew some consolation by seeing how far I had come from the agitated and miserable young man in Dalhousie. My neuroses subsided more quickly than by psychiatry and more permanently than by confession; my awareness and my diligence increased noticeably; and my harmony and my patience with myself, others, and the vagaries of life improved remarkably.

However far I still have to go to realize Truth completely, I consider myself fortunate to have found such a direct and effective path whose rewards are apparent here and now as well as if and when. It is only one of many effective paths, of course, that fall within the three broad ways common to all spiritual traditions: Contemplation, Devotion, and Action. As a contemplative technique, it aims at achieving wisdom through an experience of the illusions of the material world and the oneness of the spiritual universe. In other words, like aspects of native spirituality or New Age mysticism, it uses an intense and solitary focus on nature to pass beyond the divisions of self and other, mind and body, immanent and transcendent. It is an experience only reached by terrific effort and terrifying surrender, because it demands a dismantlement of everything protective and familiar.

The very power of Contemplation makes it the least popular of the three ways. Most people want protection and familiarity from their religions, and though the ends of pure Devotion and pure Action are no less threatening to the ego than those of pure Contemplation, their means are often a great deal more comforting. Devotion appeals to the heart.

Usually it prostrates itself before the image of a transcendent Other, male or female but often with the masculine characteristics of law and order, which tend to make devotees conservative, private, and obsessed with being good. Appropriate to its prostration, Devotion tends to stress obedience to authority on earth as well as in Heaven, and authority is given to those popes, preachers, and prophets who claim privileged access to God's Truth. But Action challenges such authority. It speaks to the head, honours reason above emotion, and prefers to search for Truth in the history and cultures of the world. Not surprisingly, it usually finds change and relativism instead of constants and absolutes, and immanence tends to make the activists more liberal, more contextual, and more obsessed with doing good. Authority is shared among the faithful, who have to struggle through ambiguity and conflict to adapt outmoded beliefs, rites, and moral codes to the signs of the times.

From a height, surveying Canada, it looks to me as if two armies have been positioned at the edge of a battlefield to fight each other in the name of faith. From every tradition there have emerged two distinct and often antagonistic wings, which then have cut across old divisions to form into new makeshift alliances. As I moved across the country, I was struck by how much more all the activists had in common with each other than with the devotees of their own denominations, and vice versa. In general theological outlook as well as on particular social issues, I discovered a sympathetic bond among United Church feminists, Anglican supporters of the *Book of Alternative Services*, Roman Catholic liberation theologians, Reform Jews who welcome gay rabbis, Presbyterian Social Gospellers, liberal Lutherans and Mennonites, and others centring their faith in the world and its cultures. Often allied to fight unemployment or apartheid in ecumenical organizations such as the World Council of Churches or GATT-fly, they seem kindred spirits too, however much they may disagree on doctrinal details or church structures. That becomes especially clear when they are set against Roman Catholic conservatives, Anglican traditionalists, United Church evangelicals, Protestant fundamentalists, Orthodox

389

Jews, or pious Sikhs, many of whom are allied informally in their own campaigns against abortion, sexual permissiveness, or the Soviet Union, though their dogmas and otherworldliness work to keep them apart.

There is nothing new about two warring camps claiming to have God on their side in matters of belief and politics. But the forging of new interdenominational coalitions is changing the religious dynamics of the past. As the rigid identification with a church or sect loosens, as the intricate points of dogma lose focus in face of mass secularism, religions are experiencing the same pressures as governments and corporations toward integration and globalization. Yet, though Truth must be one, there is as little chance of one religion as of one world government or a single multinational. More likely, as with the grand divisions between East and West or North and South, is a broadening distance between those who want to challenge the world on its own terms and those who want to confront it on theirs.

Despite their differences, both Devotion and Action share the propensity to institutionalize their spirituality into churches and doctrines. Both, therefore, risk losing the sparks of their wisdom in the maintenance of their organizations. At this level, as Carl Jung once put it, religion becomes "a defence against the experience of God," for the experience of Truth shatters all such structures and ideas. Instead of putting the burden for enlightenment on each individual, Devotion tends to package saviours and priests and rituals to do the heavy work, while Action tends to press its people no further than the visible world of human affairs. Instead of exploring natural realms, Devotion tends to turn away from this world, while Action has been more successful in making mankind sacred than in finding Truth in nature.

If that is true universally, I found it especially true during my passage across Canada. Devotion was caught up in its formal vehicles, whether Sunday services or traditional prayers or chanting in the temples; Action was caught up in its social vehicles, whether extraparliamentary politics or welfare services or base communities; and almost everyone was caught up in institutional issues of authority, sexuality, pluralism, finances, and contemporary culture. How often have I approached a church in this country for a few moments of meditation, only to find the door locked to protect the valuables or the silence shattered by tourists and meetings! I remember Archbishop Ambrozic telling of a friend who advised him, at the time of his appointment as coadjutor, to spend five hours a day in prayer, but the Archbishop had to reply that no Canadian bishop can afford to do that. Even the United Church, for all its ambiguities, is basically a multimillion-dollar organization that emerged out of 150 years of effort to harness Methodism's spiritual fire into a stable and pragmatic order.

Order was the priority in nineteenth-century Canada, when religion was at its most powerful in both the French and English settlements, and the churches were a major presence in the garrisons that protected civilization from nature and native people. Indeed, the "garrison mentality," to use Northrop Frye's brilliant phrase, perfectly expresses the character of Canada's religions, which retreated into psychologically confined spaces behind physically massive walls to escape the ego-threatening reality of infinite wilderness, savage beasts, and prophetic shamans. They are a classic illustration of the old adage that religion ends where mystery begins. As Frye himself wrote about the deep terror often found in Canadian poetry in regard to nature, "It is not a terror of the dangers or discomforts or even the mysteries of nature, but a terror of the soul at something that these things manifest."

Nature is not only without, of course, but also within; and the same terror has kept Canadian society from penetrating too deeply into its imagination, its body, and its soul. Just as Canadians prefer journalism to fiction and hockey to ballet, they prefer their religion to be more practical than mystical. Even the monks are pressed to be useful. It is no surprise, then, that Action has been stronger than Devotion in Canada, with the divine mission of New France or the evangelistic zeal of Upper Canada, with the power of the Quebec bishops or the influence of the Social Gospel. And since the churches have never been excluded from matters of state to the extent they were in the United States or parts of Europe, they have often operated at the highest levels of law and politics. Even many devotees have been drawn into that mundane arena, as Catholics fighting for abortion laws or Pentecostals fighting against pornography, for example.

Devotion has always been strong in the pews, of course, and it has been enjoying a new energy and dignity in recent years. Confronted by economic uncertainties and revolutionary change, drowning in a mass society that overwhelms individualism, more and more people are clinging to law and order, eternal truths and standard values, old rites and familiar communities. In Canada and around the world they tend to share the advantages of high births and simple faiths, earthly consolations and ethereal rewards. But, in Canada at least, Action is likely to remain the established way. The culture is essentially liberal and prosaic; many of the devotees' children will defect to it; Devotion's weak intellectual base and high sexual standards scare off many modern Canadians; and traditionalism has a long way to catch up to Action's numbers and clout.

Action has its own problems, on the other hand, evident in the declining membership of the mainline churches and the growth among the devotees. He who sups with the Devil had better have a long spoon, goes the warning, and it seems as if Action's spoons were often too short while it worked in the world and made compromises with culture. Political, relative, and shying away from authority, its messages have become confused and confusing. While it flows with the cultural tide on sexual mores, for example, it tries to stem it on capitalist greed. Generally it lacks the straightforward codes and mystical convictions to suit the needs of some and earn the respect of others.

Meanwhile, most of the society goes about its own business, indifferent to or suspicious of this struggle between Devotion and Action at its periphery. The majority of Canadians may define themselves as members of a religion for social or statistical purposes; they may show up from time to time at spiritual events out of duty or nostalgia; they may even preserve a combination of reverence and guilt toward those who have kept the old ways alive; but their real faith is in science and materialism. Theologians and sociologists sometimes argue that, far from having lapsed, the religious beliefs of these people are finding new and personal expression away from churches and ceremonies. In my experience, however, most people have made the Faustian pact and bartered their souls for technological knowledge and material power. For all their professions of belief, they rarely make the smallest efforts to seek Truth beyond better health and more wealth. Ultimately, indifference is always much more devastating to faith than persecution.

Like Faust, many of them have come to rue the deal. The comforts and wonders of secular materialism have brought a cost in personal harmony, social integrity, and ecological balance. With so little sacred any more, life has less meaning beyond the vain pursuit of pleasure and possessions, the past and the earth are ravaged for immediate gratifications, and individuals lose compassion and community to the insatiable demands of their egos. The effects are everywhere: politics has gone from being a service for others to a helping of oneself, great wealth has become severed from a responsibility to share one's good fortune without making generosity another vanity, assistance to the poor and the ill is less an act of mercy than a begrudged concession, intolerance has increased towards minorities and regions, morality gets defined as staying out of prison, and man struts unchallenged over the wretched beasts and brutalized environment.

Mankind cannot be made wise and the world cannot be made sacred by legislation, yet nothing less than wisdom and consecration seem to be required for peace of mind and the survival of the planet. In that sense, religion is not an escapist fantasy: it is a realistic need. Better to prop up God or Gaia, some say, even if they make no sense. But religion alone is not enough, for even when it ruled in Canada and elsewhere, it did not eradicate pride, envy, anger, covetousness, sloth, gluttony, and lust – even in its own halls. Too often Devotion substituted love with fear and kindness with guilt. Too often Action substituted knowledge with book-learning and faith with arrogance. The priests grew fat and stupid, the rites became dull and empty, and the churches lost purpose and credibility. All across Canada, therefore, I found religion trying to get back to Truth, in order to purify itself so that it could purify others.

In many ways, in fact, I found both Devotion and Action moving fitfully toward Contemplation. Devotees were shifting from the obedience of Law to the experience of Spirit, though morality and prayer remain basic. Activists were shifting from the realism of society to the reality of nature, though deeds and reason remain central. Whether through neo-orthodoxy or post-liberalism, there was a trend to integrating the transcendent with the immanent, the male with the female, the heart with the head, authority with conscience, to know the unity that is Truth and to make life itself both a prayer and an act of compassion. It was a trend to more personal discipline, more rigorous effort, and more exploratory practices too. It was in the ecstasies of Catholic charismatics and Protestant evangelicals; it was in the withdrawal of the Hutterites and the Hassidim; it was in the fascination of United Church theologians and Catholic creation spirituality with process and feminism; it was in New Age therapies, Christian and Jewish mysticism, Benedictine and Buddhist meditation, the Divine Light of the Emissaries, and the Great Spirit of the Dene. As the theologian Karl Rahner expressed it, "The Christian of the future will be a mystic, or he or she will not exist at all."

That does not mean that everyone in Canada, or even in Canadian churches, will be meditating in cells eventually. Even in India and Burma where the contemplative way is established and understood, most priests and followers prefer to make offerings to gods or serve the destitute than to know themselves. But something profound is happening below the surface of society and religion. As the gods of science and materialism increasingly fail their worshippers, as the world seems to be growing as old at the end of this millennium as it seemed at the end of the first one, people are starting to take new interest in faith. More are attracted to Devotion, because traditional forms and strict definitions are precisely the need, and even Action is being pulled toward tradition and authority in response. At the same time, however, Devotion and Action are being hit by the socio-economic transformation of the post-Christian world.

The Catholic momentum has gone from Europe to Latin America; the Anglican forces are gathering in Africa, not England; Islam is on the rise; the Jewish population in Canada and the United States is estimated to drop by half within the next seventy-five years, because of intermarriage and fewer births; priests, monks, and nuns are becoming older and scarcer; all sorts of native spiritualities and mystic traditions are entering the crumbling fortresses of established faith; and an infinite number of unpredictable factors can restore God in a moment, as happened in the 1950s, or kill Him off with a yawn, as happened in the 1960s. In other words, there is a major transition occurring, and only a fool or a prophet would presume to guess the outcome. But the current mood is not unlike the feeling Matthew Arnold described – more than 150 years ago! – of "wandering between two worlds, one dead, the other powerless to be born."

After 2,000 years of the laws of the Father and 2,000 years of the actions of the Son, it may be the turn of the Holy Ghost. While the spirit is formless, Contemplation needs instruments to pierce the illusions of form. So far the contemplative attributes have not solidified into cosmologies or practices that offer the immediately acceptable panaceas most people are seeking, though they seem to be trying to find shape in the West. The New Age churches have a semblance of set paths and immediate answers – which makes their leaders and methods attractive to many – but they usually lack the authority and respectability of tradition. Gnostic teachings, Sufi and cabbala techniques, and native spirituality have tradition, but not mainstream tradition. The Eastern religions have set paths, immediate answers, and mainstream traditions – which explain their quick rise in North America – but they also have a cultural barrier that impedes a widespread acceptance. None of them, therefore, has been born yet into a comprehensive alternative to Devotion and Action, welding

Devotion's transcendence and discipline to Action's immanence and compassion.

Given time, whether decades or centuries, it seems probable that such an alternative will arise. God has been dying since the Enlightenment, after all, and it may take as long for His replacement to be found. Perhaps a messiah will appear, as Jesus Christ did, to pull together the strands of a new faith from the tatters of the old one and create a radiant garment with which to adorn nature and spirit again. Perhaps a cult will emerge supreme and be given the name of religion; perhaps there will be a new enthusiasm for some old mysticism; perhaps an Eastern philosophy will adapt itself successfully to Western culture; perhaps science itself will create an ethics and purpose to match its mystical discoveries. Until then, and no doubt even after that, the old ways will use their power and tradition to contain any alternative, not necessarily because they monopolize the Truth, but because their continuity is too useful to social stability and individual complacency.

Of course, the planet may not have decades or centuries to await its reconsecration – and we, as individuals, may not have weeks or years to find the Truth before we die. Modestly, realistically, each one of us has to begin simply and at once, to venture out of the garrison and learn to accept what Spanish sailors are supposed to have called this wilderness, this whiteness, this silence, this empty space: *Aca nada*, "Nothing there." This is not India or the forest: it is our true nature within. Leaving aside our quarrels over laws and gods and concepts, we can start by developing a selfless generosity toward all beings in our words and thoughts and actions. That need not be a magnificent gesture; it must not be a self-glorifying stunt; but it should involve a conscious element of gentle speech, considerate thought, or sacrificial deed, when our own interests, desires, and opinions are subordinated to those of someone else or something greater. This is the wisdom of great devotees such as Jean Vanier and Mother Teresa, of great activists such as Lois Wilson and Desmond Tutu, and of great contemplatives such as the Benedictines and the Dalai Lama.

As Aldous Huxley once remarked, it is somewhat embarrassing to have travelled so far, read so much, spoken to so many, only to conclude that people should be a little kinder to each other. That is, after all, the common stuff of sermons. It lacks the pyrotechnics of mystical visions, the sweep of political solutions, the hit of spiritual fervour. But its simplicity of expression is as much an indication of its potency as its difficulty of execution. We would rather read tomes in Greek and Sanskrit, climb on our knees to holy shrines and naked sages, or take up arms against infidels and landowners than give up a fraction of our time, money, philosophy for the love of all other beings. Occasionally we may exchange a small service for a lot of self-righteousness, give a wad of cash for a heap of pride, or make a gesture to nature for the sake of self-interest, but any real shattering of me and mine is usually too painful.

In many ways the real test of my meditation was not how long I could sit with a balanced temperament. It was how I dealt with others as well as with myself. Equanimity is an approach to the pains and pleasures of life, not just to the pains and pleasures of sensation (though a constant awareness of sensation is a valuable early warning system for anger, fear, passion, and other reactions to the world). Spending so much time with myself in minute self-examination was not designed to develop self-centredness. On the contrary, it was designed to penetrate the illusions of separation in order to develop the qualities of caring and compassion. In theory a perfect concentration applied to a perfect observation of sensation with a perfect equanimity would reveal that there is no continuing thing called self. It is a practical fantasy for everyday purposes, apparently, created by the Chain of Conditioned Arising. But that remains a theory until it can be fully experienced. In the meantime, the deeper we look into our sensations, the more we witness the rapid arising and passing of particles and thoughts, and the less we become attached to ephemeral constructions such as my likes, my dislikes, and me.

As with morality, compassion and generosity seem both preconditions to wisdom and consequences of it. A certain amount of selflessness may be needed to begin to calm the mind and undo the ignorance, while each equanimous penetration of reality can only induce kind thoughts and helpful actions. If there is no ego to defend or exalt, there is no fear or vanity. The result is neither masochistic martyrdom nor passive lethargy nor neurotic insecurity, but healthy humility and energetic service and positive confidence. In practice, of course, there loom the dangers of smugness, docility, and spiritual conceit, which often rise up to prove that a little wisdom is a dangerous thing. Once the worst pains dissolve, a more insidious attachment to pleasure and *my* truth emerges from the shadows: now I am happy, at last I feel balanced, all is right with the world if only those miserable fools would see it the way I do. That becomes a terrible trap, because the pleasure is as transitory as the pain and selfish truth is no truth at all.

The power of the least instance of pure love, which is love without expectation of reward, is the power of the briefest flash of egolessness. The flash is like an atomic light, radiating waves of mutual identification, which in turn opens the mind and heart to more love and compassion. Things follow naturally: happiness unfolds, fear diminishes, misery lifts, generosity expands, and the process accelerates into cycle upon cycle of benevolence. Like Scrooge on Christmas morning, we fling open the dark curtains and let in the light, we cannot stop laughing, and what might have begun as a terror of Hell in the future continues as a joy of Heaven in the present. And, as in the Dark Ages, when a few in remote areas kept alive the spirit of Christianity, so now just a few pure souls in desolate corners of Canada – in the backwoods of Nova Scotia, in the mountains of British Columbia, in downtown Toronto – can keep alive the spirit of love for the whole world.

As I found on my journey, there are many paths to the Truth. All are long and complex; all have their particular raptures and tribulations. But each one begins with that easy step which is so hard to take: surrender. We would prefer not to do that. Is not the purpose, after all, more power and knowledge to myself, more health and happiness for myself? What is a man profited, we say, if he shall gain his own soul and lose the world? So we pray for strength, wage holy wars, erect great cathedrals, conjure up dazzling speculations – and get nowhere – because we paid no attention to the first and final secret.

"My children, for a little longer I am with you," Jesus said to his disciples, and he taught them one last commandment. "Love one another. As I have loved you, so you are to love one another."

"Whatever is hateful to you, do not do to your neighbour," wrote Hillel, the great Talmudic scholar. "That is the whole Torah. The rest is commentary."

And the Buddhists chant, "As a mother, even at the risk of her own life, protects her son, her only son, so let there be good will without measure between all beings. Let good will without measure prevail in the whole world, above, below, around, unstinted, unmixed with any feeling of differing or opposing interests. If a man remain steadfastly in this state of mind all the time he is awake, then is come to pass the saying, 'Even in this world holiness has been found.'"

BIBLIOGRAPHY

Abel, Kerry. "Prophets, Priests and Preachers: Dene Shamans and Christian Missions in the Nineteenth Century." *Historical Papers*. 1986.

Abella, Irving. *A Coat of Many Colours – Two Centuries of Jewish Life in Canada*. Toronto: Lester & Orpen Dennys, 1990.

Adler, Margot. *Drawing Down the Moon – Witches, Druids, Goddess-Worshippers, and Other Pagans in America Today*. Boston: Beacon Press, 1986.

Allen, Richard. *The Social Passion: Religion and Social Reform in Canada 1914–28*. Toronto: University of Toronto Press, 1971.

Armstrong, Karen. *The Gospel According to Woman*. London: Pan Books, 1986.

Baum, Gregory. "Catholicism and Secularization in Quebec." *Cross Currents*, Winter 1986–7.

———. *Catholics and Canadian Socialism: Political Thought in The Thirties and Forties*. Toronto: Lorimer, 1980.

———. *Religion and Alienation: A Theological Reading of Sociology*. New York: Paulist Press, 1975.

———. *Theology and Society*. New York: Paulist Press, 1987.

Bechert, Heinz, and Richard Gombrich, eds., *The World of Buddhism*. New York: Facts on File Publications, 1984.

Berger, Peter L. *A Rumor of Angels: Modern Society and the Rediscovery of the Supernatural*. Garden City, New York: Anchor Books, 1970.

Bergeron, Richard. *Le cortège des fous de Dieu*. Montréal: Éditions Paulines, 1982.

Berton, Pierre. *The Comfortable Pew – A Critical Look at the Church in the New Age*. Toronto: McClelland and Stewart, Toronto, 1965.

Bibby, Reginald. *Fragmented Gods – The Poverty and Potential of Religion in Canada*. Toronto: Irwin, 1987.

Bissonnette, Jean-Guy, et al. *Situation et avenir du catholicisme québécois: Milieux et témoignages*. Ottawa: Leméac, 1982.

Blaise, Clark, and Bharati Mukherjee. *The Sorrow and the Terror – The Haunting Legacy of the Air India Tragedy*. Toronto: Penguin, 1988.

Blau, Joseph. *Judaism in America – From Curiosity to Third Faith*. Chicago: University of Chicago Press, 1976.

Block, Walter, Geoffrey Brennan, and Kenneth Elzinga, eds. *Morality of the Market: Religious and Economic Perspectives*. Vancouver: Fraser Institute, 1985.

Block, Walter, and Irving Hexham, eds. *Religion, Economics and Social Thought*. Vancouver: Fraser Institute, 1986.

Bokenkotter, Thomas. *A Concise History of the Catholic Church*. Garden City, New York: Image Books, 1979.

Boucher, Sandy. *Turning the Wheel – American Women Creating the New Buddhism*. San Francisco: Harper and Row, 1988.

Boyd, Doug. *Rolling Thunder*. New York: Delta, 1974.

Brandon, Ruth. *The Spiritualists*. Buffalo, New York: Prometheus Books, 1984.

Brody, Hugh. *Living Arctic – Hunters of the Canadian North*. Vancouver: Douglas & McIntyre, 1987.

Brown, Joseph Epes. *The Spiritual Legacy of the American Indian*. New York: Crossroad, 1987.

Bulka, Reuven. *The Coming Cataclysm*. Oakville: Mosaic Press, 1986.

Burghley, Michael, and Nancy Burghley. *The Rising Tide of Change*. Loveland, Colorado: Foundation House, 1986.

Campbell, Joseph. *The Power of Myth*. New York: Doubleday, 1988.

Capra, Fritjof. *The Tao of Physics*. Boulder: Shambhala, 1975.

Cardinal, Harold. *The Rebirth of Canada's Indians*. Edmonton: Hurtig, 1977.

Cayley, David. "History and the New Age." Montreal: Canadian Broadcasting Corporation, 1984.

Cecil, Lord Martin. *Being Where You Are*. New Canaan, Connecticut: Keats Publishing, 1974.

———. *On Eagle's Wings*. London: Mitre Press, 1977.

Chadney, James G. *The Sikhs of Vancouver*. New York: AMS Press, 1984.

Chadwick, Owen. *The Reformation*. New York: Penguin, 1985.

Clark, S. D. *Church and Sect in Canada*. Toronto: University of Toronto Press, 1948.

Clifford, N. Keith. *The Resistance to Church Union in Canada 1904-1939*. Vancouver: University of British Columbia Press, 1985.

Cole, W. Owen, and Piara Singh Sambhi. *The Sikhs – Their Religious Beliefs and Practices*. Delhi: Vikas Publishing, 1978.

Cook, Ramsay. *French-Canadian Nationalism – An Anthology*. Toronto: Macmillan, 1969.

———. *The Regenerators – Social Criticism in Late Victorian English Canada*. Toronto: University of Toronto Press, 1985.

Couture, Joseph. "Indian Spirituality – A Personal Experience." *Kerygma* 16 (1982).

Cox, Harvey. *Religion in the Secular City: Toward a Postmodern Theology*. New York: Simon and Schuster, 1984.

———. *The Silencing of Leonardo Boff – The Vatican and the Future of World Christianity*. Oak Park: Meyer Stone Books, 1988.

Crysdale, Stewart, and Les Wheatcroft, eds., *Religion in Canadian Society*. Toronto: Macmillan, 1976.

Danylewycz, Marta. *Taking the Veil*. Toronto: McClelland and Stewart, 1987.

de Lange, Nicholas. *Judaism*. New York: Oxford University Press, 1987.

Dhillon, Mahinder Singh. *A History Book of the Sikhs in Canada and California*. Vancouver: Shromani Akali Dal Association of Canada, 1981.

Dumont, Fernand, et al. *Situation et avenir du catholicisme québécois: Entre le temple et l'exil*. Ottawa: Leméac, 1982.

Elliott, David R., and Iris Miller. *Bible Bill – A Biography of William Aberhart*. Edmonton: Reidmore Books, 1987.

Exeter, Lord. *Beyond Belief*. Loveland, Colorado: Foundation House, 1986.

Exeter, Michael. *My World, My Responsibility*. 100 Mile House, British Columbia: Foundation House, 1987.

Exeter, Nancy Rose. *Magic at our Hand*. 100 Mile House, British Columbia: Foundation House, 1988.

Fackenheim, Emil. *What is Judaism? An Interpretation for the Present Age*. New York: Collier, 1987.

Fallding, Harold. "Mainline Protestantism in Canada and the United States of America: an overview." *Canadian Journal of Sociology*, vol. 3, no. 2, Spring 1978.

Ferguson, Marilyn. *The Aquarian Conspiracy*. Los Angeles: J. P. Tarcher, 1980.

Fields, Rick. *How the Swans Came to the Lake – A Narrative History of Buddhism in America*. Boston: Shambhala, 1986.

Forbes, H. D. ed. *Canadian Political Thought*. Toronto: Oxford University Press, 1985.

Fox, Matthew. *The Coming of the Cosmic Christ*. San Francisco: Harper and Row, 1988.

———. *Original Blessing*. Sante Fe, New Mexico: Bear and Company, 1983.

Fumoleau, René. "Missionary Among the Dene." *Kerygma* 37 (1981).

Gordon, James S. *The Golden Guru – The Strange Journey of Bhagwan Shree Rajneesh.* Lexington, Massachusetts: Stephen Greene Press, 1987.

Goulet, Jean-Guy. "Being Oneself as an Aboriginal Person – Reflections on Becoming Bicultural." *Kerygma* 18 (1984).

———. "Dreams, Identification of Others and Identity Formation among the Dene-tha." Unpublished paper, 1988.

———. "In the Local Church: Becoming Aware of Native Religious Beliefs." *Kerygma* 16 (1982).

———. "Liberation theology and our missions of Canada." Unpublished paper, 1987.

———. "Religious Dualism Among Athapaskan Catholics." *Canadian Journal of Anthropology*, vol. 3, no. 1, Fall 1982.

———. "Ways of Knowing with the Mind." Unpublished paper, 1987.

Goulet, Jean-Guy, and Achiel Peelman. "The Amerindian Reality and the Catholic Church in Canada." *Pro Mundi Vita*, Bulletin 93, 1983/2.

Grant, George. *Technology and Empire: Perspectives on North America.* Toronto: House of Anansi, 1969.

Grant, John Webster. *Moon of Wintertime – Missionaries and the Indians of Canada in Encounter Since 1534.* Toronto: University of Toronto Press, 1984.

———. *A Profusion of Spires – Religion in Nineteenth-Century Ontario.* Toronto: University of Toronto Press, 1988.

———, ed. *The Churches and the Canadian Experience.* Toronto: Ryerson, 1963.

Greeley, Andrew M. *Confessions of a Parish Priest.* New York: Pocket Books, 1986.

Guenther, Herbert V., and Chogyam Trungpa. *The Dawn of Tantra.* Boston: Shambhala, 1988.

Haiven, Judith. *Faith, Hope, No Charity.* Vancouver: New Star Books, 1984.

Hall, Douglas. *The Canada Crisis: A Christian Perspective.* Toronto: The Anglican Book Centre, 1980.

———. *The Future of the Church – Where Are We Headed?* Toronto: United Church Publishing House, 1989.

Hamelin, Jean. *Histoire du catholicisme québécois - Le XXe siècle - tome 2, de 1940 à nos jours*. Montreal: Boréal Express, 1984.

Hanson, Eric O. *The Catholic Church in World Politics*. Princeton, New Jersey: Princeton University Press, 1987.

Harrington, Michael. *The Politics at God's Funeral - The Spiritual Crisis of Western Civilization*. New York: Holt, Rinehart and Winston, 1983.

Harris, Lis. *Holy Days - The World of a Hasidic Family*. New York: Collier, 1986.

Hart, William. *The Art of Living: Vipassana Meditation As Taught by S. N. Goenka*. San Francisco: Harper and Row, 1987.

Hayward, Jeremy. *Shifting Worlds, Changing Minds - Where the Sciences and Buddhism Meet*. Boston: New Science Library, Shambhala, 1987.

Helmreich, William B. *The World of the Yeshiva - An Intimate Portrait of Orthodox Jewry*. New Haven: Yale University Press, 1986.

Hernou, Paul. "Même des oiseaux apportent des messages." *Kerygma*, 16 (1982).

Higgins, M. W., and D. R. Letson. *Portraits of Canadian Catholicism*. Toronto: Griffin House, 1986.

Hiller, Harry H. "Continentalism and the third force in religion." *Canadian Journal of Sociology*, vol. 3, no. 2, Spring 1978.

Hopkins, Jeffrey. *The Tantric Distinction - An Introduction to Tibetan Buddhism*. London: Wisdom Publications, 1984.

Hostetler, John A. *Hutterite Society*. Baltimore: Johns Hopkins University Press, 1974.

Hostetler, John A., and Gertrude Enders Huntington. *The Hutterites in North America*. New York: Holt Rinehart and Winston, 1967.

Humphreys, Christmas. *Buddhism*. London: Penguin, 1967.

Hunkeler, Leodeger. *It Began with Benedict*. St Benedict, Oregon: Mount Angel Abbey, 1978.

Huxley, Aldous. *The Perennial Philosophy*. London: Triad Grafton Books, 1985.

Ingham, Michael. *Rites for a New Age - Understanding the Book of Alternative Services*. Toronto: Anglican Book Centre, 1986.

Israel, Milton, et al. *Sikh History and Religion in the 20th Century*. Toronto: University of Toronto Centre for South Asian Studies, 1988.

Johnson, Jacques. "Native Spirituality and the Catholic Faith." *Kerygma* 16 (1982).

Johnson, Paul. *A History of Christianity*. New York: Penguin Books, 1987.

Johnson, Shawnäh. *Entity from Another World*. Vancouver: Clear Channel Publishing, 1988.

Johnston, Basil. *Ojibway Ceremonies*. Toronto: McClelland and Stewart, 1982.

Johnston, Hugh. *The Voyage of the Komagata Maru - The Sikh Challenge to Canada's Colour Bar*. Delhi: Oxford University Press, 1979.

Jones, D. G. *Butterfly on Rock: A Study of Themes and Images in Canadian Literature*. Toronto: University of Toronto Press, 1970.

Kashmeri, Zuhair, and Brian McAndrew. *Soft Target - How the Indian Intelligence Service Penetrated Canada*. Toronto: James Lorimer, 1989.

Kilbourn, William, ed. *Religion in Canada: The Spiritual Development of a Nation*. Canadian Illustrated Library. Toronto: McClelland and Stewart, 1968.

Küng, Hans, and Leonard Swidler, eds. *The Church in Anguish - Has the Vatican Betrayed Vatican II?* San Francisco: Harper & Row, 1987.

Lachance, Micheline. *Dans la tempête: le Cardinal Léger et la Révolution tranquille*. Montréal: Éditions de l'homme, 1986.

Lacroix, Benoît. "Histoire et religion traditionelle des Québécois (1534–1980)." *Stanford French Review*, Spring-Fall 1980.

Lader, Lawrence. *Politics, Power and the Church – The Catholic Crisis and its Challenge to American Pluralism*. New York: Macmillan, 1987.

LaBlanc, Philip, and Arnold Edinborough, eds. *One Church, Two Nations?* Toronto: Longmans, 1968.

Le Moyne, Jean. *Convergences*. Montréal: Hurtubise HMH, 1977.

Levi, Peter. *The Frontiers of Paradise – A Study of Monks and Monasteries*. London: Collins Harvill, 1988.

Limburg, James. *Judaism: An Introduction for Christians*. Minneapolis: Augsburg, 1987.

Mainse, David, with David Manuel. *100 Huntley Street*. Nashville: Thomas Nelson Publishers, 1983.

Mansukhani, Dr Gobind Singh. *Introduction to Sikhism*. New Delhi: Hemkunt Press, 1977.

Marmur, Dow. *Beyond Survival – Reflections on the Future of Judaism*. London: Darton Longman and Todd, 1982.

Marshall, Joyce, ed. *Word from New France: the Selected Letters of Marie de l'Incarnation*. Toronto: Oxford, 1967.

Marvin, Walter. *The Kingdom of the Cults*. Minneapolis: Bethany House, 1985.

———. *The New Cults*. Ventura, California: Regal Books, 1980.

McKenty, Neil. *In the Stillness Dancing – The Life of Father John Main*. New York: Crossroad, 1987.

McNaught, Kenneth. *A Prophet in Politics – A Biography of J. S. Woodsworth*. Toronto: University of Toronto Press, 1967.

Mealing, S. R., ed. *The Jesuit Relations and Allied Documents – A Selection*. Toronto: McClelland and Stewart, 1963.

Milton, Ralph. *This United Church of Ours*. Winfield, British Columbia: Wood Lake Press, 1986.

Mol, Hans. *Faith and Fragility: Religion and Identity in Canada*. Burlington, Ontario: Trinity Press, 1985.

Moorhouse, Geoffrey. *Against All Reason*. London: Sceptre, 1986.

Mulgrew, Ian. *Unholy Terror – The Sikhs and International Terrorism*. Toronto: Key Porter, 1988.

Murray, Peter. *The Devil and Mr. Duncan – A History of the two Metlakatlas*. Victoria: Sono Nis Press, 1985.

Neill, Stephen. *Anglicanism*. Baltimore: Penguin, 1965.

Nichols, Peter. *The Pope's Divisions – The Roman Catholic Church Today*. Toronto: Clarke Irwin, 1981.

O'Sullivan, Sean. *Both My Houses: From Politics to Priesthood*. Toronto: Key Porter, 1986.

Ouellet, Fernand. "The Quiet Revolution: A Turning Point" in Thomas Axworthy and Pierre Elliott Trudeau, eds., *Towards a Just Society – The Trudeau Years*. Toronto: Viking, 1990.

Paris, Erna. *Jews – An Account of Their Experience in Canada*. Toronto: Macmillan, 1980.

Parkman, Francis. *The Jesuits in North America*. Boston/Toronto: Little, Brown, 1963.

Peck, M. Scott. *The Road Less Travelled*. New York: Simon and Schuster, 1978.

Peelman, Achiel. "The Amerindian Church: Dream or Reality?" *Insight*, 1987.

———. "Dynamisme spirituel, sagesse et communauté." *Église et Théologie* 16 (1985).

———. "L'avenir du christianisme chez les Amerindiens au Canada: syncrétisme ou inculturation?" Unpublished paper, 1987.

———. "A Native Church for Today and Tomorrow." Unpublished paper, 1988.

Peter, Karl A. *The Dynamics of Hutterite Society – An Analytical Approach*. Edmonton: University of Alberta Press, 1987.

Petrone, Penny, ed. *First People, First Voices*. Toronto: University of Toronto Press, 1983.

Rahula, Walpola. *What the Buddha Taught*. New York: Grove Press, 1962.

Ratzinger, Joseph Cardinal, with Vittorio Messori. *The Ratzinger Report*. San Francisco: Ignatius Press, 1985.

Ridington, Robin. *Swan People: a study of the Dunne-za Prophet Dance*. National Museum of Man Mercury Series, National Museums of Canada, 1978.

Riordon, Michael. *The First Stone – Homosexuality and the United Church*. Toronto: McClelland and Stewart, 1990.

Rioux, Marcel, and Yves Martin, eds., *French Canadian Society*. Toronto: McClelland and Stewart, 1964.

Roche, Anne. *The Gates of Hell: the Struggle for the Catholic Church*. Toronto: McClelland and Stewart, 1975.

Rosenberg, Stuart E. *The Jewish Community in Canada – vol. I – A History*. Toronto: McClelland and Stewart, 1970.

———. *The Jewish Community in Canada – vol. II – In the Midst of Freedom*. Toronto: McClelland and Stewart, 1971.

Ryan, Claude. "L'Église catholique et l'évolution politique du Québec de 1960 à 1980." *Study Sessions* 50 (1983), Société canadienne d'histoire de l'église catholique.

Ryan, John. *The Agricultural Economy of Manitoba Hutterite Colonies*. Toronto: McClelland and Stewart, 1977.

Ryan, William. *The Clergy and Economic Growth in Quebec (1896–1914)*. Quebec: Presses de l'Université Laval, 1966.

Sack, B. G. *History of the Jews in Canada*. Montreal: Harvest House, 1965.

Schoenfeld, Stuart. "The Jewish religion in North America: Canadian and American comparisons." *Canadian Journal of Sociology*. vol. 3, no. 2, Spring 1978.

Sheridan, E. F., ed. *Do Justice! The Social Teaching of the Canadian Catholic Bishops*. Toronto: Jesuit Centre for Social Faith and Justice, 1987.

Shipler, David K. *Arab and Jew – Wounded Spirits in a Promised Land*. New York: Penguin, 1986.

Silk, Mark. *Spiritual Politics – Religion and America since World War II*. New York: Simon and Schuster, 1988.

Singh, Patwant. *The Golden Temple*. Hong Kong: ET Publishing, 1989.

Singh, Patwant, and Harji Malik, eds. *Punjab – The Fatal Miscalculation*. New Delhi, 1985.

Singh, Teja. *Sikhism – Its Ideals and Institutions*. Amritsar: Khalsa Brothers, 1978.

Slater, Peter, ed. *Religion and Culture in Canada/Religion et culture au Canada*. Canadian Corporation for Studies in Religion, 1977.

Slonim, Reuben. *To Kill a Rabbi*. Toronto: ECW Press, 1987.

Smillie, Benjamin G., ed. *Visions of the New Jerusalem – Religious Settlement on the Prairies*. Edmonton: NeWest Press, 1983.

Smucker, Donovan E., ed. *The Sociology of Canadian Mennonites, Hutterites and Amish: A Bibliography with Annotations*. Waterloo: Wilfrid Laurier University Press, 1977.

Snow, John. *These Mountains Are Our Sacred Places – The Story of the Stoney People*. Toronto: Samuel Stevens, 1977.

Stackhouse, John G., Jr. "Proclaiming the Word: Canadian Evangelicalism Since World War I." Unpublished thesis, Northwestern College, Orange City, Iowa.

Starkloff, Carl. "Dialogue with Native Religious Traditions: Toward the Local Church." *Kerygma* 16 (1982).

Strange, Roderick. *The Catholic Faith*. New York: Oxford University Press, 1986.

Sykes, Stephen W., ed. *Authority in the Anglican Communion*. Toronto: Anglican Book Centre, 1987.

Tendzin, Osel. *Buddha in the Palm of Your Hand*. Boston: Shambhala, 1987.

Thatcher, David. *Earthrise – A Personal Responsibility*. Loveland, Colorado: Foundation House, 1987.

Thomas, Keith. *Religion and the Decline of Magic*. London: Penguin Books, 1985.

Toker, Franklin. *The Church of Notre-Dame in Montreal – An Architectural History*. Montreal: McGill-Queen's University Press, 1970.

Trungpa, Chogyam. *Born in Tibet*. Boston: Shambhala, 1985.

———. *Cutting Through Spiritual Materialism*. Berkeley: Shambhala, 1973.

———. *Journey Without Goal – The Tantric Wisdom of the Buddha*. Boston: Shambhala, 1985.

———. *The Myth of Freedom and the Way of Meditation*. Boston: Shambhala, 1988.

———. *Shambhala – The Sacred Path of the Warrior*. New York: Bantam, 1986.

Underhill, Ruth M. *Red Man's Religion*. Chicago: University of Chicago Press, 1965.

Vallières, Pierre. *White Niggers of America*. Toronto: McClelland and Stewart, 1971.

Vardey, Lucinda. *Belonging – A Book for the Questioning Catholic Today*. Toronto: Lester & Orpen Dennys, 1988.

Wade, Mason. *The French Canadians 1760–1967*. Toronto: Macmillan, 1968.

Walker, Susan, ed. *Speaking of Silence – Christians and Buddhists on the Contemplative Way*. New York: Paulist Press, 1987.

Walsh, H. H. *The Christian Church in Canada*. Toronto: Ryerson, 1956.

Waugh, Earle H., Baha Abu-Laban, and Regula B. Qureshi, eds. *The Muslim Community in North America*. Edmonton: University of Alberta Press, 1983.

Westfall, William. *Two Worlds: The Protestant Culture of Nineteenth Century Ontario*. Kingston/Montreal: McGill-Queen's University Press, 1989.

Westhues, Kenneth. "Stars and Stripes, the Maple Leaf, and the Papal Coat of Arms." *Canadian Journal of Sociology*, vol. 3, no. 2, Spring 1978.

Woodcock, George, and Ivan Avakumovic. *The Doukhobors*. Carleton Library Series. Toronto: McClelland and Stewart, 1977.

Young, David, Grant Ingram, and Lise Swartz. *Cry of the Eagle – Encounters with a Cree Healer*. Toronto: University of Toronto Press, 1989.

Zablocki, Benjamin. *The Joyful Community*. Baltimore: Penguin Books, 1971.

Zaehner, R. C. *Hinduism*. Toronto: Oxford University Press, 1966.

Zeman, Jarold K., ed. *Baptists in Canada: Search for Identity and Diversity*. Burlington, Ontario: G. R. Welch Company, 1980.

INDEX

Aberhart, William "Bible Bill", 11, 110, 324–25
Abhisheka, *see* Tantric tradition
Aboriginal peoples, *see* Native peoples
Abortion, 19, 118, 139, 152, 153, 156–58, 161, 164, 166, 240, 313, 322, 325, 326, 328, 351, 367, 390, 392; and Supreme Court, 14, 157
Ackerley, Albert, 89
Activists, 389, 394;
    political, 169, 301
    secular, 234
    social, 139, 230, 241.
    See also Gay Liberation
Adi Granth, *see* Guru Granth Sahib
Adultery, *see* Sexual activities, extra-marital
Aetherius Society, 72
AFFIRM, 218
Africa, 181, 246, 317, 395;
    apartheid, 100, 235, 389
    New Age spiritualism in, 94
    North, 275, 276
    and Roman Catholic Church, 32, 158, 166, 220
    West, 118.
    See also South Africa
Agnostics, 17, 68, 121, 141, 149, 169, 174, 221, 299, 386
AIDS, 161, 172, 198, 209, 211, 240, 312
Aikido, 79
Ainajugoh (High Priestess), 69
Akali Dal Party (Punjab), 250, 257, 258
Akali Singh gurdwara, 254, 263
ALaun ("daughter of Demeter"), 70, 82
Alberta, 14, 51, 110, 278, 282, 335;
    fundamentalism in, 316, 324–25
    New Age spiritualism in, 80
    Northern, 38, 57, 85
Alcohol, 29, 41, 44, 74, 109, 194, 195, 207, 230, 231, 328, 359, 384–85
Alcoholism, 36, 50, 56, 57, 84, 193, 199, 200, 209, 323, 373, 385
Alkali Lake, B.C., 100
Allah, 18, 182, 265

Allied Jewish Community Service (AJCS), 276, 284, 298
Alline, Henry, 314
All Native Circle Conference, 38
Alpert, Richard, *see* Ram Dass
Ambrozic, Archbishop Aloysius, 128, 140–41, 142–51, 153–54, 156, 158, 161, 166–67, 169–70, 174–75, 240, 391
American Indian Movement (AIM), 36, 51
American Jewish Congress, 299, 303
Amish, 282, 341
Amritsar, 246, 250, 256, 259
Anabaptists, 333, 341
André, Brother, 123, 173
Angels, 37, 106, 310, 311, 334
Anglican Church of Canada, 17, 40, 78, 111, 125, 137, 138, 223–30, 241, 294, 314, 321, 395;
    hierarchy, 225–26, 233
    liberalism in, 225, 227, 228–30, 231, 238–39, 242, 389
    National Executive Council, 226–27
    and Native people, 30–31, 33, 38, 60, 79
    and ordination of women, 159, 225–26
    per cent of population, 12, 30
    Renewal Ministries, 227, 314
    synods, 223–25, 226–27
Antichrist, 78, 95, 324
Anti-Semitism, 178, 274, 276–91 passim
Anti-Zionism, 300
Antoine, Jim, 23–24, 25
Apartheid, 100, 235, 389
Apocalypse, 71, 79, 82–83, 355
Apostles, 37, 129, 158, 159, 165, 202, 334, 375
Applewood Centre for Spiritual Studies, 79–80
Aquarius, Age of, 63, 65, 90–91
Aquinas, Thomas, quoted, 161
Arapaho Indians, 52
Arcand, Adrian, 274

237, 368
visit to Fort Simpson, 21–24
    passim, 34, 42, 46–47, 59,
    60–61
visit to Quebec, 124
Johnson, Robert, 319–20
Johnson, Shawnäh (Yvette/Shawney),
    74, 79
Johnston, Wayne, 170
Jonestown, 79
Joseph, Rabbi Howard, 273, 295, 298–
    99, 302–3
Judaism, 78, 79, 80, 82, 179, 181,
    251–52, 267–306, 394;
    anti-Semitism, 178, 274, 276–91
        passim
    Conservative, 294–95, 296, 297,
        298–99
    and Israel, 264, 268, 270, 271,
        285, 286, 288–89, 290–91,
        294, 295, 297–98, 299, 301–
        3, 304, 305, 306, 307
    in Montreal, 246, 267–68, 271–
        81, 283–86, 289–90, 291,
        293, 294, 295, 298–99, 300,
        303, 304, 305
    Orthodox, 250, 251, 258, 280,
        282, 285–86, 287, 292, 294,
        295, 296, 297, 298–99, 300,
        389–90
    Reform, 286, 292–94, 295, 296,
        297, 298–99, 300, 304, 389
    and secularization, 264, 283,
        299, 300, 301, 395
    in Toronto, 137, 271, 272, 276,
        278, 286, 291, 293, 295,
        296, 297, 304
    in U.S., 272–73, 277, 280, 283,
        284, 289, 293, 294–95, 297,
        301
    and women, 285, 286–87, 294,
        297.
    See also Jews
Jung, Carl, 80, 390

Kagyu order, see Buddhism
Kakfwi, Stephen, 24–25
Kalapa Court, Halifax, 181, 192, 196–
    97, 198
Kalu Rinpoche, 193
Karma, 64, 198
    patterns, 69

Karma Dzong Buddhist Church of
    Halifax, 178
Karma Dzong, Colorado, 176
Karma Kagyu, see Buddhism (Kagyu
    order)
Karmapa, Sixteenth (Rangjung Rigpe
    Dorje), 188–89, 191, 193, 194,
    196, 198
Keegstra, Jim, 278
Keepers of the Flame Fraternity, 63–
    64, 67
Khalistan, 246, 251, 258–60, 261,
    263, 264
Khalsa (pure ones), 249, 250, 258,
    259, 262, 266
Khalsa, Babbar, 261
Khalsa Credit Union, 261
Khalsa Diwan Society (K.D.S.), 251,
    253–54, 256, 259–60
Khin, U Ba, 380
Kibbutzim, 348
Kilbourn, William, 137
King, George, 72
King, Martin Luther, 243, 328
King, William Lyon Mackenzie, 20,
    73, 231, 278
King's College, Halifax, 227
King View EDL unit, 94
Kisemanito Centre, Alta., 38
Klassen, Betty Jane, 204, 214, 215
Klein, A.M., 11, 272
Kleinsasser, Ed, 338
Kleinsasser, Eli, 332–33, 336, 338,
    339–40, 342, 343, 346, 347, 348,
    350–51, 352
Kleinsasser, Mrs Jacob, 339
Kleinsasser, Jacob, 338–40, 341, 345–
    46, 347–48, 349, 350, 351
Kleinsasser family, 338–39
Knowles, Stanley, 231
Krishna, 182, 266
Krishnamurti, 379
Kristallnacht, 16, 267, 271, 278, 288
Kristen, Pamela, 70
Krulik, Rudy, 310
Kuan Yin (goddess), 62, 65, 82
Küng, Hans, 166, 169
Kwanza, 48–49, 56, 158

Labor Party, Israel, 297, 299, 304, 305
Labour Zionist Alliance, 268
Lacroix, Benoît, 125

421

216, 218, 264, 286, 296, 346;
  inter-, 64, 275, 295, 300, 301,
    355, 369, 370, 395
Marshall, Joyce, 108
Martyrs and martyrdom, 26, 27, 56,
    121, 167, 168, 259, 266, 333, 334,
    398
Marxism, 32, 77, 84, 118, 139, 140,
    141, 231, 235, 237, 242
Mary (Virgin), 49, 62, 63, 65, 82, 105,
    108, 123, 141, 159, 199
Mass (the), 17, 34–35, 37, 40, 48, 106,
    117, 126, 141–42, 152, 158, 160,
    170, 172, 173, 199, 228, 357,
    362, 364
Massey family, 231
Mate, Bishop Martin, 224
Materialism, 32, 66, 78, 80, 82, 101,
    114, 115, 118, 121–22, 123, 142,
    174, 180, 188, 242, 243, 285,
    299, 342, 393, 394
Mayer, Prior Alfred, 356
McClure, Robert, 235
McGill University, 119, 239, 285;
  Jewish Studies Dept., 290
McLuhan, Marshall, 11
McPherson, Aimée Semple, 316
Medicine, 36–37, 74, 75;
  bad, 37, 56, 109
  bag, 35
  bundles, 54
  Dance, 54
  good, 56
  herbal, 68
  homeopathic, 74
  men, 36–37, 38, 39, 80
Meditation, 66, 69, 75, 80, 98, 176,
    180, 184, 186, 188, 189, 190, 247,
    301, 357, 378, 379–83, 384, 385,
    387, 388, 391, 394, 395, 397–98;
  Transcendental, 40, 68
Mediums, 63, 69, 73
Meeker, Lloyd, see Uranda
Meeker, Nancy, see Exeter, Nancy
  Meeker
Meeker family, 88, 96–97
Mennonite Central Committee, 236,
    328
Mennonites, 30, 33, 316, 341, 389
Mercier, Honoré, 114
Metanoia (assoc.), 203
Metaphysics, 66, 178

Methodism, 209, 213, 314
Methodist Church, 30, 33, 137, 206,
    230–31, 315, 391. See also
  United Church
Métis, 24, 29
Metlakatla, B.C., 30
Metten Abbey, Bavaria, 355
Michael, Father Matthew, 358, 362,
    368
Milarepa (Buddhist), 186
Militarism, 32, 290–91, 306
Miracles, 44, 73, 76, 79, 106, 241,
    346, 377
Missionaries, 26–31 passim, 30, 33,
    37, 38–39, 47, 49, 60, 250, 284;
  Anglican, 30–31, 225
  Catholic, 26–29, 33, 38, 40,
    105–6, 368
  Pentecostal, 30, 313
Missions, 49, 51, 52, 319, 322
Mohammed, 71, 266, 355, 366
Monasteries, 179, 182, 185, 186;
  Benedictine, 353–74
Monasticism, 353–74;
  organization of, 355, 359–62,
    364, 365
  rules of, 355, 357, 360
Monks, 94, 182, 184, 186, 187, 194,
    353–74, 379, 395;
  formation of, 359–62, 365
Montreal, 16, 69, 80, 104, 105, 106,
    110, 114, 116, 130, 132, 187, 204,
    225, 232, 271–72, 319, 375;
  Bishop of, 112, 116
  Judaism in, 246, 267–68, 271–
    81, 283–86, 289–90, 291,
    293, 294, 295, 298–99, 300,
    303, 304, 305
  Presbytery, 214
Moodie, Susanna, 73
Moon, Rev. Sun Myung, 66
Moonies, 66, 84, 284
Moral Majority, 328–29
Morley, Alta., 53
Mormons, 30, 316, 322
Moslems, see Muslims
Mounier, Emmanuel, 116
Mowat, Farley, quoted, 20
Mukpo, Lady Diana, 187, 188, 192,
    195, 196–98
Mulroney, Brian, 45, 70, 133
Music, 251, 350;

Drums, 31, 37, 38, 54, 59-60
Hymns, 15-16, 21, 22, 106, 143,
214, 232, 233, 247, 282,
339, 357
songs and singing, 16, 22, 53, 59,
60, 67, 246, 255, 270, 345.
See also Chanting
Muslims, 30, 146, 246, 247, 251, 258,
264, 322, 395;
and Sikhs, 248, 249, 250, 257,
262
Myers-Briggs analysis, 79
Mystical experiences, 26, 63, 87, 141
Mysticism, 80, 123, 162, 228, 242,
281, 284, 286, 394, 396

Nadler, Rabbi Allan, 277, 297, 307
Nalanda, India, 127, 186
Nanak, Guru, 247, 248, 266, 355, 383
Nanaksar Gursikh temple, Rich-
mond, 263
Naramata Centre for Continuing
Education, 80
Narayana, see Tendzin, Osel
Narayana, Yogi (Alfred
Schmielewski), 70
Naropa (Buddhist), 186
Naropa Institute, 177, 193, 197, 378
Naropa Institute of Canada, Halifax,
178
National Coordinating Group, see
NCG
Nationalism, 111, 113, 258-60, 278,
335;
Quebec, 114-15, 120-21, 122,
274, 275-77
Native peoples, 11, 30-61 passim,
100, 105, 109, 162, 223, 278;
and Christianity, 28, 30-40, 43,
48, 49-50, 51-53, 56, 61,
107, 220, 242, 322
elders of, 33, 36, 39, 40, 42, 44,
47, 49, 51-52, 53, 55, 57,
58, 61, 75, 317, 384
Inuit, 223
languages of, 35, 38, 39, 49, 52
"New Covenant" with, 33, 42
per cent of population, 30
and Pope's visit, 22-23
rights (land claims), 33, 223,
224, 225, 236
threats to culture of, 25, 29, 30.

See also individual tribes
Native religions, 28, 30-31, 34, 35,
36-37, 39, 43, 44-48, 49-50, 51-
61, 67, 69, 73, 82;
apprentices of, 45, 55
and rituals, 26, 35, 37, 48-49,
54, 56-57, 59-60, 79
NATO, 223, 224, 225, 243
Nature, 50, 80, 81-82;
personification of, 82, 162, 163,
167, 169
Nazarenes, 314
NCG (National Coordinating Group),
203, 204-5, 207, 208-9, 210-12,
214;
Declaration of Dissent, 211
Neem Karoli Baba, 377-78, 386
Network magazine (Calgary), 69
Neuro Linguistic Programming, 71
New Age spiritualism, 14, 17, 65-83,
162, 169, 181, 194, 220, 394, 395
New Democratic Party (NDP), 207,
231, 242, 272
Newfoundland, 14, 15-16, 257;
Roman Catholic Church in,
170-73, 199
New France, 11, 28, 29, 73, 272, 391.
See also Quebec; French Canada
Newlightism, 314
Newman, Peter, 134
New Testament, 159, 202, 207
New York City, 259, 284, 351;
Bishop of, 162
Judaism in, 273, 280, 283, 297
Ngondro exercises, 190
Nirvana, 176, 183, 200, 386
Nishga Indians, 225
Noble Eighfold Path, 183-84
Norman, Herbert, 231
North America, 137, 181, 316, 331;
and Roman Catholic Church,
32, 119, 133
Northwest Territories, 21, 31.
Notre-Dame Basilica, Montreal, 104-
5, 117, 121-22, 127, 375
Notre-Dame de Paris, 105, 106
Nova Scotia, 176, 180-81, 187, 188,
314, 398
Nuclear weapons, 14, 67, 71, 81, 82,
83, 141, 172, 207, 220, 235, 237,
238, 240
Numerologists, 68

and women, 125, 140, 156-61, 255, 370.
  See also Bishops; Monks; Popes; Priests; Vatican Councils
Roman Catholics, 13, 29, 135, 222; charismatic, 118, 124, 281, 317, 322, 394
  in Europe, 26, 32, 113
  French, 19
Rome, David (Buddhist), 178-80, 181, 188, 191, 197, 199
Rome, David (historian), 276, 302
Rome, 24, 109, 133, 146, 151, 244. See also Roman Catholic Church (hierarchy).
Romero, Oscar, 265
Rose, Fred, 300
Ross, Malcolm, 278
Ross, Sinclair, 11
Ross St. Temple, Vancouver, 251, 253, 254-56, 259, 261
Rouges (Que.), 112-13, 116
Rovena (Seneca Indian), 69
Rushdie, Salman, 265
Rutledge, Ralph, 321

Sabbath, 282, 286, 297, 355
Sack, Benjamin, 272
Sadomasochism, 123, 162, 168
Sai Baba, 377
St Augustine's seminary, 145-46
Saint-Benoît Abbey, Que., 366
Ste Anne de Beaupré, Que., 123
St John's Abbey, Minnesota, 356
Saint-Joseph, Marie de, 107
St Joseph's Oratory, Montreal, 123
St Michael's Cathedral, Toronto, 136, 254
St Michael's College, Toronto, 161
St Peter's Abbey, Sask., 353-74 passim, 380, 387
St Peter's College, Sask., 356, 358, 364, 367, 370
Saints, 56, 101, 123, 173, 324, 330; Augustine, 160, 165, 232
  Benedict, 354, 355, 362, 374
  Francis of Assisi, 132, 153
  Germain, 62, 63, 64, 65, 66, 67
  Gregory I (the Great), 355
  James, 231
  John of the Cross, 123
  John the Baptist, 15

Mark, 148
  Odo of Cluny, 159
  Paul, 207, 214, 333, 356, 370
  Peter, 22, 40
St Vincent's Abbey, Pennsylvania, 56
Sakya order, see Buddhism
Salvation Army, 30, 102, 137, 314, 323
Sambhi, Piara Singh, 248-49
Samchuk, Alex, 70
Sanat Kumara, 63, 67, 79
Satchidananda (Hindu), 195
Satmarers, 282
Saunders, Leslie, 137
Sauvé, Jeanne, 121
Schacter, Rabbi Zelman, 80
Schillebeeckx, Edward, 166
Schmiedeleut, see Hutterites
Schmielewski, Alfred, see Narayana, Yogi
Schneerson, Rabbi Menachem Mendel, 284-85
Schools, 117, 208, 220, 313, 322, 327, 331-32, 350, 359;
  Catholic, 14, 113, 119, 135, 136, 140-41, 143, 149
  Jewish, 271, 274-75, 276, 283, 284, 303
  residential, 25, 31, 364, 367.
  See also Education; Seminaries; Universities
Science and Technology, 12, 74, 80-82, 112, 141, 162, 172, 207, 227, 242, 321, 322, 341-42, 393, 394
Scott, Edward, 235
Scott, F.R. 27, 231
Scriptures, 36, 149, 202, 206, 208, 209, 210, 212, 220, 227, 242, 309, 312, 314, 318, 321, 357, 367
Sects, 67, 68, 126, 185
Secularism, 12, 19-20, 112, 117, 149, 173, 174, 220, 242, 264, 283, 299, 300, 301, 322
Self-Connection bookstore, Calgary, 69
Selfishness, 123, 265, 340
Self-mortification, 106, 108
Selkirk, Lord, 88
Seminaries, 28, 36, 118, 125, 135, 145-46, 190, 294, 296-97, 359
Sephardim, see Jews
Seth, 79
Seventh-Day Adventists, 30, 89, 315

431